Core Concepts in Sociology

Core Concepts in Sociology

Edited by J. Michael Ryan

WILEY Blackwell

Registered Office(s)
John Wiley & Sons, Inc., 111 River Street, Hoboken, NJ 07030, USA
John Wiley & Sons Ltd, The Atrium, Southern Gate, Chichester, West Sussex, PO19 8SQ, UK

Editorial Office
9600 Garsington Road, Oxford, OX4 2DQ, UK

For details of our global editorial offices, customer services, and more information about Wiley products visit us at www.wiley.com.

Wiley also publishes its books in a variety of electronic formats and by print-on-demand. Some content that appears in standard print versions of this book may not be available in other formats.

Library of Congress Cataloging-in-Publication Data

Names: Ryan, J. Michael, editor.
Title: Core concepts in sociology / edited by J. Michael Ryan, Lisbon, Portugal.
Description: Hoboken, NJ : Wiley, [2019] | Includes bibliographical references and index. |
Identifiers: LCCN 2018004195 (print) | LCCN 2018005456 (ebook) | ISBN 9781119168645 (pdf) |
    ISBN 9781119168638 (epub) | ISBN 9781119168614 (cloth) | ISBN 9781119168621 (pbk.)
Subjects: LCSH: Sociology.
Classification: LCC HM585 (ebook) | LCC HM585 .C67 2018 (print) | DDC 301–dc23
LC record available at https://lccn.loc.gov/2018004195

Cover image: © MACIEJ NOSKOWSKI/Getty Images
Cover design: Wiley

Set in 10/12pt Warnock by SPi Global, Pondicherry, India
Printed in Singapore by C.O.S. Printers Pte Ltd

10 9 8 7 6 5 4 3 2 1

Contents

List of Contributors

Barry D. Adam
University of Windsor, Canada

Julie M. Albright
University of California, USA

Christopher Andrews
Drew University, USA

Joseph Asomah
University of Saskatchewan, Canada

Rob Beamish
Queen's University, Canada

Robert D. Benford
University of South Florida, USA

Colin Bernatzky
University of California, Irvine, USA

Gurminder K. Bhambra
University of Warwick, UK

Gary Bowden
University of New Brunswick, Canada

Gaspar Brändle
Universidad de Murcia, Spain

Peter L. Callero
Western Oregon University, USA

Andrew P. Carlin
Manchester Metropolitan University, UK

Hongming Cheng
University of Saskatchewan, Canada

Valerie Chepp
Hamline University, USA

Matthew Clair
Harvard University, USA

Stewart Clegg
University of Technology Sydney,
Australia

Jay Coakley
University of Colorado, Colorado
Springs, USA

William C. Cockerham
University of Alabama at Birmingham,
USA

Peter Conrad
Brandeis University, USA

James E. Côté
University of Western Ontario, Canada

Marci D. Cottingham
University of Amsterdam, The
Netherlands

Ryan T. Cragun
University of Tampa, USA

Graham Day
Bangor University, UK

Mathieu Deflem
University of South Carolina, USA

Gerard Delanty
University of Sussex, UK

Rutledge M. Dennis
George Mason University, USA

Kylan Mattias de Vries
Southern Oregon University, USA

Robert Dingwall
Dingwall Enterprises Ltd., UK

Riley E. Dunlap
Oklahoma State University, USA

Peter Evans
Brown University, USA

Sherelle Ferguson
University of Pennsylvania, USA

Kenneth J. Gergen
Swarthmore College, USA

Erich Goode
Stony Brook University, USA

Katie M. Gordon
SUNY at Stony Brook, USA

Kevin Fox Gotham
Tulane University, USA

William Haller
Clemson University, USA

Ashley Harrell
University of South Carolina, USA

Elizabeth Hartung
California State University, Channel Islands, UK

Patrick Heller
Brown University, USA

Patricia Hynes
University of Bedfordshire, UK

Cate Irvin
Tulane University, USA

Robert Max Jackson
New York University, USA

Guillermina Jasso
New York University, USA

Ryan Kelty
U.S. Air Force Academy, USA

Michael Kimmel
SUNY at Stony Brook, USA

Roberto Patricio Korzeniewicz
University of Maryland, USA

Peter Kivisto
Augustana College, USA

Beryl Langer
La Trobe University, Australia

Annette Lareau
University of Pennsylvania, USA

Charles Lee
Arizona State University, USA

Valerie Leiter
Simmons College, USA

Rolf Lidskog
Örebro University, Sweden

John R. Logan
Brown University, USA

Sebastián Madrid
P. Universidad Católica de Chile, Chile

Amir Marvasti
Penn State Altoona, USA

E. Doyle McCarthy
Fordham University, USA

Lisa McCormick
University of Edinburgh, UK

Susan A. McDaniel
University of Lethbridge, Canada

Arthur McLuhan
York University, Canada

Jeremiah C. Morelock
Boston College, USA

Jeylan T. Mortimer
University of Minnesota, USA

Aurea Mota
University of Barcelona, Spain

Nancy Naples
University of Connecticut, USA

Leonard Nevarez
Vassar College, USA

Richard Ocejo
City University of New York, USA

Esther Oliver
University of Barcelona, Spain

Emily Allen Paine
University of Texas, Austin, USA

Sangeeta Parashar
Montclair State University, USA

Alexandra Parrs
American University in Cairo, Egypt, and
University of Antwerp, Belgium

Michael Pickering
Loughborough University, UK

Christina Prell
University of Maryland, USA

Tetyana Pudrovska
University of Texas, Austin, USA

Maria C. Ramos
Duke University, USA

Damien W. Riggs
Flinders University, Australia

George Ritzer
University of Maryland, USA

Helen Rizzo
The American University in Cairo, Egypt

Juliet B. Schor
Boston College, USA

Kathleen C. Schwartzman
University of Arizona, USA

Alan Scott
University of New England, Australia

David R. Segal
University of Maryland, USA

Linda L. Semu
McDaniel College, USA

Tracy Shildrick
University of Leeds, UK

Chris Shilling
University of Kent, UK

Leslie Sklair
London School of Economics and
Political Science, UK

Lynn Smith-Lovin
Duke University, USA

David A. Snow
University of California, Irvine, USA

Michele Sorice
LUISS University, Rome, Italy, and
University of Stirling, Scotland, UK

Alan Spector
Purdue University Northwest, USA

Liz Stanley
University of Edinburgh, UK

Jeffrey Stepnisky
MacEwan University, Canada

John Stone
Boston University, USA

Piotr Sztompka
Jagiellonian University, Poland

Shane Thye
University of South Carolina, USA

Charalambos Tsekeris
Academy of Athens, Greece

Rens Vliegenthart
University of Amsterdam,
The Netherlands

Rudi Volti
Pitzer College, USA

John B. Williamson
Boston College, USA

Nico Wilterdink
University of Amsterdam, The
Netherlands

Bronwyn Winter
University of Sydney, Australia

James D. Wright
University of Central Florida, USA

Chris Yuill
Robert Gordon University, UK

Milan Zafirovski
University of North Texas, USA

Introduction

The idea for this project was borne not only from my experience as an academic sociologist but also from my 15 years of experience working as a senior managing editor for Wiley Blackwell. Starting in my second year of graduate school until the present day, I have been involved in managing, advising on, and/or co-editing over a dozen major sociological reference works with Wiley totaling more than three dozen individual volumes. These experiences have given me an unusual perspective in that I have been continually exposed to the broad range of fields and subfields within the discipline, including topics extending far outside the realm of my own individual research and interests. This broad exposure to topics, people, and writings from across the sociological spectrum is what inspired this project.

This volume is designed to be a handy reference for anyone working in, studying, or simply interested in the field of sociology. Contributions have been written to provide the reader with a general overview of many of the concepts widely considered to be at the heart of the field today. The volume has been envisioned in such a way so as to be useful to everyone from the novice undergraduate student taking their first introduction to sociology course up to the seasoned expert in the field looking for a quick refresher on a critical concept.

The first major challenge when conceptualizing this project was to determine what exactly is a "core" concept in sociology. To do so I consulted a range of sources including introductory textbooks, headword lists from a dozen sociology-related encyclopedias, and my own experience (itself a concept that could be considered anathema to any broad-based sociological endeavor!) and came up with a list of 90 or so concepts that I thought fit the bill. That list was then circulated amongst several "big names" in the field who each came back with their own recommendations on what was missing and what might be a bit superfluous. This project represents a synthesis of that research and feedback. It is fair to assume that most readers of this volume will no doubt be able to identify concepts that they feel are glaringly absent and probably also point out a few that seem peripheral to the field. Such reactions are inevitable with a project of this nature.

Building on the above, there is no doubt that the idea of a core concept will vary depending not just on one's personal background and interests but also on where they are (no doubt such a list compiled in France or Japan or Kenya might look a bit different), when they are (one can imagine how this list might have looked 25 years ago, or will look 25 years from now), who they are (as good sociologists we recognize that one's personal

Core Concepts in Sociology, First Edition. Edited by J. Michael Ryan.
© 2019 John Wiley & Sons Ltd. Published 2019 by John Wiley & Sons Ltd.

demographics can color their perceptions), the methods they use (I can imagine quantitative, qualitative, and mixed-methods-oriented folks having some interesting discussions over this list), and even their own motivations to be interested in sociology (revolutionaries, reformers, and pragmatists would all no doubt conceive of such a list differently). That said, every attempt was made to create a volume that was as global, in both the literal and the metaphoric sense, as possible.

The contributors in this volume come from a wide range of backgrounds but nearly all are recognized names at the top of their respective fields. Thus, amongst the contributors one will find many names that will be familiar to anyone who has taken so much as an introduction to sociology course. The contributor list also draws on experts from around the world, and not just the so-called "Global North." I believe the real strength of this volume lies in that broad range of expertise. I am grateful to each and every one of these contributors for allowing me to compile their combined expertise into a single volume.

There are many people to thank on a project such as this as this volume represents the efforts of more than one hundred people. First, and foremost, I would like to thank Justin Vaughan, my publisher, who believed in me enough to let me undertake this challenging project. Justin and I have worked together on projects such as this for some 15 years now and I cannot imagine a more supportive publisher. I would also like to thank Liz Wingett, Dominic Bibby, Emily Corkhill, Louise Spencely, and the rest of the team at Wiley for their hard work and dedication to this project. They have continued to be a joy with whom to work.

An obvious thank you goes to each of the contributors to this volume. It was their hard work, expertise, and generosity of time and intellect that really made this project possible. It is with sincere gratitude that I acknowledge this project as a fruit of their labor. A special thank you goes to the anonymous reviewers who gave feedback on early drafts of the proposed headword list for this volume. Their feedback was invaluable in putting this together, and while their input only made this volume stronger, any shortcomings are strictly a fault of mine alone.

J. Michael Ryan
Editor, *Core Concepts in Sociology*
The University of Lisbon
December 2017

Aging, Sociology of

Susan A. McDaniel

University of Lethbridge, Canada

Sociology of aging takes a social lens to the complex processes of aging from birth to death. It focusses not only on older adults, but on the entirety of the life course, and how social factors such as education, income, and ethnicity, for example, contribute to life-long aging. Structural factors in societies, such as the degrees of inequality, political systems, or policy regimes also have consequences for how we age, or even whether we age or die young.

Sociology of ageing has a relatively short history among sociology sub-areas. It only became a Research Committee (which is a thematic specialization) in the International Sociological Association in 1974, although there had been a working group on "Sociology of Old Age" earlier. The Research Committee is now called "Sociology of Aging and Life Course," indicative of the expanded focus of the field. Sociologists turning their attention to aging or older people had to fight for recognition in the discipline. Identity questions arose on whether sociologists of aging were really sociologists or gerontologists. The latter focus on older populations with an interdisciplinary and often a practice-oriented lens. Sociologists studying ageing, like older adults themselves in society, were not seen as having high status.

This sociological sub-area has been both constrained and advantaged by its early focus on empirical and often policy-relevant research questions. Methods used initially were often descriptive, cross-sectional, and both quantitative and qualitative. The often practical and easily interpreted research made sociology of aging interesting for policy makers and the public. It did less to encourage acceptance in wider sociological circles which tended to see it as less than real sociology. The field has been sharply critiqued in recent decades for its lack of theory (Marshall and Bengstson 2011). That is now changing, and indeed, may have been an overplayed critique.

Age stratification theories infused some early studies in sociology of aging, essentially taking the classical sociological theories of Durkheim, Marx, and Weber and applying them to age. Disengagement theory (Cumming and Henry 1961) was a truly transdisciplinary theoretical innovation, one which brought both interest and acclaim to the field. It posited that with the physical and psychological decline of older adults, they withdrew from society, serving a purpose both for the aging individuals of whom less was expected, and for the society in preparing for eventual death of older people. Activity theory,

Core Concepts in Sociology, First Edition. Edited by J. Michael Ryan.
© 2019 John Wiley & Sons Ltd. Published 2019 by John Wiley & Sons Ltd.

which still contrasts with, and contests, disengagement, begins with the practical concept of remaining active to stay younger longer. The degree to which this is an actual sociological theory remains open to debate, but it is popular in policy and research circles, as well in the popular mind perhaps particularly in US sociology of aging.

As both sociological theories of aging such as the life course perspective (McDaniel and Bernard 2011) advanced, sociology of aging gradually moved out of the margins of sociology. It is now a vibrant field, infused with feminist sociology, globalization, theories and research on intergenerational relations and dynamics, and, perhaps most importantly, with insights and methods of biology, psychology, and public policy. The infusion of other disciplines makes sociology of aging research no less sociological; in fact, the contribution of social factors to the aging process become more not less vivid.

The current emphasis on life course theory as central to sociology of ageing is both welcome and concerning. Life course theory, with its emphasis on life transitions and linked lives, has enabled deeper understanding of aging as a social process. So central is life course theory to the sociology of aging that the ISA research committee on aging has added life course to its title. There is no doubt that life course theory as a fully complex sociological theory adds much to the sociology of ageing. That said, concerns have been expressed that it is perhaps too individual-focussed without taking social structures as much into account. Whether this is a justified critique or not remains to be seen. Matilda White Riley (1987) in her very early exposition of life course and aging, argues that individual processes of aging over the life course change social structures while, at the same time, social structures change aging.

Future directions that sociology of aging might take include a remarkable breadth and depth. Caring and care provision remains a huge topic to explore, particularly in the context of globalized care, both families that are multinational and thus caring across borders, and carers who are imported. Intergenerational supports, dynamics, and inequalities, both micro and macro are another area likely to be mined in future for new insights (Biggs and Lowenstein 2011). Social supports and their absence is another ongoing direction for research, particularly with new insights about the negative health impacts of loneliness. Changing work and non-work life course patterns and their implications for ageing in future is a big challenge. Lastly, but no less importantly, data sets that link various records about health, lifestyle, families, education, and work enable deeper understanding of the factors and forces that contribute to mortality and illness differentials as we age.

SEE ALSO: Body, the; Demography and Population Studies; Family and Kinship, Sociology of; Life Course

References

Biggs, Simon, and Ariela Lowenstein. 2011. *Generational Intelligence: A Critical Approach to Age Relations*. London and New York: Routledge.

Cumming, Elaine, and William Henry. 1961. *Growing Old: The Process of Disengagement*. New York: Basic Books.

Marshall, Victor W., and Vern L. Bengtson. 2011. "Theoretical Perspectives on the Sociology of Aging." In *Handbook of Sociology of Aging*, edited by Richard A. Settersten, Jr. and Jacqueline L. Angel, 17–33. New York: Springer.

McDaniel, Susan A., and Paul Bernard, eds. 2011. "Life Course as a Policy Lens." *Canadian Public Policy/Analyse de Politiques* 37, Supplement February. Online at: http://www.jstor.org/stable/i24463824h.

Riley, Matilda White. 1987. "On the Significance of Age in Society." *American Sociological Review* 52 (February): 1–14. Online at: http://dx.doi.org/10.2307/2095388.

Further Reading

Hyde, Martin, and Paul Higgs. 2016. *Ageing and Globalisation*. Bristol, UK: Policy Press.

McDaniel, Susan A., ed. 2008. *Ageing: Key Issues for the 21st Century*. SAGE Major Work Series. London: Sage.

McDaniel, Susan A., and Zachary Zimmer, eds. 2013. *Global Ageing in the 21st Century: Challenges and Opportunities*. Farnham, UK: Ashgate Publishing.

Settersten, Jr., Richard A., and Jacqueline L. Angel, eds. 2011. *Handbook of Sociology of Aging. Series:* Handbooks of Sociology and Social Research. New York: Springer.

Alienation

Chris Yuill

Robert Gordon University, UK

Alienation theory speaks to the lived experience of capitalist society. The basic premise is that social agents are estranged from their talents and creativity, and lose control of their ability to work meaningfully with others. Capitalist economic and social relations are the cause of that estrangement. Human activity is directed towards the creation of profit rather than working collectively to make human society a better place in which to live. The subjective lived experience of alienation is the denial of self-actualization, which results in poor health, lower all-round wellbeing, including depression, being frustrated with life, and a sense of social fragmentation.

The theory of alienation is most commonly associated with Marx, forming a crucial element of his wider critique of capitalism, but it does also share some common ground with Durkheim's and Merton's ideas on anomie. Marx identified four basic expressions or modalities of alienation:

1) *Product alienation*: where the social agent loses control of what they have produced.
2) *Process alienation*: where the social agent loses control over how they work.
3) *Human nature alienation*: where social agents cannot exercise their innate abilities to be creative, and to use their talents and skills.
4) *Other human alienation*: where social agents are distanced from each other, and other people are recast as an object of competition, threat, or hate.

Within sociology the use of alienation theory reached its peak in the 1960s and 1970s. A considerable output of research-based journal articles and theory-orientated books were published at that time, however it was often intellectually fractious, with alienation theory being the subject of much debate. The empirical research was often criticised as lacking theoretical rigor, while the reverse was claimed about the theoretical work being insufficiently tested with research. Debates also surrounded whether to focus on the subjective and psychological experiences of alienation or the objective causes of alienation within the economic and social structures of capitalist society.

The rapid decline of alienation theory from the early 1980s onwards can be traced to a number of other reasons too: the collapse of the general Marxist political project, the rise of neoliberalism, the move towards poststructural and postmodern theories within sociology and the rise of new light or immaterial service industries. By the early 1990s interest in alienation theory had waned.

Core Concepts in Sociology, First Edition. Edited by J. Michael Ryan.
© 2019 John Wiley & Sons Ltd. Published 2019 by John Wiley & Sons Ltd.

There has been a modest re-engagement with alienation theory within sociology of late. Some sociologists have begun to explore how alienation can be used to understand the modern workplace and how alienation theory can provide insights into a diverse range of areas such as technology, and health and wellbeing. This renewed interest has arisen due to what are seen as the analytical shortcomings of postmodernist theory and that the modern neoliberal corporate workplace is filled with the sort of power relations that Marx would easily recognize. Workers and social agents across the Global North and South face meaningless fragmented working conditions, where they are subject to increasing levels of exploitation and managerial control.

SEE ALSO: Anomie; Class; Marxism; Sociological Theory; Work, Occupations and Professions, Sociology of.

Further Reading

Ollman, Bertell.1976. *Alienation: Marx's Conception of Man in Capitalist Society*, 2nd ed. Cambridge: Cambridge University Press.

Rahel, Jaeggi. 2014. *Alienation (New Directions in Critical Theory)*. Columbia: Columbia University Press.

Wendling, Amy. 2009. *Karl Marx on Technology and Alienation*. Basingstoke: Palgrave.

Yuill, Chris. 2011. "Forgetting and Remembering Alienation." *The History of Human Sciences* 24 (2): 103–119.

Anomie

Mathieu Deflem

University of South Carolina, USA

Anomie refers to a society's relative degree of normlessness or an ineffectiveness of norms to regulate behavior (Deflem 2015). Derived from the Greek terms *'anomia'*, the concept was first introduced in sociology by Emile Durkheim, who had adopted the term from French moral philosopher Jean-Marie Guyau, to develop it sociologically in his study on the social division of labor (Durkheim [1893] 1984). Durkheim's concept of anomie refers to the exceptional social circumstances under which the division of labor is not, or not sufficiently, regulated. In his seminal study on suicide, Durkheim ([1897] 1951) similarly employs anomie to differentiate that social type of suicide which results from a sudden or chronic lack of regulation.

In modern sociology, anomie was popularized in Robert K. Merton's work on deviance where he argues that various types of deviant behavior result from the strain that is exerted under conditions of a lack of opportunities to legitimate means of advancement (Merton 1957a, 1957b). Anomie results from the great emphasis that is placed in American society on attaining the cultural dominant goal of individual success irrespective of the means by which those goals are to be attained. Merton argues this de-institutionalization of means to be characteristic of American society as a whole.

In contemporary sociology, the anomie concept has lost the centrality it enjoyed in post-World War II sociology when structural-functionalism was the dominant paradigm. Yet, a resurgence of anomie has since also taken place. Merton's anomie concept has continued to be of intellectual interest via the popularity of the related strain theory of deviance. Moreover the Durkheimian concept of anomie as societal deregulation has also remained of significance, both theoretically in view of the continued centrality of Durkheimian thought as well as empirically to describe the impact of dramatic societal changes such as the fall of communism and the globalization of capitalism.

SEE ALSO: Alienation; Class; Deviance

Core Concepts in Sociology, First Edition. Edited by J. Michael Ryan.
© 2019 John Wiley & Sons Ltd. Published 2019 by John Wiley & Sons Ltd.

References

Deflem, Mathieu. 2015. "Anomie: History of the Concept." In *International Encyclopedia of Social and Behavioral Sciences, Second Edition*, Volume 1, edited by James D. Wright, 718–721. Oxford: Elsevier.

Durkheim, Emile. [1893] 1984. *The Division of Labor in Society*. New York: The Free Press.

Durkheim, Emile. [1897] 1951. *Suicide: A Study in Sociology*. New York: The Free Press.

Merton, Robert K. 1957a. "Social Structure and Anomie." In his *Social Theory and Social Structure*. Revised and Enlarged Edition, 131–160. New York: The Free Press.

Merton, Robert K. 1957b. "Continuities in the Theory of Social Structure and Anomie." In his *Social Theory and Social Structure*. Revised and Enlarged Edition, 161–194. New York: The Free Press.

Body, the

Chris Shilling

University of Kent, UK

Body matters have long been viewed as the province of the natural rather than the social sciences, as evident in Durkheim's insistence that sociology involves studying "social facts" that are qualitatively different from the subject matter of biology. Yet sociology has, since the early 1980s, focused increasingly on the physical constitution, the senses and affects of human being. Indeed, it is no exaggeration to say that the "rise of embodiment" has been one of the most influential sociological developments over the last thirty years, culminating in the establishment of an interdisciplinary field of "body studies." It is not just the social sciences, moreover, that have recognized the societal importance of bodies. Epigenetics has acknowledged that *social* factors can determine the expression of genes, for example, while bioarchaeology has revealed how human bones can illuminate patterns of migration and gender differences in diet. Perspectives from outside as well as inside the discipline have thus recognized the importance of studying the body as a social as well as an organic phenomenon.

It is social developments themselves, however, that have highlighted most visibly the importance of the body for understanding modern societies. The rise of consumer culture from the 1950s was associated with a proliferation of "slim, sexy and youthful" body images in advertising and social media. Relatedly, people's pursuit of the "body beautiful" has intensified recently, with 15.6 million cosmetic procedures performed in the United States alone during 2014. This obsession with bodily perfection has also been associated with social problems, including eating disorders, and the invention of new terms such as "muscle dysmorphia" and "tanorexia" to denote obsessions with physical appearance. The prominence of such issues helps account for why sociologists, interested in an array of contemporary developments, have felt compelled to incorporate body matters into their research.

Classical Foundations

Sociology has also become interested in the body as a means of reinterpreting its heritage in order to enhance the discipline's explanatory power. In this context, while the status of the body may have been submerged within classical sociology, analysts have unearthed a "secret history" of relevant writings. These include Spinoza's monism, Marx's materialism, and Nietzsche's analyses of Apollonian rationality and Dionysian sensuality. Within sociology itself, Comte linked morally harmonious societies with actions informed by mind *and* heart, while Tönnies understood the shift from medieval to modern societies as the outcome of contrasting embodied wills. It was the writings of Durkheim, Weber, and Elias, however, that have arguably proven of most enduring worth to sociological studies of the body.

Despite associating sociology with the study of institutions, Durkheim developed a theory of religion and society based on a concern with the body's social potential. While bodies generate egoistic appetites, they conceal "a sacred principle that erupts onto the surface" via markings or adornments that facilitate the circulation in social assemblies of a collective effervescence enabling individuals to become attached to and *embold-ened by* entities greater than themselves (Durkheim [1912] 1995: 138, 233). These themes continue to resonate in studies of forms of embodiment, forms of sociality, and diverse manifestations of the sacred.

Emanating from the contrasting methodologically individualist tradition of German thought, Weber also recruited the body to his writings on the Protestant ethic and the spirit of capitalism. Weber analyzed how religious beliefs shaped bodily identities and behavior. Eschewing sinful pleasure, and immersing themselves in labor while search-ing for worldly signs of election, the physical habits stimulated by the Reformers pro-vided a corporeal basis for rational capitalism. Weber's writings continue to influence body studies of rationalization, diet, frailty, and religion.

Norbert Elias's writings on long-term civilizing processes (recognized increasingly as an essential contribution to the foundations of the discipline) have inspired contempo-rary analyses of the intercorporeal interdependences that drive social developments. Elias explored how codes of body management gained increasing importance in almost every European country from the Renaissance onwards, promoting a heightened ten-dency among people to monitor and mold themselves in relation to these criteria. These developments were assisted by wider social contexts: in contrast to earlier periods, sur-vival depended less on physical battles and more on skills of impression management in which the body became a location for social codes.

Embodying Structure and Agency

Classical sociological resources continue to influence contemporary studies, but two areas in which considerations of the body have exerted a particular effect across sociol-ogy concern conceptions of *social structures* and *human agency*. Social structures have often been conceived of as operating via ideological forces, while people's capacities to act have been linked to status or class-based capacities for cognitive thought. Yet this focus on the mind ignores the corporeal correlates of constraint and enablement, as evident in the work of two of the most important figures within the sociology of the body: Michel Foucault and Marcel Mauss.

Foucault (1975) wrote extensively on the operation of disciplinary structures. In the European penal system, for example, medieval displays of monarchical power focused upon destroying the bodies of offenders. In the late early modern era, however, there emerged a new "art of penal government" in which disciplining the body became more important than destroying it. Focused upon improving the population's human capital, this "art" was exemplified by the English philosopher Jeremy Bentham's design for a "panopticon" conducive to rehabilitation. Evident in developments across hospitals, asylums, prisons, and schools, the recent culmination of these more "positive" means of control is exemplified by a consumer culture that eschews "control by repression" in favor of control by stimulation.

In relation to human agency, in contrast, Marcel Mauss's ([1934] 1973) writings on "techniques of the body" have been central to analyses of culture and action. Mauss identifies social, psychological, and biological dimensions to body techniques, and emphasizes that our knowledge is intimately related to how we sense and move within our environment. In contrast to conventional Western philosophical conceptions of a "brain-bound mind" trapped within an irrational body, learning involves *transactions* with our environment; taking our surroundings into our bodies through breath, sight, hearing, etc., while also transforming them through our actions. This approach towards the embodied basis of human agency has been complemented by studies of "body pedagogics" that draw on the writings of the pragmatists Dewey, Mead, Peirce, and James - and also on the phenomenologist Merleau-Ponty - in suggesting that action passes through cycles of habit, crisis and creativity as individuals experience equilibrium or disturbance within their environment.

If body matters are key to understanding structures and agency, so too they are for comprehending related social processes. Social divisions and power relations are articulated through various features of the body. Racism is a prominent example, with the history of plastic surgery highlighting how discrimination and persecution operate through the medium of the body. Social solidarities also emerge through the body. Tattooing and scarification have long been used to signify tribal and communal membership, while the food incorporated into or excluded from bodies during periods of religious observance including Ramadan has traditionally been associated with the promotion of collective experiences of belonging. Such examples suggest the body is our most *natural symbol* (Douglas 1970). It is often experienced intensely as a sign and vehicle of identity and belonging that can also signal deep differences between peoples.

Contested Bodies

Having outlined the background to and foundations of body studies, it is important to highlight the diverse trajectories associated with the subject as well as the contemporary conflicts with which it is associated. The distinctive factors that have shaped current writings on embodiment include "second wave" feminism's focus on gendered bodies, and ecological concerns about "one-dimensional" consumption-oriented lifestyles. Elsewhere, there has been a focus on commodification processes and the body, ranging from the brutal selling of women and children into the sex industry, to the global problem of organ trafficking and the pervasive standing of appearance as a form of physical capital. The significance of the body as a commodity has also added to the valuation placed upon youth, and the stigma associated with ageing and dependence.

From a different perspective, current sociological trajectories involving the body have also been influenced by the rise of embodied artificial intelligence in the form of robotics. This helped validate the discipline's concern to view the body as a constructed phenomenon. Scientific advances in medicine encouraged a distinct concern with the body in sociological writings on the rise of self-governance, while the discipline has maintained its concern with "heavy and ponderous" means of governance following the Bush government's "war on terror" and the intensified concern with "alien bodies." Finally, while the body used to be seen as natural, determined by the parameters of nature, advances in science and technology have resulted in it being viewed as alterable and subject to the designs of individuals; a *project* amenable to alteration as a consequence of individual, national, religious, or other agendas.

These developments highlight very different aspects of the body. From its gendered, constructed, governmental, exchange, and medical values, the body slips and slides, metamorphosing in terms of its meaning and status. At a time when scientific and technological interventions into the body have increased our capacity to alter our physical appearances and capacities to unprecedented levels, body matters have become increasingly contested as well as being increasingly visible. In this context, if we consider the current relevance of Durkheim's work, it is reasonable to explore whether bodies are now prized and even rendered sacred on the basis of varied and opposing factors that are likely to keep them central to sociology for the foreseeable future.

SEE ALSO: Emotion, Sociology of; Gender; Identity

References

Douglas, Mary. 1970. *Natural Symbols. Explorations in Cosmology*. London: Cressett.
Durkheim, Emile. [1912] 1995. *The Elementary Forms of Religious Life*. New York: Free Press.
Foucault, Michel. 1975. *Discipline and Punish: The Birth of the Prison*. Harmondsworth: Penguin.
Mauss, Marcel. [1934] 1973. "Techniques of the Body." *Economy and Society* 2: 70–88.

Further Reading

Elias, Norbert. [1939] 2000. *The Civilising Process*. Oxford: Blackwell.
Gilman, Sander L. 2000. *Making the Body Beautiful: A Cultural History of Aesthetic Surgery*. Princeton, NJ: Princeton University Press.
Shilling, Chris. [1993] 2012. *The Body and Social Theory*, 3rd ed. London: Sage.
Shilling, Chris. 2016. *The Body: A Very Short Introduction*. Oxford: Oxford University Press.
Turner, Bryan S., ed. 2012. *Routledge Handbook of Body Studies*. London: Routledge.

Capital: Cultural, Social, and Economic

William Haller

Clemson University, USA

Cultural, social, and economic capital are three of various forms of capital distributed unevenly in human populations. It is the instrumentality of these forms of capital for enabling social mobility, and how their lack can prevent or restrict said mobilities, which makes them particularly important for sociological analysis. Other forms of capital exist and may operate similarly as enablers or restrictors of social mobility and esteem.

"Capital is … derived from … *capitalis* (Latin root *caput*, head), meaning principal, chief" (Fetter 1930: 187). For Fetter in 1930 capital was solely economic, referring mainly to ownership of commercial and technological goods, and real estate. Application of adjectives to the term, capital, denoting other kinds of resources owned or controlled by individuals or corporate entities appeared later. Conception of the economic value of skills accruing from education began appearing in the years immediately following WWII (Teixeira 2014), developed in the early work of economist Gary Becker, in writings on *human* capital. Generally, resources of persons that are accumulable to an indefinite extent and that provide potential access to other kinds of (economic or non-economic) resources are capital.

Propagation of "capital" as a generalized concept emerged from the writings of Bourdieu. DiMaggio (1979: 1463) explained that Bourdieu diverged "critically from conventional economics in his recognition that capital need not be strictly economic" and elaborated that "capital, defined implicitly as attributes, possessions, or qualities of a person or a position exchangeable for goods, services, or esteem, exists in many forms – symbolic, cultural, social, or linguistic, as well as economic." However, as "capitals proliferate … the metaphorical currency undergoes inflation" (1468–1469). Despite this, Bourdieu is the premier social theorist who has addressed the cultural, social, and economic forms of capital, and their interrelationships, within a broader theoretical framework of social actors operating within their respective fields of action.

Cultural Capital

In "The Forms of Capital" Bourdieu (1986) discusses three subtypes of cultural capital: embodied, objectified, and institutionalized. Embodied cultural capital is vested "in the form of long-standing dispositions of the mind and body" and "presupposes a process of

Core Concepts in Sociology, First Edition. Edited by J. Michael Ryan.
© 2019 John Wiley & Sons Ltd. Published 2019 by John Wiley & Sons Ltd.

embodiment, incorporation, which, insofar as it implies a labor of inculcation and assimilation, costs time, time which must be invested personally by the investor." It is "external
wealth converted into an integral part of the person [and] cannot be transmitted instan-
taneously (unlike money, property rights, or even titles of nobility) by gift or bequest,
purchase or exchange" (47–48). Although it cannot be shorn from its possessor, neither
can it "be accumulated beyond [a person's] appropriating capacities" (49).

Objectified cultural capital adheres to material artifacts "such as writings, paintings,
monuments, instruments [and] is transmissible in its materiality." However, to "consume"
objectified cultural capital requires embodied cultural capital. Objectified cultural capital
thus exists only if there is a receiver or audience with the literacy to understand, interpret,
and appreciate it.

Institutionalized cultural capital, according to Bourdieu, permits "a form of objectification that must be set apart because … it confers entirely original properties on the
cultural capital which it is presumed to guarantee" (47). Particularly in the case of educational credentials it protects its bearer because "the objectification of cultural capital
in the form of academic qualifications is one way of neutralizing some of the properties
it derives from the fact that, being embodied, it has the same biological limits as its
bearer" (50). Academic qualifications provide "a certificate of cultural competence
which confers on its holder a conventional, constant, legally guaranteed value … which
has a relative autonomy vis-à-vis its bearer and even vis-à-vis the cultural capital he
effectively possesses at a given moment in time" (50–51). Bourdieu thus points to a
social function of institutionalized cultural capital as buffering individuals from their
own (embodied) fallibility. Thus, the cultural capital accrued from educational credentialing is separate and distinct from the human capital developed and transmitted in
even the very same institutions.

Social Capital

The key conceptual definition of social capital is also from Bourdieu. He defined social
capital as "the aggregate of the actual or potential resources which are linked to possession of a durable network of more or less institutionalized relationships of mutual
acquaintance or recognition" (Bourdieu 1986: 248).

As alluded to above, a basic feature of all forms of capital is convertibility. One form
of capital can be converted into at least one other (but not necessarily "any") form of
capital. Social capital is important not because of some nebulous potential for bridging
one individual or group with others, or for the subjective sense of solidarity (or bonding) it brings, but because it involves the social determination or influence over peoples'
fates, both positive and negative.

The importance of social capital is much more than simply being embedded more or
less deeply in social networks. It is about the resources disproportionately available
through social networks and, indeed, the strategies and tactics of intergenerational status transmission even when equalization of opportunity is increasingly codified into law.
"[T]he holders of capital have an ever greater interest in resorting to reproduction strategies capable of ensuring better-disguised transmission … by exploiting the convertibility
of the types of capital" (Bourdieu 1986: 55). Thus what frequently and officially passes for
talent or accomplishment may be cultural capital purchased through elite university

educations which, through a combination of credentialing (institutionalized cultural capital) and connections (social capital), opens doors to well-salaried positions (DiMaggio 1979: 1466). Though universalism and particularism are commonly portrayed as opposites, attention to cultural and social capital reveals that particularism can operate within universalism. Although "social ties can ... provide privileged access to resources; they can also ... bar outsiders from gaining access to the same resources through particularistic preferences" (Portes 1998: 21).

Economic Capital

Bourdieu asserts that economic capital is the most basic of the various forms of capital. It is undeniably a powerful attractant of human endeavor, tied to the material resources necessary for human cultural maintenance and survival. It is also calculable to very precise degrees within established or negotiated price structures. Economic capital provides the necessary motivation to carry out work, including that which is dirty and dangerous (and sometimes demeaning) across the full range of economic sectors and occupations. Thus, as viewed from the labor theory of value, economic capital involves much more than the ownership of commercial and technological goods, and real estate and includes human capital.

SEE ALSO: Class; Class, Capitalist; Culture, Sociology of; Economic Sociology; Marxism; Power and Authority; Social Network Analysis; Stratification and Inequality

References

Bourdieu, Pierre. 1986. "The Forms of Capital." In *Handbook of Theory and Research for the Sociology of Education*, edited by J.G. Richardson, 241–258. New York: Greenwood.

DiMaggio, Paul. 1979. "On Pierre Bourdieu." *American Journal of Sociology* 84: 1460–1474. DOI:10.1086/226948.

Fetter, Frank A. 1930. "Capital." In *Encyclopedia of the Social Sciences, Vol. 3*, edited by Edwin R.A. Seligman and Alvin Johnson, 187–190. New York: The MacMillan Company.

Portes, Alejandro. 1998. "Social Capital: Its Origins and Applications in Modern Sociology." *Annual Review of Sociology* 24: 1–21. DOI:10.1146/annurev.soc.24.1.1.

Teixeira, Pedro Nuno. 2014. *IZA Journal of Labor Economics* 3: 12. DOI:10.1186/s40172-014-0012-2.

Capitalism

Rob Beamish

Queen's University, Canada

Contemporary capitalism is a global phenomenon; no society is untouched by it. The word is used in everyday conversations, on daily newscasts, and in tweets and posts on social media; "capitalism" appears everywhere. One asks, "what's to learn about it that I don't already know?" In fact, capitalism is a very complex, highly multi-faceted term. A short overview of its etymology is a good starting point for understanding the concept fully.

Capital, Capitalists, and Capitalism

Capitalism is a derivative of "capital" which stems from the Latin "*caput*" (meaning head, principal, or chief). It is not until the eighteenth century that capital is defined as a productive form of stock, funds, or money. This meaning is further consolidated in the late eighteenth century by early political economists (e.g., François Quesnay, Jean Baptiste Say, and Adam Smith) and becomes the dominant meaning by the late nineteenth century.

The term "capitalist" first appears in the mid-seventeenth century as one of several words describing the wealthy (others included moneyed men, men of means, *nouveau riches*). Each term carried a negative connotation. Even as capitalist is used more widely by the late eighteenth century, it remains a negative term. Capitalist, as a scholarly term describing individuals who employed workers, begins in the nineteenth century. Nevertheless, even though capitalist, as a technical term, gains wider acceptance as industrial capitalism is established in Europe, it still retains several negative associations.

Capitalism is the most recent term used first, in the mid-nineteenth century, to describe the conversion of things into capital. It quickly becomes a technical term designating an economic system in which capital expands but it is not positively associated with the benefits of the emerging industrial market economy. French radicals like Louis Blanc, Joseph-Pierre Proudhon, and August Blanqui use capitalism as a negative reference point to glorify the future societies they predict will come into existence.

Core Concepts in Sociology, First Edition. Edited by J. Michael Ryan.
© 2019 John Wiley & Sons Ltd. Published 2019 by John Wiley & Sons Ltd.

This overview of capitalism's etymology leads to three important points. First, one is reminded that words like capital, capitalist, and capitalism have not always had the meanings commonly associated with them today. The emergence and changing meaning of capital, capitalist, and capitalism parallel the shifts in Europe's economy and social structure from the twelfth century onwards as trade began to expand. As a fledgling economic term, capital began as a stock of agricultural goods (crops and livestock) which were exchanged for other goods of capital or chief importance. As trade expanded, money was loaned at interest (*capitalis pars debiti*) to merchants who purchased a stock of goods to trade. Because capital was not the primary source of wealth, the words capitalist and capitalism did not exist during the medieval period. Those words emerged with the changing nature of trade, production, and wealth accumulation.

Second, although Smith is regarded as the father of free market capitalism, he did not use the terms capitalist or capitalism in *The Wealth of Nations*. Furthermore, rather than calling his preferred system "*laissez faire* capitalism" – the term so closely associated to his name – Smith (1776: 290) identified it as the "system of natural liberty." This would be an economy where all preferences or restraints are removed and a "simple system of natural liberty establishes itself of its own accord." Every individual is left perfectly free to pursue his or her own interests "and to bring both his industry and capital into competition with those of any other man, or order of men." This, Smith maintained, is the economic system that is most conducive to expanding the wealth of nations.

The third point concerns Marx. Although capitalism originated as a negative term and is frequently associated with Marx, he rarely used the word. Capitalism does not appear anywhere in the *Communist Manifesto* and occurs only once in *Capital's* three volumes.

Capitalism as an Analytical Term

Although nineteenth-century economists used capitalist as a term, only those influenced by Marxism wrote about capitalism. Werner Sombart and Max Weber are the first to use capitalism as a scholarly, analytical concept.

Sombart (1902) argues that capitalism is driven by an "acquisition principle" which makes increasing wealth the real goal of economic activity rather than producing goods for specific human needs or wants. In addition, the "economic rationalism" that capitalism establishes results in capitalists pursuing the most expedient and efficient means to capitalist acquisition.

Weber distinguishes early merchant capitalism from "modern" capitalism by the particular frame of mind found in the latter. Regarding modern capitalism, Weber ([1904/5] 2002: 19, 12) writes that the "spirit of capitalism" involves "*the pursuit of a calling [berufsmäsig]*" in which the capitalist seeks "profit for its own sake in the manner exemplified by Benjamin Franklin [i.e. an ethic of 'the *making of money* and yet more money, coupled with an avoidance of all uninhibited enjoyment']."

Three points arise from Sombart's and Weber's analyses. First, they recognize that capitalism has gone through different phases. Moreover, while some aspects are found in all of capitalism's phases, certain characteristics are unique to each phase.

Capitalism is not one overarching social formation – its different periods have specific, identifiable, distinguishing characteristics.

Second, despite Sombart's, Weber's, and subsequent analyses, people rarely view capitalism as a neutral, analytical term; it remains a controversial one. The word is so strongly associated with the politicized critique of nineteenth-century industrial capitalism that many economists, sociologists, commentators, and laypersons avoid it; they prefer allegedly "neutral" terms like market economy, free enterprise system, or something similar. Capitalism's use as an analytical term and a politicized one is the outcome of capitalism's history and the term designating it as a social system.

Third, for Sombart, modern capitalism is an economic system involving owners of the means of production and propertyless workers. The primary goal is profit and owners' use economic rationalism in concert with the acquisition principle.

Weber's image of modern capitalism is similar, although he emphasizes the dominant spirit of modern capitalism in which the quest for more and more money is a calling and a duty. In addition, Weber ([1904/5] 2002: 120–121) laments that modern capitalism and its relentless pursuit of profit, through the planned, long-term rationalization of economic activity, has created the "mighty cosmos of the modern economic order" which affects everyone "born into this mechanism," trapping them within a housing as hard as steel (*stahlhartes Gehäuse*). And there appears to be no escape.

Capitalism: A Dynamic, Expanding, Unstable, Dialectical, Social Formation

Just as the word capitalism is derived from the word capital, the innermost core of capitalism is capital itself. That core has two fundamental elements. The first is the unique nature of private ownership. Unlike feudal Europe or state socialist societies such as the former Soviet Union, where a king or the ruling party held and controlled the wealth or capital of the society, the ownership and control of capital in capitalist societies is different. Three particular aspects merit attention.

First, ownership can be direct – an individual owns a business and its assets. It can also be indirect through the ownership of corporate stocks or shares. Through share ownership, individuals or corporations may gain access to capital resources well beyond a single individual's wealth, enabling firms to enter into, and dominate, increasingly larger markets. Share ownership also allows individuals to be involved in several capital-expanding enterprises and, under the right conditions, one or more individuals can control a large corporation without owning the majority of shares.

Second, there are two types of ownership – public (governments) and private. Although private capital dominates economic production as a whole, publicly held capital has been crucial to the success of capitalism in the modern period.

Third, although only a minority of citizens own the bulk of private capital, capital holdings are, nonetheless, more dispersed than under any other economic system.

The second core element is precisely and concisely captured in Marx's (1872: 129) depiction of "the general formula of capital" as $M-C-M'$. Capital is money (M) that purchases commodities (C) which are handled and processed and then sold for more money than the original investment (M'). Building out from that core introduces the dynamic, expanding aspects of capitalism as well as many of its unstable, contradictory features. The four most significant are highlighted below.

First, capitalism is the result of a centuries-long revolutionary process that completely transforms the social and economic landscape everywhere it is established. The transition from feudalism to merchant capitalism, through industrial capitalism to the contemporary period, is a complex history of struggle and conflict that has resulted in a social system within which the results of production are unequally allocated (frequently resulting in significant social inequality) and an ongoing instability.

Second, the general form of capital – M–C–M' – displays the primary objective of capitalist enterprise – the production of profit in the pursuit of potentially unlimited wealth. Marx, Sombart, Weber, and others emphasize that the pursuit of profit is a *structural* feature of capitalism. It is not simply a pure, freely made, subjective choice. To remain competitive and in existence, firms must continuously pursue increased expediency and efficiency.

Capitalism requires continual expansion and growth. The coupling of the acquisition principle and economic rationalism with the general formula of capital creates the conditions for the mutual encroachment of capitalist enterprises. Seeking greater and greater profits, individuals and firms search the market for opportunities to expand, pitting firm against firm in sectors of high profitability. There is an internally generated tension among firms within a capitalist economy creating an ongoing dynamic instability.

In the competition for profits, successful firms often purchase their competitors or force them out of business. The result is an inevitable pressure to turn an openly competitive market into an oligopoly where a small number of large corporations dominate. Apple and Microsoft are high-profile examples but the tendency exists throughout the economy: for example, in the retail sector (Walmart, Amazon, and McDonalds), social media (Facebook, Instagram, Snapchat, and Twitter), telecommunications (AT&T, Verizon, Comcast, Time Warner, and Bell), agribusiness (Adler Seeds, Agria Corporation, and Agrium), or oil and gas (Imperial Oil, Suncor Energy, and Shell).

Capitalist production continually seeks out new markets leading to its global expansion by either meeting an existing want with a less expensive or higher status product than locally available or a producer creates new wants for consumer goods not previously found in the local economy.

The third significant element to consider is the production process where money (M) is advanced to purchase specific commodities (C) (raw materials, machinery, and workers' ability to do work) to produce commodities of greater value than the original investment (M'). The capital/worker (or employer/employee) relationship is a structural property of capitalism which, like competition among firms, creates ongoing tension, instability, and complexity within the social system.

Fourth, capitalism involves the role of government and publically held capital. Two major points are noteworthy.

First, capitalism requires an enduring, predictable legal system. To flourish, capital markets need stability and governments play a crucial role. Capitalist enterprises must have certainty over property and ownership rights, their purchase and sale, and the existence of enforceable contracts in order for them to make short- and long-term investments. Corporations also require clarity on the legal status of any products or services they may choose to pursue in the quest for profit. Marijuana is a good example;

wherever it is legalized, corporations need to know what restrictions will remain before making any long-term investment.

Governments provide stability through tariff barriers and trade agreements such as the North American Free Trade Agreement. These allow corporations to know, in advance, what international opportunities exist as well as potential international competition in domestic markets. Part of President Trump's electoral success stemmed from his promise to "bring back jobs to America" by tearing up existing trade agreements, erecting tariff barriers, and pursuing protectionist policies despite the fallacies that lay behind his promise and those strategies.

Second, national governments exert enormous economic influence through the central bank's control of currency production, the prime interest rate, taxation, and budgetary expenditures. The public sector is one of the largest players in the economy so where and how governments invest public capital has far-reaching consequences. It is also a site of significant political struggle.

From 1945 into the 1970s, pursuing Keynesian economic policies, governments became heavily involved with the economy to eliminate the large fluctuations of the business cycle and provide various social programs to protect those in need. By the 1970s, Western economies stagnated, prices increased through inflation, and some governments incurred debts which they struggled to pay. By 1980, political parties advocating reduced government involvement in the economy and a return to more *laissez-faire* principles came into power. Their neoliberal policies created an emphatic change in political–economic practices. The economic collapse of 2008 reopened the debate around government involvement in the economy. Despite those policy changes, although people tend to associate capitalism with private capital and the market, decisions around public capital and government involvement are fundamentally part of contemporary capitalist society.

In *Capital*, Marx (1872: 9) argues that wealth in capitalist societies "appears as 'an immense accumulation of commodities.'" The commodity seems "at first sight a self-evident, trivial thing." Upon closer examination, it turns out to be "a very tricky thing, full of metaphysical subtleties and theological peculiarities" (47). Capitalism also seems like a simple, familiar thing but even more than the commodity, it turns out to be a highly complex phenomenon, filled with dynamic tensions and contradictions that ensure its ongoing instability, change, and transformation.

SEE ALSO: Capital: Cultural, Social, Economic; Class; Class, Capitalist; Consumption; Economic Sociology; Globalization; Inequality, Global; Poverty; Stratification and Inequality

References

Marx, Karl. 1872. *Das Kapital (Capital)*, 2nd ed., Vol. 1. Hamburg: Otto Meissner.

Smith, Adam. 1776. *An Inquiry into the Nature and Causes of the Wealth of Nations*, Vol. 2. London: W. Strahan and T. Cadell.

Sombart, Werner. 1902. *Der moderne Kapitalismus* (Modern capitalism), Vol. 1. Munich: Duncker & Humbolt.

Weber, Max. [1904/5] 2002. "The Protestant Ethic and the 'Spirit' of Capitalism." In *The Protestant Ethic and the "Spirit" of Capitalism and Other Writings*, edited and translated by Peter Baehr and Gordon Wells. Toronto: Penguin Books.

Further Reading

Hodgson, Geoffrey. 2015. *Conceptualizing Capitalism: Institutions, Evolution, Future*. Chicago: The University of Chicago Press.
Kocka, Jürgen. 2016. *Capitalism: A Short History*, translated by Jeremiah Riemer. Princeton, NJ: Princeton University Press.

Citizenship

Charles Lee

Arizona State University, USA

In common parlance, citizenship most often designates the legal status of state membership, with a corresponding set of rights and duties conferred upon official members of the nation-state. This basic understanding of citizenship as a national institution involved in the dispensing of rights and duties is solidified in the sociologist T.H. Marshall's classic work, which conceives an evolutionary development of citizenship that began with civil rights in the eighteenth century and extended to political rights in the nineteenth century and social rights in the twentieth century.

Since Marshall's time, researchers and scholars have developed a broader notion of citizenship that encompasses three general dimensions: (1) status and membership (with stipulated rights and duties); (2) political participation and empowerment; and (3) identity, belonging, and social inclusion. This broader conception signals that citizenship should not only be understood as a *de jure* institution; rather, the concept may also characterize and accentuate how people actually experience citizenship in a *de facto* sense. In fact, given the long-noted discrepancy between states' professed commitment to universal citizenship that includes every citizen and particular social groups' actual experiences of unequal access to rights, political participation, and social recognition, often due to those groups' marked differences (e.g., race, indigeneity, class, gender, sexuality, culture, homelessness, and/or disability) from the dominant sociocultural norm, this broader conceptualization of modern citizenship not only provides a more comprehensive definition of the term, but also offers a useful set of criteria in legal, political, and sociological study to assess and investigate the extent of these groups' exclusion from citizenship and the implications of such disparity on achieving justice and equality in the larger polity.

This line of inquiry also suggests that the concept of citizenship has long had a close association with the democratic ideal. Indeed, much of the scholarly research on citizenship demonstrates a democratic aspiration to make the system of citizenship more inclusive, egalitarian, and just. In the West, this democratic association of citizenship has its intellectual lineage in political philosophy. While classical political thought on direct democracy in the city-states of ancient Greece provides an entry point to the concept of citizenship, modern political thought on liberal individualism and civic republicanism has led to two contrasting articulations of democratic citizenship.

Core Concepts in Sociology, First Edition. Edited by J. Michael Ryan.
© 2019 John Wiley & Sons Ltd. Published 2019 by John Wiley & Sons Ltd.

Specifically, while the liberal conception of citizenship places emphasis on the protection of personal autonomy, individual rights, and rational pursuit of self-interests, the republican ideal of citizenship focuses on the cultivation of common good, civic virtue, and active democratic participation. Despite the fact that liberal individualism has prevailed over civic republicanism in the modern conception of citizenship, these two schools of thought – with their respective focus on individual rights/interests and civic virtue/participation – set the foundational intellectual contours to understand citizenship as a democratic institution.

But both liberalism's and civic republicanism's relative inattention on how social group differences and inequalities have produced internal hierarchies and boundaries of citizenship in actually existing democracies has led to challenges to this Western philosophical foundation. In particular, influenced by the new social movements arising in postindustrial societies since the 1970s, a progressive cluster of social and political theorists have advanced an alternative, activist vision of radical democratic citizenship. This approach advocates for a pluralistic notion of political activism that addresses social recognition and economic redistribution for the excluded and subordinate communities, and focuses on disagreement, contestation, and counter-hegemony *vis-à-vis* sovereign power and capitalist power as embodying the essence of democratic citizenship.

Among these radical democratic iterations, Engin Isin (2002) has specifically suggested that social exclusion is not simply an external occurrence that happens to citizenship but is imminent to its constitution. In other words, citizenship is only made possible by what it excludes: the alterity/other (i.e., strangers, outsiders, aliens). The very formation of citizenship "requires the constitution of these others to become possible" (Isin 2002: 4). But while exclusion is always embedded in the mechanism of citizenship, this is not a static relationship, for citizenship is not only defined by membership but also dynamically constituted through political subjectivity (Isin 2002). Significantly, by centering political agency in the conceptual analysis of citizenship, Isin carves out an intellectual path to consider how excluded subjects (including those without status) may invent new ways of political enactment to constitute themselves as citizens.

Focusing on citizenship as fundamentally about political subjectivity, recent literatures in the field of "critical citizenship studies" have precisely chronicled the agency of excluded noncitizen subjects such as undocumented migrants and refugees in participating politically in the democratic process to claim rights and make themselves count in spite of their lack of status. These democratic activities range from regular assemblies, public demonstrations and marches, organizing others in the workplace and community, deliberating with legislators, and leafleting against deportations, to campaigning to change existing laws. By participating democratically even though they do not have legal status or authorized political standing, these nonstatus subjects are expanding the meanings and ways of enacting citizenship. Researchers and scholars have accentuated the dynamic nature of these vitalizing citizenship practices by naming them varyingly as "insurgent citizenship," "acts of citizenship," "noncitizen citizenship," or "democratic cosmopolitanism."

Yet even this radical democratic conception may not fully capture the variable trajectories and heterogeneous constitutions of citizenship as it is actually exercised and manifested in the human social world. In one significant direction, scholars influenced by Foucault's notion of biopower have come to see democratic citizenship not as constituting an autonomous opposition to power structures, but as itself entangled in the biopolitical webs of subjectivization and normalization as a constitutive part of liberal governance in the making of citizen-subjects (Cruikshank 1999). Situating her analysis in the context of the increasingly globalized economy, cultural anthropologist Aihwa Ong thus conceives citizenship in advanced liberal societies as encapsulated in an array of technologies of power (i.e., policies, programs, practices, rules, discourse, and expert and knowledge systems) that instill market values in citizen-subjects and induce them to become self-reliant and self-enterprising individuals, or flexible "homo economicus" (2006: 6, 13–14). Importantly, this assemblage of technologies does not so much override the possibility of resistance as create a "strategic field" that sets the possibilities and limits of a space of political calculations and determines the range of possible actions (Cruikshank 1999: 115). As such, subjects may enact themselves politically via "nondemocratic" forms of resistance or negotiation even as they are molded by and enfolded into the neoliberal (market-based) logic. For instance, Ong (1999) has examined how Chinese immigrant businessmen and investors maneuver migration strategies and exploit rules of global capitalism in accumulating capital overseas and optimizing opportunities for their families in transnational forms of "flexible citizenship." She has also investigated the ways in which NGOs in Southeast Asia appeal to both the local moral regimes and neoliberal calculations in demanding better treatment of migrant workers not in terms of political citizenship but in terms of biological welfare, health security, and market flexibility (Ong 2006). Further expanding this line of inquiry, Charles Lee (2016) has analyzed the everyday actions and practices of abject subjects from migrant domestic workers, global sex workers, and transgender people to suicide bombers as often subversive improvisations of citizenship undertaken in complicity with liberal capitalism, and suggests that these inventive and complex ways of resistance offer unorthodox lessons for more fluid and polymorphous forms of social movement activism.

In all, this ever-continuing reinvention and expansion of the concept of citizenship from its competing democratic articulations to its nondemocratic improvisations suggests the pliable nature of the concept that has offered much intellectual–political fruit for ongoing interdisciplinary investigations. While citizenship will always involve the distribution, mediation, and contestation of rights, participation, and inclusion, the fact that its form and meaning may be revised and innovated by subjects based on their particular contexts and changing circumstances also make it resist a fixed definition and static understanding. In fact, it is precisely because of its inherent connection to rights-claiming *and* its resistance to a fixed mode of practice that has animated citizenship's dynamic intellectual–political trajectories and expansive (re)configurations. The recent interdisciplinary turn to examine how affect, biosociality (shared genetic or somatic conditions), and consumerism engender respective formations of "affective citizenship," "biological citizenship," and "consumer citizenship" point to yet other significant future steps and directions in tracing and investigating the unending transformations of citizenship as lived human experiences.

SEE ALSO: Globalization; Homelessness; Identity; Immigration, Migration, and Refugees; Modernity; Nationalism; Political Sociology

References

Cruikshank, Barbara. 1999. *The Will to Empower: Democratic Citizens and Other Subjects.* Ithaca, NY: Cornell University Press.

Isin, Engin F. 2002. *Being Political: Genealogies of Citizenship.* Minneapolis: University of Minnesota Press.

Lee, Charles T. 2016. *Ingenious Citizenship: Recrafting Democracy for Social Change.* Durham, NC, and London: Duke University Press.

Ong, Aihwa. 1999. *Flexible Citizenship: The Cultural Logics of Transnationality.* Durham, NC, and London: Duke University Press.

Ong, Aihwa. 2006. *Neoliberalism as Exception: Mutations in Citizenship and Sovereignty.* Durham, NC, and London: Duke University Press.

City, the

Leonard Nevarez

Vassar College, USA

The city is a developed form of human settlement space. Physical emblem and cultural synonym for "civilization," the city indicates the settling of nomadic groups, the emergence of divisions of labor, and the instrument for creating and preserving material and literary cultures. First appearing by some estimates as early as 9000 BC, cities spread unevenly throughout premodern history, then grew steadily in size and number as industrial capitalism drew far-flung people, goods, ideas, and capital to specific places. In much the same way, cities organize the forces of modernization in today's developing world. The United Nations estimates the 54 percent of world population living in urban areas in 2014 will grow to 66 percent by the year 2050.

Within sociology, the city is traditionally understood as the quintessential setting for society. Sociology's classical theorists viewed cities as the original setting where the multiple dimensions of modernity came together. As the city expanded into the metropolis with its outer-lying suburbs (also counted in estimates of "urban areas"), the universality by which sociologists once theorized the urban experience changed. Increasingly, the city expresses larger inequalities: segregation by race, class, and ethnicity; fiscal crises in municipal governments and public services; and, with contemporary gentrification, the uneven capacity to mobilize changes in the built environment. Sociological theory has since transcended its initial urban focus, with the formal study of city form and organization now relegated to the field of urban sociology.

In its simplest denotation, "the city" refers to a territorial form, and "urban" its associated physical and population characteristics. These descriptive terms are distinguished from two analytical concepts associated with cities.

Urbanism refers to the ways of life found in cities. Within urban studies, a number of properties fall under this concept, from interactional and community dynamics to architectural aesthetics and planning protocols to the functional diversification of civic, economic, and cultural activities across space. In sociology, urbanism is a behavioral concept that bears the imprint of two competing theses. Georg Simmel ([1903] 1950) theorized that cities promote an individuating mode of human subjectivity; urbanites, he proposed, are calculating, blasé, and inclined to artifice in social interactions as they respond to intense stimuli of modern life, such as population density and the money economy. By contrast, the community studies tradition (e.g., Fischer 1982) emphasizes

Core Concepts in Sociology, First Edition. Edited by J. Michael Ryan.

the persistence of primary groups and collective identifications in modern life; urban neighborhoods and enclaves sustain relations shaped by solidarities around ethnicity, lifestyle, and shared institutions.

Urbanization refers to the development, growth, and proliferation of cities. In urban studies, this structural concept denotes various processes, from population growth, expansion of the built environment, institutional activities like municipal annexation and zoning designations, to rising exchange values in urban economies and real estate. Sociology tends to stress the development of social relations that promote and accompany urbanization, following Max Weber ([1905] 1958), who conceptualized the city of antiquity as a political–economic ideal type in which market exchange is territorially defended and administered.

It's one thing to theorize the city as a primary context for modernity. It's another to assign the city a causal role – the legacy of the Chicago School of Sociology, early twentieth-century sociologists at the University of Chicago who studied the city as a natural laboratory for social life. The Chicago School's *urban ecology* paradigm analyzes social structure as spatial form, inquiring into the functional differentiation and spatial dispersal of social groupings and economic activities ("natural areas") across the metropolis. Population growth and technological advance are thought to fuel ecological dynamics and their social manifestations: enclave formation, deviance clustered in "zones of transition," immigrant competition and assimilation in the form of neighborhood succession, and city life as a "mosaic" of discrete social worlds. Louis Wirth (1938) distilled urban ecology's causal model into three variables: population size, density, and heterogeneity.

In hindsight, Wirth's thesis pointed towards later trends that eclipsed the causal role urban ecologists attributed to the city. In some ways, population size, density, and heterogeneity explain the ways of life found in mass institutions across society: prisons, universities, refugee camps, theme parks, the internet, and so on. Conversely, the spatial extension (now globalization) of social networks and economic activity means urban functions can touch down in settings with apparently little urban to them, like suburban immigrant enclaves and rural towns transformed by tourism migration. Consequently, urban sociologists have mostly retreated from urban ecology's spatial determinism, reconceptualizing urbanism as an interactional/network dynamic and urbanism as a political–economic process.

Furthermore, while retaining the focus on cities as significant forces for the organization and signification of social life, urban sociology refrains from generalizations about "the city" as a monolithic dynamic. Notably, the exodus of white and/or middle-class populations out of older cities that once characterized the twentieth-century "urban crisis" in North America and elsewhere has reversed in others; economic restructuring and ethnic/racial patterns appear to explain this urban variation. Still, the multiplicity of urban types, relations, and prospects that sociologists observe today may perhaps be understood as spatial processes of concentration and dispersal. Contemporary mega-urbanization in many developing nations may represent conventional regional/national patterns of population concentration, now amplified by political and economic turbulence (see Sassen 2012). Elsewhere, the global dispersal – of people, money, goods and services, images and ideas – suggests that life in some cities may be affected by activities across the world more than by ways of life found in their hinterlands.

SEE ALSO: Capitalism; Community; Environment, Sociology of the; Modernity; Space and Place; Urban Sociology

References

Fischer, Claude S. 1982. *To Dwell Among Friends*. Chicago: University of Chicago Press.

Sassen, Saskia. 2012. *Cities in a World Economy*, 4th ed. Thousand Oaks, CA: Sage.

Simmel, Georg. [1903] 1950. "The Metropolis and Mental Life." In *The Sociology of Georg Simmel*, edited by K.H. Wolff, 324–339. Glencoe, IL: Free Press.

Weber, Max. [1905] 1958. *The City*. Glencoe, IL: Free Press.

Wirth, Louis. 1938. "Urbanism as a Way of Life." *American Journal of Sociology* 44: 1–24.

Class

Rob Beamish

Queen's University, Canada

The concept of class is central to sociology although it is a complex and contested term. The best way to understand class is to focus on four sociologists whose work has most influenced how class is understood.

From *The Communist Manifesto*'s assertion that "[t]he history of all hitherto existing society is the history of class struggles," the term is intimately tied to Karl Marx. But Marx did not discover the existence of classes or their struggles. All of the early political economists – Adam Smith, David Ricardo, James and John Stuart Mill, for example – identified three classes – the proprietors of land, owners of capital, and workers – and their conflicting interests. Marx built on their work and although he left the question, "what constitutes a class?" unfinished at his death, he wrote enough to establish the basic elements for class analysis.

For Marx, there are three fundamental aspects to class. The first is the "objective" or structural aspect of class which is determined by one's place within the economy. Marx ([1852] 1935: 109) wrote: "In so far as millions of families live under economic conditions of existence that divide their mode of life, their interests, and their culture from those of other classes, and put them in hostile contrast to the latter, they form a class." Class begins with one's place in the social division of labor. This is often referred to as "class in itself."

The second aspect concerns the "subjective" dimension of class (i.e., class consciousness). In the transition from feudalism to capitalism, economic circumstances transformed the rural masses into urban workers. While creating "a common situation, common interests," it is only in the struggle against capital that "this mass becomes united, and constitutes itself as a class for itself" (Marx [1847] 1936: 145). By becoming conscious of its particular class interests and struggling for them, a "class in and for itself" is formed.

Once the separate individuals become members of a class, in and for itself, then the class itself takes on an independent existence such that the individuals are assimilated and encompassed by their class. Classes, not autonomous individuals, now become the major actors in the drama of history and it is the different classes that are stratified and conflict with each other.

Core Concepts in Sociology, First Edition. Edited by J. Michael Ryan.
© 2019 John Wiley & Sons Ltd. Published 2019 by John Wiley & Sons Ltd.

There were sound reasons for early political economists and Marx to identify three classes as the major forces in nineteenth-century Europe. All of the major social changes they witnessed appeared to be shaped by the concentration of power within each class. By the beginning of the twentieth century, however, it was apparent that Marx's conception did not encompass the complexity of class, class conflict, and social power. Max Weber introduced important changes into the concept of class.

Like Marx, Weber studied power and class in capitalist society. He argued that identifiable groups of people exercise power *within a community*. Furthermore, power results from the interaction of class, status, and politics within a community.

Second, Weber ([1956] 1968: 927) maintained that classes "are not communities; they merely represent possible, and frequent, bases for social action." To the predominant threefold conception of class, Weber argued that there are significant differences among the types of property that owners hold, what they produce, and the nature of the market. Similarly, those without property are highly differentiated depending on the skills they have and how they are deployed. Seeing greater diversity in the objective dimensions of class (class in itself), Weber was skeptical about the development of a class in and for itself.

Third, Weber emphasized the significance of status groups (*Stände*) within a community. Individuals within a community form associations based on shared lifestyles or worldviews. Although there is overlap between class situations and status groups, it is not absolute. Furthermore, status groups can exercise power that is inconsistent with their economic or class position.

Finally, Weber recognized that political parties wield significant power in the modern period. Through the formal political process, individuals or groups can exercise considerable political power without holding high-status positions or inordinate economic power. Political parties enable individuals outside the dominant class groups to exercise power and create change.

While Weber's conception of class and power was more multi-dimensional than Marx's, sociologists continued to refine the idea of class as the complexity of contemporary societies grew.

Drawing upon Marx and Weber, Pierre Bourdieu develops class around three key concepts: field, capital, and habitus. A field is a hierarchically arranged, delimited, conceptual "space" where individuals, with different abilities and resources (capital), compete for positions and standing (Bourdieu [1980] 1990). The configuration of positions defining the field result from, and contribute further to, the types of power and the demands made upon the players/actors in the field.

Bourdieu identifies four types of capital: economic (money and productive property), social (social and institutionalized networks, group memberships, etc.), cultural (types of knowledge, cultural goods such as books, or in an institutionalized form as educational qualifications, etc.), and symbolic. Players use their capital to compete for positions in the field. Depending on the field, one type of capital may be more significant than the others but all are brought into play most of the time.

Habitus refers to a system of deeply embodied "dispositions" that individuals draw upon as they act in the field. Habitus is the practical sense guiding one's actions; it is how one is "disposed" (inclined, predisposed, internally prompted) to act in response to the actions of others. Because social action occurs in a field, habitus and the field shape and constitute social action.

Bourdieu's conceptions of capital and habitus allow him to draw together, in a manner that goes beyond Weber, the (inter)relationship of class and status groups. Social networks, knowledge, and tastes create "communities" in the Weberian sense, and they also create and stem from a class habitus that overlaps significantly but not necessarily fully with economic capital. The volume of capital possessed and the ability to transpose it from one form to another, as needed in different situations, create identifiable class groupings in the contemporary world and explain how power and class are interrelated.

Like Bourdieu, Anthony Giddens' theory of "structuration" seeks to integrate human agency with elements of social structure. Giddens emphasizes that structures in social action are not "things," like the girders of a building or organs in an organism. They are rules (informal and formal ways of acting) and resources (those one possesses and those over which one has control) that individuals use to create and recreate social practices across space and time. Due to what Giddens terms "the duality of structure," these rules and resources simultaneously enable and constrain social action.

Like Marx and Weber, Giddens (1973) regards class as a basis for social power and an outcome of the ownership or non-ownership of productive resources. In and through their economic, political, and social activities, individuals in capitalist society produce and tend to reproduce a class structure. "[P]roperty ownership" Giddens (1973: 271–272) maintains, "remains of primary importance within the economic order."

Second, Giddens (1973: 273) agrees with Weber that divisions within classes are numerous and complex: "Class divisions cannot be drawn like lines on a map, and the extent to which class structuration occurs depends upon the interaction of various sets of factors." But, Giddens emphasizes, "this is not the same as saying that class is a 'multidimensional' phenomenon which can be analyzed as an aggregate of several hierarchical 'dimensions', as is sometimes claimed by certain of those (mis)interpreters of Weber who identify 'class' and 'stratification.'" Class structuration, Giddens notes "is most strongly developed at three levels, separating the upper, middle and working classes."

Finally, Giddens' notions of the duality of structure and the way formal and informal rules enable and constrain social action allow him to draw nonclass factors into the analysis of social inequality while keeping them distinct from the impact of class. Gender, racialization, (dis)ability, age, and sexual identity, for example, are, along with class, intertwined in the social practices ordered across space and time which constitute social action as a whole. While those factors must be taken into account, that cannot occur in the same way that class factors are included. The unique impact of nonclass factors should be distinguished from the impact of class because their integration in recursive, social practices is different than the rules and resources pertinent to class.

SEE ALSO: Capital: Cultural, Social, Economic; Class: capitalist; Inequality, Global; Stratification and Inequality

References

Bourdieu, Pierre. [1980] 1990. *The Logic of Practice*. Stanford, CA: Stanford University Press.
Giddens, Anthony. 1973. *The Class Structure of the Advanced Societies*. London: Hutchinson.
Marx, Karl. [1847] 1936. *The Poverty of Philosophy*. London: Martin Lawrence Limited.

Marx, Karl. [1852] 1935. *The Eighteenth Brumaire of Louis Bonaparte*. New York: International Publishers.
Weber, Max. [1956] 1968. *Economy and Society*. New York: Bedminster Press.

Further Reading

Giddens, Anthony. 1984. *The Constitution of Society*. Berkeley: University of California Press.
Wright, Erik. 2006. *Approaches to Class Analysis*. New York: Cambridge University Press.

Class, Capitalist

Leslie Sklair

London School of Economics and Political Science, UK

The capitalist class has traditionally been defined as those who own the means of production and act directly or indirectly as a ruling class. The original theory of the capitalist class as elaborated by Marx and Engels in the middle of the nineteenth century saw this as an international phenomenon and scholarly research has tended to concentrate at the level of the nation-state, particularly in large and economically powerful countries. With the rise of globalization and neoliberalism as new features of the economic, political, and cultural spheres in the second half of the twentieth century, attention started to focus on transnational corporations. Novel theories abounded around ruling classes and elites and new concepts multiplied, for example: international managerial bourgeoisie; international networks; intercorporate relations; triple alliance of multinational, state and local capital. A key source of insight into a global ruling class emerged from the Gramscian turn in International Relations. The concept of the transnational capitalist class (TCC) within the global capitalist system can be seen as an attempt to build on this rich literature, a step towards consolidating the theoretical link between capitalist globalization and the ruling class. This implies, conceptually, that the state (represented by the state fraction of the TCC) is only one, albeit important, level of analysis and that state actors are losing power in some key areas of economic, political, and societal decision making to nonstate global actors – a transition from the international to the transnational mode of analysis.

TCC theorists generally focus around three working hypotheses. First, a transnational capitalist class is emerging that is beginning to act as a global ruling class in some spheres; second, that the key feature of the globalization of the capitalist system in recent decades has been the profit-driven culture-ideology of consumerism organized by this class; and third, that the TCC is working consciously to obscure the effects of the two central crises of global capitalism, namely the simultaneous creation of increasing poverty and increasing wealth within and between countries, and the ecological unsustainability of the global capitalist system. Despite its relatively short history there are already several ways of conceptualizing the transnational capitalist class. Prominent among these are the materialist approach of Robinson and Harris (2000), the network-oriented approach of Carroll (2010), and the global system approach of Sklair (1995, 2001). In this latter formulation, the TCC is analytically divided into four main often overlapping fractions: corporate, political, technical, and consumerist.

Core Concepts in Sociology, First Edition. Edited by J. Michael Ryan.
© 2019 John Wiley & Sons Ltd. Published 2019 by John Wiley & Sons Ltd.

The transnational capitalist class is transnational (or global) in the following respects: (a) The economic interests of its members are increasingly globally linked rather than exclusively local and national; (b) the TCC seeks to exert economic control in the workplace, political control in domestic and international politics, and culture-ideology control in everyday life through specific forms of global competitive and consumerist rhetoric and practice; (c) members of the TCC have outward-oriented global rather than inward-oriented local perspectives on most economic, political, and culture-ideology issues; (d) members of the TCC tend to share similar lifestyles, particularly patterns of higher education (increasingly in business schools) and consumption of luxury goods and services; (e) finally, members of the TCC seek to project corporate global visions of themselves as citizens of the world as well as of their places of birth. The concept of the transnational capitalist class implies that there is one central inner circle that makes system-wide decisions, and that it connects in a variety of ways with associates in each community, city, country, and region. A crucial component of the networking of the TCC is that its members will typically occupy a variety of interlocking positions. Members of all four fractions of the TCC serve on corporate boards, think tanks, charities, scientific, sports, arts, and culture bodies, universities, medical foundations, and similar institutions. Business, particularly the transnational corporation sector, then begins to monopolize symbols of modernity and postmodernity like free enterprise, international competitiveness, and the good life, and seeks to transform all social spheres in its own image.

It is no exaggeration to say that there is now a flourishing community of scholars – largely but not exclusively connected with the Network for Critical Studies of Global Capitalism (NCSGC) – who are building a substantial foundation for research on the transnational capitalist class all over the world. This group maintains an active database of work on the subject that can be found here: https://drive.google.com/open?id=1SzooNM4_4pQUkPPK-vIwYSGE46ijFlTqRVGsMMgAAH0.

SEE ALSO: Capital: Social, Cultural, and Economic; Capitalism; Class; Consumption; Globalization; Inequality, Global; Marxism

References

Carroll, W. 2010. *The Making of a Transnational Capitalist Class: Corporate Power in the 21st Century*. London: Zed Books.
Robinson, W., and Harris, J. 2000. "Towards a Global Ruling Class? Globalization and the Transnational Capitalist Class." *Science & Society* 64 (1): 11–54.
Sklair, L. 1995. *Sociology of the Global System*. Baltimore: Johns Hopkins University Press.
Sklair, L. 2001. *The Transnational Capitalist Class*. Oxford: Blackwell.

Further Reading

Scott, J., ed. 1990. *The Sociology of Elites*. 3 vols. Aldershot: Edward Elgar.
Sklair, L. 2002. *Globalization: Capitalism and Its Alternatives*. Oxford: Oxford University Press.

Sklair, L. 2016. *The Icon Project: Architecture, Cities, and Capitalist Globalization.* New York: Oxford University Press.

Stokman, F.N., R. Ziegler, and J. Scott, eds. 1985. *Networks of Corporate Power: A Comparative Analysis of Ten Countries.* Cambridge: Cambridge University Press.

Useem, M. 1984. *The Inner Circle: Large Corporations and the Rise of Business Political Activity in the US and UK.* New York: Oxford University Press.

Colonialism and Postcolonialism

Gurminder K. Bhambra

University of Warwick, UK

Colonialism created the modern world and yet is absent from most sociological discussions of how that world came into being and what its specific character might be. Standard discussions of the modern world, or modernity, present it as being a consequence of the industrial and French revolutions. These establish a market economy based on private property and a political system based on the sovereignty of the individual. They are united through ideas of reason and progress, with reason itself understood as the handmaiden of progress. The defining events of modernity are presented as endogenous to Europe; the broader global conditions that enabled these events are elided and other events, which could also claim to be world-historical, are silenced (see Bhambra 2007).

The strong association of reason, progress, and rights with the emergence of the modern world involves representing Europe as initiating a project of Enlightenment (or subsequently emancipation), against authority and tradition. However, the relations of domination in which this self-claimed European project were embedded is rarely part of its own account. Scholars such as Quijano (2007) and Mignolo (2007) have argued for colonialism to be understood as the context for the emergence of the modern world. As Quijano suggests, it was with the conquest of the lands that we now call Latin America that the new world order was constituted, "culminating, five hundred years later, in a global power covering the whole planet" (2007: 168). Colonialism, then, has to be understood as the world-historical process that has shaped the modern world both materially and epistemologically.

In its intellectual resistance to colonial forms of knowledge, postcolonialism offers more than simple opposition (see Lugones 2011). It is the basis from which to reclaim, as Spivak argues, "a series of regulative political concepts, the *supposedly* authoritative narrative of whose production was written elsewhere" (1990: 225). With this, Spivak builds on Said's ([1978] 1995) foundational work in *Orientalism* where he opens up the question of the production of knowledge from a global perspective. Said unsettles the terrain of any argument concerned with the "universal" by demonstrating how this idea is based both on an analytic division of the world and an elision of that division. It is a double displacement in that by focusing only on the "modernity" aspect of "modernity/coloniality," "modernity" is highlighted while "coloniality" is silenced. In the process, the

Core Concepts in Sociology, First Edition. Edited by J. Michael Ryan.
© 2019 John Wiley & Sons Ltd. Published 2019 by John Wiley & Sons Ltd.

West's material domination of the "other" is naturalized and justified. It is this complicity between academic knowledge production and historical processes of colonialism that the best of work within postcolonialism seeks to uncover.

The challenge posed by postcolonialism to dominant conceptual frameworks is encapsulated also within the work of Bhabha (1994) whose essays in *The Location of Culture* coalesce around a dual engagement with social ethics and subject formation on the one hand, and (the representation of) contemporary inequalities and their historical conditions, on the other. Postcolonialism, for him, is not about the establishment of separate trajectories or multiple and parallel interpretations. Rather, it attempts to interrupt the standard discourses by re-inscribing "other" traditions into narratives of modernity and thus transforming those narratives from within (see Bhambra 2014).

The insistent association of modernity with the French and industrial revolutions, for example, reveals the Eurocentered nature of standard discourses. By bearing witness to different and interconnected pasts, such as of the Haitian Revolution (see Trouillot 1995), one is able to turn from interrogating the past to initiating new dialogues about it and thus bringing into being new histories and, from those new histories, a new present and new futures. Postcolonial critical discourse at its best, Bhabha suggests, "contests modernity through the establishment of other historical sites, other forms of enunciation" (1994: 254) and, in so doing, rearticulates understandings of modernity as located in colonial endeavors.

This has also been at the heart of earlier scholarly works by those involved in anticolonial movements. Fanon (1963), for example, argued that the breakup of the colonial world was not about the establishment of *two* zones – the previously colonized and the previous colonizers – but, rather, the abolition of one – the colonial world – and the subsequent restructuring of the relations that had sustained it. Césaire ([1955] 1972) and Memmi ([1957] 1965) similarly regarded the colonial world as constituted by the interconnected histories of the "moderns" and "nonmoderns" through colonialism.

Working with "a self-contained version of the West," as Spivak argues, "is to ignore its production by the imperialist project" (1988: 289). This does not mean that the histories of imperialism or colonialism are the only significant histories of modernity, but that there is a need more explicitly to address the question of how what is currently dominant and hegemonic came to be so. Postcolonialism, then, is a provocation to think of the world that colonialism has brought into being, not to examine a world in which colonialism is over.

SEE ALSO: Development, Sociology of; Globalization; Inequality, Global; Modernity; Political Sociology

References

Bhabha, Homi K. 1994. *The Location of Culture*. London: Routledge.
Bhambra, Gurminder K. 2007. *Rethinking Modernity: Postcolonialism and the Sociological Imagination*. Basingstoke: Palgrave.
Bhambra, Gurminder K. 2014. *Connected Sociologies*. London: Bloomsbury Academic.
Césaire, Aimé. [1955] 1972. *Discourse on Colonialism*, translated by Joan Pinkham. New York: Monthly Review Press.

Fanon, Frantz. 1963. *The Wretched of the Earth*, translated by Constance Farrington. New York: Grove Press.

Lugones, María. 2011. "Toward a Decolonial Feminism." *Hypatia* 25 (4): 742–759.

Memmi, Albert. [1957] 1965. *The Colonizer and the Colonized*. Boston: Beacon Press.

Mignolo, Walter. 2007. "Delinking: The Rhetoric of Modernity, the Logic of Coloniality and the Grammar of De-Coloniality." *Cultural Studies* 21 (2): 449–514.

Quijano, Aníbal. 2007. "Coloniality and Modernity/Rationality." *Cultural Studies* 21 (2): 168–178.

Said, Edward W. [1978] 1995. *Orientalism: Western Conceptions of the Orient*. London: Penguin.

Spivak, Gayatri Chakravorty. 1988. "Can the Subaltern Speak?" In *Marxism and the Interpretation of Culture*, edited by Cary Nelson and Lawrence Grossberg, 271–313. Chicago: University of Illinois Press.

Spivak, Gayatri Chakravorty. 1990. "Post-Structuralism, Marginality, Postcoloniality and Value." In *Literary Theory Today*, edited by Peter Collier and Helga Geyer-Ryan, 219–244. Cambridge: Polity Press.

Trouillot, Michel-Rolph. 1995. *Silencing the Past: Power and the Production of History*. Boston: Beacon Press.

Community

Graham Day

Bangor University, UK

At its broadest, "community" refers to things which people have in common and which bind them together socially. People form a community when they share goals, values, or experiences and inhabit a common framework of social relationships. Communities are thought of as informally organized social groupings which mediate between the individual and society as a whole. Community is not a term which has emerged from any particular social theory or scientific analysis. Like other familiar sociological concepts, it is borrowed from and circulates widely within popular discourse, including everyday speech, media reportage, and political commentary. When used by sociologists it carries over much of the significance it has for these other types of enterprise, and can mean a variety of things according to context. This creates confusion and disagreement due to lack of certainty about its exact meaning. Consequently, although some sociologists regard community as a fundamentally important idea, others contend that it is too vague and elusive to be useful. A substantial literature concerned with definitional problems demonstrates that its value as a concept remains contested. The German sociologist Ferdinand Tönnies ([1887] 1955) introduced a key distinction between community (*Gemeinschaft*) and "association" or society (*Gesellschaft*), a contrast echoed in the works of Marx, Durkheim, and Weber. Community represented the spontaneous, organic type of relationship in which people are familiar with one another personally, as rounded individuals. Tönnies compared the warmth and intimacy of such relationships with the impersonality and distance typical of more rational contacts, when individuals meet primarily for specialized, instrumental purposes. He made a strong connection between community and traditional social order, whereas association was more a feature of modern society. Given the positive tone of his version of community, this encouraged a negative reading of social change, whereby processes like industrialization and urbanization resulted in the "loss" of community. Many later analyses follow this lead, associating modernization and development with issues of loneliness, alienation, and disorder.

Locating community in the past, alongside tradition, tended to equate actual communities with rural or small-town contexts, where settled populations dominated by ties of kinship and religion engaged in patterns of dense and repeated interaction. Communities were expected to display internal coherence and an integrated pattern of

Core Concepts in Sociology, First Edition. Edited by J. Michael Ryan.
© 2019 John Wiley & Sons Ltd. Published 2019 by John Wiley & Sons Ltd.

social existence, assumptions closely aligned with functionalist social theories. Led by examples from social anthropology, the idea of community was taken up in empirical investigation of particular locations, to see how they worked as social entities, and to describe and explain their distinctive features. Although each community was said to be unique, its identity was often disguised behind generic labels, like "Yankee City" and "Middletown." A common criticism of such "community studies" is that they fail to produce generalized knowledge, offering instead a series of one-off, novelistic depictions. A counter argument would be that they provide detailed local ethnographies enabling in-depth, multidimensional analysis of distinctive "ways of life."

Despite theoretical predictions that modern industries and city life would be intrinsically hostile to community formation, urban sociologists have discovered cohesive communities organized around class, ethnic, occupational, and religious identities. Special attention has been paid to the "unexpected" persistence of aspects of community, including extensive networks of social interaction, amongst working-class populations, and in areas of deprivation. Close examination reveals however that far from being marked by social homogeneity and consensus, community life is often riddled with division and conflict, while members are preoccupied with determining who belongs, and who can or should be excluded. Research challenges the presumption that communities have an objective status, as collectivities with clear boundaries in space and time. The sense of local distinctiveness is undermined by the realization that communities are not exclusively geographical, tied to particular localities, but embedded in wider connections, subject to changing technologies of communication, and shaped by forces of mobility and globalization. When the limits of community proved to be contested, and unstable, attention shifted to how communities are conceptualized by members themselves.

The prevailing view is that most contemporary communities are social constructions which people actively engage in producing and reproducing. Since individuals may participate simultaneously in several communities, great importance attaches to how they choose to symbolize and maintain the nature of each community. Examples include: diasporic communities of migrants, which by definition are not territorially confined; elective communities in which people exercise choice to come together, according to lifestyle preferences or possessing similar interests and resources; and "imagined" communities organized along lines of nationality, faith, or ideology. These diverge from everyday conceptions, still common among policy makers, which cling to the old vision of communities as self-contained units rooted in place. An extreme instance would be virtual communities, formed online or through social media, which have no physical presence and may involve little direct interaction.

In a world where boundaries are subject to constant negotiation, yet people value their differences from one another, community remains a proposition which many find attractive. There is ongoing debate between "communitarians" and liberals as to the positive attributes of community (social support, trust, and solidarity) versus their negative counterparts (relationships can be inward-looking, oppressive, and exclusionary). Many dimensions previously associated with community research are discussed now under the headings of identity and belonging, whilst the theme of community decline has mutated into discussions of "social capital." Those who find the idea of community altogether too woolly or old-fashioned advocate examining instead the properties and effects of different types of social networks. Finally it should be noted that contrary to the frequently romanticized image of community, it has a downside in which strong identification with a particular group can have anti-social consequences, as people gather together into narrowly defensive or sometimes aggressive combinations.

SEE ALSO: Ethnography; Social Network Analysis; Urban Sociology

Reference

Tönnies, Ferdinand. [1887] 1955. *Community and Association*. London: Routledge and Kegan Paul.

Further Reading

Bauman, Zygmunt. 2001. *Community*. Cambridge: Polity Press.
Cohen, Anthony. 1985. *The Symbolic Construction of Community*. London: Ellis Harwood.
Day, Graham. 2006. *Community and Everyday Life*. New York: Routledge.
Putnam, Robert. 2000. *Bowling Alone: The Collapse and Revival of American Community*. New York: Simon and Schuster.

Constructionism vs. Essentialism

Kenneth J. Gergen

Swarthmore College, USA

Constructionism typically refers to a conception of knowledge proposing that our accounts of the world are not pictures of the world as it is, but the outcomes of negotiated agreements, assumptions, traditions of interpretation, and representational demands. Accounts of the world are not required by the way the world is, but are employed by groups of people in achieving valued ends. The distinction between genders, for example, is not required because there are simply two genders within the human species. Rather, the distinction is useful for a variety of social purposes. And, if the distinction is made, it may be based on different criteria for different groups (e.g., chromosomes, genitals, secondary sex characteristics, clothing, or hair styles) and at different times (e.g., Olympic trials, mating traditions, nursery school). What we take to be knowledge of the world, then, is a social construction. Although there is no single, unified theory of social construction, contributions to constructionist theory of knowledge emerge from multiple disciplines, including the history of science, the sociology of knowledge, the social studies of science, critical theory, feminist studies, rhetorical studies, and poststructural literary theory, among others. The term *social constructivism* is often used interchangeably with *social constructionism.*

Essentialism typically refers to a view emerging in the philosophical writings of Plato and Aristotle, holding that for any specific entity in the world there is a set of attributes or properties necessary to its identity and its functioning. These attributes or properties inhere within the entity itself, independent of the viewer. This orientation later came to serve as the basis of scientific taxonomy, and a realist view of scientific research as revealing or illuminating the character of the world as it is. As in the case of constructionism, essentialism is not a single unified theory, but an historically extended dialogue with many variations.

Core Concepts in Sociology, First Edition. Edited by J. Michael Ryan.
© 2019 John Wiley & Sons Ltd. Published 2019 by John Wiley & Sons Ltd.

Principal Points of Contention

For constructionists, the essentialist tradition is flawed in two major ways:

Political conservativism and social oppression. As a host of critics point out, particularly within the social and biological sciences, essentialist assumptions can be inimical to cultural life. Categories of race, gender, sexual preference, intelligence, and mental illness, for example, function in ways that freeze stereotypes that are culturally divisive. Distinctions between races and genders are also insensitive to enormous ranges of difference, and carry with them normative implications that anyone who does not fall neatly into a category is "unnatural" or "queer." In anthropology the traditional practice of describing other cultures has similarly been criticized for its essentializing the other in ways that primarily reflect the biases of Western researchers.

Constraints on the growth of knowledge. As constructionists also point out, presuming a world fixed within the categories shared by a given people at a given period of history constrains the growth of knowledge. It delimits the range of what is intelligible to study, and how it might be characterized. It is here important to note that in using the phrase "growth in knowledge" constructionists do not mean incremental understanding of the way the world is. Such a view would be more consistent with an essentialist orientation. Rather, the phrase refers to pragmatic gains in our capacities for action in the world. Thus, for example, to presume that various forms of culturally unacceptable behavior constitute "mental illness" (with a biological cause) radically constricts our potential for creating practices of caring, coping, or controlling.

Essentialists, in contrast, find constructionist proposals problematic in two important ways:

Inability to account for scientific progress. Many essentialists see within constructionism a nihilistic undertone. If all science is a social construction, then what is the value of scientific research? Such nihilism seems wholly unwarranted in light of the enormous success of science in curing illness, generating energy, enhancing practices of farming, creating weapons, and so on. Essentialism is productive, while constructionists offer little but critique. In reply, constructionists point to an enormous literature on the social processes essential to bringing about what we call scientific progress.

The incoherence of skepticism. For essentialists, constructionism represents a form of skepticism, and is thus subject to Plato's critique, to whit: "If there is no truth, objectivity, or empirical knowledge, as skeptics claim, then on what grounds should skepticism be accepted? By its own account, the skeptic's proposal cannot be true, objective, or empirically based." Yet, most constructionists do not argue that their arguments are true, objective, or empirically grounded in this sense. Rather, on its own account, constructionism should be evaluated in terms of a *reflective pragmatism*, that is, in terms of its social utility in a global context of plural values. In effect, constructionists do not seek to have a final word, but offer an orientation to knowledge claims that would sustain multiparty dialogue.

Possible Resolution

For many, conflict between these competing positions is largely resolved by embracing a *situated essentialism*. This position initially emerged in feminist critique of gender essentialism. To argue against such essentialism simultaneously undermined the very male/female binary on which the conception of feminism was grounded. By adopting a position of situated essentialism, one could rationalize the irony of both embracing a distinction and simultaneously undermining it. Situated essentialism also facilitates an appreciation of widespread research demonstrating the utility of essentialist discourse in everyday life. We may recognize the utility without committing to the suggested ontologies. Finally, such a position is coherent with reflective pragmatism: a scientist may thus be an essentialist within any given line of inquiry, while neither committing to the assumptions nor avoiding reflection on the line of inquiry itself.

SEE ALSO: Deviance; Epistemology; Frames, Narratives, and Ideology; Knowledge, Sociology of; Medicalization; Postmodernism and Poststructuralism; Social Theory

Further Reading

Gergen, K.J. 1994. *Realities and Relationships: Soundings in Social Construction.* Cambridge, MA: Harvard University Press.

Gergen, K.J. 2017. "Human Essence: Toward a Relational Reconstruction." In J. Dovidio and M. van Zomeran (eds.), *Oxford Handbook of Human Essences*, 247–260. New York: Oxford University Press.

Oderberg, D.S. 2008. *Real Essentialism*. London: Routledge.

Quine, W.V.O. 1960. *Word and Object*. Cambridge, MA: MIT Press.

Consumption

Juliet B. Schor

Boston College, USA

Sociology is an essential discipline for understanding consumption. In contrast to economics and psychology, which understand the consumer as rational economic man, an isolated, infinitely desiring agent whose essential characteristics are unvarying across space and time, sociology understands consumption as always determined by social and cultural context. In this, it stands with anthropology and history as disciplines which situate consumption within social structures and social dynamics. The sociology of consumption contains two major themes. First, social inequality structures consumption. Class has been the most commonly studied differentiator, but gender, race, and ethnicity are also important. Second, that consumption takes on a particular character within modern capitalism. In these "consumer societies" people use goods and services to define and display their identities, enact moral projects, and connect with others. Consumer societies develop "consumer cultures," which are the foundation of much social interaction.

Consumption and Social Inequality

For decades, the dominant sociological approach to consumption emphasized its role as a communicator of social difference, and particularly social class. Thorstein Veblen's 1899 classic, *The Theory of the Leisure Class,* introduced the concept of "conspicuous consumption." Veblen saw visible consumption as the means by which the wealthy maintained social position and the upwardly mobile made status claims. Here, consumer goods are instrumental, a marker of status, rather than desirable for its functional benefits. Furthermore, Veblen's model of vertical emulation, i.e., people replicating the consumption patterns of those who are wealthier than they, explains how new, expensive consumer goods such as fancy cars, apparel, homes, and possessions diffuse throughout the population and help affirm an unequal social order. A key assumption of this approach is that goods have widely agreed-upon social meanings which can be "de-coded" by observers and that the status value of a good is determined by its expense.

Core Concepts in Sociology, First Edition. Edited by J. Michael Ryan.

For decades, the Veblenian model remained the dominant approach to consumption within American sociology. Classic accounts of small-town America by Andrew Warner and Robert and Helen Lynd focused on how people used consumer goods to signal and solidify status within their communities. After World War Two, this approach continued to dominate, especially during the 1950s when influential popular books such as Vance Packard's *The Status Seekers* and John Kenneth Galbraith's *The Affluent Society* also explained consumption largely in terms of social communication in the service of class positioning.

In the late 1980s, scholars began abandoning this approach. They argued that the consensus about the status values of goods was eroding, and consumption was becoming more uniform across the social spectrum. In addition, postmodernists such as Jean Baudrillard described fragmentation of the market and inflation of consumer symbols on account of pervasive advertising. This proliferation of consumer goods was undermining consumers' ability to decode status symbols.

The Bourdieusian Turn

The field reconsolidated with the publication of Pierre Bourdieu's *Distinction*. Bourdieu affirmed the class patterning of consumption but added "cultural capital" as a determinant of "taste." Cultural capital is knowledge of elite taste, manners, and habits, and is transmitted through family upbringing and elite educational institutions. Consumers high in cultural capital sought "distinction" through consumer practices that were rare and inaccessible. Bourdieu analyzed dynamics between wealthy, but less "cultured" elites (akin to Veblen's status seekers), and high cultural capital consumers with taste but not money. The "working class" was consigned to consumer lives dictated mainly by "economic necessity." Like Veblen, Bourdieu's model accounted for the pattern of consumption goods and practices across society, but using both culture and economics as explanatory variables.

Bourdieu's contribution reignited controversy about the structure of the consumer field, and whether the high vs. low distinction had collapsed, as scholars discovered that high cultural capital consumers were "omnivores," i.e., had tastes that spanned the class spectrum. Lively debate ensued on the extent to which Bourdieu's approach accurately captured the pattern of consumption. Survey-based studies of musical genres and other cultural goods attempted to map tastes across socioeconomic categories, with mixed results by country and time period. Qualitative research focused on how omnivorous consumers jockeyed for distinction by consuming low-class products in elite ways. Johnston and Baumann's work on "foodies" emphasized the importance of exotic and authentic food, including peasant and working class cuisines. However, the meaning of omnivorousness continues to be debated, as its relevance to a Bourdieusian framework remains contested.

Bourdieu's framework spread to other contexts. Scholars studied subcultural capital and the ways in which musical, artistic, and consumption subcultures developed expertise and habits as they perfected specific practices of consumption that defined membership and gave status within their communities. Others examined the relevance of Bourdieusian analysis in the Global South, focusing on the contrast between national consumer cultures and the status to be gained by orienting towards Western culture.

Consumption and Capitalism

An alternative approach emphasizes the capitalist character of consumption. The classic account is the mid-twentieth-century contribution by Frankfort School theorists Theodor Adorno and Max Horkheimer. They argued that capitalism had spawned a degraded, lowest-common-denominator popular culture which lulled people into accepting economic alienation and exploitation. In this account, consumption created the ideological legitimacy for the capitalist system. Advertising and marketing were developing ever-more sophisticated tools of segmentation and classification to manipulate and dominate, as shown by high levels of media use, shopping time, and acquisition. This perspective was popular during the counter-culture of the 1960s and 1970s, exemplified most famously by Herbert Marcuse's *One-Dimensional Man.* Sociologists in this tradition studied the influence of marketing and advertising, and saw consumption as a force for social conformity and passivity.

This perspective came under fire in the 1980s. Mirroring larger debates within sociology over agency and structure, the consumer literature engaged in its own "agency vs. manipulation" debate. In contrast to "agentic" consumers who acted in their own interests, critics were accused of seeing consumers as "cultural dupes." Underlying this debate was disagreement about where market power was situated – in the hands of powerful monopolistic corporations who could dictate outcomes, or sovereign consumers who knew what they wanted. Douglas Holt provided a potential resolution with the insight that the relation between corporations/marketers and consumers had changed over time. At mid-century, corporations did hold enormous "cultural authority" over consumers, as Adorno and Horkheimer argued. However, the counter-culture of the 1960s led to a rejection marketers' influence. As a result, they adopted a new model, in which they no longer told people *what* to want, but researched emergent cultural trends and sold them back to consumers.

In the 1990s, scholars again turned to capitalist dynamics to understand emergent consumer patterns, this time in the context of consumerism in the Global South. They studied rising demand for branded products such as Coca-Cola, blue jeans, and American music and considered the ways that Western consumer culture was transforming formerly colonized countries. A vigorous debate with anthropologists ensued about how consumer objects affect culture and whether product meanings crossed boundaries or were "indigenized." Was McDonaldization, to use George Ritzer's term, standardizing culture? While the anthropologists convincingly debunked the idea that product meanings are static across cultures, the world was clearly becoming more culturally hybrid. And because consumer changes are typically accompanied by economic development and new patterns of work, time use, and family life, the sociological perspective of growing cultural conformity is likely to be more accurate in the longer term.

Consumption and Identity

Anthony Giddens's *Modernity and Self Identity* provided a second approach to the ways in which capitalism affected consumption. Giddens argued that in late modernity individuals were forced to enact a project of the self, creating a self-aware, or "reflexive," identity with a unique personal narrative. (He contrasted this with "traditional" identities, which are determined by social roles.) Consumer goods were at the core of the late modern identity. Indeed, some scholars went further and argued that consumption had become *the* privileged site of sovereignty. Scholars also began studying the ways that consumer goods and practices constructed group identities other than class, such as race and ethnicity, and gender and sexual identities. Consumer choices in cuisine, hair and beauty regimes, and apparel were seen as vital to creating and reproducing race and ethnic difference. Scholars such as Karyn Lacy and Cassi Pittman contributed to a growing literature on consumption among the American black middle class that complicated notions of status and identity. Masculinity and femininity were also studied as they were inscribed in clothing, food choices, automobile consumption, and other consumer practices. Consumption rituals created bonding within groups, and defined symbolic boundaries. This work contributed to a turn away from consumer critique to an interpretive framework which relied on consumers' own interpretations of meanings and practices, rather than scholars' views.

Ecological Crisis and Consumption

As ecological crisis intensifies, sociologists have been studying the ways in which consumers are responding, through the purchase of "green" products as well as engaging in "ethical consumption" to punish and reward companies for their environmental and labor practices. Echoes of earlier debates resonate in this literature. Is it possible to "shop" for a greener, safer, or fairer world, or does consumption remain a socially pacifying activity *à la* Frankfurt School, as Andrew Szasz has argued? Are high-priced green products like Priuses and Teslas merely elites' newest status symbols? Finally, we may consider a question that goes beyond the sociology of consumption to the question of society itself. Can consumption be transformed from a major source of carbon emissions and ecological degradation, into a positive force for achieving a sustainable world?

SEE ALSO: Capital: Cultural, Social, Economic; Capitalism; Class; Consumption; Environment, Sociology of the; Globalization

Further Reading

Bourdieu, Pierre. 1984. *Distinction: A Social Critique of the Judgement of Taste.* Cambridge, MA: Harvard University Press.

Holt, Douglas. 2002. "Why Do Brands Cause Trouble?" *Journal of Consumer Research* 29: 70–91.

Johnston, Josée, and Shyon Baumann. 2007. "Democracy versus Distinction: A Study of Omnivorousness in Gourmet Food Writing." *American Journal of Sociology* 13 (1): 165–204.

Sassatelli, Roberta. 2007. *Consumer Culture: History, Theory and Politics.* London: Sage.

Schor, Juliet B., and Craig J. Thompson, eds. 2014. *Sustainable Lifestyles and the Quest for Plenitude: Case Studies of the New Economy.* New Haven, CT: Yale University Press.

Crime and Juvenile Delinquency, Sociology of

Joseph Asomah and Hongming Cheng

University of Saskatchewan, Canada

Crime and juvenile delinquency are universal public concerns all over the world although they differ in extent from country to country. The legalistic approach to crime and juvenile delinquency sees crime and juvenile delinquency solely as acts which have been legally prohibited by the state such that, if done, it renders the actor liable to formal punishment or treatment or both. The sociology of crime and juvenile delinquency, on the other hand, is the body of knowledge regarding crime and juvenile delinquency as violation of social conduct norms or as deviance from social expectations. The sociology of crime and juvenile delinquency is thus interested in the relationship between crime/juvenile delinquency and social factors. It uses established sociological methods, such as records, experiments, surveys, historical data, content analysis, etc. to study definitions, causes, and patterns of criminal behavior and juvenile delinquency in the social context, as well as formal and informal social control of crime and juvenile delinquency.

Deviance, Crime, and Juvenile Delinquency

The main concepts of the sociology of crime and juvenile delinquency include deviance, crime, and juvenile delinquency. Deviance refers generally to any departure from the social expectations, including violation of laws. Adults commit a crime when they break the criminal law. On the contrary, however, youth or minors commit a delinquent act when they violate the social expectations and/or the law. Juvenile delinquency is a sociolegal term articulating the behavior of youth or minors who have broken the law or violated social norms, including anti-social behavior. A country's legal framework set the age limit for those described as minors or juvenile. In many Western countries, such as the United Kingdom (except Scotland), the United States, and Canada, those under the age of 18 are considered minors in the eye of the law. Minors commit status offenses, which refer to the breaking of laws for which adults are legally exempted. In many places, for example, children under the age of 16 may not buy and drink alcohol. When minors break such law that does not affect adults, they have committed status offenses and hence are considered as juvenile delinquents.

Juvenile delinquency is a growing universal concern. The nature, the extent, and the gravity of juvenile delinquency, however, vary from one context to the other. The sociology of crime and juvenile delinquency typically pays much attention to theories of crime causation by focusing on answering either of these two questions: Why do some people break the rules? Why do most people conform to the rules? The next section explores the evolution of these theories, and the main linkages between and among these theories with a central focus on juvenile delinquency.

Sociological Theories of Crime and Juvenile Delinquency

In the 1830s, Belgian statistician Adolphe Quetelet pioneered the collection and analysis of crime data and suggested that the occurrence, increase, and decrease of crime, as well as the type of crime, are associated with social factors. In 1884 Enrico Ferri published *Criminal Sociology*, a book that marked the formation of the sociology of crime. Since the twentieth century, the sociology of crime, especially the sociology of juvenile delinquency, has been further developed. In this process, strain, social learning, control theory, social learning theory, labeling, social disorganization theory, critical and conflict theories have all played an important role. These social explanations of crime and delinquency emerged to question the individualistic explanations in the United States in particular from the 1930s.

Social Structure Theories of Delinquency

Social structure theories generally propose that the social structure creates crime and delinquency. These theories are based on the assumption that each of society's structures fulfills functions that are needed for the maintenance of social stability. As Emile Durkheim suggests, crime and delinquency emerge from society when a certain structure is no longer fulfilling its functions. For example, the Chicago School's social disorganization theory links causes of delinquency to limited support systems in slum or poor neighborhoods during urbanization, which weaken social control, and facilitate the learning of deviant culture. Shaw and McKay (2006), in particular, uses Burgess's concentric zone model to explore the relationship between geographical locations and delinquency. Their study suggests that youths from disadvantaged neighborhoods participate in a subculture which generates delinquency. Current research also indicates that delinquency rate is generally high in most slum or poor neighborhoods.

In a slightly different way than Durkheim's theory did, Merton's (1938) strain traditions generally argue that the American dream (the widely shared notion that anyone can achieve financial success in the United States through hard work) sets a high cultural standard. The pressure to conform to this cultural standard in the wake of limited economic opportunities for youths in a poor inner-city neighborhood create crime and delinquency, as they adopt illegitimate means to achieve this dream.

Following both the Chicago School and Merton's strain traditions, Albert Cohen's (1955) theory of status frustration suggests that boys residing in city slums find difficulty in meeting the middle-class measuring rod that characterizes the school system. As a result, they create delinquent subcultures (i.e., reaction formation) and join with other lower-class boys (i.e., mutual conversion) in malicious youth gangs.

Cloward and Ohlin's (1960) differential opportunity theory, on the other hand, expands on Merton's theory by arguing that the structure of society creates differential access to both legitimate opportunities and illegitimate opportunities. They argue that people are not free to choose to become a particular type of deviant. Instead, the availability of illegitimate means – the illegitimate opportunity – regulates the selection of the particular mode of adaptation in society. Their theory focuses attention to the role of differential opportunity in creating varieties of delinquent behavior and different types of youth gangs (criminal gangs, retreatist gangs, and conflict gangs).

Learning Theories of Delinquency

Learning theories propose that crime and delinquency are learned from others. For example, Edwin Sutherland's (1947) classic theory of differential association suggests that juvenile delinquency and conformity are both learned through the same process. Within small, intimate groups, minors are exposed to the techniques of and motives for deviance and/or conformity. If a minor is exposed to relatively more "deviant" than "conforming" techniques and motives, he or she is likely to become delinquent.

Other theories also indicate that delinquent behavior may be learned in the process of learning conventional behavior. For instance, in Sykes and Matza's (1957) neutralization theory the emphasis is on those "motives" of deviance that Sutherland referred to. They argue that juveniles are able to rationalize their delinquency with certain techniques of neutralization, including denial of responsibility ("It's not my fault!"), denial of injury ("I'm not hurting anyone!"), denial of the victim ("He deserved it!"), condemnation of the condemners ("Who are you to tell me that I'm doing something wrong?"), and appealing to higher loyalties ("I did it for a higher purpose").

Social Control Theories and the Life Course

In contrast with social structure theories and learning theories, social control theories ask a different question: "Why don't we all act in deviant ways?" Based on Durkheim's notion that deviance can occur when the egoistic self (personal selfish interests) rules over (dominate) the social self (the internalized cultural norms), social control theories generally propose that personal relationships, commitments, values, norms, and beliefs prevent them from rule breaking. A number of earlier theorists have proposed various versions of social control theories, such as Edward Ross, Albert Reiss, and Walter Reckless.

Among all contemporary social control theories, Travis Hirschi's ([1969] 2006) social bonds theory probably has the greatest influence on the sociology of crime and delinquency. According to Hirschi, four different types of social bonds – attachment (emotional bonds), involvement (amount of time spent in the conventional world), commitment (investment in the conventional world), and belief (the extent to which most children accept the norms and values of the conventional world) – restrain most children from deviance. When a bond is weakened or broken then delinquent behavior for that child may occur. More recently, Hirschi and Michael Gottfredson (1990) have developed a new social control theory known as the general theory of crime. This theory proposes that low levels of self-control resulting from ineffective parenting encourage some children to be delinquent. The empirical research of social control theories remains divided on whether these theories are sustainable but has generally confirmed some of the predictions.

Finally, John Laub and Robert Sampson (1993) argue that youths are not necessarily locked into a specific delinquent and criminal path through life to the degree that low-level self-control would suggest. They believe instead that certain events may occur to offer the social capital and change the direction of the juvenile delinquent who is on a path to criminality.

Interpretive and Critical Theories

Conventional sociological theories as discussed above do not focus on how power, capitalism, the behavior of authorities, and the intersection of race, class, and gender can affect the perceptions of and reactions to crime and delinquency in society. Following World War Two, interpretive and critical theories emerged to emphasize the perceptions of and reactions to the criminal or delinquent act or person, as well as the role of power in determining such perceptions and reactions.

In this regard, labeling theory is critical of the behavior of state authorities. Labeling theory argues that the problem of crime and delinquency, or recidivism, lies in the stigmatizing reactions, including formal and informal social control to crime and delinquency (Becker 1963). When children have deviant labels attached to them, others start to perceive and treat them differently, which affects how they perceive themselves and may create their criminal lifestyles. A number of empirical studies support this claim. In terms of policy implications, labeling theory suggests decriminalization of juvenile delinquency in which victimless and minor cases (such as gambling) shall not be criminalized. It also argues for de-institutionalization to reduce incarceration of youths and prison populations.

Conflict theorists generally argue that crime and delinquency are a result of conflict between various interests in society, usually between those who have power and who do not. Conflict theories focus on how government and other powers can produce higher rates of crime and delinquency among lower-class youths. These theories draw attention to the behavior of authorities that affect the criminalization of the poor in society. They are also used to explain the overrepresentation of minority juveniles in all stages of the juvenile justice system, particularly in secure detention and other juvenile lockups.

Feminist theories are another category of critical theories. They criticize mainstream sociological theories for assuming that research on the boys' experience can be generalized to the girls' experience, and encourage more equal studies on female experiences and their divergence from male experiences. Some integrated critical theories attribute crime and delinquency to the combined effects of patriarchy, masculinities, and the intersection of race, class, and gender.

In conclusion, the sociology of crime and delinquency is important because different perspectives on why juveniles offend are essential to improve the criminal and juvenile justice systems. The history of sociological theories and empirical research on crime and delinquency represents the cumulative development of knowledge, with each new perspective building upon the insights of past theories. The future of the sociology of crime and delinquency may depend on the capacity of theorists and empirical researchers to cooperate with each other to create more integrated models to understand the problems and thus design more effective prevention and control programs.

SEE ALSO: Anomie; Capital: Cultural, Social, and Economic; Capitalism; Deviance; Feminist Theory; Power and Authority; Social Psychology; Socialization; Stigma

References

Becker, H. 1963. *Outsiders: Studies in the Sociology of Deviance*. New York: Free Press.

Cloward, R.A., and L.E. Ohlin. 1960. *Delinquency and Opportunity: A Theory of Delinquent Gangs*. New York: Free Press.

Cohen, A.K. 1955. *Delinquent Boys: The Culture of the Gang*. New York: Free Press.

Gottfredson, M.R., and T. Hirschi. 1990. *A General Theory of Crime*. Stanford, CA: Stanford University Press.

Hirschi T. [1969] 2006. *Causes of Delinquency*, 5th ed. New Brunswick, NJ, and London: Transaction.

Laub, J.H., and R.J. Sampson. 1993. "Turning Points in the Life Course: Why Change Matters to the Study of Crime." *Criminology* 31 (3): 301–325.

Merton, K.R. 1938. "Social Structure and Anomie." *American Sociological Review* 3: 753–758.

Shaw, C.R., and H.D. McKay. 2006. "Juvenile Delinquency and Urban Areas." In F.T. Cullen and R. Agnew (eds.), *Criminological Theories: Past to Present*, 3rd ed., 106. Los Angeles: Roxbury.

Sutherland, E. 1947. *Principles of Criminology*, 4th ed. Chicago: J.B. Lippincott.

Sykes, G.M., and D. Matza. 1957. "Techniques of Neutralization." *American Sociological Review* 22: 664–670.

Culture, Sociology of

Lisa McCormick

University of Edinburgh, UK

Sociologists who study culture are attuned to the expressive and symbolic dimensions of social life. Culture is generally understood to consist of shared beliefs about reality, norms that orient action and behavior, values that anchor moral commitments, and the communication of these beliefs, norms, and values through symbols. Studying culture sociologically involves explaining the dynamics of cultural processes, identifying cultural patterns in groups and institutions, and investigating the influence culture has on other aspects of society.

"Cultural Sociology" versus the "Sociology of Culture"

The discipline of sociology is characterized by (and sometimes criticized for) the wide range of theoretical perspectives, methodological approaches, and empirical topics it encompasses. Nowhere is this more apparent than in sociological engagements with cultural matters. This rich diversity stems only in part from the central concept – culture – which is notoriously complex and polysemic. Other contributing factors are the linguistic differences, intellectual histories, and institutional arrangements that shape the various national contexts where the sociological study of culture has become established.

In the United States, the "sociology of culture" is routinely distinguished from "cultural sociology." Outsiders might take these to be interchangeable terms, but for those who identify with either label, they signal research agendas that are not just separate but antagonistic as well. Simply put, the "sociology of culture" applies mainstream sociological methods, ideas, concepts, and orientations to the domain of culture. Richard Peterson's work is widely recognized as the archetype; having studied with Alvin Gouldner, a scholar of industrial bureaucracy and labor disputes, Peterson approached popular music as an industry and drew from organizational sociology to explain its content, social legitimization, and innovation patterns. Peterson's studies of jazz and country music laid the groundwork for what was to become the "production of culture" perspective which informed studies of "symbol fabrication" in both high and low cultural industries (Peterson and Anand 2004). Similarly, the idea motivating Howard Becker's (1982) *Art Worlds* was to apply the

Core Concepts in Sociology, First Edition. Edited by J. Michael Ryan.
© 2019 John Wiley & Sons Ltd. Published 2019 by John Wiley & Sons Ltd.

sociology of occupations, as defined by Everett Hughes and the Chicago School, to artistic activity. As with the production of culture, meaning was deliberately bracketed in order to focus on the social context, which was held to be the more suitable subject for sociological expertise.

In contrast, American "cultural sociology" aims to transform the discipline at large by taking a meaning-centered approach. For those who call themselves "cultural sociologists," the "cultural turn," which had emerged earlier in cognate disciplines such as history and anthropology, created new methodological possibilities and opportunities for theoretical development in sociology. The most distinctive and zealous version of American cultural sociology is the neo-Durkheimian "Yale School" founded by Jeffrey Alexander. Advocates of this approach criticize the "sociology of culture" for being a "weak program" because it is essentially reductive, having relegated culture to a dependent variable that can be explained by recourse to "real" social forces and "hard" social structures. What makes theirs a "strong program" by comparison is the insistence on the relative autonomy of culture, and the beginning premise that "every action [...] is embedded to some degree in a horizon of affect and meaning" (Alexander and Smith 2012).

The cleavage between the "sociology of culture" and "cultural sociology" makes more sense when the history of American sociology is taken into account. A mainstay of Parsonian structural functionalism was a theory of culture that emphasized value integration to anchor a consensual view of society. With the demise of the Parsonian paradigm in the 1960s, cultural explanations became suspect. What ultimately forced the issue was Oscar Lewis's "culture of poverty" argument, which politicized and polarized debates in stratification research by appearing to blame the victims of racial inequality for their own problems. Once that debate subsided, culture became actively avoided in sociology, allowing institutional explanations and conflict theories to dominate. Culture began to return to research agendas after Richard Peterson (1979) "revitalized" the concept, and its rehabilitation was secured when "sociologists of culture" successfully lobbied the American Sociological Association to create a Culture Section. But the production of culture perspective was never intended to be a formal theory, which left an opening for a new generation of scholars to define a truly *cultural* sociology in more theoretically ambitious terms. Through their efforts, culture has become more than a subfield, and an unmistakably cultural approach is infusing the full range of sociological topics and issues.

In Europe, we find a different set of divisions and complications. "Cultural sociology" in the United Kingdom was never so much a subfield as a general concern across most of the discipline. Given the early influence of European Marxist theory, the success of the Birmingham School of cultural studies, and the strong interest in poststructuralist and postmodern theories of agency and identity that emerged in the 1980s, the "culturalization" of British sociology in the 1990s was an unsurprising and uncontroversial development that consisted mainly of reworking existing areas of study, such as class analysis (Inglis 2016).

In France, the "sociology of culture" is a well-defined and dynamic subfield, but it is framed differently still, causing frequent misunderstandings between Anglophone and Francophone scholars. Since the 1960s, culture has been strongly associated with the arts in French academia; this close identification is the product of an institutional unity that maintains the connection between the study of what French political institutions define as art, and the study of its consumption. The important distinction that arises in the French context is between "sociologie de l'art" – which refers to empirical investigations of artistic production, reception, and mediation – and "sociologie de la culture," which signals a more democratic attitude and the inclusion of leisure activities, such as watching television and reading comic books, along with more traditional cultural ones, such as visiting museums and going to concerts. So far, cultural studies has had no French counterpart, and the broader issues associated with the Anglo-American meaning of "culture" are typically dealt with by historians.

While the Americans had Parsons, the pivotal figure in European sociology of culture is Pierre Bourdieu. Previous generations of European sociologists, from Weber to the Frankfurt School, never questioned the value of high culture or its power to resist the forces of rationalization and massification in modern capitalist society. What Bourdieu accomplished through his work, especially *Distinction* (1984), was the redefinition of the sociology of culture as a critique of the arts and humanities. He laid out in no uncertain terms the sociologist's central task as a "contextual critique of culture," which would expose the role of taste in sustaining privilege and reveal cultural authorities' claim to disinterestedness and universalism as a power play. The themes and techniques that Bourdieu pioneered might have taken on a different flavor when they were exported from France to the Netherlands, Germany, and further afield but his style of contextual critique and his way of dividing cultural production and consumption were widely established as the default position in sociological studies of culture.

Methodology and Methods

One of Bourdieu's legacies is the incorporation of conventional social science tools, namely surveys and quantitative analysis, to accomplish contextual critique and test theoretical arguments about culture. The popularity of multiple correspondence analysis can be traced to his inventive use of this statistical method in developing his concept of the field and relational analysis. Bourdieu can also be credited with inspiring the vast literature on cultural omnivores; the effort to refute his findings involved the deployment of an entirely different set of multivariate models to examine groups that consumed high-, middle-, and low-brow cultural forms.

Those more interested in processes of meaning-making than in patterns of consumption have tended to prefer qualitative approaches. Even before "cultural sociology" emerged as we know it, ethnography was introduced into sociology to investigate culture as ordinary, everyday life. While the Chicago School has traditionally prioritized description over explanation, this has not prevented others from using participant observation and interviews to ground theoretical explanations of general cultural forms. The methodological approach of the Yale School is a "structural hermeneutics" that marries anthropological "thick description" with Saussurian linguistics; discourse and narrative analysis have typically been the methods of choice to explore the symbolic dimension of culture.

Controversy surrounds whether cultural sociology can or should be a science. Some scholars remain committed to bringing scientific measurement practices to bear on questions of meaning. But others object to the abstraction involved in coding and cluster analysis methods on the grounds that they decontextualize meaning, allowing the analyst to impose their own values and encouraging a dangerous disregard for truth-seeking.

Social network analysis similarly inspires either enthusiasm or skepticism, regardless of whether it is used in a mixed-method strategy with a more familiar method such as ethnography.

New Developments

Several theoretical innovations have already emerged from American cultural sociology. Cultural pragmatics informs studies on a wide range of empirical topics, such as election campaigns, central banking, and arts organizations. The model of cultural trauma continues to offer new insight into how nations and social groups respond to events such as war, assassination, and natural disaster. Civil sphere theory has just entered a second stage of development where it is being globalized through the examination of civil societies beyond the context of the United States. An interest in materiality is taking shape; this includes attending to the ways that material properties (and the disintegration of materials) shapes interpretation, as well as examining the processes through which images, buildings, objects, persons, and brands become "iconic." While the sociology of culture has traditionally drawn on the humanities for inspiration, some are calling for a new form of interdisciplinarity through a serious engagement with cognitive neuroscience and social psychology to develop "dual process" models (Lizardo et al. 2016).

Meanwhile, European sociology of culture is entering a post-Bourdieuian stage. For some, "after Bourdieu" means turning to different approaches, such as actor network theory or contemporary anthropology, for new ways to conceptualize agency, ontology, subjectivity, and the relation between the aesthetic and the social. For others, it means returning to Bourdieu's original intentions to create a renewed relational sociology, or rediscovering neglected aspects of his work to fuel new research agendas. Apart from these debates surrounding Bourdieu, a collective effort aims to transform historical sociology into a more globally oriented research program by questioning its conceptual basis and critiquing the colonial geopolitics of knowledge that has traditionally legitimated sociological thinking. Sociologists of culture are not getting any closer to reaching a consensus about the topics they should study, the methods they should use, or the theories that orient their investigations, but few will find this a cause for concern. It is not in spite of these disagreements but because of them that the sociology of culture thrives.

SEE ALSO: Capital: Cultural, Social, and Economic; Colonialism and Postcolonialism; Consumption; Ethnography; Everyday Life; Media, Sociology of the; Popular Culture; Social Network Analysis

References

Alexander, Jeffrey C., and Philip Smith. 2012. "Introduction: Cultural Sociology Today." In Jeffrey C. Alexander, Ronald N. Jacobs, and Philip Smith (eds.), *The Oxford Handbook of Cultural Sociology*, 3–24. New York: Oxford University Press.

Bourdieu, Pierre. 1984. *Distinction: A Social Critique of the Judgement of Taste*. Cambridge, MA: Harvard University Press.

Inglis, David. 2016. "Introduction: Culture/Sociology/Sociology of Culture/Cultural Sociology." In *The SAGE Handbook of Cultural Sociology*, edited by David Inglis and Anna-Mari Almila, 1–7. London: SAGE Publications.

Lizardo, Omar, Robert Mowry, Brandon Sepulvado, Dustin S. Stoltz, Marshall A. Taylor, Justin Van Ness, and Michael Wood. 2016. "What Are Dual Process Models? Implications for Cultural Analysis in Sociology." *Sociological Theory* 34 (4): 287–310.

Peterson, Richard A. 1979. "Revitalizing the Culture Concept." *Annual Review of Sociology* 5: 137–166.

Peterson, Richard, and N. Anand. 2004. "The Production of Culture Perspective." *Annual Review of Sociology* 30: 311–334.

Democracy

Kathleen C. Schwartzman

University of Arizona, USA

Democracy designates a type of political regime. It is a system of representation and a system of governance. Because it is exceptionally germane for human wellbeing, countless scholars have dedicated their careers to defining, measuring, uncovering social origins, determining conditions of stability and survival, and assessing its social and economic implications.

Democracy differs from pre-capitalist autocratic states, for example, the Aztec empire, feudal states, or absolutist monarchies, which derived their legitimacy from a deity and or inheritance. Democracy also differs from other capitalist states, for example, fascism, authoritarianism, or military dictatorships. In contrast to all of these, democracy grounds its legitimacy, its stability, and its survival in the continuous consent of its citizens.

Democratic states are systems of representation – they embody procedures by which "citizens" who are granted suffrage may elect individuals to represent them. Democracies have varied with respect to the classes of people entitled to participate in electing representatives. Franchises have been limited to individuals with: a certain quantity of property or wealth; a minimum level of education; or of a certain race or gender. In Argentina, for example, women over the age of 18 were first enfranchised in the 1951 presidential race. In South Africa, Africans were first given the vote in 1994.

These "systems of representation" differ with respect to the voluntary or obligatory nature of exercising the franchise. Democratic regimes also vary in the electoral laws which determine how the votes of citizens are translated into representative positions in government. Some electoral laws, for example, determine winners through a simple majority (winner take all), others through an absolute majority, or one of many formulas of proportional representation.

Democratic states are systems of governance – blueprints by which a nation generates and enforces public policies. Inscribed in constitutions and laws, blueprints specify who has power to do what. Democracy is a system of authority rooted in the legal-rational system of elections and a system of domination by consent. In short democracy is an institutional arrangement for arriving at political decisions which reflect the common good by having citizens elect individuals who are to assemble in order to carry out their will.

The interaction of these two dimensions (representation and governance) gives rise to a multitude of democratic forms (and definitions). Some definitions emphasize

Core Concepts in Sociology, First Edition. Edited by J. Michael Ryan.

institutional arrangements: an inclusive franchise, regular elections, one person one vote, individual and political rights, and freedom of speech, assembly, and the press. Power may be centralized or devolved to multiple branches and levels with many veto points. Definitions based on institutional arrangements may include the degree of separation of powers and balance among separate branches. Some have referred to states which score high on these institutional dimensions as polyarchies. Polyarchy has come to be the accepted essence of democracy among most US scholars and politicians.

Political regimes may score high on formal institutional arrangements, but lack a clear path to policies which reflect the will of the people and the common good. Dictatorships and authoritarian regimes may hold elections which are non-competitive and insignificant, and in no way bind rulers to the will of the people.

Measuring the "democraticity" of any regime has been a central task of scholars. The definitional complexities have led to a plethora of indices for cross-national and overtime comparisons. There are many, but often cited measures include Polity IV, Freedom House, and the Economist Intelligence Unit. These measure emphasize the "procedural" dimension of democracy and not social or economic outcomes.

Understanding the delinking of a high-scoring "procedural democracy" from a "common good" democracy is the research domain of those who investigate the degree of state autonomy from unelected dominant classes. That somewhat contentious debate viewed the state on a continuum between totally autonomous or captured. The autonomous state (neutral in the terms of "pluralists" scholars) aggregates individual preferences in a more or less equitable fashion. The captured state (biased toward the interests of the bourgeoisie in the terms of some Marxists scholars) discounts citizen preferences as a result of lobbying, redistricting, or elite domination of government posts. Power Elite research falls on the continuum between those two. Despite their sometimes heated disagreements, scholars reflect on the link, or lack thereof, between the expressed will of the electorate (the process) and the policies (the greater good).

Scholars have also investigated the social origins, institutional stability, and societal consequences of democracy. The *origins* scholarship can be divided very roughly into the earliest democracies, cases clustering around the two world wars, the "third wave," and a post-third wave. Regarding the transition from autocratic states, for example, monarchies, to more inclusive systems of representation, authors point to the rise of parliamentary bodies that counterbalanced the power of the king. Often this followed a bourgeois revolution and an increase in the size of the middle classes. Regarding later democracies which broadened preexisting "limited" ones, scholars have identified the role of mobilization for national liberation and/or foreign wars. Following World War I, the number of democracies increased from three to ten. World War I accelerated pressures for inclusion leading to the British Reform Act of 1918 abolishing property qualifications for men and extending limited suffrage to women over 30. Likewise the Nineteenth Amendment to the US constitution (1919) granted female suffrage. The "Third Wave" refers to democratic transitions beginning with the 1974 Portuguese revolution, continuing with Spain, Greece, Latin American countries, Former Soviet Republics, and then South Africa.

One critical facet of the "origins" research is determining the endogenous versus international roots of democracy. The fact that the "Third Wave" nations were considered underdeveloped and lacking the presumed demographic, cultural, and economic preconditions suggests that endogenous factors alone are inadequate for understanding democratic origins. The fact of 500 years of chronological clustering of the advent of democratic waves also suggests that we must look beyond endogenous factors.

Evaluating preconditions and origins is crucial for international policy makers. Democratic imposition was successful in post-World War II Japan following its surrender. Washington, partnering with Japan's pre-World War II government, arranged for a general election, suspended laws which restricted political, civil, and religious liberties, extended the franchise to women, and drafted a constitution embodying elements of the British system, the American Bill of Rights, and some New-Deal-like economic freedoms. This model, along with "democracy-promotion" in post-World War II Germany, were the inspiration for President Bush's "global democratic revolution." It failed abysmally in Iraq.

Nations may be convinced to embrace democratic procedures as the quid-pro-quo for foreign aid or loans. In 1961, the Alliance for Progress hoped that funding would help Latin Americans resist communist influences. By the 1970s, thirteen Latin American democracies were overthrown and replaced, not by communism, but by military rule. In 1991, the US Congress tied guidelines regarding democracy and human rights to foreign aid. In 1991 and 1992 the United States and the Paris Club declared a moratorium on aid to Kenya and to Malawi pending the implementation of pro-democratic political reforms.

Democratic regimes and democratic stability may be somewhat illusive, but researchers and politicians alike are convinced that it is the route to global peace and prosperity.

SEE ALSO: Class, Capitalist; Marxism; Power and Authority

Further Reading

Domhoff, G. William. 2016. Class-Domination Theory of Power. Online at: http://www2. ucsc.edu/whorulesamerica/power/class_domination.html.

Moore, Barrington. 1993. *Social Origins of Dictatorship and Democracy*. Boston: Beacon Press.

Przeworski, Adam. 1985. *Capitalism and Social Democracy*. Cambridge: Cambridge University Press.

Rae, Douglas. 1967. *The Political Consequences of Electoral Laws*. New Haven, CT, and London: Yale University Press.

Schwartzman, Kathleen. 1989. *The Social Origins of Democratic Collapse: The First Portuguese Republic in the Global Economy*. Lawrence: University Press of Kansas.

Demography and Population Studies

Sangeeta Parashar

Montclair State University, USA

Demography (Greek, *demos* or "people," *graphein*, "to write about") is the scientific study of the "size, territorial distribution, and components of population, changes therein, and components of such changes" (Hauser and Duncan 1959: 2). Based on differences in subject matter and methodological approaches, demography can be subdivided into formal demography and population studies. Formal demography, whose foundation is credited to John Graunt (1620–1674), focuses on the demographic processes of fertility, mortality, and migration when applied to the size, age structure, and spatial distribution of human populations. Built on mathematical principles, it uses research tools such as model life tables, cohort and period analyses, Alfred J. Lokta's 1922 stable population model (extended to non-stable populations), indirect estimation, and stochastic processes. Access to population-level data is assumed. Population studies, whose origin is traced to Thomas Malthus (1766–1834), approaches population composition and change through an interdisciplinary lens that straddles formal demography and another social or natural science, for instance, sociology, economics, biology, geography, or anthropology. It relies on the principles of statistical inference, the bedrock of these fields, tested through a wide range of multivariate techniques including econometric models, event history models, path analysis and structural equations, log-linear models, etc. using sample survey and population data. Qualitative methods (for instance, participant observation and focus groups) are also employed. Put simply, formal demography examines relationships between demographic phenomena in isolation (for example, how age structure influences fertility or vice versa), and population studies examines the interaction of demographic and non-demographic phenomena (for example, how social structure, economic incentives, culture, fecundity, or even population policy influences fertility and vice versa). The former is descriptive or analytic in nature, while the latter is explanatory. Although it is important to highlight the distinctions between the two subfields, the boundary between them is not rigid or impermeable.

Achille Guillard coined the term "demography" for his 1855 publication, *Éléments de statistique humaine ou démographie comparée*, but the discipline has significantly older roots in terms of methodology and thought. Governments of the ancient civilizations of Egypt, Babylonia, China, Palestine, and Rome carried out the first censuses (*census*,

Latin for "assessing" or "taxing") to register taxpayers and their property, prospective laborers and military recruits, or the political status of free citizens. In the seventh century CE, the Prophet Mohammed conducted a written census of the Muslim population (total of 1500) in the city-state of Medina, Saudi Arabia. After conquering England in 1086 CE, William I stipulated the Domesday Book (*domesday*, Middle English for day of final judgement; here, final proof of legal title to land) to catalog the landed wealthy. These efforts often yielded imprecise counts due to flawed data collection (self-reporting versus census takers), partial geographic coverage, and restrictive age–sex selection, usually adult males. The rise of the modern nation-state in France and elsewhere during the eighteenth century led to a genuine quest for accurate statistical information (*statistic*, German for "facts about a state"). In 1794, Sweden became one of the first European nations to track its residents through a combined population register and census administered by local clergy in each diocese. The United States and United Kingdom initiated their censuses in 1790 and 1801 respectively, and, by the end of the nineteenth century, it was re-envisioned as a powerful scientific tool, not just for enumeration, but to gather data related to various aspects of society.

Population censuses are now conducted every five or ten years in almost all countries, although they have faced resistance in some (the Netherlands, England, Switzerland, Germany, Nigeria, and Lebanon) due to privacy concerns and political–religious conflicts. Data collection includes the short-form count of everyone plus the detailed long form of a large sample (usually 10%) of the population. People are included on the basis of usual residence, rather than *de facto* or *de jure*. In the case of the United States, the monthly American Community Survey (ACS) replaced the long form in 2010. Besides the census, other primary sources of data include registration of vital events, sample surveys, and administrative data. Vital events such as the number of births, deaths, marriages, divorces, and abortions are routinely recorded by government agencies although their completeness and accuracy varies substantially, being almost nonexistent in some developing countries. Sample surveys, whether probability or non-probability, are crucial sources of demographic and non-demographic data where census or vital events are not collected or prone to error, questionnaires are restrictive in content, and the cost of census collection is high. Examples include the National Health Interview Survey (NHIS), Demographic and Health Surveys (DHS), and the European Social Survey (ESS). Administrative records such as social security checks, tax reports, medical records, utility connections data, school enrollments, etc., are important sources if linked with other datasets. Finally, new and innovative sources of data now include: (1) geographic information systems (GIS) that combine maps with demographic data and (2) DNA and biomarker information useful for health and aging studies.

Concomitant with the development of scientific methods is the advancement of population thought from premodern doctrines to modern theory. Until about 2500 years ago, populations grew slowly due to universally high mortality and fertility. Hence, philosophers were preoccupied with size and mortality: Confucius espoused population growth and transmigration, while Plato and Aristotle preferred stability through delayed marriage, abortion, and infanticide. Ibu Khaldun (~1380), a Tunisian historian, argued that population growth created occupational specialization, leading to higher incomes concentrated in urban areas, an idea partially echoed by Durkheim a few centuries later. After an intellectual hiatus during the Middle Ages, mercantilism (reflecting the Colombian Exchange) dominated European thought from the sixteenth through the eighteenth century. It viewed a nation's population as a form of wealth: larger population implied a larger labor supply, markets, and armies. John Graunt, who laid the foundation of modern demography and statistics in *Natural and Political Observations ... Made Upon the Bills of Mortality* (1662) supported mercantilist ideas of population size. Using weekly records of deaths and baptisms in London, he constructed the first life table that suggested high (infant) mortality levels; in other analyses, he highlighted regular patterns of death in different parts of the city. The subsequent development of the actuarial profession and growing attention to public health sustained attention to mortality studies.

Adam Smith (1723–1790), one of the first modern economists, changed the course of demographic thought when he reversed the relationship between population and economic growth. From being an independent variable causing change in society, population size became a dependent variable being altered by societal change. Thomas Malthus, building on Smith's work in his *Essay on the Principle of Population* (1798), argued that population growth, which is generated by the urge to reproduce, is ultimately checked by the means of subsistence. Societies that did not practice "moral restraint" through delayed marriage and celibacy would suffer "positive checks" of poverty since population has a tendency to grow faster than the food supply. Malthus considered other "preventive checks" such as birth control and abortion as immoral, although neo-Malthusians embraced them. Karl Marx, on the other hand, argued that poverty is the product of capitalism and the evils of social organization instead of population growth. Although both theorists shared a strong concern for the poor, they differed on the solution: for Malthus, it was individual responsibility, and for Marx, it was a social revolution leading to socialism. Malthus's empirically unsupported and misdirected theory, however, launched a debate that has lasted more than two hundred years.

Fertility studies gained visibility when demographers noted a considerable decline of birth rates in industrialized countries and population increases (or a "population explosion") in developing countries during the twentieth century. The classic explanation of this trend, initially proposed by Notestein, is the demographic transition theory. It emphasizes the importance of economic and social development (reflecting modernization theory) in first stimulating mortality decline, followed by a corresponding decline in fertility. Hence, societies transition from high birth and death rates (low population growth, Phase I), to low death rate and initial fertility decline (rapid population growth, Phase II), to low birth and death rates (zero or negative population growth, phase III). The macro-level theory was later reformulated to downplay the role of economic development, introduce "ideational" factors, and consider micro-level theories, for example, rational choice theory, Caldwell's intergenerational wealth flows theory (1976), and Easterlin and Crimmins (1985) supply–demand theory as possible explanations. To explain lowest low fertility and weakening family structure in Europe, Lesthaeghe and Van de Kaa (1986) formulated the "second demographic transition" theory. They ascribed these changes to personal freedom, especially among women, postponement of marriage, rise in single living, cohabitation, and divorce, and the acceptance of modern contraceptives.

In developing countries, on the other hand, population growth led to a resurgence of Malthusian thought and, despite mixed results from several empirical studies that supported or negated it, many national family planning programs were implemented, the most stringent ones being in India and China. However, a 1986 statistical study commissioned by the US Academy of Science and coordinated by Preston, Lee, and Greene concluded that the initial effects of rapid population growth are negative, but they can be improved or even reversed in the long run through effective institutional changes. It qualitatively concluded that slower population growth would be beneficial for economic development, although these benefits are context dependent and possibly conditioned by the quality of markets, the nature of government policy, and features of the natural environment. However, the debate between population and economic growth has far from ended.

Based on past trends, the main areas of future inquiry are in aging, migration, health, and environmental sustainability. Due to rapid fertility and mortality declines and increasing life expectancy, the elderly are a large segment of the population in many societies. Importantly, the process is occurring at a much faster pace in developing countries that lack adequate economic and social welfare programs. This affords demographers several research opportunities in aspects related to retirement, health, forecasts in residence, economic security, and family support. Accompanying aging and corresponding labor shortages is migration from poor to wealthy countries, which affects both origin and destination regions. This, along with the challenges created by massive internal migration within developing countries and refugee flows internationally, presents interesting research prospects. With increasing globalization and human activities, the debate about population growth and environmental sustainability, including food availability, land use, water resources, energy, and climate change, has also gathered momentum. Finally, global health continues to be an important area of research in the context of the double burden of infectious and chronic diseases in poor countries, HIV/AIDS, and aging.

In conclusion, as a field of inquiry, demography has experienced immense growth during the twentieth century due to critical queries as well as an expansion of data sources and computing technology. Its quantitative, interdisciplinary, and applied nature has made it indispensable to politics (e.g., apportionment of seats in the US House of Representatives, redistricting), social planning (social security, school districts, job creation), health, and business (e.g., product targeting and segmentation, human resource management, investment, cluster marketing). Thus, by providing statistical information pertaining to human population, demography is instrumental in laying the foundation for social science research.

SEE ALSO: Aging, Sociology of; Development, Sociology of; Economic Sociology; Family and Kinship, Sociology of; Immigration, Migration, and Refugees; Sexualities

References

Caldwell, John C. 1976. "Toward a Restatement of Demographic Transition Theory." *Population and Development Review* 2 (3–4): 321–366.

Easterlin, Richard A., and Eileen M. Crimmins. 1985. *The Fertility Revolution*. Chicago: University of Chicago Press.

Hauser, Philip M., and Dudley O. Duncan. 1959. *The Study of Population: An Inventory and Appraisal*. Chicago: University of Chicago Press.

Lesthaeghe, Ron, and Dirk van de Kaa. 1986. "Twee Demografische Transities?" In Dirk J. van de Kaa and Ron Lesthaeghe (eds.), *Bevolking: Groei en Krimp*, 9–24. Deventer: Van Loghum Slaterus.

Preston, Samuel H., Ronald Lee, and Geoffrey Greene. 1986. *Population Growth and Economic Development: Policy Questions*. Washington, DC: National Academy Press.

Development, Sociology of

Peter Evans and Patrick Heller

Brown University, USA

Over the course of the last several hundred years, human society has arguably been transformed more rapidly and fundamentally than in any comparable era. The transformation of agriculture and the subsequent growth of industry have created vastly increased capacity to satisfy human needs. Changes in transportation and communication have made isolated communities anachronisms and ensured that events and ideas reverberate almost without regard to geographic distance.

Over these recent centuries, social scientists have been searching for ways of conceptualizing and analyzing this conglomerate of revolutionary and largely irreversible transformations in human social life. "Development" became the dominant conceptual tool for promoting more interdisciplinary perspectives that could grapple with the complex interactions among the different aspects of this transformation. Unlike nineteenth-century conceptualizations of "progress," "development" is not necessarily seen as a transformation to be embraced and valued. Some social scientists have raised the alarm, horrified by the destructive consequences of development.

The expanded scale of social organization, which nearly everyone agrees is a component of development, increases the potential for freedom and satisfying human needs and wants, but also introduces new potential for inequality, injustice, oppression, and ecological catastrophe. Nonetheless, regardless of their evaluation of the effects of development, all of those who study it would agree that there is, indeed, an interrelated set of historical processes which have, for better or for worse, revolutionized human society over the course of the past several centuries, and that understanding these changes is critical to informing scholarly, public, and policy debates.

One of sociology's principle contributions to debates on the concept of development has been to challenge the hegemony of "economic growth" as the dominant metric of development. Sociologists have provided an important counter to the reductionism of the "economic growth" paradigm by showing how economic life is embedded in institutions, organizations, identities, and patterns of collective action and that these areas of social life have dynamics of their own. In doing so, they have tried to avoid slipping into formulations that are teleological, that is imply some sort of predetermined goal or

Core Concepts in Sociology, First Edition. Edited by J. Michael Ryan.

endpoint (e.g., "modernity," economic advancement), instead recognizing the contingencies of history, the centrality of social and institutional conflict, and the resulting variety of patterns of transformation.

In its post-World War II infancy, the study of development was dominated by teleological perspectives, including in sociology. These perspectives projected the institutions and practices of Western societies as a road map for "developing" societies. Against this modernization view, sociologists in the tradition of dependency theory and theories of underdevelopment (both inspired by the Marxist tradition) raised two sets of critical questions. First, they challenged the assumption in economics that market-led growth is necessarily welfare-maximizing and raised the questions of power and equity. Second, they linked questions of distribution not only to the role of classes (long a central sociological variable) but also to relations between nations which they argued were governed by a hierarchal global political economy in which the nations of the North prospered at the expense of the nations of the South (or Third World as it was then called). Sociologists specifically called into question the power relations that constitute economic systems, in effect arguing that asymmetrical social or international relations were the obstacle to more just forms of development. In many ways these contributions anticipated the emergence of the literature on globalization of the 1990s and a new preoccupation with questions of inequality.

A critical juncture in the sociological study of development came in the 1980s. By then three new developments were forcing a rethinking of both the trajectories and the substance of development. First, the rise of the East Asian tigers called into question the determinism of world systems and dependency models. It was becoming clear that underdevelopment was not the inevitable fate of the Third World and that there were clearly multiple paths to development for the "periphery." New comparative research also made it clear that the success of the East Asian tigers was in large part explained by the role of the state in nurturing and accelerating industrial transformation and making economies of the South more globally competitive. This triggered a revival of work on state institutions and bureaucracy in the Weberian tradition, work that in many ways anticipated the "institutional turn" that has dominated the development literature across all social science disciplines for the past two decades. Second, sociologists were at the leading edge of recognizing that the global economy was undergoing profound transformation in the 1980s, and in particular shifting for nation-based systems of production associated with Fordism, what were increasingly globalized networks of value production. This spawned both work on making sense of the post-Fordist economy – flexible accumulation – as well as very rich research on global commodity chains and transnational modes of governance. Third, transitions to democracy in Eastern Europe and Latin America spawned a revival of political sociology in the study of development, and in particular new work on civil society and social movements as transformative actors.

These three developments have in many ways set the stage for very new ways of thinking about development. First, globalization and the new information economy have required a re-scaling of the units of analysis. Sociologists today are more aware than ever of global dynamics, but also recognize the significance of regional and sub-national scales, including a rapidly growing literature on cities. In this new perspective, forces that cut across the traditional political and economic boundaries of the nation-state, including networked forms of governance, ideas, and norms, and a range of transnational actors ranging from corporations to movement activists, are receiving much more attention. Second, the normative definition of development itself has shifted from the traditional focus on material wellbeing to a more complex set of human flourishings, including most importantly the capacity of self-expression and the exercise of basic civic and political rights. This shift, driven in no small part by social movements of the past two decades, has been accompanied by an increasing preoccupation with inequality. On the one hand, sociology has provided powerful analytical tools for exposing the mechanisms through which social and economic elites have secured and even extended their power even as societies have developed and democratized. On the other hand, sociologists have drawn attention to the ways in which durable inequalities organized around categories of gender, race, class, ethnicity, and other variables continue to pose significant obstacles to promoting inclusive and sustainable forms of development. Finally, sociology also offers tools for understanding the exercise of agency, the ways in which people are able to realize their goals and aspirations by creating new ties and acting together collectively. Analysis of both structural constraints and opportunities for agency is done at all levels of scale, from interactions in families to the restructuring of rules governing flows of goods and capital at the global level. This has included the exploration of new and more participatory forms of democratic governance, including a vast and growing body of research that examines how social movements and various civil society formations have engaged with states and economic forces in pursuing more inclusive, just, and sustainable forms of development.

SEE ALSO: Class; Colonialism and Postcolonialism; Economic Sociology; Globalization; Marxism; Modernity; Poverty; Social Movements and Social Change; Stratification and Inequality

Further Reading

Centeno, Miguel, Atul Kohli, and Deborah Yashar with Dinsha Mistree, eds. 2017. *States in the Developing World*. Cambridge and New York: Cambridge University Press.

Deviance

Erich Goode

Stony Brook University, USA

Deviance is the violation of a social norm, the discovery of which is likely to result in the members of the society ("audiences") sanctioning or stigmatizing the violator; the norms may be formal (laws) or informal (mores). More broadly, some sociologists define deviance as the violation of anything that activates, or is likely to activate, negative, stigmatizing reactions or sanctions from audiences. Designations of deviance are not random; societies are highly likely to sanction violators of behavior that, if left unchecked, would threaten their survival. Looked at from the other end of the telescope, however, cross-culturally, the variability in sanctioned acts – as well as expressed beliefs and physical conditions – is substantial. Moreover, postmodern or postindustrial society is fragmented into collectivities whose members hold and act on diverse, competing interpretations of right and wrong; hence, what's regarded as wrongful varies substantially even within a given society. Nonetheless, cohesiveness within such a society may prevail in the face of great perceived threat, such as, in the United States, subsequent to the attack on the World Trade Center in 2001, and in France and Belgium following the ISIS bombings of 2015 and 2016.

The term "deviance" originated from the Latin word *deviare*, to "turn aside" – *de*, meaning "off" or "from," and *via*, the, or a, "way" or "path." But what sort of departure from what sort of path? The sociology of deviance is a contentious discipline that lacks coherence and unity; its subject matter is ambiguous, unclear (Downes and Rock 2011: 1–23). Some sociologists regard the investigation and explanation of violations of society's norms as the field's central mission. Other sociologists delineate the field of deviance as the study of whatever generates negative, sanctioning, stigmatizing reactions from audiences. While not contradictory, the differences between them are crucial and consequential. Advocates of the normative approach typically investigate deviance by applying one or another *explanatory theory*; in contrast, reactivist sociologists adopt the *constructivist* approach. The forms of deviance to which authors of deviance textbooks most typically devote a chapter comprise drug use, sexual unconventionality, alcoholism, mental disorder, street crime, and white-collar crime; sociologists have investigated all of them adopting both of these perspectives.

Core Concepts in Sociology, First Edition. Edited by J. Michael Ryan.
© 2019 John Wiley & Sons Ltd. Published 2019 by John Wiley & Sons Ltd.

Explanatory Theory

Positivists argue that the only basis of valid knowledge is by means of scientific investigation. In sociology, positivism refers to the application of the scientific method to the study and explanation of human behavior. Explanatory theory is positivistic; it raises the question: *What causes someone to engage in deviant behavior?* Positivism is based on three fundamental assumptions. *Empiricism* refers to relying on the evidence of the senses, often aided by instruments (such as a microscope or a telescope), as well as more indirect geological, archaeological, historical, or interview indicators, and downplaying or ignoring intuition, unwarranted speculation, spiritualism, esthetics, ethics, and moralism. *Objectivism* holds that phenomena in the material and social world are identifiably real and possess a common core of properties that is sufficiently internally consistent as to distinguish it from unlike phenomena. *Determinism* maintains that cause-and-effect relationships prevail in the social and material worlds; with the use of valid evidence, the scientist can discover and explicate these relations. Positivistic sociologists of deviance argue that specific, identifiable conditions cause or influence actors to engage in behavior that violates society's norms, and that the scientist can demonstrate the influence of these conditions with verifiable, concrete evidence. Such conditions include anomie, community disorganization, weak neighborhood efficacy, social interaction with parties who advocate normative violations, low self-control, ineffective or weak social control, and inconsistent or ineffective childhood socialization. Some of these conditions operate on the macro or the meso level; they influence entire societies or neighborhoods. Others influence identifiable individuals or members of social categories.

All positivistic theorists recognize that laws and norms are culturally, historically, and societally constructed; few sociologists of deviance believe they can locate a universal *essence* or inherent property to wrongfulness. (A few do; such absolutists wish to resurrect the notion of *mala in se*, or absolute evil; they argue that what's "really, truly" deviant is not the same as *social constructions* of deviance.) Still, explanatory approaches of deviance assume that all deviancies share a common core; otherwise, there would be nothing to explain. Hence, *deviance is a type of action* that violates dominant or hegemonic norms; positivists believe all forms of deviance have something in common, above and beyond the label itself. Comparatively speaking, they argue, norms – particularly criminal statutes – tend to sanction the most harmful types of behavior. Worldwide, we see something of a consensus regarding the objective seriousness of the offense and the severity of the penalty; hence, deviance is not as relative as the constructionists and the labeling theories claim. *Why do they do it?* is the central concern of the positivistically oriented explanatory theorists.

Constructionism

Constructionists examine the deviance-defining and labeling processes in collectivities of all sizes, both society-wide as well as in smaller, specific social circles. Social constructionists do not examine deviance as a specific type of action. To them, the positivistic approach seems to imply that there is something inherently or intrinsically deviant, distinctly or qualitatively different, about acts that violate the social norms

(Becker 1963: 3); hence, they regard the objectivist assumption that deviance is a concrete, identifiable form of behavior as unsound and empirically erroneous. To the constructionist, a norm is not an entity with clear-cut, particular features; instead, what is considered wrongful, unacceptable, sanctionable, and stigmatizing is interpreted variably by diverse audiences as well as according to situation and circumstance. The mission of the constructionist is to explicate how audiences devise notions of undesirable behavior, beliefs, and conditions, and how such audiences respond to persons who engage in, express, or manifest them. Moreover, societies assemble novel categories of deviance over time. Consider a few twentieth-century constructions – some generated by new technology, some a consequence of the reconfiguration of social statuses: Identity theft, cybercrime, cyberporn, sexting, digital shaming, sexual harassment, bioterrorism, road rage, hate crime, and juvenile delinquency did not exist *as a conceptual category* until the relevant parties created the label. In addition to generating new conceptual categories over time, societies may *redefine* previously acceptable, tolerated, or unknown behaviors or conditions as wrongful or objectionable: for instance, homosexuality, alcohol use, marijuana possession, trafficking, and use, the sale and consumption of pornography, vagrancy, homelessness. And the reverse is also true: Today, in the industrial West – for the majority, at least – numerous sanctioned behaviors or conditions virtually no longer exist as categories of wrongful behavior: blasphemy, heresy, witchcraft, sorcery, consorting with the devil, godlessness.

In short, social and legal definitions of right and wrong vary over time; societies may define and redefine deviance both "up" (Krauthammer 1993) and "down" (Moynihan 1993). The sociologist does not have to observe every reaction to every act, expression of a belief, or physical condition beforehand to know that some are *likelier* to draw such reactions than others; we observe many commonalities in one society through time as well as from one society to another. Still, deviance categories are fuzzy around the edges; what acts *constitute* or fall under the penumbra of prostitution, pornography, vehicular homicide, murder, ecocide, cowardice, and treason is subject to endless disputation between and among lawmakers and sectors of the population.

Once a grouping of undesirable phenomena is conceptualized then applied, or revived, as a particular *type* of deviance – thereby *creating a deviant category* – the next step in the deviantization process is the interpersonal or legal reaction to a given putative violator. Audiences apply deviant *labels* to an actual person who, given abstract norms, presumably deserves being sanctioned. What do these audiences *do*, specifically, *to* that person? Do they shun, isolate, stigmatize, imprison, execute, denounce, or socially humiliate the violator? Is the violator *a pariah* in the community? And are different violators sanctioned in an unequal fashion according to their social statuses – by age, for instance, or gender, race, or socioeconomic status? And does this differentiality in material negative reactions vary over time and from one locale and society to another? And why? Constructionism *problematizes* the sanctioning process administered to persons linked to these categories. Audiences give the abstractions of the social and legal code a concrete embodiment. Deviance texts typically discuss labeling theory, conflict theory, "controlology," Marxism, feminism, phenomenology, and postmodernist theory as the chief constructionist perspectives.

Poverty and Disrepute

Designations of contempt and dishonor are not confined to behavior. Members of many, especially industrial, societies believe that failures to live up to the norm of economic success manifest a corresponding inability to live up to society's moral standards on a broad range of fronts. David Harvey argues that poverty "carries with it a *moral stain* as vexing as material uncertainty itself" (2007: 3589). A clear-cut manifestation of the deviantization of persons living in poverty is that, according to Erving Goffman, the poor tend to be *disqualified from full social and civic participation* – "members of the lower class who quite noticeably bear the mark of their status in their speech, appearance, and manner, and who, relative to the public institutions of our society, find they are second class citizens" (1963: 145–146). But though many deviance theorists, researchers, and textbook authors have discussed poverty as a *source* or breeding ground for deviant behavior, very few have regarded it as a *form* of deviance. Sharon Anleu is a major exception, holding that the unemployed, the homeless, the beggar, and the welfare recipient are decidedly stigmatized. The negative terms that the affluent apply to the poverty-stricken operate as if they were "magnets," she states, attracting other deviant labels, such as drug abuser, criminal, and mentally ill persons (2006). In short, poverty is more than simply a factor in generating deviant behavior; it is *itself* stigmatizing, denigrating – *deviantizing*. But the members of the society construct being poor as undesirable and consequently, wrongful, and correspondingly, treat the poor in a disparaging, disrespectful fashion. Affluent people often feel that those at the bottom of the income ladder are inferior to themselves; though they may feel genuine compassion, what they more often feel is condescension, pity, and contempt – and they tend to act accordingly.

Physical Characteristics

Positivists and social constructionists of deviance sharply part company when it comes to undesirable physical characteristics. Sociologists who regard deviance as *a particular and identifiable form of behavior* quite obviously do not discuss physical characteristics as deviance. Contrastingly, the constructionist approach, which views deviance not as a type of action but *that which provokes a negative, stigmatizing reaction*, addresses the matter of deviant bodies, which includes disability, disfigurement, and illness – including leprosy and HIV/AIDS – as well as extreme bodily alterations. The possession of undesirable physical characteristics may or may not be the result of the person's willful choice, and often, sociologists frequently overlook it as a form of deviance. But many attributes that are not chosen by the individual have likewise resulted in stigmatization, humiliation, and discreditation. Researchers often include obesity as a stigmatizing physical condition; many observers regard being fat the fault of person who is overweight, citing gluttony and inactivity as the main causes. But at one time, children born out of wedlock shared their mothers' shame; they were "bastards," illegitimate – and deviants – though their bastardy wasn't their fault. And clearly, today, getting visibly inked is chosen. Goffman singled out a specific type among non-fault stigmatizing conditions – which he referred to as *abominations of the body* (1963: 4–5), possessed by the disfigured and disabled. "Normals," or intact, abled individuals, often discredit or negatively label persons who possess such abominations, regarding them as inferior and socially undesirable; they stigmatize, shun, and socially isolate them. Though distinctly unfair, this labeling process is a fact of social life – though thankfully, it is a waning tendency.

Tribal Stigma

Goffman pointed to "tribal stigma of race, nation, and religion" as a major source of personal and collective ignominy or moral shame (1963: 4), but few deviance textbook authors have devoted much attention to it. The first edition of Marshall Clinard's text (1957, Chapters 16 and 17) represented a major exception – though later editions omitted racism as a form of stigmatization. Tribal stigma is a form of racism; dominant categories of humanity attempt to *inferiorize* subaltern or less powerful humans. Tribal stigmata are "transmitted through lineages and equally contaminate all members of a family" (Goffman 1963: 4). Though the distribution of identifiable genetic markers is far from randomly distributed the world over, socially designated "races" do not exist as distinct biological or genetic categories; they are cultural, historical, and social constructs – a human invention – but *belief in their ontological reality* justifies the oppression of humans thereby socially inferiorized. The inattention to race by deviance sociologists may be changing. Daniel Dotter suggests that "individuals may be defined as deviant more for *who* they are … than for *what* they have done" (2004: 89), mentioning race (along with gender) as a major example. Interbitzin, Bates, and Gainey's deviance text (2013) includes discussions and readings on race and homelessness, "shopping while black," racial profiling in immigration law enforcement, violent police–citizen encounters, and employees' unwillingness to hire certain applicants. Tribal stigmata as a source of deviance-imputation operate in human endeavors as diverse as mortgage-loan inequality, housing discrimination; racial steering and redlining; educational tracking, re-segregating schools; standards of beauty, the use of certain models to advertise products; the reporting of news; and disparities in health and disease. Over time, tribal stigma is declining in toxicity, although slowly and fitfully; the fact is, racism is still alive and well in the United States.

SEE ALSO: Crime and Juvenile Delinquency, Sociology of; Symbolic Interactionism

References

Anleu, Sharon L. Roach. 2006. *Deviance, Conformity and Control*, 4th ed. Sydney: Pearson.

Becker, Howard S. 1963. *Outsiders: Studies in the Sociology of Deviance*. Glencoe, IL: Free Press.

Clinard, Marshall B. 1957. *Sociology of Deviant Behavior*. New York: Reinhart.

Dotter, Daniel. 2004. *Creating Deviance: An Interactionist Approach*. Walnut Creek, CA: AltaMira Press.

Downes, David, and Paul Rock. 2011. *Understanding Deviance: A Guide to the Sociology of Crime and Rule-Breaking*, 6th ed. Oxford: Oxford University Press.

Goffman, Erving. 1963. *Stigma: Notes on the Management of Spoiled Identity*. Englewood Cliffs, NJ: Prentice-Hall/Spectrum.

Harvey, David L. 2007. "Poverty and Disrepute." In George Ritzer (ed.), *The Blackwell Encyclopedia of Sociology*, 3589–3594. Malden, MA: Blackwell Publishing.

Interbitzen, Michelle, Kristin Bates, and Randy Gainey. 2013. *Deviance and Social Control: A Sociological Perspective*. Thousand Oaks, CA: Sage.

Krauthammer, Charles. 1993. "Defining Deviancy Up." *The New Republic*, November 22, 20–25.

Moynihan, Daniel Patrick. 1993. "Defining Deviancy Down." *American Scholar* 64 (Winter): 25–33.

Further Reading

Adler, Patricia A., and Peter Adler, eds. 2016. *Constructions of Deviance: Social Power, Context, and Interaction*, 8th ed. Belmont, CA: Wadsworth.

Barkan, Steve E. 2014. *Criminology: A Sociological Understanding*, 6th ed. Englewood Cliffs, NJ: Prentice Hall.

Ben-Yehuda, Nachman. 2013. *Atrocity, Deviance, and Submarine Warfare: Norms and Practices During the World Wars*. Ann Arbor: University of Michigan Press.

Goode, Erich, ed. 2015. *The Handbook of Deviance*. Malden, MA: Wiley Blackwell.

Disability, Sociology of

Valerie Leiter

Simmons College, USA

The sociology of disability examines how societies draw boundaries between people who are labeled as having disabilities and those who are not, and addresses the social, political, and economic consequences of disabilities. Many different physical, intellectual, and psychological experiences are lumped together under the term "disability." People who are blind, have Down Syndrome, are paraplegic, have dementia, or are schizophrenic may be described as having a disability. What individuals with disabilities have in common is that the society in which they live has placed them in a social category together because their bodies deviate from societal norms. Disability is a fact of life at some point for most people. Irving Zola, one of the founders of the sociology of disability, suggested that "The issue of disability for individuals … is not whether but when, not so much which one but how many and in what combination" (1993: 18).

Definitions of disability vary by time and place. Social models of disability examine how societies construct disability, imbedded in barriers and attitudes. They draw attention to how social and physical spaces are constructed in ways that marginalize people with disabilities. For example, people who use wheelchairs can face architectural barriers, such as stairs that prevent entry into a building, the necessity of using a back door or service elevator to gain access, or hazardous sidewalks (Leiter 2015). Institutional barriers may separate people on the basis of disability, including segregated "special education" programs in schools. Social attitudes can exclude people, such as when individuals withhold job offers, birthday party invitations, and other social opportunities.

In contrast, medical models of disability have traditionally classified individuals based on how their bodily functions result in impairment (measured by experts as deviation from biomedical norms of the body), and focus on individual-level interventions to maximize bodily functioning. Some critics of social models of disability argue that they go too far in response to medical models, "exiling" the body, and that a sociology of impairment is needed to bring the body back into how we think about disability (Hughes and Patterson 1997). There is lively debate about how best to bring people's bodies into sociological work on disability without reinforcing individual-level approaches.

Sociologists have been very interested in how the disability rights movement has made tremendous strides toward gaining civil rights for people with disabilities. Parents

Core Concepts in Sociology, First Edition. Edited by J. Michael Ryan.
© 2019 John Wiley & Sons Ltd. Published 2019 by John Wiley & Sons Ltd.

of children with disabilities started organizing after World War II, resulting in federal legislation in the United States guaranteeing children the right to a public education (Leiter 2012), and later international parental activism. In the 1970s, adults with physical disabilities mobilized to press the federal government to outlaw discrimination against people with disabilities, as described in Richard Scotch's book, *From Good Will to Civil Rights*. Self-advocates, parents, and professionals all contributed to the civil rights movement for people with intellectual disabilities, as Allison Carey outlines in her book, *On the Margins of Citizenship*. In the United States, disability activists' work culminated in the passage of the Americans with Disabilities Act (ADA) in 1990, which protects individuals against disability-based discrimination. Internationally, activists in many countries use the United Nations Convention on the Rights of Persons with Disabilities, which came into force in 2008, as a foundation to press for change.

While civil rights for individuals have improved, social inequalities remain. Disability status is a powerful determinant of unemployment, underemployment, and living in poverty. In the United States, among people ages 16–64, only 27 percent of people with a disability are employed, compared with 72 percent of those without a disability. The unemployment rate for individuals with disabilities is twice that of people without a disability: 11.7 percent versus 5.2 percent (US Bureau of Labor Statistics 2015). As of 2013, 28 percent of adults with disabilities who were not living in institutions were living in poverty (Cornell University 2016). Increasing longevity, advances in medical treatment, and broadening definitions of disability (to include conditions such as Attention Deficit Hyperactivity Disorder) have contributed to growth in the number of people with disabilities, suggesting that recognition of inequalities based on disability may become even more widespread over time.

Sociologists were arguably slow to recognize the importance of disability as a social phenomenon. Through the end of the twentieth century, many sociologists accepted the legitimacy of individual-level theories, and took disability-related inequality for granted. While some of the early work on the sociology of disability was done in the United States, much critical work was also done by scholars in the United Kingdom. Colin Barnes, Len Barton, Jane Campbell, Mark Priestley, Mike Oliver, Tom Shakespeare, Carol Thomas, and others in the United Kingdom have made major contributions to disability theory and research.

There is growing recognition within sociology that, like race, gender, and sexual orientation, disability shapes individuals' life opportunities, and also interacts with other statuses in powerful ways. The next generation of scholars in the field is examining a wide range of issues, including how medical technology is being used to reduce disability (Laura Mauldin), how social policies create or constrain opportunities for integration (Brian Grossman), material wellbeing since the passage of the ADA (Julia Drew), disability pride (Jan Grue), intellectual disability and the life course (Scott Landes), and approaches to independent living (Chen Yang). The sociology of disability is still a relatively new field, but one that is growing, maturing, and spurring critical and creative scholarship.

SEE ALSO: Aging, Sociology of; Body, the; Deviance; Life Course; Medical Sociology; Medicalization; Mental Health and Illness; Stereotypes, Prejudice, and Discrimination; Stigma

References

Cornell University. 2016. Disability Statistics: Online Resource for US Disability Statistics. Online at: http://www.disabilitystatistics.org/reports/acs.cfm?statistic=7.

Hughes, Bill, and Kevin Patterson. 1997. "The Social Model of Disability and the Disappearing Body: Towards a Sociology of Impairment." *Disability & Society* 12: 325–340. Online at: http://dx.doi.org10.1080/09687599727209.

Leiter, Valerie. 2012. *Their Time Has Come: Youth with Disabilities on the Cusp of Adulthood*. Piscataway, NJ: Rutgers University Press.

Leiter, Valerie. 2015. "A Bricolage of Urban Sidewalks: Observing Locations of Inequality." In *Disability and Qualitative Inquiry: Methods for Rethinking an Ableist World*, edited by Ronald Berger and Laura Lorenz, 13–28. Burlington, VT: Ashgate Publishers.

United States Bureau of Labor Statistics. 2015. Persons with a Disability: Labor Force Characteristics Summary. Online at: http://www.bls.gov/news.release/disabl.nr0.htm.

Zola, Irving K. 1993. "Disability Statistics, What We Count and What I Tells Us." *Journal of Disability Policy Studies* 4 (2): 9–39.

Dramaturgy

Robert D. Benford

University of South Florida, USA

Dramaturgy refers to a perspective and an analytic tool that enhances awareness of how people collaborate to foster impressions, derive shared understandings, and create meaning in their everyday lives. Every social act – conversations among friends or strangers, exchanges between customers and cashiers, interactions in the workplace, classroom, or home – entail performances which can be viewed and analyzed through a dramaturgical lens.

Two interrelated yet distinctive schools of thought can be gleaned from those who operate from a dramaturgical perspective (Brisset and Edgley 1990). The first, based on the Erving Goffman's *Presentation of Self in Everyday Life* (1959), conceives of the use of theatrical concepts in analyzing social acts as a useful metaphor. From this vantage point everyday life is *like* a theater. Life is replete with dramas and includes performances by actors (a cast of characters that includes protagonists and antagonists), audiences, costumes, props, sets, front and back stages, plots and subplots, and scripts. Thus the theater provides a template for understanding how people communicate, negotiate meaning, and accomplish life's myriad of tasks. A second school of thought, derived from Kenneth Burke's (1969) "dramatism," contends that life *is* theater. From this view life is not like drama and the theater is not simply a metaphor for analyzing social life. Instead, life is drama and the theater portrays life's dramas. Plays on the theater stage feature all the elements of ordinary social life to present to an audience a new take on a particular dimension of the human condition. Regardless of one's ontological position concerning the relationship between the theater and real life, dramaturgical analysis illuminates how people construct reality, develop and present a self, and sustain the interaction order.

Numerous academic disciplines have contributed to the dramaturgical perspective, including sociology, anthropology, psychology, social psychology, political science, communication studies, linguistics, philosophy, cultural studies, performance studies, and film studies. Researchers have employed dramaturgical analysis to illuminate the dynamics of social movements, protests, media dramas fanning public fears concerning domestic terrorism, the performative body and body impression management, gender performances, transsexuals' self-presentations, museum dramas, leisure activities, policing, symbolizing

Core Concepts in Sociology, First Edition. Edited by J. Michael Ryan.

in the drama of human evolution, and electoral politics, to name but a few applications (Edgley 2013). Dramaturgical scholars have recently turned to the analysis of digital and social media to examine the ways in which the advent of the digital age has transformed social interaction and impression management in the twenty-first century.

SEE ALSO: Everyday Life; Self, the; Symbolic Interactionism

References

Brissett, Dennis, and Charles Edgley, eds. 1990. *Life as Theater: A Dramaturgical Sourcebook*, 2nd ed. New York: Aldine de Gruyter.

Burke, Kenneth. 1969. *A Grammar of Motives*. Berkeley: University of California Press.

Edgley, Charles, ed. 2013. *The Drama of Social Life: A Dramaturgical Sourcebook*. Farnham, UK: Ashgate.

Goffman, Erving. 1959. *The Presentation of Self in Everyday Life*. New York: Anchor.

Economic Sociology

Milan Zafirovski

University of North Texas, USA

The concept of economic sociology signifies the sociological conception and analysis of the economy, the sociology of economic life, the sociology of economic actors, actions, and outcomes, including organizations firms and markets, and the like. Economic sociology is usually defined as the "sociological perspective applied to economic phenomena" (Smelser and Swedberg 2005). This includes such "sociological perspectives" as social structures involving institutions, social controls like sanctions, norms, and values, cultural settings, social interactions, groups, and networks, in short society as a whole in relation to economy. According to this definition, economic sociology involves the "application of the frames of reference, variables, and explanatory models of sociology to that complex of activities concerned with the production, distribution, exchange, and consumption of scarce goods and services," simply to the economy, including firms and markets (Smelser and Swedberg 2005: 3). Thus defined, economic sociology is a distinct and autonomous field in relation to conventional economics instead mostly characterized with a non-sociological or individualistic orientation to the economy. The latter discipline involves, however, certain exceptions to this orientation such as social economics, socioeconomics, early institutional economics, historical economics, behavioral economics, and other unorthodox variants approximating or converging with economic sociology.

Methodologically, economic sociology constitutes a coherent sociological approach to the economy. It applies a sociological method to analyzing economic actors, activities, processes, and outcomes, in particular business enterprises and markets. Economic sociology is an essentially interdisciplinary concept and field placed at the intersection of sociology and economics. In this sense, it is often described as a "no man's and everyman's land" located between and representing a special field of both economics and sociology. Substantively, economic sociology represents a conception and analysis of the relationship between economic actions and other forms of social action on a micro level and between economy and society on a macro level. In micro terms, economic sociology conceives economic and analyzes actions as embedded in and influenced by what Weber calls the "autonomous structure of social action," including interpersonal relations and social networks. In macro terms, economic sociology focuses on the impact of society, including polity and culture, on the operation and outcomes of the economy, in particular markets and firms. It places a special emphasis on the economic effects of social institutions and other societal structures. Therefore, economic sociology posits and analyzes the micro- and macro-social embeddedness of economic actors, actions, and organizations regarded as embedded in and impacted both by personal interactions and social networks and by overarching societal, including political and cultural, institutions. Moreover, the social embeddedness of the economy, including markets and business organizations, is established as the main assumption of the new economic sociology as especially emerging and expanding since the 1980s.

A special and probably most important subfield of economic sociology is the sociology of the market. The latter is based on the social conception and analysis of the market, as distinct from its non-sociological or individualistic, psychological, and mechanical notion and study (for example, markets as automatic mechanisms) prevailing in orthodox economics. Economic sociology distinctively treats the market as a social structure, social system, social institution, political creation, cultural construction, and the like. The social-structural, in particular institutional, concept of the market is applied to various types of market such as production, consumption, financial, and labor markets. This concept is also applied or applicable to different forms of market structure, including perfect or free competition, monopoly and monopsony, duopoly and oligopoly, monopolistic and imperfect competition, and so on.

In historical perspective, economic sociology has developed as a distinct specialty within classical and contemporary sociology, as well as in certain segments of early and later economics. Since its inception within sociology and economics alike, it has characteristically conceptualized and analyzed the "economic process as an organic part of society, constantly in interaction with other forces" (Smelser and Swedberg 2005: 7). In this historical account, the historical development of a "social perspective on the economy," as well as its economistic alternative, in sociology and economics involves several and distinctive phases and representatives. Among these the first phase is the "original societal approach" to the economy characteristic both for classical economics and sociology and represented by such figures as the early sociologist or social philosopher Montesquieu and classical economists Quesney and Smith. The second phase consists of the "original economistic approach" identified in classical economics after Smith and of which the main representatives are deemed Malthus and Ricardo. The "return to societal approach" represents the next stage observed in some versions of unorthodox economics, as well as classical sociology, with Marx being invoked as the best-known example. This is followed by the "return to economistic approach" associated with neoclassical economics or marginalism and exemplified by its early exponent Menger (the founder of the Austrian economic school). The last phase is considered to be the "synthesis" of the previous societal and economistic approaches and especially represented by Weber's conception of economic sociology. In particular, this phase encompassing the period of the 1890 to the 1920s is often estimated to be the highest point in the development of classical economic sociology, also represented by other sociologists and economists such as Durkheim, Pareto, Marshall, Schumpeter, and others.

Within sociology, its founder Comte provides the first conception of economic sociology as the study of the "social economy," by treating the economy as an integral element of the "social system" in interconnections with its other elements. Weber defines economic sociology as the analysis of the influence of non-economic social forces on the economy, of "sociological categories of economic action," "sociology of economic action," and "a sociological theory of economic action," which is expected to build its "own theoretical constructs" in relation to pure economics. He classifies economic sociology into "social economics" which also encompasses pure economics and economic history. Durkheim conceives economic sociology as the investigation of the "genesis and functioning" of social institutions, specifically of their strong and pervasive impact on the economy. In particular, this concept involves the economic sociology of the market investigating the non-contractual social, especially institutional, underpinnings of exchange contracts, money values treated as institutionally conditioned and as collective representations, etc. Weber and Durkheim are often regarded as converging on a sociological, social "value-integration" conception of the economy, in particular on the social construction of economic actions and institutions, as exemplified by the notion of monetary value.

Economic sociology also develops within segments of economics and thus shows its interdisciplinary roots. A classical instance comprises "elements of the economic sociology of Adam Smith" (Schumpeter 1954) or Smith's "sociological economics," who is classified among the representatives of the "original societal approach" to the economy (Smelser and Swedberg 2005). Other classical instances or proxies are J.B. Say's concept of "social economy" as the study of the "economy of society" and a "proper name" for economic science, "sociological elements" in Ricardo, the significant share of "economic sociology" in J.S. Mill's rendition of political economy as well as in that of Marx, etc. A neoclassical example is Jevons's explicit concept of "economic sociology" defined as the "science of the evolution of social relations" and their effects on the economy, and recognized as a branch of and helping extricate economics from its "confused state." Also, Wicksteed implies the concept by proposing economics "must be the handmaid" of sociology because of the impact of social forces on the economy, notably the market. So does economist-sociologist Pareto by suggesting that many economic facts cannot be properly studied "without the aid of sociology" on the basis that they are only particular states of social facts and the economy an inseparable component of the "sociological system" as more extensive and complex. Other instances or proxies of economic sociology within neoclassical economics include Walras's conceptions of "social economy" regarded as a part of economic science, along with "pure" economics, Wieser's concept of "social economics" focusing on the "sociological problems of economic theory," Marshall's historical "economic sociology" of modern capitalism, Keynes's sociological or sociopsychological assumptions, etc. Cases or approximations of economic sociology within unorthodox economics comprise Veblen's and other institutional economics, the Historical School, in particular Sombart, alongside Weber, etc.

Within later mainstream economics, similar to Weber and Durkheim, Schumpeter (1954) defines economic sociology as the "analysis of social institutions" and their vigorous and constant influence on the economy in distinction from theoretical economics instead defined as the "analysis of economic mechanisms." In particular, Schumpeter outlines the "sociology of enterprise" and thus entrepreneurship and economic development, as well as of business cycles, as a subfield of economic sociology. Like Weber and Jevons, Schumpeter (1954) incorporates economic sociology into "economic analysis," together with economic theory, economic history, and other fields. In addition, other economists recognize economic sociology, especially in its version of institutionalism, within sociology and economics, and particularly propose the economic sociology of the market viewed as part of the social system, involving "sociological" and related explanations of market phenomena. Also, some leading contemporary economists adopt and apply the main premises of economic sociology by incorporating various "sociological assumptions" in economic analysis, and in particular point to the "sociology of the corporation" as its subfield. Other contemporary economists as well as sociologists imply the concept of economic sociology through such concepts as "sociological economics," "socioeconomics," "social economics," (classical) "institutional economics," "political economy," and the like.

Generally, early classical economic sociology is continued in and distinguished from its new, contemporary variant regarded as emerging with the conception of "social embeddedness" of the economy (Granovetter 1985). The shared core of the old and new economic sociology consists in certain "central propositions" treating economic actions as special cases of social action and as socially embedded in and influenced by social relations and structures, and economic institutions as societal constructions (Granovetter and Swedberg 2001). Relatedly, economic sociology, old and new, revolves around characteristic analytical lines such as the "sociological analysis of economic process," the "analysis of the connections between the economy and the rest of society," and the "study of changes in the institutional and cultural parameters that constitute the economy's societal context" (Smelser and Swedberg 2005).

Economic sociology encompasses such subfields as sociology of the market, sociology of business organizations, sociology of work or industrial sociology, sociology of consumption, sociology of wealth and income distribution, fiscal sociology, sociology of economic growth and development, sociology of traditional economies (or "substantive" economic anthropology), and so on. Future directions in theory, research, and methodology particularly include a better communication and integration between the new economic sociology and the incorporation of sociological concepts and assumptions in contemporary economics.

SEE ALSO: Consumption; Development, Sociology of; Organizations, Sociology of; Sociology; Work, Occupations, and Professions, Sociology of

References

Granovetter, Mark. 1985. "Economic Action and Social Structure: The Problem of Embeddedness." *American Journal of Sociology* 91: 481–510.

Granovetter, Mark, and Richard Swedberg. 2001. "Introduction." In *The Sociology of Economic Life*, edited by Mark Granovetter and Richard Swedberg, 1–26. Boulder: Westview Press.

Schumpeter, Joseph. 1954. *History of Economic Analysis*. New York: Oxford University Press.

Smelser, Neil, and Richard Swedberg. 2005. "The Sociological Perspective on the Economy." In *The Handbook of Economic Sociology*, edited by Neil Smelser and Richard Swedberg, 3–26. Princeton, NJ: Princeton University Press.

Further Reading

Friedland, Roger, and A.F. Robertson, eds. 1990. *Beyond the Marketplace*. New York: Aldine de Gruyter.

Martineli, Alberto, and Neil Smelser. 1990. "Economic Sociology: Historical Threads and Analytical Issues." *Current Sociology* 38: 1–49.

Swedberg, Richard. 2003. *Principles of Economic Sociology*. Princeton, NJ: Princeton University Press.

Weber, Max. [1920] 1968. *Economy and Society*. New York: Bedminster Press.

Zukin, Sharon, and Paul DiMaggio, eds. 1990. *Structures of Capital*. Cambridge: Cambridge University Press.

Education, Sociology of

Annette Lareau and Sherelle Ferguson

University of Pennsylvania, USA

Regardless of the circumstances that children are born into, education is meant to level the playing field. Schools teach children that *merit* – not social background – is crucial in determining how much they can accomplish. Further, educational success matters. Not only does education influence the kinds of jobs available to young adults, but degrees lead to higher earnings. If the advice of the nineteenth century was "Go west young man," the advice today is, "Go to college." Nevertheless, parents' social position predicts educational success throughout the life course. College graduation is much more likely for children born into affluent homes than for children born into poverty.

Sociologists of education illuminate how children from different social groups fare in educational systems including classrooms, schools, and colleges. Scholars investigate how social origins are related to social destinations. They also trace everyday interactions within institutions and unpack how adults and children understand their successes and failures. Sociologists study schools as organizations, examine the curriculum, and place education within the context of other institutions like family and politics. We will provide a brief overview of some of the most important themes in the sociology of education. In particular, we describe how sociologists focus on the role of families and schools in students' success, variations in students' experiences, and how schools have changed.

Overall, family background is the best predictor of educational outcomes. Families differ in their abilities to give their children a start in life that promotes the skills which are rewarded by schools. Compared to children from poor families, more affluent parents talk to children more, read to them more, provide less stressful home environments, and live in safer neighborhoods with better schools (Duncan and Murnane 2014).

Before children even enter kindergarten, their families shape their readiness for school. Teachers want children to enter school knowing the letters of the alphabet, being able to recognize shapes and colors, and being able to count to 100. But middle-class and upper-middle-class parents (hereafter middle-class), who have a college degree, are much more likely than working-class parents to teach their children these skills before they enter kindergarten. For example, social class shapes how much

Core Concepts in Sociology, First Edition. Edited by J. Michael Ryan.
© 2019 John Wiley & Sons Ltd. Published 2019 by John Wiley & Sons Ltd.

parents talk to children. While working-class parents talk to adults or talk *about* children, middle-class parents see children – even babies – as conversation partners. Middle-class parents are also more likely to ask children questions while working-class parents issue directives (Lareau 2011). Hence, children enter school with different levels of educational training.

Schools do help to socialize students to important social expectations. For example, in addition to the reading and math curriculum, children learn to follow classroom rules, play games, and cooperate with peers. As students progress through school, however, parents play different roles in their children's education. All parents want their children to be successful, but working-class parents are more likely to depend on educators – who have vastly more education than they do – to offer a professional training to their child. Middle-class parents, by contrast, see more interdependency between themselves and educators. They do not hesitate to intervene on educational matters. Middle-class parents are also more likely to enroll their children in extracurricular activities and hire tutors, while working-class parents grant children more autonomy to play outside, negotiate activities with peers, and watch television. These out-of-school activities matter for children's growth. All children learn during the year, but during the summers children of the middle-class continue to learn at a faster rate than more disadvantaged children in a pattern known as the "summer setback."

Significant achievement gaps exist in early childhood, and they remain from preschool to high school. There is a class gap in educational achievement, and racial gaps that cannot be fully explained by class differences. Black, Latino, and Native American students have lower academic outcomes compared to their white and Asian peers; for example, a majority of white students are "proficient" in math and reading, but less than one-quarter of black students are proficient (Duncan and Murnane 2014; Kena et al. 2016). Yet, the class gap has grown larger over time. The gap between children in the top 10 percent of income and bottom 10 percent of income is twice as large as the black–white gap (Reardon 2011; Duncan and Murnane 2014). Gender is also important; girls now outperform boys in many aspects of schooling.

While it is undeniable that family background plays an important role in educational outcomes (Coleman et al. 1966), schools also are consequential. Hence, researchers examine the variety of educational experiences available to children both in the United States and globally. Overall, students in many countries, including China, Taiwan, and Korea, spend many more hours per day on educational matters. This "time on task" contributes to the higher test scores of their students compared to US students (Kena et al. 2016). Within the United States, however, schools vary. There are elite boarding schools with state-of-the art facilities as well as under-resourced public schools in neighborhoods with high crime rates. Yet, it is less clear what aspects of a school environment matter for a student's outcomes. Recent research suggests a number of ways in which schools matter.

Scholars have looked at variation across school types, especially the relative merits of private and public schools. A wave of research in the 1980s and 1990s debated whether attending private schools increases students' learning opportunities and outcomes. It is difficult to separate private school effects on achievement from the effects of smaller class sizes, stronger college counselling programs, and the fact that, on average, private school students come from more affluent families than public school students. Some also argue that Catholic school students have higher achievement than their public schools peers. Still, the magnitude of these differences remains unclear.

Recently, charter schools have had a surge in enrollment. Between 2003 and 2013, public charter school enrollment increased from 0.8 million to 2.5 million (Kena et al. 2016). In many cities over one-quarter of students attend publicly funded charter schools. Typically, charter schools have much more autonomy than traditional public schools. A survey of available research suggests that charter schools perform similarly to average public schools: some do better, some do worse, and some do the same. There is not a body of evidence that shows that charter schools, as a whole, are better schools than traditional public schools. Although there have been media campaigns highlighting the success of select charter schools, the quality of charter schools varies widely.

Another way that schools differ is in the composition of their student body. For a brief period (from about the mid-1950s to the mid-1980s), policy makers and researchers pursued efforts to reduce educational inequalities by racially integrating schools. After the ruling of *Brown v. Board of Education* (1954), school desegregation peaked in the 1980s. But, in *Milliken v. Bradley* (1974), the US Supreme Court refused to mandate desegregation across district boundaries. The role of the courts in promoting desegregation subsided. Over the past few decades, many cities have seen white flight and increased white enrollment in private and magnet schools. By the 2000s, schools were more segregated than they were in the 1970s. Schools with student bodies that are predominantly black, Latino, or Native American have lower average test scores than those that are white or Asian. Even in some areas where racial segregation has decreased, income segregation has increased. In the 2013–14 school year, 25 percent of traditional public schools were high poverty, meaning more than 75 percent of students were considered low income (Kena et al. 2016). Nonwhite students are more likely to attend these high-poverty public schools. Schools with high proportions of low-income students have lower attendance rates, lower graduation rates, higher rates of disorder, and higher student and teacher turnover rates. There is evidence that peers' achievement and behaviors can impact students' learning opportunities.

Even within the same school, students may not have the same learning opportunities. Schools with grades K–12 commonly engage in ability grouping or tracking. Educators divide students into classes based on prior academic performance or perceived ability. In theory, teaching and learning is more efficient when students are homogeneously grouped. Critics argue, however, that tracking actually reproduces inequalities. Students in high-track classes are often taught by more experienced teachers, spend more time on instruction, and engage in more complex tasks than their peers (Oakes 2005). Low-income, black, Latino, and Native American students are more likely to be assigned to lower-track classes. Further, students' pathways are often set early their school career and mobility between tracks is rare.

Recent research suggests that being consistently taught by skilled teachers may improve students' chances for educational success. Scholars have struggled to determine the best measures of teacher quality. Number of years of education or credentials do not seem to explain teachers' effects. Some studies show that teachers' level of experience matters for how much students learn. Yet, high-quality teachers are unequally distributed across schools and districts. Disadvantaged students are more likely to have a teacher with little experience or teachers teaching outside of their subject expertise (Duncan and Murnane 2014). Schools in urban and rural areas also struggle to retain teachers. More experienced teachers often seek better pay and less challenging working conditions at better resourced schools with fewer disadvantaged students (Duncan and Murnane 2014).

The United States is in the middle of a demographic transition which impacts schools. Nationally, the majority of school children are nonwhite. In addition, the United States has been transformed by an influx of immigrants. On average, immigrant youth have more educational success than one might predict from their parents' educational backgrounds. Recent studies have investigated the impact of foreign-born students, particularly those who speak little English, on student achievement. Patterns of immigration exacerbate school segregation as low-income immigrant students are more likely to attend schools with low-income, native-born black and Latino students.

In recent decades, there has been a reduction of support for public education. Many school districts are struggling to meet costs. Teachers' salaries are very low relative to other professions; teacher turnover is high. In higher education, public funding has plummeted. Tuition has risen, and student debt has also increased. As educational institutions continue to change, an important task will be to understand the degree to which schools offer realistic opportunities for mobility or, rather, act to reproduce social inequalities in the broader society.

SEE ALSO: Family and Kinship, Sociology of; Poverty; Socialization; Stratification and Inequality

References

Coleman, James S., Ernest Q. Campbell, Carol J. Hobson, James McPartland, Alexander M. Mood Frederic D. Weinfeld, and Robert L. York. 1966. *Equality of Educational Opportunity*. Washington, DC: US Government Printing Office.

Duncan, Greg, and Richard Murnane. 2014. *Restoring Opportunity: The Crisis of Inequality and the Challenge for American Education*. Cambridge, MA: Harvard University Press.

Kena, Grace, William Hussar, Joel McFarland, Cristobal deBrey, Lauren Musu-Gillette, Xiaolei Wang, Jijun Zhang, Amy Rathbun, Sidney Wilkinson-Flicker, Melissa Diliberti, Amy Barmer, Farrah Bullock Mann, and Erin Dunlop Velez. 2016. *The Condition of Education 2016*. National Center for Education Statistics. NCES 2016-144.

Lareau, Annette. 2011. *Unequal Childhoods: Class, Race, and Family Life*, 2nd ed. Berkeley: University of California Press.

Oakes, Jeannie. 2005. *Keeping Track: How Schools Structure Inequality*, 2nd ed. New Haven, CT: Yale University Press.

Reardon, Sean. 2011. "The Widening Academic Achievement Gap Between the Rich and the Poor: New Evidence and Possible Explanations." In R. Murnane and G. Duncan (eds.), *Whither Opportunity? Rising Inequality and the Uncertain Life Chances of Low-Income Children*. New York: Russell Sage Foundation Press.

Emotion, Sociology of

Marci D. Cottingham

University of Amsterdam, The Netherlands

Emotion is a fundamental feature of human experience and as such has shaped the discipline of sociology. Though relatively young as a recognized subfield, emotion has played a role in classic and contemporary sociological work. Durkheim's notion of collective effervescence reimagined in Collins's (2004) Interaction Ritual theory or Hochschild's (1979) groundbreaking theory of emotion management with clear lineage to Marxist feelings of alienation are all examples of the ways in which emotion has been present in sociological theory. Even an expansive reading of Weber's notion of *verstehen* as empathic understanding can speak to emotional as well as intellectual goals set to guide the sociological endeavor. The subfield of the sociology of emotion has struggled to distinguish a distinctly social definition of emotion as the set of modes of being and processes that can animate both individual and collective bodies in tandem with cognitions and beliefs. Parallel to theorizing emotion, the subfield has created space for empirical investigations across institutions, groups, and specific emotions.

One defining characteristic of sociological approaches to emotion has been a focus less on what emotions *are* – the focus of philosophical and psychological approaches – and more on what emotions accomplish or *do* for the self and the social collective. In this vein, emotions can serve as the "glue" that binds social groups (in the case of ritual theory) or a signal of ill fit between self and environment (in the case of identity and affect control theory). Constructivist approaches and Symbolic Interactionism situate emotion and the self as emergent from, or at least heavily formed through, real and imaginative interactions with others. Certain emotions are notable for how clearly they demonstrate the influence of social context on felt emotion. For example, embarrassment, guilt, and shame all work in operation with one's internalized expectations of how others (specific and generalized) see the self. To feel embarrassed is to feel the presumed negative judgments of others, even without direct, verbal communication of such judgments. Social expectations can be so thoroughly shared and internalized that a publicly discovered violation of shared norms can evoke strong negative emotions, even if only imagined by the individual.

Hochschild's (1979) work examines emotion within postindustrial capitalism and the service economy. Her emotion management theory has dominated sociological treatments of emotion as well as scholarship in healthcare, organizational studies, and psychology. Her approach connects social structure and individual emotion through feeling rules, emotion management, and deep and surface acting. Feeling rules define the social norms surrounding what, when, and how to feel certain emotions. These vary across cultures, institutions, and situations and provide the internalized guidelines for when to mask, repress, or evoke certain emotions. Weddings are generally happy affairs, while funerals demand certain emotions and comportment that affirm their somber quality. Feeling rules specific to the workplace elicit emotional labor from workers expected to produce a certain affect in themselves and others as a part of paid employment. The work of masking or cultivating expected emotional expressions is captured in terms like surface acting – focused on what is expressed and seen – and deep acting – focused on the work involved in cultivating actual felt emotion.

Underlying many sociological approaches to emotion is a biological basis. Reflective of the mind/body dualism, the experience of emotion is located in the body. Changes in pulse, pupil dilation, sweat production, and breathing might all be seen as biological indicators of emotional arousal. Certainly in biological studies, such clustering of phenomena is often seen as the emotion itself. Sociobiological approaches to emotion privilege the interface between the social and biological while structural approaches to emotion focus less on the biological experience and more on the effect of two aspects of one's social position – power and status – on the type of emotion experienced.

Poststructuralism has also stimulated new considerations of emotion. Moving away from the dialectic of the self and the social, which seems to privilege atomistic individuals and their numerical grouping, Foucault's move to discourse and Bourdieu's emphasis on practice emphasizes social processes across time and space. Ways of being move through space in the form of practices while discourse is the mechanism through which past practices live on in present conditions. As a result, recent work has looked at emotional discourses, emotional capital, emotion-as-practice, emotional habitus, and emotional regimes as ways to use the conceptual tools of poststructuralism to make sense of what emotions accomplish in social life.

Empirical investigations of emotion have proliferated over the last 40 years; from sports fans to nation-states, legal work to rescue missions, and grassroots movements to online forums, emotions permeate. Gender, given its tie in Western cultures to (non) emotionality, has overlapped a number of fruitful studies of emotion. Race and social class have received less attention from emotion scholars, though this is changing. This work has benefitted other subfields as well as catalyzed methodological critique of the rational, dispassionate actor (and researcher) at the center of much sociological work. Debates persist on how to investigate emotion. McCarthy's (1989: 51) question remains: are emotions to be "measured and sifted like flour?" Ethnographic methods of observation and interviews in line with McCarthy's approach are common, but surveys and experiments on emotion also proliferate. More innovative data-collection methods include diary and photo elicitation and analysis of new and emerging digital communications. With these new methods, new questions emerge about how societies and their emotional features might be changing.

SEE ALSO: Body, the; Gender; Identity; Social Psychology; Self, the

References

Collins, Randall. 2004. *Interaction Ritual Chains*. Princeton, NJ: Princeton University Press.

Hochschild, Arlie. 1979. "Emotion Work, Feeling Rules, and Social Structure." *The American Journal of Sociology* 85 (3): 551–75.

McCarthy, E. Doyle. 1989. "Emotions Are Social Things: An Essay in the Sociology of Emotions." In *The Sociology of Emotions: Original Essays and Research Papers*, edited by D.D. Franks and E.D. McCarthy, 51–72. Greenwich, CT: JAI Press.

Further Reading

Bericat, Eduardo. 2015. "The Sociology of Emotions: Four Decades of Progress." *Current Sociology* 64 (3): 491–513.

Stets, Jan E., and Jonathan H. Turner, eds. 2006. *Handbook of the Sociology of Emotions*. Boston: Springer.

Environment, Sociology of the

Riley E. Dunlap

Oklahoma State University, USA

Sociology has a complex history with the biophysical environment. Although early sociologists often acknowledged environmental conditions, concerns about determinism and anti-reductionism led the discipline to ignore the environment during much of the last century, while awareness of major environmental problems in recent decades has led to the emergence of a vital field of environmental sociology.

Founding figures, including Marx, Durkheim, and Weber, gave the biophysical environment some attention, but Durkheim's anti-reductionism taboo combined with excesses of geographical and biological determinism led most sociologists by the mid-twentieth century to ignore and even dismiss the societal relevance of environmental conditions. This tendency was reinforced by the sense that scientific and technological advancements were making economic growth and progress the natural state of affairs for modern industrial societies. The result of these trends is that sociology, along with other social sciences, adopted an implicit "human exemptionalism paradigm" that viewed modern societies as exempt for the ecological restraints faced by other species. Thus, in the process of reacting against earlier forms of determinism, sociology adopted a staunch form of sociocultural determinism, one that fetishized Durkheim's anti-reductionism dictum to the point of dismissing the relevance of all nonsocial conditions for sociological analyses. In this context, in sociological analyses "environment" came to refer to social surroundings or context (Dunlap and Catton 1979).

These disciplinary trends limited sociology's response to the rapid growth in societal awareness of environmental problems in the 1960s and 1970s. Early research tended to focus on public attitudes toward environmental issues, the nature of environmentalism, and governmental responses to environmental problems, basically involving applications of traditional sociological specialties such as social psychology, social movements, and political sociology. Such work represented a "sociology of environmental issues." However, the energy crisis of 1974, which gave credence to growing concerns about "limits to growth," led to analyses of the relationships between energy, resources, and social structure. These analyses, complemented by increased attention to the impacts of housing and

Core Concepts in Sociology, First Edition. Edited by J. Michael Ryan.
© 2019 John Wiley & Sons Ltd. Published 2019 by John Wiley & Sons Ltd.

the built environment on human behavior, involved the study of "societal-environmental interactions," and stimulated the emergence of a distinct field of environmental sociology (Dunlap and Catton 1979).

The launch of this new field was also enhanced by societal attention to a widening array of environmental problems, and practical concerns such as enhancing sociological contributions to social impact assessments (as part of congressionally mandated environmental impact assessments) and strengthening sociological research for natural resource agencies such as the US Forest Service. All of these interests were involved in the formation of a Section on Environmental Sociology within the American Sociological Association in 1976, regarded as the official birth of the new field. Over the ensuing four decades environmental sociology has slowly, if irregularly, evolved into a well-established specialization within the larger discipline, one with an ever-growing range of foci.

The discovery of toxic wastes at Love Canal in the late 1970s was quickly followed by environmental hazards being identified in numerous communities across the nation, and sociologists led the way in focusing on the impacts of hazardous conditions on residents and community life more broadly. It was soon recognized that environmental hazards were disproportionately found in poor and minority communities, leading to "environmental justice" (EJ) becoming a critical focus of environmental sociology. The societal impacts of environmental hazards, often stemming from technological accidents, are an obvious example of societal-environmental interactions, and thus EJ research became a core component of environmental sociology, as well as an interdisciplinary specialization in its own right. Over time EJ research has become increasingly sophisticated, thanks to better data and use of GIS and other advanced analytical techniques, although debate continues over the relative roles of social class and race in generating disproportionate vulnerability to hazards. EJ work has also been extended to the international level in recent decades, exploring the dynamics that led to some nations becoming waste sites for others and the unfortunate consequences for the former's populations (Mohai, Pellow, and Roberts 2009).

While the core of environmental sociology was being strengthened by research on environmental hazards as well as continuing work on energy and resources, the application of traditional sociological perspectives to environmental issues continued to flourish into the 1980s and beyond. Research on public attitudes became more theoretically sophisticated and fed into efforts to promote pro-environmental behaviors, research on environmentalism broadened to incorporate local EJ movements as well as national-level organizations and activism, and studies of both activism and public opinion were extended to the international level. And finally, disciplinary work on social problems led to a spate of studies of the social construction of environmental problems, with sociologists highlighting the crucial roles played by claims-makers in getting conditions (ranging from local toxic contamination to global warming) defined as problematic and then widely accepted as such.

These highly insightful constructivist analyses, especially when applied to global environmental problems, led to a schism within the field in the 1990s related to sociology's cultural turn and embrace of postmodernism. Constructivist analyses of global warming in particular emphasized the importance of science in discovering, defining, and dealing with the problem, and uneasiness with such strong reliance on natural science led some sociologists to adopt an agnostic view of warming. This challenged the materialistic core of environmental sociology, and led to heated debates between constructivists and realists. While the debates have subsided, with constructivists noting they are not challenging the reality of environmental problems and realists acknowledging that evidence of such problems is socially mediated, their echoes are apparent in contemporary treatments of materiality within environmental sociology (Murphy 2016).

Nonetheless, over the past two decades growing evidence of the seriousness of global environmental problems such as tropical deforestation and human-caused climate change have created rich opportunities for sociological analyses, and environmental sociologists have responded. Measurements of biophysical phenomena such as greenhouse gas emissions, forest loss, and ecological footprints created valuable data sets at various scales – from local to national – that can be combined with a vast array of social, economic, and political data into highly sophisticated quantitative analyses employing techniques like multi-level modeling. The result has been an explosion of cross-national studies shedding light on the driving forces and societal impacts of these problems, insights that have enriched understanding of climate change and deforestation and enhanced the status of sociology across the environmental sciences. Sociological research on climate change in particular has offered unique insights into its driving forces and impacts, ameliorative and adaptive strategies, as well as the social, economic, and political forces hampering efforts to curb greenhouse gas emissions (Dunlap and Brule 2015).

In general, while qualitative field studies continue to make crucial contributions to environmental sociology and our understanding of the nature and impacts of environmental problems, the "quantitative turn" in environmental sociology (both in micro-level EJ studies as well as macro-level, comparative studies) has generated insights into societal-environmental interactions that were unimaginable when the field was young. Both qualitative and quantitative studies make use of and contribute to core theoretical concerns in the larger discipline, and the success of these efforts is reflected in the increase in environmental sociology research being published in elite disciplinary journals (Scott and Johnson 2016).

The growing salience of environmental problems, from toxic contamination to climate change, is also creating pressure for more courses, programs, and jobs in environmental sociology. The result of these trends is that the field is moving from the fringe to the core of sociology, a major intellectual shift for a discipline that just a few decades ago largely ignored the biophysical environment.

SEE ALSO: Risk: Science and Technology, Sociology of; Social Movements and Social Change; Space and Place

References

Dunlap, Riley E., and Robert J. Brulle, eds. 2015. *Climate Change and Society: Sociological Perspectives*. New York: Oxford University Press.

Dunlap, Riley E., and William R. Catton, Jr. 1979. "Environmental Sociology." *Annual Review of Sociology* 5: 243–273.

Mohai, Paul, David Pellow, and J. Timmons Roberts. 2009. "Environmental Justice." *Annual Review of Environment and Resources* 34: 405–430.

Murphy, Raymond. 2016. "Conceptual Lenses to Bring into Focus the Blurred and Unpack the Entangled." *Environmental Sociology* 2: 333–345.

Scott, Lauren N., and Erik W. Johnson. 2016. "From Fringe to Core? The Integration of Environmental Sociology." *Environmental Sociology* 3: 17–29.

Epistemology

Liz Stanley

University of Edinburgh, UK

Epistemology covers such matters as what knowledge is, how it is known, and under what circumstances. Although fundamental to disciplinary (and other) claims to produce knowledge, when discussed in sociology textbooks it is often presented round comments about its abstraction or being just a minority special interest, with the emphasis instead on addressing "knowledge what," rather than the "knowledge how" or "knowledge who" questions of epistemology. Such questions are however actually intertwined and separated only to the detriment of sociological understanding.

Epistemological ideas underpin work in the sociology of knowledge, which has been an established presence since Mannheim's (1925) *Sociology of Knowledge*. Epistemology deals with foundational issues in knowing, including who knows, under what conditions, using what criteria, with what challenges and counter-claims, and whether certain or absolute knowledge of the social world can be gained. When a branch of philosophy, epistemology is generally considered abstractly. However, within the framework of sociology it has been shaped differently, bringing matters of epistemology and the sociology of knowledge closer by treating epistemology in social terms and grounded ways. A concern with epistemology has impacted significantly on the sociological agenda in recent decades, stimulated in particular by the presence of feminist sociologists exploring the relationship between feminist epistemology and sociological research, and also through the development of social epistemology.

In substantive work, sociologists are concerned with producing conclusions about, for example, contemporary family life or changes in employment opportunities and so on. But for the people concerned, this may involve "the facts" being subject to speculation, disagreement, and competing claims-making. In other words, the what, how, and who of knowledge about these matters are closely connected. This conveys that fundamental matters of epistemology are relevant both for sociology and for understanding the fabric of social life. In consequence, sociological work concerned with epistemology has developed around practical concerns, with key areas concerning: the craft and claims of sociology; constructions of reality in different historical and present-day contexts; epistemologies of the South; black, lesbian, feminist and other "Other" epistemologies; and the production of scientific knowledges. Key debates include whether social reality is best understood in foundationalist, constructionist, or

Core Concepts in Sociology, First Edition. Edited by J. Michael Ryan.
© 2019 John Wiley & Sons Ltd. Published 2019 by John Wiley & Sons Ltd.

"fractured foundationalist" terms; if "who knows" makes a difference to what is known, in particular regarding the gender of the knower and whether they are situated in the North of the world; the craft of sociology and researcher-reflexivity and how these shape what is known; and whether epistemological privilege exists for researchers and other specialist kinds of knowers. Present epistemological hotspots are "race" and "the South."

SEE ALSO: Constructionism vs. Essentialism; Feminist Theory; Knowledge, Sociology of

Reference

Mannheim, Karl. 1925. *The Sociology of Knowledge.* London: Routledge.

Further Reading

Benton, Ted, and Ian Craib. 2011. *Philosophy of the Social Sciences*, 2nd ed. Basingstoke: Palgrave Macmillan.
Santos, Boaventura de Sousa. 2014. *Epistemologies of the South.* London: Routledge.
Stanley, Liz, and Sue Wise. 1993. *Breaking Out Again: Feminist Ontology and Epistemology.* London: Routledge

Ethnography

Richard Ocejo

City University of New York, USA

Ethnography is a social science research method that entails the researcher analyzing a social problem by directly engaging with a group over an extended period of time. Related terms include "fieldwork," or when researchers gather data in a specific setting, and "participant observation," or when a researcher becomes both a participant and an observer of the action in a field site. The philosophical foundation of ethnography is the idea that sociologists can understand how people socially construct and make sense of their own lives by observing them behave up close in their natural settings. It is considered a qualitative method, since ethnographers are focused on learning the significance behind the meanings and interpretations of the people they study by examining their behavior. What people say and how they act represent the data ethnographers collect, primarily through handwritten field notes as well as other data-collection techniques (e.g., audio recorders, photos, and video). While ethnographers can take either an inductive (ground-up) or a deductive (top-down) approach in their work, most take the former. In other words, ethnographers generally enter a field site like explorers, with a varying amount of knowledge about what explains the behavior they will find, and with the goal of gradually building a theory, or explanation, of the social problem. Some, however, enter the field with a theory of the behavior and social problem in mind, with the goal of revising it with new data.

Anthropologists originated the ethnographic method in the early twentieth century, and lived among the tribes and native peoples they studied. Sociologists, such as W.E.B. Du Bois and Robert Park and other scholars in the "Chicago School," quickly adopted it, primarily to study urban life. While some of these early sociologists lived among the people they studied, as anthropologists did and often still do, many did not (this mix is similar today). But there has been a historical progression among sociologists who use ethnography toward greater and greater immersion in their field sites and among the people they study. Early ethnographers were more detached from the people they studied, and played the role of an "observer" more than a "participant observer." While they were able to document the behaviors they saw of the people in the setting, they did not necessarily gain access to their meanings and interpretations of their situation. In other words, they hadn't really immersed themselves in the cultures they were studying. During the course of the twentieth century and continuing into the twenty-first,

Core Concepts in Sociology, First Edition. Edited by J. Michael Ryan.
© 2019 John Wiley & Sons Ltd. Published 2019 by John Wiley & Sons Ltd.

ethnographers have generally aimed to get close to the people they study to best see the world from their perspective, or "take the role of the other" (Geertz 1973). As a result, ethnographers often live in the same neighborhoods as their participants (including violent areas) (Contreras 2012; Duck 2015), work alongside them in their jobs (Desmond 2007), and participate in a variety of activities, like playing blues music (Grazian 2003).

But in doing so, ethnographers are careful to maintain a critical distance between themselves and their participants. They want to get close to the people they study, but not so close that they end up misrepresenting or glamorizing them. Ethnographers therefore try to carefully maintain the relationships they have with their participants, and always be aware of situations when they become too intimate with them, potentially compromising their ability to accurately analyze their lives. Maintaining relationships is also important because ethnographers must be aware of how who they are in terms of their social identities (their gender, race, ethnicity, age, sexuality, social class, etc.) influences the behavior they are observing. For instance, because of the divisive nature of race, white ethnographers who study blacks can "miss" significant meanings in the behaviors they observe, which can lead to an incomplete and/or inaccurate study (Duneier 1999).

Related to these points, of all the popular research methods sociologists use, ethnography presents researchers with the greatest ethical challenges. Unlike with questionnaires, it is impossible for ethnographers to not know the identities and intimate details of the people they study. Ethnographers also often observe people's private lives, or aspects of themselves they would rather keep secret. It is therefore easy for sensitive information to become public through various publications, which can have significant consequences for participants. They can lose their jobs, lose their standing in their communities, or become imprisoned if their actions become connected to their identities as a result of participating in an ethnographic research study. As in any research project, it is the researcher's responsibility to ensure their participants do not come to any harm because of their participation. They must therefore be very protective of the data they collect, and careful in their publications to not reveal the identities of the people they study if they do not want them revealed.

SEE ALSO: Everyday Life; Frames, Narratives, and Ideology; Knowledge, Sociology of; Qualitative Methods; Symbolic Interactionism

References

Contreras, Randol. 2012. *The Stickup Kids: Race, Drugs, Violence, and the American Dream*. Berkeley: University of California Press.

Desmond, Matthew. 2007. *On the Fireline: Living and Dying with Wildland Firefighters*. Chicago: University of Chicago Press.

Duck, Waverly. 2015. *No Way Out: Precarious Living in the Shadow of Poverty and Drug Dealing*. Chicago: University of Chicago Press.

Duneier, Mitchell. 1999. *Sidewalk*. New York: Farrar, Straus and Giroux.

Geertz, Clifford. 1973. *The Interpretation of Cultures: Selected Essays*. New York: Basic Books.

Grazian, David. 2003. *Blue Chicago: The Search for Authenticity in Urban Blues Clubs*. Chicago: University of Chicago Press.

Ethnomethodology

Andrew P. Carlin

Manchester Metropolitan University, UK

Ethnomethodology is the study of social order, a preoccupation in sociology since Émile Durkheim, where the "problem" of order is theorized as a feature of the forms of society being studied, e.g., as characterized by mechanical versus organic solidarity. Harold Garfinkel (1917–2011) developed ethnomethodology in response to his close reading of Talcott Parsons. Garfinkel sought to "dissolve" the problem of order, which he regarded not as a problem for sociologists, but as an everyday matter that is produced in an ongoing manner by members of society.

A useful way to approach ethnomethodology is to consider the distinction made by Garfinkel's students, between *topic* and *resource* (Pollner and Zimmerman 1970). Sociology proceeds by theorizing what people do and their relation to "society." However, this presupposes a detailed "procedural" knowledge of *how* people do things. Ethnomethodology suggests that sociology takes for granted this procedural aspect of people's lives and uses it as a resource for its studies; ethnomethodology, on the other hand, takes this aspect as topics, not resources, for analysis. This gives the sense to Garfinkel's claim that ethnomethodology is an "alternate" approach.

Garfinkel's first book, *Studies in Ethnomethodology*, was received with hostility in sociology. It was misread as critical of sociology when Garfinkel was highlighting procedural difficulties with doing sociological studies. To illustrate this, his studies (Garfinkel 1967) of patient records at a psychiatric clinic demonstrate that previous inquiries failed to meet standards of "methodological adequacy" that sociologists had set for themselves; furthermore, the reasoning analysts used in order to "do" sociology relied, in unexplicated ways, upon the common-sense reasoning used by members of society. Garfinkel's point was not that members used the same reasoning as professional sociologists in conducting their ordinary affairs; but that professional sociologists used the self-same common-sense reasoning procedures in doing sociological theorizing.

This is the import of the emphasis on "practical sociological reasoning." For Garfinkel, members used "practical" sociological reasoning rather than "professional" sociological reasoning; a key point in ethnomethodology exemplified by his study of jurors' decision-making activities (Garfinkel 1967). Garfinkel showed not only how practical sociological reasoning was incorporated into sociological studies; he established that an explicative sociology should study members' methods for making sense of society.

Core Concepts in Sociology, First Edition. Edited by J. Michael Ryan.
© 2019 John Wiley & Sons Ltd. Published 2019 by John Wiley & Sons Ltd.

However, even though Garfinkel pointed out methodological "troubles," e.g., how statistics are produced, how interview responses are thematized, ethnomethodology is not, despite what the word suggests, a method of doing sociology. Nor does ethnomethodology suggest how existing methods could be improved. As long as sociology takes procedural knowledge (members' practical reasoning) as "resources" for analyses, then increasingly precise research methods cannot address the research problem. They are doing what they should be studying.

Ethnomethodology is a "radical" approach in the sense that in order not to "lose the phenomenon" of investigation in each and every actual case, methods suited to the specificities of the phenomenon are selected as opposed to a particular "one size fits all," perspectival approach. As recent studies show, using methods fitted to phenomena of inquiry ("unique adequacy") implicates a more sophisticated, explicative analysis (Sormani 2014).

Among these "methodological policies" are the principle of "ethnomethodological indifference," where the ethnomethodologist abandons any preconceptions of a body of knowledge or "literature canon" that must be addressed in order to consider a particular topic. Instead, the ethnomethodologist cites "classic" studies on a topic to show "What More" is to be investigated in sociological studies. Ethnomethodological indifference requires the analyst to set aside epistemological assumptions, concentrating on members' practical sociological reasoning free from professional sociological conceptualization (Bittner 2013).

It is important to note that ethnomethodological investigations do not follow all Garfinkel's methodological policies, such as meeting the unique adequacy requirement, within the same study, and may be conducted under various ethnomethodological auspices. Nevertheless, Garfinkel's methodological injunctions show the intellectual debt he owed to phenomenologists; as do the major topics of explication within ethnomethodology, such as "accountability," "indexicality," and "reflexivity."

With Garfinkel's follow-up to *Studies* (Garfinkel and Sacks 1970), which enjoined ethnomethodology to engage with the later work of Ludwig Wittgenstein, and contained explication of forms of theorizing he called "constructive analysis," it became clearer that sociology was merely an example of a sustained methodological argument. Subsequently, demonstrating the "alternate" approach of ethnomethodology to phenomena, or "respecification," became more dominant (Button 1992; Garfinkel 2002). While the Wittgensteinan profile within ethnomethodology matured, the phenomenological aspects of Garfinkel's work persisted throughout his career.

Textbook caricatures of ethnomethodology rely on outdated notions of the approach, illustrating its scope with reference to early "breach experiments" conducted in the 1960s, as described in *Studies in Ethnomethodology*. Others recycle the mistake that ethnomethodology is a form of "qualitative" sociology, which allows sociologists to rehearse objections to it as a particular "type" of sociology (concentrating on "agency" at the expense of "structure," which suggests that it is "subjective") (Sharrock and Watson 1988). For example, ethnomethodology is accused of being unable to address "macro" issues, such as "power." This is disingenuous: it does address these issues, not by theorizing but by studying the concrete details of its use. This illustrates another confusion, whereby ethnomethodologists are also accused of focusing on "trivial" issues, such as the organization of queues and ordinary texts (Watson 2009); yet the analysis of mundane phenomena affords the surfacing of how social order is endogenously produced and maintained by parties to those phenomena, or "local production cohorts."

Whilst ethnomethodology remains a thoroughly sociological approach to members' methods, there is current debate regarding the disciplinary aegis of ethnomethodology (Quéré 2012) and it has been abstracted into various fields. With its program of "respecification" ethnomethodology has changed, but its core problematic – how is social order possible – remains the same.

SEE ALSO: Everyday Life; Knowledge, Sociology of

References

Bittner, Egon. 2013. "The Concept of Organization." *Ethnographic Studies* 13: 175–187.

Button, Graham. 1992. *Ethnomethodology and the Human Sciences*. Cambridge: Cambridge University Press.

Garfinkel, Harold. 1967. *Studies in Ethnomethodology*. Englewood Cliffs, NJ: Prentice-Hall.

Garfinkel, Harold. 2002. *Ethnomethodology's Program: Working Out Durkheim's Aphorism*. Lanham: Rowman & Littlefield.

Garfinkel, Harold, and Harvey Sacks. 1970. "On Formal Structures of Practical Actions." In *Theoretical Sociology: Perspectives and Developments*, edited by John C. McKinney and Edward A. Tiryakian, 337–366. New York: Appleton-Century-Crofts.

Quéré, Louis. 2012. "Is There Any Good Reason to Say Goodbye to 'Ethnomethodology.'" *Human Studies* 35 (2): 305–325.

Pollner, Melvin, and Don H. Zimmerman. 1970. "The Everyday World as a Phenomenon." In *Understanding Everyday Life: Towards a Reconstruction of Sociological Knowledge*, edited by Jack D. Douglas, 80–103. Chicago: Aldine Publishing.

Sharrock, Wes, and Rod Watson. 1988. "Autonomy Among Social Theories: The Incarnation of Social Structures." In *Actions and Structure: Research Methods and Social Theory*, edited by Nigel G. Fielding, 56–77. London: Sage.

Sormani, Philippe. 2014. *Respecifying Lab Ethnography*. Farnham, UK: Ashgate.

Watson, Rod. 2009. *Analysing Practical and Professional Texts*. Farnham, UK: Ashgate.

Everyday Life

Arthur McLuhan

York University, Canada

Sociologies of everyday life focus on the common features and processes involved in people's day-to-day experiences of the world. This includes investigating how people become involved in groups, acquire perspectives, achieve identities, develop relationships, perform activities, experience emotionality, and form and coordinate group associations (Prus 1996). The emphasis is on the doing or accomplishing of human knowing and acting. Therefore, in many ways, the study of everyday life is one of the most central – as well as relatable – tasks of the sociological discipline. Any comprehensive understanding of society must address and be grounded in what people actually do as members of the group.

The focus on everyday life has a rich history in sociology, but "everyday life" as a distinct theoretical, methodological, and substantive area of specialization in sociology has only occurred within the past three decades. Everyday life sociology is usually identified with a group of sociological approaches that have historically focused on social interaction, including symbolic interactionism, dramaturgy, phenomenology, social constructionism, ethnomethodology, and existential sociology, among others. These approaches, while having notable differences, cohere in their concerted examination of the perspectives, practices, and problems that people develop and manage in their day-to-day experiences and encounters. As Adler, Adler, and Fontana (1987) note, several "major tenets" unite sociologies of everyday life: the critique of macro-sociological determinism and reductionism; the primacy of interpretive processes and the use of qualitative methods to examine those processes; the conceptualization of human actors as symbolic–interactive beings; and the analysis of social structure as not only patterned and obdurate but also negotiable and contextual joint actions.

While research in everyday life sociology is often associated with micro-sociological examinations of social interaction, the study of everyday life can provide links among the micro-, meso-, and macro-sociological levels of analysis. For example, the empirical examination of everyday life allows researchers to link structural inequalities to group-based cultures, situated interactions, and interpretive processes. Some of the recent and important work in everyday life sociology has contributed to this type of multi-level analytical bridging.

The sociology of everyday life has also been the subject of several criticisms. These include a set of overlapping yet distinct charges that everyday life sociologies cannot account for or do not incorporate matters of social structure, history, morality, politics, or power. Various everyday life scholars have addressed these criticisms, citing the critics' misinterpretation and misapplication of everyday life theory and research. There is, however, at minimum a kernel of truth in most of these criticisms, as they concern features of social life that have typically been the domain of macro-sociology. In order to distinguish themselves from macro-sociologies, everyday life sociologies historically tended to focus on the day-to-day, situational practices usually neglected in mainstream sociology. In doing so, everyday life sociology often avoided developing explicit theory and research on social structures and forces. This analytical neglect has shifted, however, recently, as everyday life perspectives have offered several influential explanations for social structural issues that were once exclusively the domain of macro-sociology.

A group of critical approaches to the study of everyday life have also emerged and become prominent voices in recent decades, which, in part, address the aforementioned critiques of conventional everyday life sociology. Critical approaches to everyday life represent multiple theoretical traditions, including feminism, cultural studies, poststructuralism, and postmodernism. Rather than focusing their analyses on how people experience and make sense of everyday life, critical approaches not only attempt to reveal the inherent inequalities, forms of oppression, and relations of power that shape everyday experiences, but also develop their analyses as a means of deconstructing, subverting, and changing reality in the pursuit of social justice, progress, and emancipation.

Looking ahead, everyday life as an area of theoretical, methodological, and substantive interest for sociology will become increasingly important as it is incorporated further into mainstream sociology. The challenge for many of the traditional sociological approaches to everyday life will be maintaining distinctive identities as their analytical contributions become taken for granted and common sense reference points in the mainstream sociology that subsumes them.

SEE ALSO: Dramaturgy; Ethnography; Ethnomethodology; Qualitative Methods; Self, the; Social Psychology; Symbolic Interactionism

References

Adler, Patricia A., Peter Adler, and Andrea Fontana. 1987. "Everyday Life Sociology." *Annual Review of Sociology* 13: 217–235.

Prus, Robert. 1996. *Symbolic Interaction and Ethnographic Research: Intersubjectivity and the Study of Human Lived Experience*. Albany: SUNY Press.

Further Reading

Gardiner, Michael E. 2000. *Critiques of Everyday Life*. New York: Routledge.

Kalekin-Fishman, Devorah. 2013. "Sociology of Everyday Life." *Current Sociology* 61: 714–732.

Maines, David. 2001. *The Faultline of Consciousness: A View of Interactionism in Sociology*. New York: Aldine de Gruyter.

Family and Kinship, Sociology of

Linda L. Semu

McDaniel College, USA

Kinship and Family: An Overview

Kinship can be viewed as an important source of social structure in communities: it impacts many aspects of an individual's life whereby relations and connections are systematically constructed and conducted to better serve the fundamental good. The emergence of capitalism in the nineteenth century resulted in the elevation of the family as a social institution through which an individual's sociopolitical, economic, cultural, legal, and ideological norms were grounded. Industrialization and its attendant demographic transition inevitably led to a kinship transition in which declining fertility rates resulted in fewer kin networks such that by the 1950s, the media and popular culture elevated heteronormative constructions of the nuclear family, comprised of married heterosexual parents and children. However, various social movements – namely the civil rights, women's rights, gay rights, and marriage rights movements – and the resultant social, political, and legal changes in the past 50 years – have challenged the dominance of the traditional nuclear family model. In fact, recent literature shows that the traditional heterosexual nuclear family has never really been the norm in the United States. This is more so now when families are being created in unconventional ways, ranging from adoption and assisted reproduction, to gay and heterosexual, single and coupled parenting, and multi-generational parenting; in some cases, aided by technological, medical, and legal innovations and choices. Stacey's 2011 study of unconventional family, kinship, and intimacy patterns in the United States, South Africa, and China provides evidence of creative social arrangements that are contrary to the Western nuclear hetero-patriarchal norm and calls for a nuanced attention to, and institutionalized support for, the diversity of the family form (Stacey 2011).

An examination of living arrangements helps to illuminate the nuanced nature of family and kinship. Almost one-fifth of individuals in the United States live with extended family members (that is, non-nuclear family of spouse and children) and non-kin. These households typically tend to be multi-generational. Although economic and housing constraints are typical causes, the recent trend is also attributed to an increase

Core Concepts in Sociology, First Edition. Edited by J. Michael Ryan.

in high median age at marriage and immigration from countries in Latin America and Asia whose customs and cultural practices lean toward family cohesiveness, support, and nurture (Zonta 2016). Historically, in the United States, African-American families have been characterized by intergenerational and multi-generational families. These were a carry-over of African traditions and were a necessary survival strategy in the face of slavery, Jim Crow, decades of segregation, racism, and marginalization. They have become ever more important in contemporary times in response to drug and alcohol addiction, health disparities and HIV/AIDS, high incarceration rates, unemployment, and poverty (Waites 2009).

Extended families provide care for children when parents are unable to do so. Informal kinship care is the most common care of related children: the number of children who are raised by kin other than their parents has recently grown faster than the United States child population, buoyed by public policy as the preferred living arrangement for children who are unable to live with their parents. A somewhat similar pattern in children's living arrangements exists among the Maasai of southern Kenya where child circulation is widespread despite increasing institutional discourse that depicts the "modern" family as small, settled, and nuclear. This practice is grounded in the Maasai worldview where family and home are fluid concepts. This, in turn, reinforces the notion that belonging is not biologically constituted hence children circulate within and across households, rather than belonging to a single location and single set of parents (Archambault 2010). For the Maasai, family and parenthood is much broader than the typical Euro-American family and kinship conceptualization.

Fictive Kin: By Any Other Name?

The idea of a blood relationship as a basis for kinship is culturally constrained, and is mostly a Euro-American expression of the biogenetic connection between parents and children through the act of procreation. When extended to the social realm, the idea of blood relationship and altruism are equated such that family members are thought to be recipients of stable and enduring kin and reciprocal altruism, while friends can only get temporal reciprocal altruism. Yet kinship extends beyond blood relations and marriage. In many cultures, kinship claims based on solidarity, feeling, and stipulated relatedness have been shown to exist historically and cross-culturally. For example, the most common substance-based metaphors for kinship relatedness in the Bible are seed (denoting semen: the lineal relationship between parents and descendants), and bone and flesh. However, Israelites understood breastmilk as a kinship-forging substance through which a mother or wet-nurse conferred her tribal identity and status to a child. Similar notions of breastmilk as a conduit for forging kinship bonds have been found in diverse cultures spatially and over time among Trobriand islanders, Abkhazian of central Eurasia, the Irish, and Arabs. Similarly, well-off Nantwich women in England (1603–1685), reinforced kinship relations and emotional investment in female-centered families by passing on their wealth to other women as a way of providing for the welfare of the less fortunate.

Sociologists call the relationships where family-like relations exist among individuals who are not related by the usual practice of blood, marriage, or adoption as "fictive kin." For example, homeless youth form street families, the self-supportive networks from which they obtain acceptance, support, security, and companionship, and which they also utilize to combat feelings of alienation and loneliness and to mitigate the demands of life on the streets. Although there is no direct evidence that the phenomenon is any more common within one group than it is in any other, scholars tend to look for and analyze evidence of fictive kin with respect to people who are marginalized in terms of age, race, sexual identity, family structure, and country of origin; and yet are less likely to use it to describe relationships within the mainstream white population. Different terms are used for different groups ranging from: *intentional families* (among LGBTQ), *voluntary kin* (among predominantly white), urban tribes (college-educated urban youth), *othermothers* (among African-American women), and *compadrazgo* (among Latino/a). The racialization is not lost on scholars who note how images of dependency are implicit in describing minorities' relationships while terms implicit of agency are used for gay, lesbian, and white populations. This way of analyzing the relationships has been problematized as ethnocentric, heteronormative, and fetishizing biological forms of relatedness over other kinds of solidarity. Furthermore, fictive families are conceptualized on the basis of their deviation from the conventional family model, where emphasis is on what they are not, rather than what they are, thereby reinforcing the stigmatization that implies that they are not "real." On the other hand, a social constructionist view acknowledges that families come in different forms other than the traditional heterosexual nuclear model. Thus, it provides a broader perspective that not only includes conventional views of the family based on marriage, blood, or law, but also includes perceptions of family and kin based on shared history and functioning.

Lesbian, Gay, Bisexual, and Transgender (LGBT) Family and Kin

The law codifies societal norms of what is acceptable and what is not, thereby contributing to the challenges experienced by gay, lesbian, bisexual, and transgender (LGBT) parents and their children as they attempt to establish their family and kinship conditions. This is because parenthood has been historically embedded in conventional notions of the heterosexual nuclear family hence legal and policy barriers have been historically enacted to prevent non-heterosexuals from creating families and parenting. Although the right to parent children is now a visible part of the mainstream LGBT movement, this has not always been the case. Major societal and legal transitions have occurred from the end of World War II to the present. Rivers (2013) identifies the following as some key historical points in the fight for change: from being in the shadows (1945–1969); to fights for parental rights through the legal system in the 1970s to 1980s; activism of lesbian mothers; gay fathers and the fight and politics for gay family respectability; and the gay and lesbian baby boom, facilitated by reproductive technologies. Acceptance of LGBT family life is more common-place now than was the case in the past, at least in many parts of the world. This is evidenced by the growing number of countries that now allow same-sex marriage, as well as the legal establishment of legal domestic partnerships same-gender marriage, and the opening of foster parenting and adoption to LGBT persons.

Double-Edged Sword: Frontiers and Reinforcement of Kinship and Family Through Reproductive Technologies

The sociological implications of the definition, meaning, and role of family intersect political, economic, sociocultural, and religious realms. This is the case now as the family has acquired a new meaning in the era of reproductive technologies that have facilitated the bearing of offspring by breaking some of the traditional rules of family formation. This is simultaneously played out in two areas: reproductive technology and genetics (medicine). Assisted reproductive technologies (donor-conceived families) are transforming common conceptualizations of families: the law currently does little to foster establishment of ties between donors and their offspring, with state laws varying from precluding donors from any relationship and responsibility, to granting them some sort of nominal relationship. Hence, various familial outcomes are possible: for a single parent, where a donor is used outside of official surrogacy, s/he is officially identified as a parent. However, if the donation is done in an official context, there is the option to either be anonymous or known prior to conception, each of which has different relationship outcomes with the offspring. On the other hand, when heterosexual, lesbian, and gay couples make families through gamete donations, they introduce third-party genetic material and an offspring biologically related to one parent. Although spouses are considered legal parents, for non-marital couples, the nonbiological parent must establish legal parenthood through judicial action or they are not legally considered a parent. Furthermore, a donor-conceived family has additional potential relationships: between the donor and the resulting offspring and between discrete families whose offspring share the same donor. Although such offspring share genetic ties, there is no legal recognition of their relationship: they cannot designate to them financial and health powers of attorney; cannot be their standby guardians; and cannot provide for inheritance through wills or other forms of gifting. Yet at the same time, children from the same donor have used social media to connect via online forums, opening up new terrains of kinship. Clearly, the fertility industry is not just about biotechnology, but is also about creating social institutions with legal, social, cultural, and psychological implications.

Although family and kinship are fluid, genetic identity is grounded in biological ties where a kinship is not just a present relationship but is also a repository of connections with the past and the future. Genetics in contemporary medicine has medicalized family and kinship relations: for example, a family medical history at the doctor's office reinforces the notion of the relationship between kinship and health hence stressing and giving cultural significance to genetic transmission. Hence, although everyday social processes are arguably taking people away from traditional ideas of family and kinship, biomedicine is arguably pulling people back closer to notions of consanguinity.

SEE ALSO: Feminist Theory; Gender; Life Course; Patriarchy; Sexualities; Social Psychology

References

Archambault, Caroline. 2010. "Fixing Families of Mobile Children: Recreating Kinship and Belonging Among Maasai Adoptees in Kenya." *Childhood* 17: 229–242.

Rivers, Daniel Winuwe. 2013. *Radical Relations: Lesbian Mothers, Gay Fathers and Their Children in the United States Since World War II*. Chapel Hill: University of North Carolina Press.

Stacey, Judith. 2011. *Unhitched: Love, Marriage and Family Values from West Hollywood to Western China*. New York: New York University Press.

Waites, Cheryl. 2009. "Building on Strengths: Intergenerational Practice Within African American Families." *Social Work* 54: 278–287.

Zonta, Michela. 2016. *Housing the Extended Family*. Center for American Progress. Online at: www.americanprogress.org.

Feminist Theory

Nancy Naples

University of Connecticut, USA

Feminist theory refers to a diverse set of related epistemologies that share a basic concern with gender inequality and social justice. The formalization of feminist theory followed the analysis of gender discrimination, violence against women, and other struggles for gender equality in different social movements and social institutions. This understanding of the origins of diverse feminist theories relates to the term "feminist praxis" that refers to the recursive relationship between struggles for equality and social justice and the knowledge generated from these experiences. This is evident in a variety of different contexts. During the 1970s in the United States, women began to form what became known as consciousness-raising groups that encouraged women to share their experiences in personal relationships, families, and work, among other settings. Through these conversations, women recognized that their personal troubles were shaped through larger patterns or structures of gender inequality and patriarchy. Sites for the production of feminist theory also included community settings such as those analyzed by Patricia Hill Collins ([1990] 2008) in her now classic book *Black Feminist Thought*. Collins identified a number of themes that run through black feminist thought including an ethic of caring, an emphasis on the importance of experience, dialogue as a way to assess knowledge claims, and personal accountability.

During the late 1970s and early 1980s, women in the academy identified several different strands of feminist theory: liberal, radical, cultural, Marxist, and socialist feminisms. Liberal feminists challenged the tradition of liberal political thought that positioned women as unequal to men. They argued for equal representation of women in politics, religious institutions, the military, education, and the workplace. Liberal feminist strategies for equality in the workplace include calls for gender-neutral job ads, equal pay for equal work, family medical leave, and policies against sexual harassment.

Radical feminist theory developed from analyses of patriarchy defined as a system of oppression that asserted the dominance of men over women and over any man who exhibited traits associated with women. In contrast to liberal feminist thought, radical feminist theorists argue that since all social institutions are founded on patriarchal and androgenic practices, women's inclusion would be insufficient for ending women's oppression.

Cultural feminist theory focuses attention on "essentialist understandings of male and female differences as the foundation of women's subordination" (Wolff 2016: 637) and the valuation of characteristics associated with women such as nurturing and non-violence. Radical feminists also promoted the development of women's cultural spaces free from control by men and offering women the safe environment in which to express their views and develop strategies to counter the male privilege in the wider society. They encouraged the establishment of women-owned and women-led bookstores, women's centers, educational programs, and music and arts festivals. They also called for the development of women-owned economic enterprises such as women's banks, land cooperatives, and others businesses like bakeries and restaurants.

Marxist and socialist feminist theories were generated in dialogue with Karl Marx's analysis of capitalism and class oppression. Marxist feminists utilized his framework to analyze women's oppression as a sex-class and identified the ways in which women's socially assigned role in the family contributes to their unpaid labor and social reproduction of the working class. Socialist feminists argued that this approach did not fully incorporate the many ways that women were also oppressed in their homes and workplaces by husbands and co-workers, nor did it acknowledge factors contributing to violence against women and sexist cultural images of women. Their theoretical perspective drew on both Marxist analyses of class as well as feminist analyses of patriarchy. Feminists of color further developed this materialist epistemology by identifying how racism and white supremacy shaped women of color's social, economic, and political experiences. Attempts to incorporate racism alongside class oppression and sexism led to the development of so-called standpoint epistemologies that built upon feminists of color's articulation of black, Latina, Chicana, Asian American, and Native American feminist theories.

As women of color developed strong critiques of the white-centered approaches to feminist theory, they articulated diverse ways in which racism, xenophobia, and nativism intersected with sexism and class oppression. These approaches were variously named, as noted above, centering the analytic and experiential understanding of different racial ethnic groups. In response to these challenges an approach termed multi-racial feminism was developed to reflect the intersectional understanding and experiences of women of color in the United States.

In another effort to go beyond theorizing multiple oppressions through an additive approach, a paradigm emerged in the form of standpoint epistemology. Standpoint epistemologies offered a materialist analysis of the ways in which knowledge is generated from different social experiences and shapes understandings of social, economic, and political life (Naples 2009). Intersectional feminism also moves beyond the additive approach (gender plus class plus race), but is more self-consciously derived from anti-racist praxis than many previous feminist epistemologies.

Third-World feminist scholars further noted the inability of different feminist approaches to account for the ways that colonialism also shaped the intersection of what sociologist Dorothy Smith (1990) calls "relations of ruling." Third-World feminism was developed in the context of nationalist struggles against colonialism and imperialism and Third-World women's struggles against gender oppression. Feminist scholars and activists in different parts of the world generated localized feminist perspectives that foregrounded knowledge about gender relations, inequalities, and anti-colonial and anti-imperialist struggles. For example, Mehta (2016) discusses the development of Indo-Caribbean feminism as rooted "in the history of Indian indenture, in the capitalist pre- and post-plantation economy of the Caribbean island, and in patterns of resistance to colonial and patriarchal subjugation" (654).

The theoretical framework of postcolonial feminism offered a broadened analysis of the dynamics between Western feminisms and feminism developed by feminists in the so-called Third World. Among the many different avenues of investigation, postcolonial feminists explore how and in what ways political alliances can develop across the many differences that contour women's lives. For example, Mohanty (2003) argues that feminist solidarity is possible through anti-capitalist struggles.

Other feminist theoretical frameworks developed from engagement with different theoretical traditions. Existential feminism and anarchist feminism are not as widely utilized by contemporary feminism as some of the other traditions described above, although the former has been reinvigorated through contemporary social justice movements such as the World Social Forum and Occupy Wall Street. As with other forms of feminism, they build on previous political-theoretical frameworks and insert a feminist intervention that provides an intersectional theoretical angle of vision. Feminist anarchists "agree with socialists, socialist feminists, and radical feminists that the factors involved in understanding social inequality – and sexual inequality in particular – go beyond mere discrimination" (Ackelsberg 2005). In her study of the anarchist women's organization Mujeres Libres, Ackelsberg noted that "[i]nstead of treating either class relations or sexual divisions as the most basic form of subordination on which all others depend, anarchists saw hierarchy, formalized authority, as an equally crucial problem" (33).

As new theoretical frameworks such as poststructuralism and postmodernism emerged in the academy, feminist scholars engaged with them in ways that demonstrated the gender blindness and their limitations to explicate gender discourses and practices. Poststructuralist feminist theories assert that language gives meaning to experience. This epistemology includes a variety of strands including the so-called French feminisms of Luce Irigary, Helen Cixous, and Julia Kristeva. Since "experience has no essential meaning," it is "given meaning in language through a range of discursive systems of meaning which are often contradictory and constitute conflicting versions of social reality, which in turn serve conflicting interests" (Weedon 1987: 34). Discourses are seen as "integral to the maintenance and contestation of forms of social power, since social reality has no meaning except in language" (ibid.). Postmodern feminisms are related to poststructuralist approaches in the attention to discourse. Following postmodern epistemology, postmodern feminists critique the very idea of "truths" and the notion of unitary subjects. They argue against the singular explanatory narratives of many previous feminist theories.

In response to what some feminist scholars saw as the privileging of social construction over materiality, feminist scholars refocused attention to the materiality of the body and the physical environment we inhabit, along with other material consequences of social inequalities and injustice. They distinguish their approach from the materialist approaches influenced by Marxism by challenging the analytic division between materiality and discourse.

Feminist scholars have also engaged with queer theory to develop intersectional and materialist analyses of gender and sexuality. They challenge the privileging of heterosexuality and cisgenders as well as homonormativity which centers white, cisgender, Eurocentric, and class privilege within the LGBT community.

As this brief review demonstrates feminist theorizing is an active, on-going, and reflexive practice that engages with progressive and revolutionary social change and theoretical traditions in the academy to further deepen analyses of the relations of ruling that contour everyday life as well as cultural practices, discursive formations, and social institutions.

SEE ALSO: Gender; Homophobia and Heterosexism; Inequality, Gender; Intersectionality; Marxism; Masculinities; Patriarchy; Postmodernism AND Poststructuralism; Sexualities; Social Justice

References

Ackelsberg, Martha A. 2005. *Free Women of Spain: Anarchism and the Struggle for the Emancipation of Women.* Oakland: AK Press.

Collins, Patricia Hill. [1990] 2008. *Black Feminist Thought.* New York: Routledge.

Mehta, Brinda. 2016. "Indo-Caribbean Feminism." In *Wiley Blackwell Encyclopedia of Gender and Sexuality Studies*, edited by Nancy Naples, 634–658. Oxford: Wiley Blackwell.

Mohanty, Chandra Talpade. 2003. *Feminism Without Borders: Decolonizing Theory, Practicing Solidarity.* Durham, NC: Duke University Press.

Naples, Nancy A. 2009. "Teaching Intersectionality Intersectionally." *International Feminist Journal of Politics* 11 (4): 566–577.

Smith, Dorothy E. 1990. *Texts, Facts and Femininity: Exploring the Relations of Ruling.* New York: Routledge.

Weedon, Chris. 1987. *Feminist Practice and Poststructuralist Theory.* Oxford: Basil Blackwell.

Wolff, Kristina. 2016. "Cultural Feminism." In *Wiley Blackwell Encyclopedia of Gender and Sexuality Studies*, edited by Nancy Naples, 637–647. Oxford: Wiley Blackwell.

Frames, Narratives, and Ideology

Rens Vliegenthart

University of Amsterdam, The Netherlands

How people assign meaning to reality is an important question in the social sciences. A wide plethora of concepts related to meaning construction has been coined, that differ in terms of focus, scope, and analytical approach. Most notably, *narratives* and in particular *frame* and *framing* have gained prominence in sociological research and in particular in social movement, as well as mass communication, research. Both are used to describe the outcome of individual or collective processes of meaning construction, and are used as independent variables to explain individuals' attitudes and behavior (e.g., participation in protests) or to assess movements' impact on institutional politics (e.g., policy making processes), or as dependent variables to investigate how frames and narratives come about, diffuse, and change over time.

A Framing Perspective

The sociological origins of the framing concept can be traced back to the work of Gregor Bateson. He argues that the meaning of communication depends on the context in which it takes place, as well as on the way the message is being constructed (or "framed"). Erving Goffman elaborates in his book *Frame Analysis* (1974) a symbolic-interactionist approach toward communication. He addresses the question of how people develop orientations to situations based on their interpretation of social cues. Other scholars picked up this idea and applied it to issue interpretation and the analysis of communication in particular. These analyses focus on the content features of news and other (mainly written) texts and more specifically on the presence of certain *frames*. *Framing*, in contrast, focuses on process or contextual features of news making and receiving. Thus, while a frame is a tool to describe the content of communication, framing involves the process by which this frame is constructed and impacts others.

Frames

Students of social movements and collective behavior – both from a critical as well as a constructivist perspective – have been early adopters of the framing approach and further developed and investigated framing and frames, both by movements as well as by media. When it comes to the latter, scholars rely on qualitative or quantitative content analysis of (mainly) texts. Gitlin (1980), for example, falls in the critical paradigm and investigates the framing of the New Left by US media. He defines frames as "principles of selection, emphasis and presentation composed of little tacit theories about what exists, what happens, and what matters" (1980: 7). His analysis shows how the framing of the New Left in the media is the result of an ongoing struggle between activists and journalists, where both structural factors (such as news routines and journalistic practices), together with internal organizational struggles in the movement, in the end resulted in a framing of the New Left as a chaotic, leaderless amalgam of radicals. Constructivist Gamson (1992) argues in his study on media and public opinion on the US nuclear movement that frames are part of "interpretative packages" in which an "organizing idea," or a frame, is central. He identifies a whole range of different frames, including, for example, a "progress frame" and a "free enterprise frame," that are all present in the media coverage on the US nuclear energy debate.

Framing

Snow and Benford (1988) distinguish three framing "tasks" or elements –"diagnostic" (focusing on the question of what the problem is and who is responsible), "prognostic" (what is the solution and who should provide it?), and "motivational" (a "call to arms" from the movement). This distinction is part of much of the recent conceptualizations and definitions of (media) framing. Snow and colleagues (2007), for example, investigate how media from different countries frame the riots that took place in many French cities in 2005 in diagnostic and prognostic terms. Their analysis shows, for example, that, overall, the "law and order" prognostic frame, emphasizing police intervention as the solution to the riots, is the most prevalent one. In their article, they introduce the idea of *frame variation* which refers to the idea that an issue or event can be presented in multiple ways – and, depending on a wide range of issues, source and temporal characteristics – certain frames are more prevalent than others.

If we consider framing to be a contest or struggle over the meaning of an issue and event, *frame resonance* is indeed of crucial importance. Frame resonance refers to the extent to which larger audiences accept a frame that is propagated by a certain actor. Social movements, and other actors for that matter, are only able to obtain general support and policy success if their claims resonate more widely, especially under those with formal political power. It is through framing that social movements try to gather support for their claims and to mobilize potential participants by offering interpretations of events. Successfully aligning frames of potential participants with those of the movement is key in obtaining support and increasing participation. The study by Snow and colleagues (1986) has been very influential and addresses the effects of framing by movements on citizens. They argue that in order for individuals to participate in a social movement, *frame alignment* between movement and individual has to take place.

In other words, individuals have to adopt the movement frame before they will participate in the movement. Depending on the difference between the movement frame and the individual frame, this frame alignment can range from frame bridging – which is the linkage of two ideologically congruent frames and is easily achieved – to frame transformation – that requires the transfer of new values and is a long-term process.

Narratives

While probably not as widely used as frames and framing, narratives have received ample attention in the context of, for example, studies of social protest. According to Polletta and Gardner (2012: 3), a narrative is "an account of a sequence of events in the order in which they occurred to make a point". Some researchers consider narratives a subcategory and concretization of frames. Others argue that they should be considered as something with distinctive features, with the main distinction being that they play a crucial role in the formation and expression of collective and individual identities by providing a larger and often personalized story that people can relate to, rather than a "simple" and rationalized frame in terms of diagnosis, prognosis, and motivational elements. The (empirical) questions that relate to narratives are, however, similar to those relating to framing and deal with the content of narratives, their origins, and their impact, for example, in terms of mobilization.

Connection to Ideology

For both framing and narratives it is important to emphasize their connection to ideology. While ideology can be considered as a coherent set of beliefs with a certain orientation toward politics and society more broadly, both frames and narratives can be considered an explicit, manifest translation to a certain situation (or issue) at a particular moment in time. Ultimately, much collective action, for example, is driven by ideological considerations, but those are often abstract and implicit. Thus, first, ideology both informs and constrains framing and narratives. Second, in some instances framing and narratives might also translate back, because they present extensions of ideology, or disclose inconsistencies or gaps in ideological beliefs. In that way, sense-making processes take place in a continuous interaction between ideological values and beliefs and manifest translations in frames and narratives.

SEE ALSO: Ethnography; Identity; Knowledge, Sociology of; Media, Sociology of the; Social Movements and Social Change; Social Network Analysis

References

Gamson, William A. 1992. *Talking Politics*. New York: Cambridge University Press.
Gitlin, Todd. 1980. *The Whole World Is Watching: Mass Media in the Making and Unmaking of the New Left*. Oakland: University of California Press.
Goffman, Erving. 1974. *Frame Analysis: An Essay on the Organization of Experience*. Cambridge, MA: Harvard University Press.

Polletta, Francesca, and Beth Gharrity Gardner. 2012. "Narrative and Social Movements." In *The Oxford Handbook of Social Movements*, edited by Donatella Della Porta and Mario Diani, 1–19. Oxford: Oxford University Press.

Snow, David A., and Robert D. Benford. 1988. "Ideology, Frame Resonance, and Participant Mobilization." In *From Structure to Action: Comparing Social Movement Research Across Cultures*, edited by Bert Klandermans, Hanspeter Kriesi, and Sidney G. Tarrow, 197–217. Greenwich: JAI Press.

Snow, David A., E. Burke Rochford Jr., Steven K. Worden, and Robert D. Benford. 1986. "Frame Alignment Processes, Micromobilization, and Movement Participation." *American Sociological Review* 51 (4): 464–481.

Snow, David A., Rens Vliegenthart, and Catherine Corrigall-Brown. 2007. "Framing the French Riots: A Comparative Study of Frame Variation." *Social Forces* 86 (2): 385–415.

Gender

Michael Kimmel and Katie M. Gordon

SUNY at Stony Brook, USA

Defining Gender

In popular discourse, the terms "sex" and "gender" are often used interchangeably. However, social and behavioral scientists frequently differentiate between the two. Sex refers to an individual's membership in a biologically distinct category based on genital appearance (e.g., male, female, intersex, or hermaphroditic). Gender is a socially constructed classification system which categorizes individuals, traits, and institutions based on societal definitions of male and female.

Social Construction and the Gender Binary

Some behavioral scientists believe that early childhood socialization leads to gender identities that become fixed, permanent, and inherent in our personalities. However, many sociologists disagree with this notion today. As they see it, gender is less a static component of identity that we take with us into our interactions, but rather the product of those interactions. This is the social constructionist approach, which frames gender and identity as a fluid (rather than fixed) combination of traits and characteristics which is constructed through our interactions with other members of society. In contrast, the gender binary is a concept that refers to the implicit assumption that there are only two ways to express gender: male or female. These two options are linked to one's biological sex assigned at birth, although current sociological theory contends that few, if any, attributes of human behavior are determined in this way.

Social constructionists acknowledge that using male/female categories is not the only way of classifying individuals. For instance, while many nations describe people in this way, other societies include gender-variant classifications such as *hijras* or *berdaches*. In South Asia, *hijra* is an ancient term used to describe gender-nonconforming individuals who identify as a "third gender." *Berdaches*, a term used by some Native American cultures, rejects the binary classification system altogether, allowing for wider variety and freedom of expression with regard to gender identity.

Core Concepts in Sociology, First Edition. Edited by J. Michael Ryan.
© 2019 John Wiley & Sons Ltd. Published 2019 by John Wiley & Sons Ltd.

"Doing Gender"

Acknowledging that gender is a social construction allows us to make visible the implicit and performative elements of identity. We are constantly "doing" gender. That is, we are continually engaged in the performance and activities which either exhibit or reject sociocultural gender norms. As we interact with others, we are held accountable to display behavior that is consistent with the prescribed gender norms for that particular situation. Thus consistent gender behavior is less a response to deeply internalized norms or biologically informed personality characteristics, and more a negotiated response to the consistency with which others demand that we act in a recognizably masculine or feminine way. We create and re-create our own gendered identities within the contexts of our interactions with others and within the institutions we inhabit.

Gender Identity and Expression

Gender identity refers to, quite simply, the gender with which one identifies. It originates in the mind and can differ from or conform to the sociocultural gender norms of an individual's particular environment. For some, gender identity is implicit and unquestioned, while others may actively engage in and explore this aspect of themselves. On the other hand, gender expression is the way an individual performs or "does" gender through actions, dress, and demeanor. It is also the way those presentations are interpreted by society. In sum, gender identity is an internal experience while gender expression consists of external actions which society then assigns value and meaning to.

An individual's gender identity may or may not align with their gender expression or their biological sex. For example, gender-nonconforming individuals reject conventional notions of binary gender expression, while transgender is a term that refers to individuals whose gender identity does not correspond with their assigned sex at birth. Cisgender is a term that describes those individuals where these three elements of identity match. For instance, a biological male who identifies and expresses himself in this way can be described as cisgender.

Fluid, Not Fixed

Because gender is a social construction that is being continuously negotiated throughout our lives, we cannot speak of gender identity, masculinity, or femininity as though they were constant, unchanging, universal essences common to all individuals, in all places, at all times. Rather, gender is a fluid assemblage of meanings and behaviors. In this sense, we must speak of gender *identities*, *masculinities*, and *femininities*. By pluralizing these terms, we acknowledge that gender identity means different things to different groups of people at different times.

What gender means will vary over four different dimensions; thus four different disciplines are involved in understanding gender. First, gender varies from one culture to another. Anthropologists have documented the ways that gender varies cross-culturally. Some cultures encourage men to be stoic and to prove masculinity, especially by sexual conquest. Other cultures prescribe a more relaxed definition of masculinity, based on civic participation, emotional responsiveness, and collective provision for the community's needs. Some cultures encourage women to be decisive and competitive; others insist that women are naturally passive, helpless, and dependent. And still other cultures embrace non-binary systems of categorization. What it means to be a man, woman, or gender-nonconforming individual in France or among Aboriginal peoples in the Australian outback are so far apart that it belies any notion that gender identity is determined mostly by biological sex differences. The differences between two cultures' definition of gender identity is often greater than the differences between the sexes.

Second, definitions of gender vary considerably in any one country over time. Historians have explored how these definitions have shifted in response to changes in levels of industrialization and urbanization, position in the larger world geopolitical and economic context, and with the development of new technologies. What it meant to be a gendered individual in seventeenth-century France or in Hellenic Greece is certainly different from what it might mean to be a French or Greek person today.

Third, definitions of gender change over the course of a person's life. Psychologists have examined how a set of developmental milestones lead to difference in our experience and our expression of gender identity. Both chronological age and life-stage require different enactments of gender. For instance, an individual's gender identity may change as they age, as will the social institutions in which they will attempt to enact those experiences. Major benchmarks, such as finishing one's education, moving away from home for the first time, joining the workforce, or becoming a parent, may all yield different forms of gender expression from the same individual.

Finally, gender meanings vary considerably within any given society at any one time. At any given moment, several meanings of gender expression coexist. Simply put, not all American or Brazilian or Senegalese men, women, or gender-nonconforming individuals are the same. With this in mind, sociologists take an intersectional approach to explore the ways in which class, race, ethnicity, age, ability, sexuality, and geographic region all shape gender identity. Imagine, for example, two "American" men, one, an older, black, gay man in Chicago, the other, a young, white, heterosexual farm boy in Iowa. Or imagine a 22-year-old wealthy Asian-American heterosexual woman in San Francisco and a poor white Irish Catholic lesbian in Boston. Or a transgender individual who grew up in New York City and another who was raised in North Carolina. Each of these individuals likely define and experience their gender identity differently, and yet each of these people is deeply affected and shaped by the norms and power arrangements of their society.

The use of the plural – *identities, masculinities,* and *femininities* – recognizes the dramatic variation in how different groups define gender. Although social forces operate to create systematic differences between individuals, on average, these differences between them are not as great as the differences among them.

Gender and Power

This is not to imply that there is great freedom in the range of acceptable expressions of gender. On the contrary, gender performance exists within a highly rigid regulatory frame. Dominant, or culturally preferred, versions of gender expression act as the models against which we are expected to measure ourselves. We come to know what it means to "be a man" or "be a woman" in our culture by setting ourselves in opposition to a set of "others": racial, sexual, class minorities, etc.

Definitions of gender identity are not simply constructed in relation to the hegemonic ideals of masculinity and femininity, but also in constant reference to each other. Gender is not only plural, it also relational. Surveys in Western countries indicate that men construct their ideas of what it means to be men in constant reference to definitions of femininity. What it means to be a man is to be unlike a woman; indeed, social psychologists have emphasized that while different groups of men may disagree about other traits and their significance in gender definitions, the "anti-femininity" component of masculinity is perhaps the single dominant and universal characteristic.

Women contend with an equally exaggerated ideal of femininity, which Connell calls "emphasized femininity" (Connell 1987). Emphasized femininity is organized around compliance with a system of gender hierarchy which places men in the dominant social position (specifically Western, white, middle-class, heterosexual men). One sees emphasized femininity in "the display of sociability rather than technical competence, fragility in mating scenes, compliance with men's desire for titillation and ego-stroking in office relationships, [and in the] acceptance of marriage and childcare as a response to labor-market discrimination against women." Emphasized femininity exaggerates gender difference as a strategy of "adaptation to men's power" stressing empathy and nurturance; "real" womanhood is described as "fascinating"; and women are advised that they can wrap men around their fingers by knowing and playing by the "rules" (Connell 1987: 183, 188, 187).

These socially constructed gender differences are based on biological distinction of the sexes. In other words, gender expression is thought to be a "natural" extension of one's corporeal structure. Used in this way, gender shapes access to power and resources, which in turn shapes relations between men and women. This is when using the term gender synonymously with sex becomes problematic: biological differences between the sexes become tools with which to organize individuals into groups with power and groups without power, based on what is perceived to be the "natural" order.

The Future of Gender Studies

Gender identity is one of the most fundamental aspects of our social selves and is constructed through the act of repeated performances. Gender identity is informed by interacting systems of power like class, race, ethnicity, age, ability, sexuality, and geographic region, which disadvantage many, while privileging others. Gender expression is the external representation of one's gender identity as well as the societal meanings assigned to those acts. The interpreted meaning of these acts is contingent on the society, culture, era, and life-stage they are performed in. In this way, gender can work as a system of oppression, based on what people perceive are biological differences between women and men.

The future of gender studies will focus on the incorporation and acceptance of many forms of gender expression, definitions which have nothing to do with one's biological sex or romantic attraction. By increasing our tolerance of more fluid forms of gender expression, we can create a more inclusive, safe, and supportive society for those individuals who challenge the power dynamics inherent within a binary-based gender classification system. Through this, all individuals will be given the opportunity to fully explore and celebrate the multifaceted dimensions of their gender identity with freedom from persecution and fear.

SEE ALSO: Body, the; Family and Kinship, Sociology of; Feminist Theory; Homophobia and Heterosexism; Identity; Inequality, Gender; Life Course; Patriarchy; Sexualities; Socialization; Stereotypes, Prejudice, and Discrimination

Reference

Connell, R.W. 1987. *Gender and Power: Society, the Person, and Sexual Politics*. Redwood City, CA: Stanford University Press.

Further Reading

Butler, Judith. 2011. *Gender Trouble: Feminism and the Subversion of Identity*. New York: Routledge.

Goffman, Erving. 1963. *Stigma*. Englewood Cliffs, NJ: Prentice-Hall.

Kimmel, Michael S. 2000. *The Gendered Society*. New York: Oxford University Press.

West, Candace, and Don H. Zimmerman. 1987. "Doing Gender." *Gender & Society* 1 (2): 125–151.

Globalization

George Ritzer

University of Maryland, USA

Offering simplistic generalizations about any socioeconomic phenomenon is, to put it mildly, problematic, but none are more questionable than those that relate to globalization. Globalization is *not* a single process. There is a globalization of virtually everything including the economy, politics, culture, religion, science, health and medicine, education, and sport. Further, there are profound differences within and between them in how, and the degree to which, they globalize.

In spite of globalization's wide range, most academic and popular attention is focused on its economic component. However, even that defies generalization since it, in itself, is highly diverse. One example of a simplistic, even erroneous, generalization is Thomas Friedman's (1999) contention that the world is both growing flatter and rising economically. Clearly, great barriers continue to make the world "hilly," if not "mountainous," and billions are falling further behind economically.

Ruchir Sharma (2016) has argued that the lesson of globalization's past, and of United States President Donald Trump's proposals that relate to globalization, "is that just as night follows day, deglobalization follows globalization – and can last as long." This, of course, is a deterministic "grand narrative." It is derived from generalizing from a single historical case of the great wave of globalization in the early twentieth century (there were a number of other epochs, or phases, before that) and its descent into what *might* be termed deglobalization with the start of World War I. Determinism, grand narratives, and generalizing from a single case are all "no-nos" in contemporary sociology and most other social sciences.

A more nuanced view requires a perspective on globalization that views it as a dialectic of a series of "flows" and "barriers." In fact, contemporary globalization is defined by the great liquidity of its many elements (money, social networks, people) as well as the barriers (tariffs, national borders, China's "Great Firewall," visas, terrorist watch lists) that are often erected to stem the flows that at least some see as undesirable. The idea of barriers would seem to suggest that globalization could be ended if only there were enough of them and that they were made impermeable. However, there are never enough barriers and those that exist have proven to be porous (e.g., firewalls on computers housing government secrets or valuable corporate information). Therefore, it is best to think of globalization as involving a continuing dialectic between global flows and the barriers erected to impede them. Flows of, for example, capital, immigrants, ideas, and pollution will tend to continue, even accelerate, until they reach a point where they engender strong enough opposition to begin to erect barriers to them. These efforts might be successful for a time, but it is likely that whatever barriers are created will eventually be swamped by global flows and/or dismantled by those with vested interests opposed to the barriers.

Because of the dialectic between global flows and barriers, globalization varies in terms of a number of dimensions. Globalization can vary in its extensiveness; its elements need not cover the entire globe (indeed nothing does) to be considered an aspect of globalization. McDonald's is a global phenomenon even though its restaurants are now found in "only" about 60 percent of the countries in the world. Some areas of the world will escape the ravages of climate change and perhaps even benefit from it. Intensiveness of globalization can vary everywhere from the currently "hot" spread of radical Islam to the "cool" movement of a global fashion change. In terms of velocity, some global changes occur seemingly overnight (the flow of radical new ideas and social movements), while others (the movement toward greater global economic equality) are glacial or nonexistent. Finally, there is the variation in the impact of global processes from high (the 9/11 attacks) to low (the latest fad in emoticons on the internet).

Sharma (and others) not only fails to see this, but he has a limited view of globalization as primarily an economic phenomenon (with a little politics thrown in). Such a narrow perspective means that he fails to see that globalization has continued apace, and even accelerated, in many other sectors of society, especially on the internet and, more generally, in the cultural, social, and intellectual realms (among many others).

We may be an era in which there is increasing interest in creating barriers in *some* sectors of society (e.g., trade, migration), but that is decidedly not the case in many others. Sharma, and those who adopt his perspective, need to develop a broader (especially less economistic) and less deterministic view of globalization. Yes, night does follow day (at least for the foreseeable future), but one should not leap from that to the idea that deglobalization follows globalization. There are trends, but *no inevitabilities*, in the social world.

How do we account for this near-universal tendency to equate economic globalization with globalization as a whole or, less extremely, to privilege the economy in discussions of globalization? Obviously, the economy is of enormous importance both macroscopically (e.g., for countries) and microscopically (e.g., to individuals virtually everywhere). In addition, it is implicated, at least to some degree, in all other aspects of globalization. But it is far from being alone in being of great significance and in having wide-ranging implications. Among the many other aspects of globalization that have these characteristics are borderless diseases (think of the next viral pandemic), climate change, immigration, the brain drain, the internet (especially social networking), as well as the spread of political and religious ideologies, illegal goods (especially drugs), and terrorism.

However, those who analyze the economy, especially the economists, are hegemonic in the social sciences. They are also deeply involved in the political world, especially in the United States, as, for example, Chair of the Federal Reserve. Their thoughts and ideas are also of great interest to the media and economists are often featured in newspaper articles and as "talking heads" on television. It is not surprising, therefore, that an economist, Thomas Piketty (2013), has become a global superstar and his ideas on capital and inequality, as well as the numerous criticisms of them, have globalized with unprecedented speed for a scholarly work. Ultimately, it is the capitalist economy, and its impact on all aspects of globalization and of the social world, that gives the economists their great visibility and influence. Given this reality, it is not surprising that most discussions of, and thinking about, globalization focus on its economic aspects.

However, it is wrong-headed to reduce globalization to economics, to focus so much attention on economic globalization and, of course, to over-generalize about it. No generalization about globalization is more troublesome than the idea that it, especially economic globalization, is somehow ending (a similar argument was made, erroneously, in the wake of the autarchy associated with World War I). One often hears this today in discussions, especially in the United States and Europe, of the efforts to better control, even resurrect, national borders in order to stem the flow of various unwanted products and immigrants. Muslim extremists are currently seeking to create a new caliphate that would presumably put in place barriers to the entry of all sorts of heretical ideas, to say nothing of the heretics who bear them (but not to the oil they – largely Sunnis – want and need to export including, at the moment, even to the hated Alawites (Shiites) in Syria). However, even if these barriers are put in place, we will continue to see the global flow of extremist ideas, of extremists themselves, and of oil (and the huge profits associated with it) into and out of the new caliphate. Also likely to flow freely are arms and other material support for the opponents of this development. All of this points to the continuing reality and importance of globalization even in the face of efforts to create new obstacles to it.

However, that is not to say, as Thomas Friedman has argued, again erroneously, that globalization is inexorable. There are developments such as a nuclear winter or a pandemic worse than the Spanish flu that could slow or alter the nature of globalization, although it is worth noting that both of those developments would, themselves, be global in scope.

SEE ALSO: Capitalism; Economic Sociology; Immigration, Migration, and Refugees; Inequality, Global; Internet, the; Political Sociology; Space and Place

References

Friedman, Thomas. 1999. *The Lexus and the Olive Tree: Understanding Globalization*. New York: Farrar, Straus, and Giroux.

Piketty, Thomas. 2013. *Capital in the Twenty-First Century*. Cambridge, MA: Harvard University Press.

Sharma, Ruchir. 2016. "Why Borders Close." *New York Times*. November 13.

Homelessness

James D. Wright

University of Central Florida, USA

Introduction

Homelessness has been a concern of sociologists at least since the publication of Stuart Rice's paper "The Homeless" in 1918 and the classic ethnography of homelessness, *The Hobo: The Sociology of the Homeless Man*, by Nels Anderson in 1923. In the 1950s, Skid Row stimulated another wave of interest in the homeless. The "new homeless" of the 1980s and beyond (e.g., Lee, Tyler, and Wright 2010) bring us up to the present day. Homelessness is of interest to sociologists because the condition reveals in sharp detail the extremes of poverty and social inequality in society and because it is a vivid illustration of conflict theory's argument concerning differential accessibility of resources.

The homeless are a diverse lot but three common characteristics stand out in most studies (see Wright 2009): high levels of personal disabilities (physical and mental illnesses, alcohol and drug dependence, physical disabilities, criminal records); high levels of familial estrangement; and extreme poverty.

Definition of Homelessness

The United States Department of Housing and Urban Development (HUD) defines homelessness as: "Individuals and families who lack a fixed, regular, and adequate nighttime residence including … an individual who is exiting an institution where he or she resided for 90 days or less and who resided in an emergency shelter or a place not meant for human habitation immediately before entering that institution." Three other categories are also recognized by HUD: people at imminent risk of losing their residence; unaccompanied youth and families with children; and women fleeing domestic assault. These definitions were effective as of 2009 and are used by all agencies of the United States government.

HUD further distinguishes between the *chronically homeless* and the *transitional or episodically homeless*. The chronically homeless are "homeless individuals with a disability … who live in a place not meant for human habitation, a safe haven, or in an emergency shelter; and has been homeless continuously for at least 12 months or on at least 4 separate occasions in the last 3 years where the combined occasions must total at least 12 months." Homeless persons not meeting these criteria are considered transitional or episodic.

Core Concepts in Sociology, First Edition. Edited by J. Michael Ryan.
© 2019 John Wiley & Sons Ltd. Published 2019 by John Wiley & Sons Ltd.

In Europe, homelessness tends to be defined more in terms of marginalization and social exclusion than in terms of housing status (Shinn 2010). Shinn's study shows large differences in the rates of homelessness across nations, with the highest rates in the United States and United Kingdom. Key predictors are the degree of income inequality, the amount of social or public housing, and differential rates of incarceration.

Trends and Numbers

Many efforts to enumerate the homeless have been attempted through the years, none with complete success. An apparent upsurge in homelessness in the 1980s stimulated a number of counting efforts, including census efforts in 1980 and 1990. Most observers believe that these early counts were woefully inadequate. The most recent counting effort, the 2015 national Point in Time count, found 564,708 homeless people across the United States, of whom 96,275 were chronically homeless. This represents a decline in the total number homeless of about 31 percent between 2010 and 2015 (HUD 2015). This is a count of the number homeless on a given day. The number homeless in the course of an entire year is possibly three to five times larger. All these numbers are at best approximations and cannot be taken as exact.

Shinn (2010) provides estimated lifetime rates of homelessness for the United States and five European countries. The rate is highest in the United States (8.1%), followed by the United Kingdom (7.7%), followed by Italy (4.0%), Belgium (3.4%), Germany (2.4%), and Portugal (2.0%). It has also been conjectured that comparatively higher rates of social welfare spending on the Continent mollify the effects of homelessness on people who experience it.

Subgroups

The stereotypical homeless person is an alcoholic male panhandling on the street corner and many sociologists have taken pains to dismantle this stereotype. For example, research shows that women and children are a very common subgroup; in some studies, they comprise more than half the total population. In the 2015 AHAR report, 36 percent of all persons counted were members of homeless families. Another important subgroup are minors and young adults already on their own. Many of these are runaway or "throwaway" children and a large number are LGBT youth – not "homeless by choice" as many wish to believe, but victims of unsupportive parents, violence, stigma, and other social factors. Also relevant are veterans, who comprise 11 percent of the 2015 AHAR population.

Potential Solutions

Recently, HUD has adopted so-called Housing First policies. Simplifying, homeless interventions have traditionally assumed that homeless people are broken and must be repaired before being placed in housing. Housing First rejects the idea that homeless people need repair. What they need is housing. Many also need wrap-around supportive services to be successful in a community setting. Thus permanent supportive housing options are the model proposed for most chronically homeless people. Housing First has been HUD policy for about a decade and is assumed to have been largely responsible for the declining numbers of chronically homeless people.

SEE ALSO: Inequality, Racial and Ethnic; Mental Health and Illness; Poverty; Stratification and Inequality

References

HUD: US Department of Housing and Urban Development. 2015. *The 2015 Annual Homeless Assessment Report (AHAR) to Congress.* Washington, DC: HUD Office of Community Planning and Development.

Lee, Barrett A., Kimberly A. Tyler, and James D. Wright. 2010. "The New Homeless Revisited." *Annual Review of Sociology* 36: 501–522.

Shinn, Marybeth, 2010. "Homelessness, Poverty and Social Exclusion in the United States and Europe." *European Journal of Homelessness* 40: 19–44.

Wright, James D. 2009. *Address Unknown: The Homeless in America.* New Brunswick, NJ: Transaction Publishers.

Further Reading

Hopper, Kim. 2002. *Reckoning with Homelessness.* Ithaca, NY: Cornell University Press.

Howard, Ella. 2013. *Homeless: Poverty and Place in Urban America.* Philadelphia: University of Pennsylvania Press.

Liebow, Elliot. 1995. *Tell Them Who I Am: The Lives of Homeless Women.* New York: Penguin Press.

Rossi, Peter H. 1991. *Down and Out in America: The Origins of Homelessness.* Chicago: University of Chicago Press.

Homophobia and Heterosexism

Damien W. Riggs

Flinders University, Australia

In its original use, the term "homophobia" referred to an irrational fear of homosexual people (Weinberg 1972). More recently, the term has come to refer to hatred or violence directed toward homosexual people, stemming from the assumption that homosexuality is a sin or pathology (Mason and Tomsen 1997). Whilst the term "homophobia" is typically used with reference to individuals, by contrast the term "heterosexism" typically refers to institutions, or institutionalized ways of thinking (Herek 1996). Specifically, heterosexism refers to systems that enshrine a bias that favors heterosexual people. Heterosexism may thus be implicit rather than explicit, and often takes relatively "mundane" forms (Peel 2001).

Given the individualistic focus of the term "homophobia," it has been widely criticized for its failure to address the systemic nature of discrimination targeted at non-heterosexual people. The very language of "phobia," it has also been suggested, does not adequately describe the hatred that may be expressed in homophobic acts (Kitzinger and Perkins 1993). Nonetheless, the term homophobia (typically styled as "homophobic violence") continues to be used in describing acts perpetrated against non-heterosexual people. Measures of homophobia (e.g., Hudson and Ricketts 1980) have consistently found that it is commonly expressed by men more than women, by more religious people, and by people with more right-wing views.

As noted above, the term "heterosexism" encompasses the institutionalized nature of discrimination against non-heterosexual people. Heterosexism can appear in everyday examples such as hospital intake forms that only include the relationship categories of "husband and wife," or can occur when a person speaks about their partner and it is assumed that their partner will be of a different sex. Whilst examples such as these may appear "'mundane," they nonetheless serve to exclude non-heterosexuality from many sectors of life. There is no singular scale that measures heterosexism, given the many forms that it takes and the fact that it is institutional rather than individual. Amongst the many measures that exist, most attempt to assess non-heterosexual people's perceptions of when and how heterosexism occurs (e.g., Vyncke et al. 2011).

Both homophobia and heterosexism, each in their own way, offer analytic leverage for identifying, understanding, and potentially challenging discrimination directed toward non-heterosexual people, discrimination which in turn serves to privilege heterosexual people.

Core Concepts in Sociology, First Edition. Edited by J. Michael Ryan.
© 2019 John Wiley & Sons Ltd. Published 2019 by John Wiley & Sons Ltd.

SEE ALSO: Gender; Identity; Inequality, Gender; Sexualities

References

Herek, Gregory. 1996. "Heterosexism and Homophobia." In *Textbook of Homosexuality and Mental Health*, edited by Robert P. Cabaj and Terry S. Stein, 101–113. Arlington: American Psychological Society.

Hudson, Walter W., and Wendell A. Ricketts. 1980. "A Strategy for the Measurement of Homophobia." *Journal of Homosexuality* 5 (4): 357–372.

Kitzinger, Celia, and Rachel Perkins. 1993. *Changing Our Minds: Lesbian Feminism and Psychology*. New York: NYU Press.

Mason, Gail, and Stephen Tomsen, eds. 1997. *Homophobic Violence*. Annandale: Hawkins Press.

Peel, Elizabeth. 2001. "Mundane Heterosexism: Understanding Incidents of the Everyday." *Women's Studies International Forum* 24: 541–554.

Vyncke, Johanna D., Danielle Julien, Emilie Jodoin, and Emilie Jouvin. 2011. "Development and Initial Validation of the Perceived Heterosexism Scale and the Preoccupation with Disclosure of Parents' Sexual Orientation Scale." *Journal of GLBT Family Studies* 7: 313–331.

Weinberg, George H. 1972. *Society and the Healthy Homosexual*. Basingstoke: Macmillan.

Human Rights, Sociology of

Patricia Hynes

University of Bedfordshire, UK

The gulf between human rights ideals and the lived experiences of those who face, endure, and survive human rights violations across the globe is vast, with impunity and denial central characteristics in the struggle for human rights. Whereas human rights have historically been considered within the disciplines of law, politics, and philosophy, a growing number of sociologists are arguing that a sociology of human rights is important in what has been termed an "age of rights" (Bobbio 1996). For Bobbio a positive sign of the "age of rights" is the increasing importance given to recognizing human rights in international debates.

Sociologists have long studied power, inequalities, and social problems as one of sociology's central purposes. Historically, sociological interest has been within "national container[s]" (Burawoy 2016: 950) and in citizenship, rather than in human rights more broadly. The tyranny of thinking nationally and conflation of "society" and "state" by Weber, Durkheim, Marx, and other "classical" sociologists is now being challenged. A sociology of human rights holds the potential to investigate and analyze power, inequalities, conflict, and social divisions within and beyond national borders, overcoming methodological nationalism and associated limitations of study solely within nation-states, moving toward a more cosmopolitan vision (Turner 1993; Morris 2013). A sociology of human rights recognizes global inequalities and global conflicts as the subject of study and analysis.

Sociologists have also been skeptical about the individualism of rights given the emergence of the discipline during the nineteenth century at a time of considerable social change in the "West" and advent of capitalism (Turner 1993). The individualistic nature of rights enshrined in the 1948 Universal Declaration of Human Rights (UDHR) and civil and political rights in the International Covenant of Civil and Political Rights (ICCPR) have tended to be the focus of human rights discourse above, and arguably devaluing, the International Covenant on Economic, Social and Cultural Rights (ICESCR). These postwar and post-Holocaust declarations and covenants have been critiqued as European-focused, associated with the "civilizing mission" of Western imperialists (Morris 2013: 164).

There are recurring debates around universalism versus the cultural relativism, particularism, and pluralism of human rights. There is also considerable skepticism about the universalist discourse of human rights, which has given rise to particularist rights claims. This view has, in turn, been critiqued. For example, when considering human

Core Concepts in Sociology, First Edition. Edited by J. Michael Ryan.
© 2019 John Wiley & Sons Ltd. Published 2019 by John Wiley & Sons Ltd.

rights in Asia, Amartya Sen argues that attempts at generalization about "Asian values" have often been invoked by those in power "to provide justification for authoritarian political arrangements in Asia" (Sen 1999: 231).

It was not until the 1990s that the work of Bryan Turner and Malcolm Waters, through an often-cited debate, led to the development of a sociology of human rights. Turner (1993) argued that sociology could ground the analysis of human rights in the concept of human frailty, particularly the vulnerability of the body, in an idea of the precariousness of social institutions and in a theory of moral sympathy. His suggestion was that frailty and human vulnerability as a universal human condition could be ameliorated by the "institution of rights which protect human beings from ontological uncertainty" (1993: 489). While Turner grounded human rights in a sociological theory of the body, Malcolm Waters (1996) advanced a "social constructionist" view of human rights, with human rights as "an institution ... specific to cultural and historical context ..." (1996: 593). Lydia Morris has since advanced this perspective pointing to recent and more sociologically informed understandings of natural law. Human rights are now a part of postwar globalization processes and are themselves globalizing.

Contributions from Hynes, Lamb, Short, and Waites have added to this developing sub-discipline, reflected in increasingly confident special issue titles of "new engagements" (2010) and "new directions" (2012a and b) in the sociology of human rights. A special issue for *Sociology*, which at the time attracted a record number of submissions for the journal, included papers from Kate Nash on conceptualizing human rights "from above" or "from below" and Darren O'Byrne on socially constructed language structures of human rights.

The sociological study of human rights is late but now well underway and sociology as a discipline can bring much to the analysis of human rights. Disassociating sociology with "society," the nation-state, and studies of citizenship will allow a refocus on neglected global issues such as the slow, grinding, and relentless struggle for economic rights in an unequal world and the protection and rights of refugees who have fallen between rights held within nation-states among other issues.

SEE ALSO: Citizenship; Inequality, Global; Social Justice; Sociology

References

Bobbio, N. 1996. *The Age of Rights*. Cambridge: Polity Press.

Burawoy, M. 2016. "The Promise of Sociology: Global Challenges for National Disciplines." *Sociology* 5 (5): 949–959.

Hynes, P., M. Lamb, D. Short, and M. Waites. 2010. Special Issue, Sociology and Human Rights: New Engagements. *The International Journal of Human Rights* 14 (6).

Hynes, P., M. Lamb, D. Short, and M. Waites. 2012a. Special Issue, New Directions in the Sociology of Human Rights. *The International Journal of Human Rights* 16 (8).

Hynes, P., M. Lamb, D. Short, and M. Waites. 2012b. Special Issue, The Sociology of Human Rights. *Sociology* 46 (5).

Morris, L. 2013. *Human Rights and Social Theory*. Basingstoke: Palgrave Macmillan.

Sen, A. 1999. *Development as Freedom*. Oxford: Oxford University Press.

Turner, B.S. 1993. "Outline of a Theory of Human Rights." *Sociology* 27 (3): 489–512.

Waters, M. 1996. "Human Rights and the Universalisation of Interests: Towards a Social Constructionist Approach." *Sociology* 30 (3): 593–600.

Identity

James E. Côté

University of Western Ontario, Canada

Prior to the 1950s, the term "identity" was used mainly in the psychiatric and psycho-analytic literatures. It was then introduced into the social scientific literature by the neo-Freudian Erik Erikson, and subsequently taken up in the sociological literature in theories of mass society to account for the decline in traditional forms of community and a consequent rise in problems of identity (Stein, Vidich, and White 1960). Since the 1950s, concerns about problems of identity have morphed into several approaches, with the term mass society supplanted by the concepts of postmodernity and late modernity, although similar post-traditional societal conditions remain the focus of explanations for identity problems.

Because of the interdisciplinary nature of the concept of identity, a single definition is inadequate. Instead, "identity" is multidimensional in nature, requiring different discipli-nary definitions associated with the level of analysis (Côté and Levine 2002). Even within sociology, the definition varies by theoretical tradition and the epistemological and political variants within each tradition. Even so, all variants in sociological definitions of identity involve characterizations of the person's status or position in a group or groups: it is sometimes defined in terms of the person's perception of that status (including self-perceptions of statuses, along with attempts to manage status appraisals); at other times it is defined in terms of how others impute the person's status (ranging from ascribed assignments to recognitions of achieved positions in status hierarchies). Micro-oriented approaches tend to focus on *personal identity*, whereas macro-oriented approaches in general refer to *social identity*, although these explicit designations and distinctions are not always made.

Micro-oriented approaches stem from the American pragmatist tradition rooted in the works of William James and Charles Pierce, which were interpreted by George Herbert Mead and Herbert Blumer. This tradition is often referred to as the Chicago School of symbolic interactionism, distinguished by its qualitative investigations through which social reality is understood from a nominalist perspective and therefore requires continual negotiations among actors to maintain adequate definitions of situations. The best-known heir of this tradition was Erving Goffman, whose work has introduced several generations of sociologists to the processes of context-specific identity manage-ment. A realist variation of symbolic interactionism, known as the Iowa School, was founded by Manfred Kuhn. Adherents of this perspective favored quantitative

Core Concepts in Sociology, First Edition. Edited by J. Michael Ryan.

methodologies, especially the Twenty Statements Test, also called the "Who Am I?" test. A conclusion drawn from this research is that personal identities (defined in terms of subjective assessments people make of their styles of self-presentation) have gained importance in self-definitions in relation to social identities (understood as socially recognized roles) in contemporary Western societies. Complementing this line of research, Ralph Turner postulated a similar movement from the "institutional self" to the "impulsive self" in Western societies.

Macro-oriented approaches that have taken up the identity concept since the 1950s can be traced to Emile Durkheim's classical formulations of anomie associated with the transition from premodern to modern societies. Talcott Parsons continued this concern, theorizing that as societies become more differentiated and pluralized, so do issues associated with social statuses and their maintenance. As more choices become available to people with the decline of ascribed statuses, the potentials for achieved statuses increase.

This macro tradition has influenced two contemporary sociological formulations of identity: late modernism and postmodernism.

Anthony Giddens and Ulrich Beck can be identified as the chief proponents of the late modernist perspective. For Giddens, late modern conditions have undermined certain traditional habits and customs, altering daily social life and experiences of self-identity, introducing ontological insecurities. The specter of these insecurities has made it important for the individual to develop agentic capacities with which to construct reality and manage identities. The life course can thus become a "reflexive project" in reaction to institutional de-structuring of old rites of passage and social markers as well as the introduction of new, more individualized, normative structures. Self-identity formation involves negotiating passages through life and reflecting on actions during these passages, which can be alienating and disjunctive. For Giddens, the life course in late modernity follows a large number of trajectories determined in part by individual preference (referred to as "individualization"), and in part by the uncertainty and risks of living in, and attempting to cope with, less predictable concrete, day-to-day structure than in premodern societies. Both Giddens and Beck have been concerned with linking macro formulations with micro ones, thereby addressing the concern in sociology with the structure–agency debate.

Paralleling the realist epistemology in the late modernist formulations are nominalist epistemologies in formulations that can loosely be termed "postmodernist." This caveat about characterizing postmodernism stems from a reluctance of many of those adopting politically charged forms of nominalism – especially as a vigorous anti-realism – to self-identify as postmodernists. Nevertheless, the common thread in these formulations is a confluence of interpretive and social constructionist approaches, with roots in symbolic interactionism, the sociology of knowledge, and critical theory. Most recently, the influences can be seen in cultural studies and feminism, especially with their work on "identity politics."

The genesis of postmodernist theories of identity follows the familiar path of sociological analyses, as noted above, of a deterioration in normative securities of daily experiences associated with premodern life and the rise of insecurities created by the complexities of the phases of modernity. A common theme running through sociological theories of modernity is that modern institutions create a tension between self and society, resulting in the fragmentation of self and loss of a sense of authenticity among those affected – a condition more generally referred to in the social scientific literature as *identity confusion*. Like the late modernist literature, the postmodernist literature focuses on these problematic trends to explore new forms of self and identity, but it often adds an emphasis on how both structure and agency are undermined. Poststructuralist formulations stemming from theorists such as Derrida, Foucault, and Lacan emphasize the maladies associated with the decline of traditional normative structures that produce insecurities of self, including forces acting against the development of personal agency producing a decentered, multiple, unfixed self without unity, always under construction with no overall blueprint. Some of these formulations propose that there is a constant struggle between "real" and "illusory" selves (carrying on the authenticity problem originally identified with the advent of modernity); in others, it is claimed that the postmodern self is relational and contingent, lacking a core upon which a stable sense of personal agency can be based. Thus, a common theme in postmodernist formulations is that the problems of self-formation introduced by the transition to modern societies (problems in finding one's authentic self or core) intensify in postmodern society to the point where anomie erodes the very sense that there is an authentic core. There is evidence that these maladies are experienced among those involved in youth cultures and segments of societies alienated from the mainstream, but little evidence that these maladies are widespread among those well integrated into contemporary societies.

Future Directions in Research, Theory, and Methodology

The common thread in sociological theories of identity is the erosion of securities in self-definition in post-traditional societies. However, the ways in which these identity insecurities can be interpreted depends on the epistemological and political assumptions of the theorist. Symbolic interactionists see the modern world as a stage on which people tend to be (insecure) actors, to paraphrase Shakespeare. Post-Durkheimian functionalists see these insecurities as an inevitable trend that people cope with in various ways as part of the human condition. Late modernist sociologists see opportunities in the normative declines that open up avenues for the exercise of personal agency in identity achievements over identity ascriptions. Postmodernists vary somewhat, but the overall outlook is pessimistic among those who reject an objectivist basis for personal agency; for those following this postmodernist boilerplate, the postmodern subject is metaphorically unanchored: at sea and adrift, buffeted by whatever misfortunes or fortunes await with the next weather system.

It is unclear how these opposing views of identity can be reconciled, in part because they can be based more on personal epistemologies and political orientations than on a shared body of evidence that could mediate value-based disputes. It is also not clear that reconciliation is in order so much as recognition that different theorists are often referring to different levels of analysis that involve different dimensions and manifestations of identity – in short, different subject matter. As it stands, those with the opposing views of identity tend to inhabit academic silos with like-minded theorists who offhandedly reject the work of disciplinary competitors. A comparison of four recently published handbooks in the field of identity studies illustrates this situation, with each volume tending to claim the proper approach to, and subject matter of, the field, yet there is remarkably little overlap in content among the four publications (these are listed below as suggested readings – the editor's introductions from each volume illustrate this point). However, this lack of overlap supports the contention that identity is multidimensional and constitutes a range of subject matter and manifestations whose examination requires that theorists employ a range of epistemologies and methodologies to understand the breadth of the field.

The history of symbolic interactionism illustrates the merits of both realist and nominalist epistemologies as well as their concomitant quantitative and qualitative methodologies in the study of different manifestations of personal and social identities. For example, qualitative, nominalist approaches to identity appear to be most appropriate at the level of interaction, where non-routine face-to-face encounters have emergent qualities, but less appropriate at the institutional/societal level where roles and statuses tend to be more fixed and stable. When the identity processes under consideration are more stable and enduring, realist, quantitative approaches can be more appropriate. A mature field of study is characterized by reasoned and measured approaches that are more sensitive to the contextual manifestations under investigation, with the results of investigations less contingent on the personal epistemologies of theorists.

SEE ALSO: Alienation; Anomie; Epistemology; Modernity; the Self; Structure and Agency

References

Côté, James E., and Charles Levine. 2002. *Identity Formation, Agency, and Culture: A Social Psychological Synthesis*. Mahwah, NJ: Erlbaum.
Stein, Maurice, Arthur J. Vidich, and David Manning White. 1960. *Identity and Anxiety: Survival of the Person in Mass Society*. New York: The Free Press.

Further Reading

Elliot, Anthony, ed. 2014. *Routledge Handbook of Identity Studies*. New York: Routledge.
McLean, Kate C., and Moin Syed, eds. 2015. *The Oxford Handbook of Identity Development*. New York: Oxford University Press.
Schwartz, Seth J., Vivian Vignoles, and Koen Luyckx, eds. 2011. *Handbook of Identity Theory and Research*. New York: Springer.
Wetherell, Margaret, and Chandra Mohanty, eds. 2010. *The Sage Handbook of Identities*. Los Angeles: Sage.

Immigration, Migration, and Refugees

Alexandra Parrs

American University in Cairo, Egypt, and University of Antwerp, Belgium

Theories of Migration

Migration, or the movement of people from one place to another, has always occurred; however, it is with the creation of the concept of the nation-state, associated with sovereignty and fixed boundaries, that international migration became more significant as it became politicized. Up until the nineteenth century, *emigration*, or the movement of people out of a country, was strongly regulated because states wanted to retain citizens within their boundaries – as tax-payers and potential soldiers (Zolberg 1978). With the development of labor migration in the twentieth century, *immigration*, or the movement of people into a country, started to become more regulated, and states established different control mechanisms to encourage or discourage certain types of immigration: skilled vs. nonskilled workers and migrants of specific nationalities, religions, or ethnicities. Some countries, such as the United States, are perceived as traditional countries of immigration and have relied on migrants to populate their territories. Other countries have needed labor migrants sporadically, such as European countries in the post-World War II period of reconstruction. Southern European countries and some Asian countries went from being countries of emigration to countries of immigration at the end of the twentieth century.

Different theories try to explain the causes of migration. They rely on economic, political, and social explanations and examine different levels of analysis. From the neoclassical perspective, migration occurs when there are significant differences in earnings and employment rates between states. Workers migrate from one place to the other and return home when their wages have stabilized. Migrants are assumed to be rational and well-informed about wage rates, job security, and costs of travel in order to maximize their income. This perspective tends to be ahistorical. According to the new economics of migration, the decision to migrate is not individually made, but it is the result of collective strategies at the family or community level, which can fully rely on financial remittances from migrants. Going up a level, the dual labor theory stipulates that migration is a structural requirement of industrial economies, as developed economies constantly need migrants. Concomitantly, sending countries become structurally dependent on migration (remittances, deindustrialization).

Core Concepts in Sociology, First Edition. Edited by J. Michael Ryan.
© 2019 John Wiley & Sons Ltd. Published 2019 by John Wiley & Sons Ltd.

World system theories, rooted in Marxism, contend that international migration has little to do with wage rates or employment and is linked to the development of capitalism. Wallerstein (1974) classifies countries into the core, periphery, and semi-periphery and examines the dependency and oppressive mechanisms that take place between these areas: owners of large corporations use poorer countries' raw material, corrupt elites, and destroy their productive systems, forcing their population to migrate to the core.

Other theories look at historical, political, and social elements to explain the initiation and perpetuation of migratory movements. Some countries may have specific bilateral relations due to colonization, political influence, or trade routes, like India and Great Britain. Some institutions are also crucial in the perpetuation of migration, such as humanitarian organizations, regional associations facilitating credit employment or lodging, or smugglers. The network theory focuses on the social networks established by migrants that contribute to sustaining migration from one place to another, as increased social capital reduces the uncertainties and risks associated with migration and eases integration. New theories also focus on the role that aspirations and perceptions play in the decision to migrate beyond pure economic gain. Migrants can aspire to a better education, more human rights, gender equality or healthcare; all those are based both on knowledge and perceptions that can be transmitted by media or fellow migrants.

Faist's "meso-level" (1997) embodies the intricate relations between social, political, and economic structures and different levels of analysis. After the pioneer stage, migration becomes more common in sending communities after potential migrants learn about the receiving country (language, culture, needs). In receiving countries, networks are also created, triggering a higher or lower tolerance for some migrants and specific sets of interactions. Policies, in turn, both reflect migratory flows and impact them, via border control, potential quotas and visa requirements, or the obtention (or not) of dual citizenship. Migrants can impact host nations in their relations to their home country through their political lobbying or their investments. Social remittances and the exchange of norms, practices, and beliefs between nations also impact sending and receiving countries.

Integration of Migrants

The integration of migrants can take different forms, and countries have different modes of integration, or philosophies of integration, from assimilation and multiculturalism to blatant discriminative practices. Some countries' philosophies rely on the idea that their national identity is anchored in a common culture which can be reified, while others focus on social and political norms and values associated with citizenship and belonging. Some countries offer citizenship to migrants while others keep them marginalized as a right-less underclass. Portes and Zhou (1993) developed the notion of segmented assimilation, which means that migrants can be assimilated socially, economically, or politically, but not necessarily in all these areas.

Many scholars have asked whether the increase of international migration challenges the notion of the nation-state: does migration weaken the nation-state or does it contribute to reinforcing it, as host societies tend to reify their own culture in opposition to what are perceived as foreign, perhaps threatening, cultures? What is the relationship between citizenship and culture and can individuals pay allegiance to more than one nation? Scholars examine the notion of *transnationalism*, which refers to different processes migrants engage in that transcend states' physical and symbolic boundaries culturally, financially, and politically. Individuals can have dual frames of reference and bifocal orientations. Their sentiments of belonging are multiple as they can be from "here and there." Economically, they are also involved in more than one national context, which can materialize in their investments in different countries or in diaspora philanthropy, according to which diasporas are involved in various projects to develop their home countries. Another manifestation is "brain circulation" which as its name indicates is circular, unlike brain drain that is often one-way. Finally, some individuals own multiple citizenships, and, therefore, are able to vote and be politically active in more than one nation. Increased mobility and communication technology allow for additional fluidity in terms of belonging and allegiances.

Refugees

Asylum seekers are individuals who cross borders because they can no longer be protected by their own government. According to the 1951 UN Convention, asylum seekers can be granted refugee status after proving that they are under a well-founded fear of persecution for reasons of race, religion, nationality, or membership in a particular social group or because of a political opinion. The refugee status determination (RSD) is paradoxically largely subjective, as the "well-founded fear of persecution" is difficult to assess and very bureaucratic.

Three durable solutions are possible for refugees: voluntary repatriation, local integration, or resettlement in a third country. Countries that are signatories of the 1951 convention are bound by the non-refoulement principle, which means that they cannot send asylum seekers waiting for the RSD or accepted refugees back to the countries they have fled. Individuals who have not been granted refugee status (denied asylum seekers) are either deported back or left in the country that denied them without any formal status, akin to stateless individuals.

The term refugee is both a legal and a social category and a "label" as it strips individuals of their identity pre-refuge and reconstructs them as passive victims in need of international support. The concept of the "vulnerable female refugee" is ostensibly a concept that energizes additional protection for women in order to protect them from sexual violence during the journey to refuge. This concept, though, also disempowers as it constructs women as essential victims without agency.

SEE ALSO: Capital: Cultural, Social, and Economic; Citizenship; Colonialism and Postcolonialism; Demography and Population Studies; Globalization; Inequality, Global; Nationalism; Social Network Analysis

References

Faist, T. 1997. "The Crucial Meso-Level." In *International Migration, Immobility and Development: Multidisciplinary Perspectives*, edited by T. Hammar, G. Brochmann, K. Tamas, and T. Faist, 187–217. Oxford: Berg.

Portes, A., and M. Zhou. 1993. "The New Second Generation: Segmented Assimilation and Its Variants." *The Annals of the American Academy of Political and Social Science* 530: 74–96.

Wallerstein, I. 1974. *The Modern World-System I: Capitalist Agriculture and the Origins of the European World-Economy in the Sixteenth Century.* New York: Academic Press.

Zolberg, A. 1978. "International Migration Policies in a Changing World System." In *Human Migration: Patterns and Policies,* edited by William H. McNeill and Ruth Adams, 241–286. Indianapolis: Indiana University Press.

Inequality, Gender

Robert Max Jackson

New York University, USA

Gender inequality exists when members of one sex – usually men – get a better deal than do members of the other sex. This means that members of one sex have more access to desirable opportunities and goods, have greater liberty and control of their futures, control more valuable resources, garner more respect and privilege, and occupy more positions of power. Gender inequality also refers to the hierarchical relationship between women and men as groups or population segments, such that men control the social order. Gender inequality primarily concerns men being in the superior or privileged position, and we will assume that meaning throughout this entry unless explicitly stating otherwise.

Gender inequality is a complex construct, a composite based on relative, not absolute, differences. Gender inequality does not mean that men have an advantage with respect to everything that people value. Even with significant gender inequality favoring men, for example, women could potentially live longer or have better friendships. Gender inequality also does not mean that all men live better than all women do. For example, upper-class and racially privileged women may live in greater comfort and have more authority than do men in lower-class and racially disadvantaged groups. Thus, gender inequality exists as far as men disproportionately hold the positions of power and influence in society and that, as individuals, men's advantages over women in similar social categories outweigh their disadvantages.

When the rights, opportunities, quality of life, and social influence of men are significantly and consistently better than those of women the underlying magnitude of gender inequality is unmistakable. For example, in early nineteenth-century industrial societies like the United States or United Kingdom, men controlled positions of political and economic power; women could not vote; married women ceded their legal rights to make contracts and control inheritances to their husbands; women had almost no access to higher education or professional training; and everyone expected men to dominate their families. In contrast, today women participate widely in politics and the economy; women gain considerable public recognition as high achievers and celebrities; women are becoming more educated than men are; and the public discourse regarding women's social position shows that women's circumstances and status are

Core Concepts in Sociology, First Edition. Edited by J. Michael Ryan.
© 2019 John Wiley & Sons Ltd. Published 2019 by John Wiley & Sons Ltd.

markedly better than they used to be in most ways. Such consistent and unmistakably large (or small) differences between women's lives and men's lives allow confident claims of relatively high (or low) gender inequality.

Calculating gender inequality with enough precision that we can confidently rank smaller differences between similar societies, however, is an elusive challenge. Possibly the best-known efforts to solve this problem are the Gender Inequality Index of the United Nations and the Global Gender Gap Index of the World Economic Forum. Each index uses data on a variety of enumerable characteristics understood to indicate specific inequalities between women and men, such as holding elected government posts, mortality rates, educational attainment, or employment. The index combines these inequality "components" to produce an aggregated measure of gender inequality. Unfortunately, we have no theoretical guide to choosing which inequalities between women and men merit inclusion, no common standard by which to measure different types of inequalities, no compelling theoretical logic defining their relative importance, and no systematic calculus for combining them. As a result, the existing indices do cluster countries that scholars' recognize have unmistakably high levels of gender inequality at one end of the scale and those known to have comparatively low levels at the other, but smaller differences in the indices' rankings otherwise have tenuous theoretical or empirical justification.

The distribution of gender inequality over time and space has been uneven. Hunting and gathering bands displayed little gender inequality if only because their small size, reliance on shared natural resources, and immunity from political hierarchy left little room for any persistent social inequality (although temporary inequalities could emerge anywhere due to specific historical and cultural conditions). Gender inequality seems to have become common in societies after they domesticated plants and animals, resulting in both property rights in cultivated land (or herds or fishing grounds) and significant political hierarchy. Historical records, archeological studies, and ethnographic work suggest the form and depth of gender inequality varied greatly by local cultural and historical circumstances, although it commonly became high in feudal societies around the world, where kinship organized both military power and agricultural land ownership in the hands of men. Beginning at least two centuries ago, gender inequality has declined dramatically, if unevenly, starting in nations with industrializing economies and electoral governments.

Scholars do not agree why gender inequality arose initially in early societies, why it commonly persisted through the varied economic and political transformations across the world leading toward modern societies, or why it has declined in modern states. Most believe that gender inequality originated in early "rudimentary" societies as an indirect result of a division of labor fostered, but not directly produced, by biological differences. Women's roles as child bearers and providers of breast milk to infants, possibly reinforced by men's greater average strength, encouraged a division of labor, with men responsible for hunting and (where needed) warfare, while women had greater responsibility for foraging and caring for young children. Although the division of work between women and men varied across societies, men commonly gained greater control over weapons and relationships between groups. These conditions fostered the emergence of gender inequality when an increased productivity of agricultural societies allowed some people to live on the output of others, giving rise to persistent inequality through wealth accumulation, and enabling greater political hierarchy. So long as men controlled economic and militaristic resources through kinship, and transferred them across generations to younger men, these conditions created an environment enabling sustained gender inequality. The emergence of industrial societies and representative governments gradually displaced kinship hierarchies' role as a mechanism distributing social power, thereby significantly eroding both motives and means that had fostered gender inequality.

Women's rising status and the moral rejection of gender inequality are modern phenomena. Women and men everywhere, throughout history, largely accepted the cultural legitimacy of differences in gender status. Undoubtedly, women often balked at gender inequality's implications for their lives, but resistance could secure most women only marginal gains given the overwhelming odds. This began to change noticeably in the nineteenth century, coinciding with the rise of industrial economies, electoral governments, and scientific knowledge. Families and kinship gradually lost their former economic and political roles. Over the next two centuries, modern economies drew ever more people, eventually including women, into the labor force; and modern governments extended citizenship rights to an ever larger range of people, including women. As scientific knowledge displaced religion as a basis of legitimating beliefs, an unanticipated consequence of modern schooling, business practices, and government policies was the rise of meritocratic ideals, a profound challenge to beliefs supporting gender inequality. Lacking an inherent organizational interest in preserving gender inequality, employers hired women when they saw an economic advantage and government officials supported policies that benefitted women when it served their political careers. Together, these changes undermined the supports for gender inequality, allowing women, acting both as individuals and collectively, to successfully resist the obstacles that constrained their lives. The moral transformation of women's subordinate status from a natural law to a social injustice both reflected and helped propel these accumulating changes.

Just how much gender inequality persists and what the future holds are matters of considerable controversy. While women's status has improved all around the world, the changes have been far greater in some areas than in others. In the countries where women's status has changed the most, women have far greater access to higher education, high-status professions, and government positions than was true in the past and they are much better represented in these institutions. In many places, governments have outlawed economic, social, or legal discrimination against women. Still, even where gender inequality has declined most, several aspects of gender inequality have been slow to change. Women still have only limited representation at the highest levels of business and government. Women still have significantly more responsibility for raising children, particularly infants. Women also remain highly vulnerable to sexual harassment and sexual violence from men. In short, women's status has experienced a revolutionary change over the past two centuries, but the results have been uneven. Some nations and some religions have moved slowly, and some aspects of gender inequality have changed less than others. Nonetheless, what we know of women's rising status over the past two centuries and recent empirical trends consistently point toward a continued decline in gender inequalities as far into the future as we can now project.

SEE ALSO: Feminist Theory; Gender; Patriarchy; Stratification and Inequality

Further Reading

Goldin, Claudia Dale. 1990. *Understanding the Gender Gap: An Economic History of American Women*. New York: Oxford University Press.

Jackson, Robert Max. 1998. *Destined for Equality: The Inevitable Rise of Women's Status*. Cambridge, MA: Harvard University Press.

Ridgeway, Cecilia L. 2011. *Framed by Gender: How Gender Inequality Persists in the Modern World*. New York: Oxford University Press.

Inequality, Global

Roberto Patricio Korzeniewicz

University of Maryland, USA

To a significant extent, studies of global inequality have focused on measuring the evolution of convergence and divergence between nations. Among these studies, most agree that a large gap between rich and poor nations became evident by the late nineteenth century, and continued to grow at least until roughly the middle of the twentieth century. There is less agreement about the evolution of trends after the mid-twentieth century, and about the key processes shaping inequality between nations.

For some, inequality between nations began to stabilize around the middle of the twentieth century, and there was considerable convergence between nations thereafter. Such assessments, knowingly or not, draw significantly from the long-established paradigm of modernization. "Modernization" approaches argue that in the same way as nations undergo a transition from rural (or agricultural/traditional) to urban (or industrial/ modern) arrangements, inequality between countries is caused by some nations taking the lead in becoming industrialized while others lag behind. As in economist Simon Kuznets's famous Inverted-U hypothesis, this rise in inequality was supposed to be merely transitional and lasting only as long as it would take for lagging nations to "catch-up" with the leaders. This line of interpretation perceives nations as independent and autonomous entities that embark, albeit with differences in timing, in a universal process of transformation from tradition into modernity. The relative degree of command over income is perceived to be a consequence of modernization, and the achievement of wealth by nations as indicative of relative success in embracing key elements of modernization (such as urbanization and industrialization). Over time, as all nations move toward universal practices and modes of thought, income convergence is expected to ensue and inequality between nations to decline. Along these lines, Firebaugh (2003: 23), for example, argues that "diffusion of industrialization works to compress inequality across nations" and international convergence is a product of the "deepening industrialization of poor nations."

A more updated version of a "modernization" approach explains the gap between wealthy and poor nations as an outcome of institutional differentiation (e.g., Acemoglu and Robinson 2012). Wealthy countries are so, according to these authors, because the development of inclusive institutions (centralized but pluralist government, secure but broadly distributed property and political rights, the unbiased application of law, competitive markets) allows for economic incentives that result in constant, long-term growth.

Core Concepts in Sociology, First Edition. Edited by J. Michael Ryan.
© 2019 John Wiley & Sons Ltd. Published 2019 by John Wiley & Sons Ltd.

Poor countries, by contrast, endure extractive institutions designed to maximize the ability of a small elite to plunder resources. Such plunder can thrive in the absence of a centralized state (where the power and exercise of violence by small groups tends to lead toward chaos), but also prevails under absolutist centralized states. In these environments, ruling elites seek to restrict competition and limit innovation, and this results in persistently stagnant growth. These institutional arrangements might generate ephemeral bursts of affluence (such as in the Soviet Union in the twentieth century), but no true prosperity. A rather persistent gap between wealthy and poor nations results from these patterns of institutional differentiation.

The future evolution of inequalities between nations, in this version of "modernization," is rather less certain and/or predictable. No pretense is made of producing an easy panacea for development, as there is no single model for inclusive institutions, and these bear the imprint of the evolving and changing political balance of forces in specific locales and times. What works in one place might not work in another. Moreover, the emergence and development of inclusive institutions is seldom by design, shaped instead by the particularities of a given place at a given time. Moreover, from such a perspective, the extraordinary rates of growth experienced in China over the past two decades resulted from an actually modest adoption of inclusive institutions, and unless such institutions are adopted more broadly, the persistence of extractive institutions can bring growth in China to a quick end. For all these reasons, this version of a "modernization" perspective is less sanguine about the likelihood of continued convergence between rich and poor nations.

Others have been more skeptical about the extent of convergence in the latter half of the twentieth century, but for different reasons. In part, there is some disagreement about the extent of convergence that took place in the latter half of the twentieth century. Korzeniewicz and Moran (1997) show that between-country inequality was rising as recently as the mid-1990s when using exchange rate-adjusted income values rather than purchasing power parities (PPPs). Others indicate that convergence between countries has been driven by rapid economic growth in China, and that when the latter country is removed from measures of between-nations inequality, the trend toward convergence disappears. Wade (2004) found that all measures of between country inequality are widening except for PPP-adjusted between-country inequality with China included.

But beyond empirical questions about the extent and limits of between-nation convergence, contemporary perspectives emphasizing the persistence of polarization and inequality are linked with older, critical approaches on the global processes that operate to perpetuate inequalities. Among these older approaches, Raul Prebish (e.g., 1950) and Arghiri Emmanuel (1972) argued that the gap in wealth separating rich and poor nations was maintained and/or deepened by market interactions, as wage differentials between core and periphery were at the root of a deterioration in the terms of trade (Prebisch) or unequal exchange (Emmanuel) between peripheral and center products. To different extents, the notion that the market has been a key arena for the unfolding of unequal exchange, and that unequal exchange has constituted the main force shaping inequalities between core and peripheral nations, has been central to many critical perspectives on inequalities between nations, particularly those that tend to see inequality primarily as the outcome of exploitation (by one class over another, or by rich nations over poor nations). In the more simplistic representations of these arguments, the "core" or "peripheral" status of nations in the global economy corresponds with specialization in manufacturing production in the former, raw material production in the latter.

Thus, paradoxically, many critical perspectives on inequality between nations have been just as likely as those in the "modernization" perspective to focus on explaining global patterns as driven by processes largely similar to those that drive inequality within nations. Critical perspectives might emphasize exploitation, and "modernization" studies the eventual convergence of economies and social institutions, but both tend to see inequality between and within nations as parallel but separate, self-contained processes.

When focusing only on wealthy nations, as is the practice of most of the social sciences, the institutional arrangements of wealthier nations indeed appear, as in the eyes of Acemoglu and Robinson (2012), to be characterized primarily by inclusion. With such a focus, inequality and social stratification appear to be primarily either (a) from a more mainstream perspective, the outcome of individual achievement, as measured by universal criteria, in spheres (e.g., education, labor markets) characterized by relatively unrestricted access; or (b) in a critical version, the expression of processes of exploitation linking populations contained within these institutional arrangements.

By contrast, world-systems approaches to the study of inequality and stratification call for shifting the relevant unit of analysis to the world as a whole, so as to produce a more holistic, relational, and challenging narrative of global inequality. From such a perspective, the establishment of social compacts characterized by relatively greater equity in wealthy nations and the emergence of high inequality between countries are not separate processes: rather, they are the outcome of fundamental institutional arrangements undergirding world inequality. For example, the strengthening of national barriers to entry through the twentieth century was part and parcel of an effort to restrict competitive pressures and/or reduce inequality within the wealthier nations, and was a crucial process leading to the development of high inequality between nations through the twentieth century.

Facing the persistence of world inequalities almost forty years ago, Arghiri Emmanuel admonished us to beware of "the danger that, by concentrating our revolutionary ardor inside [a] minority group of countries, we may find ourselves, in tomorrow's tempest, *on the side of* the minority. It will not be the first time in history that Rome will have fallen, not under the blows of the Romans but under those of the 'barbarians.'" Twenty years later, Giovanni Arrighi (1991: 65) echoed similar concerns, indicating that world income inequalities continued to raise a dilemma for progressive forces in wealthy countries, as "[e]ither [Western socialists] will join forces with Eastern and Southern associates and come up with an intellectual project and a political programme capable of transforming systematic chaos into a more equal and solidary world order, or their appeals to human progress and social justice will lose all residual credibility."

Twenty years later still, not all remains the same. It is now a substantive transformation in world income inequalities that is raising difficult tradeoffs, and progressive forces in the West are yet to delineate the political alignments or strategies that can provide comfortable answers to these tradeoffs. But in the midst of these ongoing transformations, we should heed more than ever the admonishments of Emmanuel and Arrighi: in pursuing protection for those in wealthy countries who suffer negative effects from the decline of world income inequalities, we must be careful that progressive forces do not stand again as advocates of exclusion for most of the world.

SEE ALSO: Capitalism; Class, Capitalist; Colonialism and Postcolonialism; Economic Sociology; Globalization; Marxism; Modernity; State, the; Stratification and Inequality

References

Acemoglu, Daron, and James Robinson. 2012. *Why Nations Fail: The Origins of Power, Prosperity, and Poverty*. New York: Crown Publishing Group.

Arrighi, Giovanni. 1991. "World Income Inequalities and the Future of Socialism." *NLR* I/189 (September–October): 39–66.

Emmanuel, Arghiri. 1972. *Unequal Exchange: A Study of the Imperialism of Trade*. New York: Monthly Review Press.

Firebaugh, Glenn. 2003. *The New Geography of Global Income Inequality*. Cambridge, MA: Harvard University Press.

Korzeniewicz, Roberto Patricio, and Timothy Patrick Moran. 1997. "World-Economic Trends in the Distribution of Income, 1965–1992." *American Journal of Sociology* 102: 1000–1039.

Prebisch, Raúl. 1950. *The Economic Development of Latin America and Its Principal Problems*. Lake Success, NY: United Nations (Department of Economic Affairs, Economic Commission for Latin America).

Wade, Robert Hunter. 2004. "Is Globalization Reducing Poverty and Inequality?" *World Development* 32: 567–589.

Inequality, Racial and Ethnic

Rutledge M. Dennis

George Mason University, USA

Racial and ethnic inequalities continue to perplex politicians, scholars and, somewhat less, the general public. This perplexity, especially in the West, stems partially from the discrepancy between the ideals associated with freedom and democracy, and the actual experiences of individuals and groups caught between, as Myrdal (1944) states it, the stated creed of societies and the actual deeds. Though Myrdal intended the discordance to represent the United States, the United States was [is] not alone in illustrating this universal social discrepancy. The United States is indeed unusual in its historic dual racial/ethnic subjugation legacy: first waging warfare against its indigenous population, then subsequently imposing restrictive reservations for them; simultaneously, it imposed legal enslavement upon Africans, then subsequently imposed legal segregation after a brutal civil war which ended slavery. The ethnic inequality of European emigrants extending mainly from the middle and late nineteenth and early twentieth centuries is yet another story of ethnic hardship, though minus the brutality experienced by Native Americans and Africans. It is this twin, or dual, legacy, especially the legacy of slavery, which makes the United States an appropriate model for extended analysis of racial and ethnic inequality. Indeed, the United States is an excellent social laboratory whereby issues related to race and ethnicity and majority–minority, or dominant–nondominant relations may be observed and tested. The ubiquity of racial and ethnic inequalities and disparities in the United States and elsewhere is the focus of this entry.

If the position is accepted that groups exploit due to a need to feel and be superior, and that color prejudice is the most persistent and the most deeply felt and accepted form of inequality, such accepted forms of inequality are bound to have consequences for groups not only culturally different, but racially different. But it is not only being racially different. It is having dark skin and African physical features. This is important, for lighter skin racial groups are more widely accepted in the United States and many Western countries. There is generally less hostility toward Chinese and Japanese, or light skin Indians, than is the case for darker skin Africans and those from the Caribbean, for example, in the United Kingdom and the United States. This silent hostility often has a great impact on the lives of darker racial groups: health, politics, economics, social life, and education.

Core Concepts in Sociology, First Edition. Edited by J. Michael Ryan.
© 2019 John Wiley & Sons Ltd. Published 2019 by John Wiley & Sons Ltd.

Historical Foundations of Racial and Ethnic Inequality

It is important to understand how feelings, attitudes, and behavior are galvanized toward specific objectives when European nations encountered the people of Africa, Asia, Australia, and Latin America. Eurocentrism to be sure resulted from this encounter, but the psychology of inferiority and superiority accompanied Eurocentrism. When the British, French, Spanish, and Portuguese set out to explore and control they already had science and technology as valuable assets. By the middle and end of the nineteenth century Darwinism, especially social Darwinism, would be an added asset. So inequality existed on two fronts. First, there was inequality between nation-states due to the technological advantages of the West. Second, there was the inequality between the people – the dominated and the dominators – which would have emotional and psychological ramifications.

The most overt, and manifest, feature in the dynamics of racial and ethnic inequality is arguably the difference in skin color and the responses to those differences by those who view skin color differences as indicants of inferiority or superiority. Stating this does not overlook the fact that skin color and skin color differences were also important in the Chinese and Japanese relations to Europeans, other Asians, and Africans. It is to say that since Europeans, those of European descent, and Americans played a major role in Western expansionism and the annexations of territories occupied by people of color, their presence in those territories, and what they did to people of color who then occupied the territories which Europeans and Americans conquered, meant they became major players in the battleground of the conflicts which involved the English, and those of English descent in the United States, Canada, Australia, and New Zealand. The French, Spaniards, Portuguese, and Dutch, along with the English, were also major players in European expansionism and annexations throughout South and Central America, and the Caribbean. The slave status of Africans in the United States was a double burden, in as much as the stigma of slavery was attached to color. Also, there were cultural assumptions which heightened the European sense of superiority over conquered societies: the lack of written languages. Europeans placed great emphasis on the written word as a reflection of refinement and one's closeness to the idea of being a "civilized person." Closely associated with skin color, the lack of a written language was the assumed lack of sexualized consciousness within their own groups, and with outsiders, which, in the European mind, represented sexual "looseness" and "licentiousness." Religion was yet another reason for treating the "others" as not only morally, emotionally, and intellectually irredeemable, but, on certain levels, almost subhuman. The seizure of land as a gift from the gods and the role of religion accompanying the seizure all worked in unison to create a highly complex network of organizations and institutions which destroyed indigenous cultures and made the laws, customs, and cultures of those of European descent the accepted laws, norms, and values.

Structural Inequality

Structural inequality is the inequality which, over generations, becomes ritualized and forms a consistent pattern which creates and shapes the nexus of intergroup ties and relations. If these consistent patterns of intergroup relations are not written into the legal system, thus forming the bases for laws fostering inequality, they may form the bases for informal norms which may be just as strong in setting guidelines for racial and ethnic relations. In the United States this structural inequality was illustrated in the treatment of Africans: from legal slavery to legal Jim Crow Laws in the South, and *de jure* segregation in the North. Group domination and exploitation are key concepts when describing structural inequality, for it is created in order to dominate, exploit and discriminate against, and exclude certain groups. In the Jim Crow South thousands of black men were targeted for lynching, the vast majority on fake charges. Structural inequality can be seen to operate in the areas below.

(a) Inequality under the law: Different legal standards are applied to many racial and ethnic groups in countries where they comprise the minority. Coptic Christians in Egypt often complain of the lack of justice in Egyptian courts and their inability to build additional churches. Black Americans and Hispanics complain of the differential justice between them and whites, and much of the inequity in both cases has been well documented. Though the United States has advanced well beyond the pre-civil rights era where blacks were routinely convicted by largely all-white juries, there is still great disparity in sentences between blacks and whites for similar crimes in similar localities. Similar inequities are experienced by Christians throughout Muslim majority countries, especially in Muslim countries living under Sharia law. Though a million plus refugees have flocked to Europe due to the strife in Syria and Iraq, Germany, Sweden, and France, and Denmark have all given the refugees equal protection under their respective national laws.

(b) Inequality of opportunity: Structural inequality creates unequal opportunities for racial and ethnic groups. The isolation, segregation, and marginalization of racial and ethnic groups places them outside of the networks crucial for knowing of, and taking advantage of, existing opportunities available in the larger dominate society, especially in the crucial areas of employment and education (King 1964). For example, in the United States, black Americans experience unemployment rates more than twice those of white Americans. In the major inner cities of America black males between the ages of 16 to 25+ face an unemployment rate of almost 50 percent. This has major, and far-reaching consequences for the cultural, political, and economic health of black communities, especially black families, institutions, and organizations. Similar patterns of inequality explain black inner-city education which is largely segregated and plagued by high levels of school drop-outs and generally low educational achievement. High levels of ethnic inequality are also evident throughout. In the pre-fractured Yugoslavia, Serbian hegemony fueled Croatian, Slovenia, Bosnia, Macedonia, Montenegro, and Kosovo's thirst for independence. In Northern Ireland and the United Kingdom the inequality of opportunity for Irish Catholics was well established. In many Muslim-dominated countries, it makes a difference if you're a Shiite in Iran, or a Sunni in Saudi Arabia.

Du Bois's ([1903] 1961) use of the term "veil" aptly describes the process by which larger and more powerful dominant groups restrict and constrain smaller and less powerful groups. For Du Bois, the exclusion of one group, racial or ethnic, from participating in the political, economic, and social processes prevents that excluded group from acquiring the means to participate, and hence compete for desired societal goals and objectives. Du Bois also uses the terms "double consciousness" and "masking" to refer to the inner subjective world, and mind, and its responses to inequality and individual and group subjugation. Thus, Du Bois understood the physicality of exclusion and its materialistic manifestations. He especially understood the subjective, psychological, and emotional responses by blacks to being, as he stated it (Du Bois [1940] 1968), relegated to being in prison and having "entombed souls."

(c) Inequality of power: In general, in most societies, power is held by the numerically largest group, South Africa, with white rule, and Rwanda and Burundi, with minority Tutsi rule, being the exception. In the United States and Europe it has normally meant that people of color will always be outvoted, unless they are able to form coalitions with segments of the larger white population, or form coalitions with other groups of color. This is how individual men and women of color have been able to rise to the top in many political arenas: ex-President Barack Obama in the United States, the current Muslim mayor of London, former African-American governors of Massachusetts and Virginia, and African-American senators from Illinois, New Jersey, and Massachusetts. This includes the Christian mayor, currently under siege, in Jakarta, Indonesia, the largest Muslim country in the world. Although individuals belonging to minority racial and ethnic groups may hold power in societies, they do so despite the massive inequality experienced by members of their own groups. The lack of political power may also parallel a lack of power in the economic sphere. There are, however, exceptions to this general rule. In Indonesia and Malaysia, the minority Chinese and Indian populations lack political power but have great economic power. When Malaysians were fearful that the Chinese and Indians might attempt to gain a degree of political power, they rewrote the Malaysian constitution so as to guarantee that only Malaysians could have political control. Thus, ethnic groups not only inveigh against dominant and more powerful Western nations. As is now clear, there are interethnic and intraethnic conflicts and antagonisms which also result in unequal group relations between ethnic and racial minorities.

Responses to Racial and Ethnic Inequality

In his various books, Du Bois succinctly and with much precision outlines and enumerates the responses of blacks to racial inequality. Various strategies were supported and tried, including: in the nineteenth century, the Back to Africa Movement; organizational strategies, for example, Negro Conferences, the American Negro Academy, the Du Boisian-proposed Talented Tenth Concept; and the Booker T. Washington strategy of black–white "economic symbiosis" and black political non-involvement. In the twentieth century, Washington launched the Business League, while Du Bois was instrumental in the formation of the Niagara Movement and the NAACP. Then the massive Civil Rights Movement began in the late 1940s and reached its peak in the 1960s under the leadership of Martin Luther King, Jr. But it was only a matter of time before the slow pace of racial and social change, or the lack of such, which prompted Stokely Carmichael and other young activists to raise the battle cry of Black Power, was soon followed by other racial and ethnic groups with their own cry of Brown Power, Yellow Power, Red Power, followed by a host of black, Hispanic, and Native American Studies Programs throughout America. These occurred simultaneously with a newly emerging Pan-African Movement and the decolonization of many African, Asian, and Latin American countries. The Black Lives Matter Movement, generally led by young blacks from working-class backgrounds, is the latest movement to surface to address racial and ethnic inequalities in the United States. The United Kingdom, though late in addressing issues germane to racial and ethnic groups, has had to address persistent inequality largely between its white and its African-Caribbean minority populations. Like blacks in the United Staets, these minority groups have coalesced around organizations and societies designed to challenge racism and discrimination.

Meanwhile, in Europe the Irish, having won independence from England in 1921, had to contend with the partition of the country and protracted guerilla warfare begun by the IRA to push the British Government and British military forces out of Northern Ireland. In Central Europe and the Balkans, the uprising of ethnic Hungarians and Poles tested Russian tolerance for limited freedom for the Iron Curtain countries which served as its buffer against Western Europe. However, arguably the most revolutionary change in Europe before the collapse of the Soviet Union occurred after the death of Tito and the collapse of Yugoslavia into small ethnic enclave nations. The idea among many ethnic minority groups historically forced into a national merger with a larger and more powerful ethnically different group is to now seek independence and go it alone as a separate nation-state. This quest failed twice for the French-Canadian Separatist Movement in Canada, failed recently for Scottish nationalists in Scotland, and Madrid has nullified the results of the recently held Catalonian referendum in which a majority of Catalonians voted to exit the Spanish federation. Leaders of the independence movement were not only threatened with mass arrest, but they were systematically deposed and Madrid sent in its officials to govern the province. In the case of French-Canadians, Scotland, and Catalonians, each believe it is getting less than it is giving in the union, and each thinks it can better prosper as a separate nation-state.

In Africa, ethnic inequality in Rwanda and Burundi of the Hutu by the Tutsi resulted in widespread slaughter, with many viewing this as genocide by the majority Hutu against the minority Tutsi. In the Sudan, the attempts by Khartoum to force Islam upon southern Sudanese, largely Christian and animist, resulted in a twenty-plus year war, ending with the creation of the new nation of South Sudan. Similar ethnic conflicts between Indonesia and East Timor led to the creation of the nation of East Timor; it was also this perception of group (religious and ethnic) injustice and inequality which resulted in the twenty-year war between Ethiopia and Eritrea, ending in the establishment of Eritrea as an independent nation, rather remaining an Ethiopian province. And we are waiting for the dust to settle in Iraq to find out if the Kurdish role in ousting ISIS from parts of northern Iraq will give impetus to the long-held Kurdish quest for an independent Kurdistan.

Conclusion

This brief survey of types of racial and ethnic inequality underscores the intensiveness and extensiveness of both types of inequality. As Du Bois asserted, equality between individuals and groups, of whatever variety, is difficult, if not impossible to attain. As one traces the plight of the African in America, as that African becomes colored, Negro, black, and African-American, what is clear is that these symbolic and name transformations had psychological consequences for both blacks and whites. White America sought to shape blacks in ways which would continue subservience to whites. Yet, blacks would shape the American cultural and political landscape in ways deemed unthinkable to many whites.

SEE ALSO: Colonialism and Postcolonialism; Crime and Juvenile Delinquency, Sociology of; Immigration, Migration, and Refugees; Race and Ethnicity; Social Movements and Social Change; Stereotypes, Prejudice, and Discrimination; Stigma

References

Du Bois, W.E.B. [1903] 1961. *Souls of Black Folk*. New York: Fawcett Books.
Du Bois, W.E.B. [1940] 1968. *Dusk of Dawn*. New York: Schocken Books.
King, M.L. 1964. *Why We Can't Wait*. New York: New American Library.
Myrdal, G. 1944. *An American Dilemma*. New York: Harper and Row.

Internet, the

Charalambos Tsekeris

Academy of Athens, Greece

The internet is a global network of interconnected computer hardware and software systems, which enables users to store, retrieve, circulate, and process information and communication across time and space. From a sociological perspective, the production, transmission, and reception of information and communication are embedded in socially and historically structured contexts and processes. This renders the internet more than a global information machine, or a communication medium, and places emphasis on the sociocultural dynamics of the constituent internet technologies, as well as on the vast complexity of new types of meaningful action, interaction, experience, subjectivity, and identity formation that stretches across the digital world (Tsekeris and Katerelos 2014).

Such complexity both enables and restricts communication and the accessing and distributing of information. But most importantly, it leads to a radical interconnection of people (and technological systems) and reorganization of social relationships in the time–space continuum, with both intended and unintended consequences for human social life, groups, and societies that need to be studied and understood.

In this context, the internet, especially after the advent of Web 2.0 (or Social Web), deserves the attention of sociologists as an important tool for collecting data and for accessing information, requiring new automated data extraction techniques, quantitative methods of rigorous analysis, and robust empirical findings about the organization and performance of online communities and virtual worlds, where the corporeal (or physical), as we have hitherto known it, is dynamically reconfigured. Of course, online techniques and methods not only change the way we do sociology (or social science in general), but also transform the very substance (object) of the modern sociological enterprise.

In other words, the very practice of these techniques and methods is performative; it is more or less constitutive of (and for) what increasingly counts as "normal" social scientific activity. In addition, the internet-based environments expand the opportunities and arenas for circulating research results and for supporting critical reflection, learning, and debate. Hence, a comprehensive understanding of the internet lies beyond the disciplinary boundaries of sociology and can only be developed jointly, from a multidisciplinary approach. This is obvious in contemporary studies of computer-mediated communication and "cyberculture," which have been taken up by researchers from diverse disciplinary backgrounds.

Furthermore, the development and use of the internet (and social media in particular) cannot be separated from the complex and contradictory changes that are taking place in our increasingly globalized, reflexive, and information-saturated world. To a large extent, the internet itself, as a technology of communication, contributes to the construction, mediation, and disclosure of what these changes are. At the same time, the internet enmeshes with the cultural transformations associated with the rise of modern societies, posing the need for a far greater awareness to the situated, cultural, and political contexts of its use (Fuchs 2015).

Sociology thus re-contextualizes critical issues of justice, power, and domination, emphasizing the communicational, political, economic, ethical, and normative aspects of the internet and its use, or a combination of these. This includes the study of how the internet, as a contested terrain, is facilitating diversity and innovation, impacting on democracy, social movements, and activism, rearranging the public sphere and civil society, reinvigorating participation and citizenship, and redefining freedom of expression and discussion (see Castells 2015). For sociologists, the various struggles for visibility and attention via information technology have become important topics of research.

Despite the rise of a wide range of alternative forms of collaboration, community building, communication, and media production, many scholars pose urgent questions around the digital divide, exploitation of digital labour, corporate dominance, ownership, and control over large parts of the media and communication technology, infrastructure, and content, as well as around data theft or fraud, security, and the systematic large-scale surveillance and massive manipulation of internet users, within an increasingly commercialized online environment. This calls for new forms of policy and regulation, able to affect internet access and content, and to promote sharing, pluralism, and the deconcentration of power, as well as to define the connections with other media.

Nowadays, a wide range of previously offline devices (such as TV sets, refrigerators, coffee machines, and cameras), smart wearable devices (such as activity trackers), and measurement sensors are connected to the internet, creating the "Internet of Things" (IoT) or "Internet of Everything" (IoE). This provokes a huge explosion in data volumes and calls for entirely new paradigms for running our hypernetworked societies (Helbing 2015). What we arguably need is to find new ways of organizing the internet, as well as new concepts, research methods, and frameworks that can be placed in the service of generating a more critical understanding of internet developments.

SEE ALSO: Media, Sociology of the; Science and Technology, Sociology of; Social Media and Virtual Communities; Social Network Analysis

References

Castells, Manuel. 2015. *Networks of Outrage and Hope: Social Movements in the Internet Age*. New York: John Wiley & Sons.

Fuchs, Christian. 2015. *Culture and Economy in the Age of Social Media*. New York: Routledge.

Helbing, Dirk. 2015. *Thinking Ahead: Essays on Big Data, Digital Revolution, and Participatory Market Society*. Berlin: Springer.

Tsekeris, Charalambos, and Ioannis Katerelos, eds. 2014. *The Social Dynamics of Web 2.0: Interdisciplinary Perspectives*. London and New York: Routledge.

Further Reading

Rifkin, Jeremy. 2014. *The Zero Marginal Cost Society: The Internet of Things, the Collaborative Commons, and the Eclipse of Capitalism*. New York: Palgrave Macmillan.

Intersectionality

Kylan Mattias de Vries

Southern Oregon University, USA

The study of intersectionality is interdisciplinary and can be found in the humanities, social sciences, health sciences, and legal studies. A key component of the application of intersectionality lies with an analysis of social power, including the analysis of power in relation to identities, inequalities, and the ways knowledge is (re)produced. Intersectionality is also closely linked with political and social change. This refers to the influence of scholar-activists in creating and implementing the study of intersectionality, the ways intersectionality continues to inform the practice of activists and social movement organizations, and how activism informs the theory of knowledge.

An intersectional framework emerged from black feminist critique and activism in the United States that challenged the essentialist categories of *woman* and/or *black*. In 1974, the Combahee River Collective released a statement calling for an "integrated analysis" that considered the multiple interconnections of systems of oppression. During this time, a number of black women scholar-activists further highlighted the importance of acknowledging and interrogating the ways oppressions interconnected within and amongst each of their identity memberships. bell hooks (1984) critiqued the universalizing of *woman* in feminist activism and scholarship and called for an examination of interlocking oppressions in her book *Feminist Theory: From Margin to Center*. In 1989, Kimberlé Crenshaw, a legal scholar, coined the term *intersectionality* in her analysis of the exclusion of women of color in the US legal system which only understood their experiences in terms of race *or* gender rather than integrated and simultaneous. Since that time, the study of intersectionality has expanded exponentially.

Cho, Crenshaw, and McCall's (2013) three groupings are helpful in understanding the numerous directions and applications of the study of intersectionality, particularly within sociology. These groupings include: 1) the application of intersectional analysis in research and teaching; 2) the interrogation of the methodological and theoretical utility of intersectionality; and 3) the application of an intersectional lens for political and social change.

A number of sociologists utilize the study of intersectionality and have influenced its development and directions. First, sociologists have applied intersectionality in their research and teaching. Influential among these is Patricia Hill Collins's work, particularly in terms of race, class, and gender. Collins (2000) not only introduced intersectionality within sociology, but she has also had a significant influence on the directions of the study of intersectionality overall.

Race, ethnicity, class, gender, sexuality, age, and nationality are facets of intersectionality more commonly explored, but additional facets include religion, (dis)ability, body size, language, culture, and (de)colonization. The applications of the study of intersectionality within sociology entail: (1) the questioning of knowledge production, theories of knowledge, and the idea of objectivity (similar to poststructuralism); (2) the analysis of power and disruption of normative structures; (3) understanding the political and social importance of identities while simultaneously addressing how they inform and are informed by social institutions and social structures; (4) the questioning of the sociological cannon and valuing of the single-axis for analysis; and (5) incorporating social justice to further social change. This fifth application in sociological research and practice overlaps with Cho, Crenshaw, and McCall's (2013) third framing of the study of intersectionality, the use of intersectionality in political and social change. In fact, since scholar-activists were, and often still are, the ones developing the study of intersectionality, it is arguably a critical component (see Collins's book *Black Feminist Thought*).

Second, scholar-activists debate the theoretical and methodological scope of intersectionality. What the study of intersectionality may bring to sociology also raises critiques. The deconstruction of knowledge and dismantling of categories brings challenges to conducting social research. In order to provide generalizations about our social world, the concern is that the application of multiple axes, facets, or categories will diminish any generalizable results. Furthermore, some misunderstandings around the application of intersectionality have included debates about identity politics; this includes questions regarding level of analysis (e.g., identities, categories, institutions, social structures, etc.). In response, intersectional sociologists highlight the connection of identities or categories with social systems and the ways these systems are interdependent of one another.

Another concern about the application of the study of intersectionality has been its roots in black feminism and thus a focus on (particular) marginalized identities, specifically with a focus on race (black) and gender (women). While marginality and social oppression are key aspects in understanding and applying an intersectional lens, because the study of intersectionality is linked to social power, scholars also apply this lens to normative and privileged categories/structures; for instance, sociologists explore intersections of whiteness, heterosexuality, and/or masculinities. Other scholars have further applied intersectionality to challenging the perpetuation of binary categorizations (e.g., woman/man, black/white, gay/straight, etc.). Sociologists have explored the experiences of groups of people that highlight the social construction and fragility of these binaries; some of these have included intersectional studies on the experiences of transgender people of color, Latinx people, queers of color, mixed-race people, and indigenous peoples.

The study of intersectionality offers a framework for sociologists to challenge single-axis methods which tend to suggest universal experiences around identities, categories, and systems. Intersectionality further supports the aim of sociology to explore our social world and the dynamics of social life from multiple perspectives, levels of analysis, and theories of knowledge.

SEE ALSO: Epistemology, Feminist theory, Poststructuralism and Postmodernism, Stratification and inequality, Structure and agency

References

Cho, Sumi, Kimberlé Williams Crenshaw, and Leslie McCall. 2013. "Toward a Field of Intersectionality Studies: Theory, Applications, and Praxis." *Signs* 38 (4): 785–810. DOI:10.1086/669608.

Collins, Patricia Hill. 2000. *Black Feminist Thought: Knowledge, Consciousness, and the Politics of Empowerment.* New York: Routledge.

Crenshaw, Kimberlé. 1989. "Demarginalizing the Intersection of Race and Sex: A Black Feminist Critique of Antidiscrimination Doctrine, Feminist Theory and Antiracist Politics." *University of Chicago Legal Forum* 1989 (1): 139–167.

Hooks, Bell. 1984. *Feminist Theory: From Margin to Center.* Cambridge, MA: South End.

Further Reading

Collins, Patricia Hill. 2015. "Intersectionality's Definitional Dilemmas." *Annual Review of Sociology* 41: 1–20. DOI:10.1146/annurev-soc-073014-112142.

Knowledge, Sociology of

E. Doyle McCarthy

Fordham University, USA

The sociology of knowledge studies the social and group origins of the entire "ideational realm" (knowledges, ideas, theories, mentalities), examining how the mental life of a group of people arises within the context of the groups and institutions in which people live and act. More recently, its subject matter has included not only a society's authoritative ideas and formal knowledges (like science, law, religion) but also those which operate in the realm of the quotidian, informal knowledges that people draw from in everyday life.

The term "sociology of knowledge" (*Wissenssoziologie*) was first used in 1924 and 1929 by Max Scheler and Karl Mannheim, respectively. In their works, the field of the sociology of knowledge reflected the nineteenth-century German philosophical interest in problems surrounding relativism that were linked to the legacies of Karl Marx, Friedrich Nietzsche, and the historicists, whose cultural philosophy of worldviews (*Weltanschauungsphilosophie*) was influential in German social science from the 1890s to the 1930s. *Wissenssoziologie* would serve as an empirical and historical method for resolving the intense conflicts of ideologies in Weimar Germany that followed political and social revolutions of the nineteenth and early twentieth centuries and produced warring groups whose battles were manifestly ideational and grounded in conflicting worldviews. The sociology of knowledge would provide a method for unmasking the assumptions of political ideologies and indicating their truth content as well. However much Scheler and Mannheim differed about the nature of truth within relativism, both agreed that truths do not exist apart from historical and social processes.

The excitement and urgency with which the framers of *Wissenssoziologie* approached the study of the social origins of ideas has been replaced today by a widespread acceptance of their premises concerning the social origins of ideas, ideologies, and worldviews. Many of the positions advanced by sociologists of knowledge operate today as working propositions for a range of social scientists as well as for specialists in other disciplines, like the history of ideas, social studies of science, feminist theories, and cultural studies. Partly because of the diffusion of the idea of the social nature of knowledge, the sociology of knowledge has been described as a field that has no unified field, but only a series of theoretical works and research agendas.

Therefore, one may speak of two ways of introducing the sociology of knowledge. The *broad approach* identifies a range of works in sociology that examines the social nature of mind and knowledge. In this broad or general sense, the sociology of knowledge is a field that systematizes the leading propositions of the modern social sciences about the social nature of mind. Furthermore, like sociology, the sociology of knowledge constitutes a tradition of inquiry that reflects and shapes the development of "modernity" itself, a construction in the making since the eighteenth century. In this respect, sociology offers a theory of the human mind that is compatible with "our time" (Wolff 1953).

A second way of defining the sociology of knowledge, the *particular approach*, considers the field as a special body of work and examines its origins, development, and future prospects. This approach begins with the original statements of Scheler and Mannheim and proceeds to later works and arguments. One of the merits of this approach is that it allows for a critical view of the sociology of knowledge over time and, in keeping with the field's presuppositions about the existential determination of thought (*Seinsgebundenheit*), opens the question of how social theories of knowledge are themselves subject to change and revision over time.

Using the particular approach, a brief history of its statements and theories offers more than a recounting of its nature and scope. It also draws attention to the reflexive features of all sociological inquiries, particularly the fact that sociology is part of the social reality it studies in that its changing concepts and insights develop out of and address particular social worlds.

For Scheler ([1924] 1980), the *forms* of mental acts, through which knowledge is gained, are always conditioned by the structure of society. For this reason, sociology of knowledge is foundational to all specialized studies of culture and to metaphysics. While Scheler's original essays provoked commentary and debate, it was Mannheim's formulation of the discipline in *Ideology and Utopia* ([1929] 1936) that defined the subject matter of the field for years to come.

Mannheim's treatise begins with a review and critique of the prevailing and authoritative Marxist theories of ideology (the "particular theory of ideology") and proceeds toward a theory of ideology in the broader sense: the mental structure in its totality as it appears in different currents of thought and across different social groups. This "total conception of ideology" examines thought on the structural level, allowing the same object to take on different (group) aspects. The "total conception of ideology" defines the subject matter of the sociology of knowledge. Like ideologies, "utopias" arise out of particular social and political conditions but they are distinguished by their opposition to the prevailing order. Utopias are the embodiment of "wish images" in collective actions that shatter and transform social worlds partially or entirely. Both concepts form part of Mannheim's theoretical apparatus for a critical but nonevaluative treatment of "ideology" that supersedes the sociohistorical determinism and relativism of Marxism while moving toward a "relationist" notion of truth; truth is always defined relative to a people's social life and its uses of religion, law, and science as authoritative bodies of knowledge.

Mannheim examines how collective actions and ideas (ideologies and utopias) emerge out of and are "determined" by the multiple social contexts and positions of their proponents. From an analysis of the various and competing social positions of ideologists and utopians, a kind of "truth" emerges that is grounded in the conditions of intellectual objectivity and detachment from the social conditions that more directly determine ideas. *Ideology and Utopia* established the criteria for a valid knowledge, albeit a *relational* knowledge, of sociohistorical processes. It raised problems surrounding the historicity of thought and did this within the newly emerging academic discourse of sociology, thereby giving legitimacy to a new set of methodological problems involving the problems of objectivity and truth for the sciences and the humanities.

Werner Stark's *The Sociology of Knowledge* (1958) prompted a redirection of the field, arguing for a place for the sociology of knowledge within the larger field of cultural sociology. His book also served as an introduction to the field, offering a comprehensive history of the sociology of knowledge and its most significant ideas: theories of ideology of Marx and Mannheim; philosophical speculations of the neo-Kantians Heinrich Rickert and Max Weber; views of the German phenomenological school of the 1920s, especially Scheler. The central argument of this treatise was that the sociology of knowledge is concerned with the "social determination of knowledge," not with the problem of ideology. This meant that all of mental life is grounded in conditions that are ineluctably social and historical and grants to "social determination" a depth that the theory of ideology does not permit, since that theory deals only with errors and misperceptions (Stark [1958] 1991: 50–55).

Berger and Luckmann's *The Social Construction of Reality* (1966) advanced a sociology of knowledge that was compatible with the view of sociology as a humanistic discipline and the notion that "human reality" is a "socially constructed reality." These authors broadened the field to include all types of knowledge, including the knowledge of everyday life. What Berger and Luckmann proposed was that knowledge and reality (by which they always mean social reality) exist in a reciprocal relationship of mutual constitution thereby placing the sociology of knowledge on an entirely new footing, one whose focus is the broad range of signifying systems that form and communicate the realm of social realities. Since its publication, the idea of a "constructed reality" has summarized a number of concerns of contemporary writers in the sciences and humanities, best described as the problem of meaning and the use of philosophical, literary, and historical approaches to study the social construction of meaning.

The methodological implications of this change in the sociology of knowledge are noteworthy since interest in the problem of meaning is linked to a methodological framework that is neither causal nor explanatory (the attitudes expressed by Mannheim's theory of "social determination") but *semiotic*. The semiotic study of culture is directed toward the study of the symbolic and signifying systems through which a social order is communicated and reproduced. These signifying systems and social practices make up a culture and its structures of meaning.

More recently, "the new sociology of knowledge" (Swidler and Arditi 1994; McCarthy 1996) can be seen as part of this larger movement in the social sciences generally, distinguished by a turn away from materialist theories or theories of social structure and in the direction of semiotic theories that focus on the ways in which a society's multifarious meanings are communicated and reproduced, how specific kinds of social organizations (e.g., the media through which knowledge is preserved, organized, and transmitted) order knowledges rather than examining social locations and group interests. These scholars also examine in light of new theories of social power and practice

(Michel Foucault and Pierre Bourdieu), how knowledges maintain social hierarchies and how techniques of power are simultaneously and historically linked to discursive forms (knowledges). They also argue that newer theories of power, gender, and knowledge depart from the economic, class, and institutional focus of the classical sociology of knowledge.

This brief overview of the sociology of knowledge from Mannheim to contemporary sociology lends itself to the type of interpretive scheme that originated with classic works in this field, one that opposes any formal understanding of knowledge. The sociology of knowledge examines how changes in the ideational realm correspond to changes in the structures and organizations of social worlds. Today, for example, sociology has witnessed a shift, roughly from since mid-twentieth century to now, from "social structure" to "culture" as authoritative schemes for describing and interpreting how social knowledges are "socially determined" and how social realities are "constructed" by knowledges.

While sociology's "cultural turn" has been effectively felt in contemporary works of the sociology of knowledge, it is likely, in decades to come, that the sociology of knowledge will take a new direction. One possible direction for social theory has been proposed by Isaac Reed (2011): an "explanatory" model that replaces the older idea that knowledges are "determined" by social factors, factors once conceived as social facts existing outside of the world of interpretations. As Reed argues, the explanations we seek in sociology always include meaning and signification as part of everything "social" that we study. Interpretations are always there framing the social facts *and* the social theories we employ as important explanations of what people do and why they do them. One implication of this argument is that all fields of sociology should move beyond the persistent opposition of "explanation" and "interpretation," the signposts that have directed us to follow one methodology versus another and to see these as fundamentally opposing viewpoints.

In place of this long opposition, social theory and the sociology of knowledge can become fields that engage the social scientist in *explanations*, studies of the effects of systems of meanings on the lives of social actors themselves and on the social movements and social communities they share with others. Described this way, Reed's proposals for the uses of social theory allow us to recapture the excitement of the framers of *Wissenssociologie*. By returning to this field of study we can work to uncover new and better explanations for how and why social actors embrace certain ideas and ideologies over others, how collective actions and ideas (ideologies and utopias) emerge out of and are "determined" by the multiple social contexts and positions of their proponents. Sociologists of knowledge can provide empirical–causal accounts – "explanation through maximal interpretation" – that provide incisive explanations about the social sources of the concepts of social life that each of us carry with us, conceptions that bear the weight of their consequences in the worlds that we share with others. This may be a much-needed approach for today's highly contentious cultural and ideological climate.

SEE ALSO: Culture, Sociology of; Epistemology; Frames, Narratives, and Ideology; Modernity; Sociological Theory

References

Berger, Peter, and Thomas Luckmann. 1966. *The Social Construction of Reality*. New York: Doubleday.

Mannheim, Karl. [1929] 1936. *Ideology and Utopia*. New York: Harcourt, Brace & World.

McCarthy, E. Doyle. 1996. *Knowledge as Culture: The New Sociology of Knowledge*. New York and London: Routledge.

Reed, Isaac Ariail. 2011. *Interpretation and Social Knowledge: On the Use of Theory in the Human Sciences*. Chicago: University of Chicago Press.

Scheler, Max. [1924] 1980. *Problems of a Sociology of Knowledge*, translated and edited by M.S. Frings, and with an introduction by K.W. Stikkers. London: Routledge & Kegan Paul.

Stark, Werner. [1958] 1991. *The Sociology of Knowledge*, with a new introduction by E. Doyle McCarthy. New Brunswick, NJ: Transaction.

Swidler, Ann, and Jorge Arditi. 1994. "The New Sociology of Knowledge." *Annual Review of Sociology* 20: 305–329.

Wolff, Kurt H. 1953. "A Preliminary Inquiry into the Sociology of Knowledge from the Standpoint of the Study of Man. In *Scritti di Sociologia e Politica in Onore di Luigi Sturzo*. Bologna: Nicola Zanichelli, III.

Life Course

Jeylan T. Mortimer

University of Minnesota, USA

The life course is a conceptual paradigm encompassing all stages of human life from birth to death within their changing social structural contexts. Emerging in the latter half of the twentieth century, this paradigm has had major influence across sociological subfields (e.g., social psychology, family, work, and health) as well as in other social sciences (e.g., history, economics, psychology, demography, epidemiology, public health). This entry considers the development of this approach, its central ideas, current research topics, and future directions.

The life course perspective originated in the "social structure and personality" school of social psychology, which recognized age as a key social location affecting individual values, attitudes, and behaviors. Rapid changes in modernizing societies (e.g., urbanization, industrialization, technological innovation, migration, and other trends) highlighted change at both "macro" and "micro" social levels, spurring dissatisfaction with static conceptualizations. Increasingly, both social structures and individuals were seen as moving targets. Glen Elder's classic, *Children of the Great Depression* (1974), served as a catalyst, as it introduced what were to become dominant life course concepts. Using archival methods applied to longitudinal data, Elder showed that even short distances between birth cohorts, when coupled with dramatic historical events, fundamentally altered the course of individual lives. Children born in the years 1928–1929 were very young when the Great Depression struck; they had little comprehension of the reasons their parents were distraught and could do nothing to help them. In contrast, those born in the years 1920–1921 experienced the Depression as adolescents; they understood why their families suffered economic hardship, and they could assist them. These contrasting experiences had major repercussions throughout their lives.

Several key themes guide scholars of the life course (Elder, Johnson, and Crosnoe 2003). Individual lives unfold within, and are shaped by, their historical contexts; the life course of a woman born in 1920 differs markedly from one born in 1960. Cohort replacement, as older cohorts die off and newer ones replace them, drives social change. Moreover, within cohort heterogeneity (e.g., by gender, social class, ethnicity) affects life patterns. Human biographies may be characterized as sequences of age-graded

Core Concepts in Sociology, First Edition. Edited by J. Michael Ryan.
© 2019 John Wiley & Sons Ltd. Published 2019 by John Wiley & Sons Ltd.

social roles or trajectories within institutional spheres (e.g., family, work, civic participation), marked by transitions signaling new expectations, opportunities, and constraints. The timing and sequencing of these transitions are important (e.g., parenthood will have distinct developmental and social consequences if it occurs at age 17 versus 28). The life course is a quintessentially social phenomenon; life course transitions and events reverberate via linked lives throughout the social network. For example, a divorce affects not only the marital partners, but also their children, parents, and close friends. People take on new identities as they move through their lives. These characterize the life course as a whole – e.g., child, adolescent, adult; as well as within institutional careers – e.g., worker and retiree. Normative expectations govern major life transitions (e.g., taking on adult role markers), which are accompanied by shifts in age-linked identities and realizations that one is "on time," "early," or "late." The concept of bounded agency recognizes that individuals may be considered architects of their lives, as they set goals, devise action strategies, and enlist others to attain their objectives. In doing so, they may undergo turning points, altering multiple trajectories (e.g., from a delinquent to a law-abiding youth) at once, with widespread repercussions. However, agentic processes are constrained by social structural location. Individual attributes and circumstances at any given time cannot be understood without considering earlier experiences (e.g., resources and opportunities in retirement reflect the entire work history). Mounting evidence points to complex reciprocal processes of development, as individuals exercise agency in selecting life course contexts, in molding their environments in accord with their interests, values, and behavioral dispositions, and as these contexts simultaneously feed back on, and often accentuate personal traits.

Understanding the life course is enriched by a variety of methods, including large-scale multi-wave prospective surveys and qualitative approaches, such as in-depth life history interviews, ethnographic studies, and mixed methods research. The diversity of research questions, conceptual developments, methodologies, and analytic techniques animating contemporary life course studies are explicated in Volumes I and II of the *Handbook of the Life Course* (Mortimer and Shanahan 2003; Shanahan, Mortimer, and Johnson 2016). Recent institutional and historical changes have led life course researchers to extend their investigations beyond family, education, and work trajectories to new substantive territory (e.g., military service, incarceration, and disaster). Mechanisms through which inequality throughout the life course affects trajectories of cognitive functioning, and both mental and physical health, are of major contemporary concern. Theoretical critiques have prompted reconceptualization of agency and other psychological and behavioral phenomena as structurally determined, grounded especially in stratification processes; the reconsideration of age as a continually changing social construction; and increased attention to the legal-regulatory contexts of aging. Growing interdisciplinary collaboration between the life sciences and social sciences draws attention to genetic transmission as potentially contributing to individual/environment interactions that affect trajectories of health and other life outcomes. Recent methodological work grapples with causality, analytic procedures to elucidate trajectories of individual growth and decline, and spatial studies of neighborhood, peer group, and other micro-level contextual influences. With the recent institutionalization of this paradigm through the interdisciplinary and international *Society for Longitudinal and*

Life Course Studies, life course concepts are diffusing rapidly across the social sciences and increasingly informing policies surrounding state intervention to alleviate life course risks.

SEE ALSO: Aging, Sociology of; Family and Kinship, Sociology of; Frames, Narratives, and Ideology; Identity; Social Psychology; Social Theory; Socialization

References

Elder, Glen H., Jr. 1974. *Children of the Great Depression: Social Change in Life Experience.* Chicago: University of Chicago Press.

Elder, Glen H., Jr., Monica Kirkpatrick Johnson, and Robert Crosnoe. 2003. "The Emergence and Development of Life Course Theory." In Jeylan T. Mortimer and Michael J. Shanahan (eds.), *Handbook of the Life Course,* Vol. I, 3–19. New York: Kluwer Academic/Plenum Publishers.

Mortimer, Jeylan T., and Michael J. Shanahan, eds. 2003. *Handbook of the Life Course,* Vol. I. New York: Kluwer Academic/Plenum Publishers.

Shanahan, Michael J., Jeylan T. Mortimer, and Monica Kirkpatrick Johnson, eds. 2016. *Handbook of the Life Course,* Vol. II. New York: Springer.

Marxism

Alan Spector

Purdue University Northwest, USA

The inherently interdisciplinary nature of Marxist social theory makes it difficult to completely differentiate Marxist sociology from Marxist philosophy, Marxist history, Marxist political science, Marxist economics, Marxist anthropology, and even Marxist cultural criticism. Sociology, itself, did not come into much prominence until decades after the Communist Manifesto formalized Marxism as a world view (1848), and many of the social scientists who have contributed to a Marxist-oriented sociology were themselves not sociologists.

Karl Marx (1818–1883) – along with Emile Durkheim (1857–1917) and Max Weber (1864–1920) – is considered one of the foundation theorists of modern Western sociology. It is not simply the work of these three that makes them important, but also how they reflect the key processes of human social life – material labor, culture, and ideas respectively. (One can find a rough analogue in folklore: body, soul, and mind.) It is simplistic to categorize all three in absolutist ways. Durkheim, with his emphasis on the division of labor and culture is considered a "functionalist" and yet he was a socialist interested in economics and ideas. Weber was interested in economics and religion, in addition to his emphasis on ideas and their manifestations in organizational structures and processes. Marx, along with his long-term associate Friedrich Engels (1820–1895), is often wrongly stereotyped as being narrowly interested in economics despite the fact that his interest derived from human labor, alienation, and freedom and his writing of over 50 books demonstrates some interest in the world of ideas! However, it is true that these three had sharply different emphases and analyses of how social forces, social processes, and social institutions interact.

Marx is the only one who has had an "ism" attached to his name because Marxism is a sociological analysis/framework, a philosophical analysis/framework, a cultural analysis/framework, an economic analysis/framework, a political analysis/framework, and the loose framework for political movements that have influenced, in one way or another, hundreds of millions of people worldwide including artists, economists, presidents of major sociology organizations, and even many important biologists and physicists. There have been massive movements that, at one time, governed perhaps one third of the Earth's population. As such, there are hundreds of variations of "Marxism" – sometimes hostile to each other. Within sociology there are similar debates

Core Concepts in Sociology, First Edition. Edited by J. Michael Ryan.

over to what degree "agency" (individual decisions) and "structure" (political–economic institutions and processes) influence various aspects of society, although virtually everyone within Marxian frameworks agree that both are important and that there is a dialectical interaction between them.

The core of the Marxist sociological perspective comes from the question of what makes us human (our activity/our labor including our relationships with others) and what prevents us from becoming fully human (what constrains, controls our labor and alienates us from ourselves and others.) From this comes Marx's focus on human labor and production. Contrary to popular conception, the important contribution of Marx's analysis was not simply about "unequal distribution and sharing" but rather was especially focused on *what constrained humankind's ability to produce – material goods but also constructive culture and non-exploitative human relationships.* Why and how human activity, human labor is created, controlled, and directed is a reflection of our humanity. Production, broadly defined, becomes the link between the philosopher's quest for "freedom" and the economist's focus on economic processes. Grasping this dialectical process can overcome the false dichotomy within Marxist social thought about "human freedom" and "economic determinism."

Most sociologists including Marxists understand that social processes and social institutions don't simply come from ideas in a one-directional way but rather that ideas themselves are generated and nurtured by social structure and social relationships. For that reason it is impossible to accurately discuss a sociological framework, including Marxist ones, out of the context of their interaction with society. Actual social movements had a profound impact on the direction that various forms of Marxist social theory took over the past century and a half.

Young Marx was particularly focused on questions of human freedom and alienation. Later, Marx, along with Engels, seemed to emphasize economics more. That has led some to argue that there were two different Marxs. Others believe that Marx's economic theories flow organically from his earlier views on freedom, alienation, and human labor. It is the tension between those who put heaviest emphasis on psychology and culture versus the perspective that emphasizes economic processes and structures (or as expressed above: between "human freedom" and "economic determinism") that frames the major debates within Marxist social theory. However, a structural analysis based on understanding the economic processes of production and distribution can fully incorporate political and cultural trends without doing it in a narrow, mechanical way. It is not necessary to "choose sides" in the debate between "agency" and "structure."

In activist social movements, another central debate is between "reformism" and "revolution." Some in the Marxist tradition are not concerned with analyzing internal contradictions or dialectics and are primarily focused on the material reform aspects of Marxism including especially alleviating poverty and creating economic equality. Some others in the Marxist tradition focus on dialectics but emphasize ideas, culture, and psychological processes without fully taking into account the material-structural processes. However, there have been reformist-minded and revolutionary-minded theorists from both orientations.

Marxism is concerned with trends rather than predicting individual events. The mode of analysis used by Marx and Engels has been called "dialectical materialism," although Marx never used that term. Dialectical materialism is based both on two inseparable concepts: "materialism" – that the material world preexists the world of ideas – and "dialectics" – that the material world itself is constantly changing as a result of internal contradictions within every process and the interactions between that process and other processes, and further, that some of those changes are profoundly irreversible rather than simply quantitative back and forth.

Political leaders sometimes took shortcuts and summarized aspects of Marxist social theory in ways that rationalized and justified their strategies, often "freezing" aspects of Marxist social theory and treating it as if it were some kind of mechanical dogma. Marx believed that class relations were key to understanding social change; this was often narrowly misinterpreted to mean that taking wealth away from the rich and giving it to the working class was the fundamental goal of the movement. Marx discussed "stages of history" as stages of economic production in a broad way; this was often mistaken to be a precise roadmap for social change. Marx believed that ideas, in the main, reflected the social–economic relations of the society; this was often mistaken to assert that all ideas were mere mirror reflections of economic battles. The dialectical core of Marxist analysis, the core that emphasizes contradiction and change, was often ignored or applied in mechanical ways that actually were undialectical!

As a reaction against this, there were those in the Marxist tradition who moved sharply away from economic analysis. The *Frankfurt School* combined aspects of Marxist dialectics with an emphasis on culture and psychology, including psychoanalytical perspectives. This tension over the emphasis between "ideas" and "social structure" exists today, although there have been many in all fields of social science who understand how ideas may originate in social relations but they become profoundly important in shaping the material world. V.I. Lenin to some degree, in politics, and Gramsci and Lukacs in social theory, were among the earlier Marxists who developed the understanding of the relationship of the "economic base" to the "idea superstructure" without expressing it in narrow, shallow ways.

Marxist theory is not mechanically deterministic. It utilizes a kind of "probabilistic determinism," not unlike the way sophisticated scientists develop theory. There are patterns, not necessarily "laws," but patterns that can be broadly predictable. In the same sense that a game will generally go through certain stages beyond the complete conscious control of individual people, so too do economic processes (as manifestations, ultimately of humans' struggle to control our activity/labor) go through certain stages. This does not mean that every case follows exactly the same pattern but that there is a general pattern. Marxist theory sees itself as "scientific" rather than "moralistic" and while its goals may be consistent with many people's visions of morality – economic equality, no exploitation, no sexism or racism, no alienation or psychological domination – Marxist theory sees social processes unfolding in ways that are broadly highly probable to the point of being "virtually inevitable." (Of course an asteroid can slam into the Earth and put a stop to all these processes and of course, on a smaller level, a revolutionary movement can be sidetracked by certain cultural developments).

What is distinctive about Marxism is not simply its concern for improving the material wellbeing of people nor its use of a dialectical method of analysis. What is distinctive is the concept of class and class struggle as the driving force in human society. Class is not simply how much money someone has – the "common sense" quantitative concept using terms such as "upper class, middle class, lower class." It is much more complex. Class is a relationship, a qualitative concept referring to what is someone's relationship to why and how goods, services, culture, and ideas are produced in society. In that sense, the "class struggle" can be seen as a struggle to reorganize society rather than a struggle to acquire material goods. While many socialists today eschew the strategy of armed revolution, Marx himself believed that the struggle to reorganize society would most probably be forced for self-protection to use violence to counter the violence of the capitalist class. That does not mean that Marxists support terrorism or random violence.

In every organized society some people own and control the means of production and other people work for them. Of course there are some intermediary groups and some people with aspects of both classes, but the main struggle was between the owners and the producers, the laborers. This is not the same as the haves and the have-nots struggling over material products or about simple inequality, as Piketty and others emphasize, although it sometimes takes this form. *At its core Marxism is struggle over control of production*, where decisions are made about what is produced and how it is produced. Of course how it is distributed is a key part of that process.

Central to this is Marx's concept of the "labor theory of value." The Labor Theory of Value asserts that the ultimate value of a commodity is determined by the minimum amount of labor it takes to produce it or an exact copy plus, on a societal level, also the cost of reproducing the labor force. Competition forces the rate of profit to drop, leading first to overproduction and then to economic stagnation. This does not mean that the price of something is immediately reducible to the cost of producing it, but it does set the limits of what a business or a system of businesses can tolerate before it is forced to cease production. As with other social theorists, Marxists understand that social institutions do not function exactly the way individual people do. There are certain patterns of behavior that are different for institutions than for individuals. This is a rejection of reductionist pro-capitalist theories of so-called "human nature" which tries to justify exploitative social systems by asserting that they merely reflect "selfish human nature."

The broad stages of history that Marx used were based on how production (and distribution) were organized. Various class societies constrained production, both material production and scientific/cultural production. Eventually that would create crisis and if the exploited classes were conscious and organized, they would replace it with a system that freed up production (and human potential) more, until eventually class society would disappear and society would be organized on the basis of "From each according to ability; to each according to need" – communism.

While primitive societies experienced a kind of primitive communism for tens of thousands of years, communist society based on modern social organization and science has not come into existence. Socialism was seen as a stepping stone, but major socialist movements made compromises with capitalism that led to its return. Marxists believe that revolutionary change is eventually possible; anti-Marxists believe that it is not.

Marxism has been strongly critiqued by supporters of capitalism, generally by those who rationalize exploitation by asserting that it is fundamental to human nature or society. Within the framework of critical sociology, Marxism has also been critiqued. In recent decades, there has been strong criticism of Marxism as being inadequate to be able to explain discrimination and oppression based on sex/gender and on "race" and ethnicity. Some critique Marxism as not taking into account the global spread of capitalism. While Marxism is sometimes accused of one-sided *"economic determinism"* that does not take psychological factors into account, some Marxists argue that anti-Marxist perspectives on gender and "race-ethnic" oppression may be one-sided as a kind of *"psychological determinism"* asserting that the systems of oppression come from the "mind" rather than from exploitation and social structure. These debates cannot be solved philosophically but rather depend on looking at actual social processes and social structure in various contexts.

Many Marxists acknowledge that Marx's analysis was a product of its historical times and that Marx set out a framework, not a recipe. Just as Darwin set out a general theory of biological evolution, but could not incorporate into that latest developments in genetic research, so too could Marx, writing before automobiles, before the widespread use of electricity, not be able to predict every particular event. But just as Darwin's overall framework of evolution maintains its core even as parts of it have been modified, so too can Marxism retain its core while incorporating new understandings of the complex nature of gender and "race–ethnic" relations. Marx and Engels did address the oppression of women in strong terms, and Marx did address the question of racism, particularly with respect to how black slaves in the United States were exploited and oppressed and how the Irish were mistreated by Britain. That is why many of the strong-est fighters against racism were influenced by Marxism and why, as a case in point, International Women's Day, now celebrated all over the world, was actually first created by the socialists of the early Soviet Union.

While modern imperialism had not fully developed, one can find in Marx's work ele-ments of the critique of how Britain, in particular, was exploiting workers and peasants in its colonies. There are, however, always nuances to be explored in social processes, including gender and "race–ethnic" relations and there are also changes that take place over time. Marxism, then, shares some of the concerns and concepts of some aspects of feminist theory, of anti-racist theory, of World Systems analysis, and of cultural criticism, but Marxism maintains the concept that exploitation of labor, class exploitation, is at the core.

One other controversial updating of Marxism stems from the writings of V.I. Lenin. Lenin analyzed imperialism and saw the processes of capitalism on a global level. As a result, he argued that anti-colonial and anti-imperialist movements were struggles against capitalist exploitation and should be supported. However, there is a fine line between supporting national struggles against imperialism and supporting the nationalism, as an "ism" as a positive, pro-Marxist perspective. Many of the revolu-tionary movements that began as Marxist have devolved into nationalist movements that defend, protect, and even aggressively advance the interests of capitalist interests. This is one of the main reasons for the current decline in the influence of Marxist movements.

Within the revolutionary wing of Marxism, the embracing of nationalism as a positive "ism" and the use of the term "revolutionary nationalism" has clouded the discussion about how to understand the struggle against imperialism as a positive force without embracing nationalism as an "ism." Marx's most famous words, after all, are "Workers of all countries, unite!"

Marxist social science should be understood as a living science, not a dead pseudo-science of static concepts nor its opposite as a philosophical "free for all" based on someone's subjective notions of morality. It is a method of investigation, using exploitation of labor as its fundamental core, but capable of broadening and deepening its analysis to incorporate new understandings and developments in economic, political, social, and cultural processes.

SEE ALSO: Alienation; Capitalism; Class; Class, Capitalist; Economic Sociology; Inequality, Global; Modernity; Poverty; Social Justice; Social Movements and Social Change; Social Theory

Further Reading

Marx and Engels wrote over fifty books. Thousands more have been written about Marxism with many important insights. For those starting to learn about Marxism as a social theory, some basic books are:

Anderson, Kevin B. 2016. *Marx at the Margins: On Nationalism, Ethnicity, and Non-Western Societies*. University of Chicago Press.
Fischer, Ernst, and Franz Marek. 1996. *How to Read Karl Marx*. Monthly Review Press.
Gabriel, Mary. 2012. *Love and Capital: Karl and Jenny Marx and the Birth of a Revolution*. Back Bay Books.
Knapp, Peter, and Alan J. Spector. 2011. *Basic Questions of Marxist Sociology Today*. Rowman & Littlefield.
Ollman, Bertell. 1977. *Alienation: Marx's Conception of Man in a Capitalist Society*, 2nd ed. Cambridge University Press.
Rius. 2003. *Marx for Beginners*. Pantheon.

Masculinities

Sebastián Madrid

P. Universidad Católica de Chile, Chile

Although the vast majority of sociological work during the last century has been done by men, and concerns men (class analysis is an extraordinary example of this), it was not until the late 1970s that men began to be studied as part of gender relations, recognizing the gender dimension in their lives. This change reflects the influence of feminisms of different kinds that, trying to overcome the subordination and oppression of women, started to direct their gaze to the situation of boys, men, and masculinities. The study of men and masculinities is an interdisciplinary and diverse field of knowledge that is generally critical of the current gender order.

The theoretical perspectives in the study of men and masculinities are rich and diverse, ranging from psychoanalysis to poststructuralism, including sex role theory and different strands of Marxism. These approaches have varying conceptions of masculinities and their relations to men and women. They have been shaped through four turning points in the conceptualization of gender: from notions of "male" and "female" (relating to biological sex) to "masculinity" and "femininity" (relating to gender identity) to "masculinities" and "femininities" (recognizing diversity, complexity, and relationship) to the disembodiment of gender (gender as performativity, uncoupled from the sexed body).

Nowadays, the latter two approaches, the materialist and the discursive, are the predominant ones in the Global North (Europe and North America). However, it is important to note that in the Global South there are no sharp distinctions but an eclectic use of both. For instance, in Latin America men's identities have always been studied in relation to other identities, relating the production of those identities to historical changes in economy and politics.

Taking as a basis the materialist or social practices approach, we can define masculinities as a relational concept that emerges as an object of sociological study within gender relations. Although the concept of masculinities refers to men, it goes beyond men, and includes the cultural ideas of what it means to be a man and, especially, the position of men in the gender order. Thus, the concept concerns social practices, and their consequences, in relation to both men and women. Sociologically, then, the concept of masculinities is much more than an assemblage of individual traits, attributes, and behaviors. It follows

Core Concepts in Sociology, First Edition. Edited by J. Michael Ryan.
© 2019 John Wiley & Sons Ltd. Published 2019 by John Wiley & Sons Ltd.

that masculinities are not an individual or psychological characteristic; rather they are part of the interactive process of the making of gender relations.

Currently, there is agreement in the social sciences that masculinities are socially constructed. This means that masculinities have a dynamic character. Masculinities vary historically (through time), culturally (among different societies), contextually (within a given society), and psychologically (during the life course of one individual in the context of gender relations). These variations have led sociologists to speak of "masculinities" in the plural, and rarely treat masculinity as a homogeneous unity or an immutable essence grounded on sex differences. On the contrary, sociological research in recent decades around the world has shown that masculinities can change and that they are complex; research has emphasized their ambiguities and contradictions.

The dynamic process of constructing masculinities occurs at several levels. First, at the personal level, involving the making of identities and definitions of the self in relation to others (for instance, against women and homosexuality). Second, through interactions with other people in the course of everyday life in specific situations. Third, in institutions such as the state or schools where collective practices organize different masculinities and femininities. Fourth, at a cultural or ideological level that involves discourses, meanings, and social norms.

The fact that multiple masculinities exist should not allow analysis to collapse into a typology. On the contrary, we should recognize hierarchies among different patterns of masculinities. Some patterns are more respected and get more benefits from the gender order than others. This idea is expressed in the concept of "hegemonic masculinity" developed by the Australian sociologist Raewyn Connell, one of the main proponents of the materialist approach in the field. Currently, there are debates about whether there are different patterns of hegemonic masculinities, for instance, in different institutional situations or between different cultures.

The social construction of masculinity is a collective and historical process. In the making of masculinities we see the effects of various social divisions, like social class, race, sexuality, and geography. From those divisions emerge different patterns of masculinities. Likewise, the social construction of masculinities is shaped by macro processes like imperialism, colonialism, postcolonialism, globalization, and neoliberalism. For instance, while the media often speak about the crisis of masculinity (in the singular), they commonly obscure the fact that most power positions in society are still held by men, whether in the economic, political, or military fields. Media give little attention to the fact that worldwide domestic violence has not declined yet; nor to the fact that with neoliberal globalization, it is specific groups of men who are in crisis. Those most affected are working-class young men who depend on precarious jobs, indigenous men who have lost their land, and migrant men displaced by war or economic restructuring.

The study of men and masculinities has grown considerably in the last decade; it is now an integral field within sociology. However, there is still much to research and to advocate. Changes in masculinities have arisen in some social sectors and specific contexts, yet the collective privilege of men and masculinities – in bodies, institutions, and culture - is still overwhelming. Sociologically, it is important then to stress the material basis of masculinities. This means not only focusing on the ways in which men as a group are in positions of power and privilege, but also addressing the costs of those privileges for both men and women, and the disadvantage of some groups of men in relation to others. The study of men and masculinities is most effective when carried out as part of an intellectual and political project that aims for social justice and gender equity.

SEE ALSO: Body, the; Constructionism vs. Essentialism; Family and Kinship, Sociology of; Feminist Theory; Gender; Homophobia and Heterosexism; Inequality, Gender; Intersectionality; Patriarchy; Socialization; Sport, Sociology of

Further Reading

Aboim, S. 2010. *Plural Masculinities*. Farnham, UK: Ashgate.

Connell, R. 2005. *Masculinities*, 2nd ed. Cambridge: Polity Press.

Ouzgane, L., and R. Morrell, eds. 2005. *African Masculinities: Men in Africa from the Late Nineteenth Century to the Present*. London: Palgrave.

Pini, B., and B. Pease, eds. 2013. *Men, Masculinities and Methodologies*. London: Palgrave.

Viveros, M., N. Fuller, and J. Olavarría, eds. 2001. *Hombres e identidades de género: Investigaciones desde América Latina* (Men and gender identity: Research from Latin-America). Bogotá: Universidad Nacional de Colombia.

Media, Sociology of the

Michele Sorice

LUISS University, Rome, Italy, and University of Stirling, Scotland, UK

The sociology of the media studies the relationship between communication tools (the media that play a mediating role in the communication among individuals and institutions) and society, using the methods traditionally established within the discipline of sociology, media, and cultural studies. The media, conceived at the same time as framework and content of cultures, are often analyzed as a public space; they also play an important role in the re-shaping of the public sphere. Many media and communications researchers define the relationship between media and democracy as well as the media and the social and political identities as being primarily a sociological one.

Political communication is sometimes framed as a key subject of media sociology, considering the history of the two scientific fields and their common "founding fathers" (Harold Lasswell, Paul Lazarsfeld, Robert Merton and, more generally, so-called *communication research*, a broad area of studies developed in the United States in the first half of the twentieth century).

The sociology of the media has devoted great attention to the basic principles of socio-communicative behavior. In particular, John B. Thompson (1995) has identified some key features of mass communication. They can be summarized as follows: (a) the commodification of symbolic goods and attribution of an economic value to cultural products and, consequently, the birth of the imaginary market; (b) the structural separation between the production of symbolic forms (as media texts and products of imaginary) and their reception (this separation of the study of production and reception of media messages constitutes an important reference point for research into the sociology of the media and has been evident with the emergence of cooperation between production and reception scholars in the internet age); (c) extended accessibility of symbolic forms in space and time; (d) public diffusion of symbolic forms; (e) importance of the technological dimension of communication technologies (but in a theoretical framework which rejects technological determinism).

Thompson's analysis highlights the need to review the relationship between media and society. Several general models have attempted to explain this controversial relationship. A simple classification is the one which lists the different theoretical approaches following the linkages between media and society. We can use a tripartite division which refers to: (1) macro-social models; (2) micro-social models; (3) dynamic models. The macro-models are those who consider the media able to impose itself on society, influencing or determining specific behavioral effects. In this frame we can link certain sociological approaches to the idea of communication as transmission, approaches including determinism, some Marxist perspectives, some aspects of the political economy of the media and most of the functionalist theories and interpretation models. The micro-social models are those that are based on the idea that society "uses" the media: the media, in other words, operate in social dynamics and provide tools for connection and/or self-representation that the society uses more or less consciously. In this area we can place reception studies, some Cultural Studies-based approaches and some tendencies of the Audience Studies (in particular those adopting an *ethnographic approach* to audience analysis). Finally, dynamic models, refer to those approaches, theories, and modeling which consider the media and society as always interconnected, in an interactive way activating a dynamic of mutual influence. Dynamic models reject the idea of the media that deterministically intervene to change the society (macro-social models), or the idea that the media are used by people without any consequences (micro-social models). With dynamic models scholars moved toward the rejection of effects theories, however accepting the logic of social influence. In other words, the dynamic model refuses the simplistic deterministic approach in favor of a holistic look at the relationship between media and society. In this area we can also place studies on the relationships between new/digital media and society. However, the growing importance of digital communication (new media, Web 2.0, social networks, etc.) has facilitated the birth of a new area of study (the *sociology of new/digital media*) which is part of the sociology of the media but which also enjoys a semi-autonomous scientific status.

The sociology of the media uses interdisciplinary approaches and hybrid methods (qualitative and quantitative). Some of its aspects overlap specific areas of other disciplines, such as psychology, performing arts, economics, and political science. Given its interdisciplinary nature, many different topics can fall under the domain of sociology of the media. The media themselves – conceived as media institutions – are one of the topics along with the study of markets, technological innovation, audience reception, political influences, and formal regulations.

The most influential scientific handbooks agree in identifying the emergence and development of the sociology of the media with the birth and growth of electric media in the late nineteenth and early twentieth century. A symbolic term for the birth of the sociology of the media can be represented by the development of the *Payne Fund Studies* (late 1920s, early 1930s) which looked at the impact of movies on children's behavior, as well as the publication of Harold Lasswell's book *Propaganda Techniques in the World* War (1927).

The consolidation of the press and the development of cinema and radio between 1900 and 1920 accompanied the process known as "technical reproduction" of art, defined by the German philosopher Walter Benjamin as a cultural turning point. Benjamin identifies the technical reproducibility of cultural products as a shift in the relationship between masses and art. In the same period a new collective subject emerges: the mass public, viewed with suspicion by the psychologists of crowds and analyzed with contradictory feelings by both US and European scholars. The concept of audience very quickly became a major "sociological issue," in the scientific works of Gabriel Tarde, Georg Simmel, Emile Durkheim, and the Chicago School (whose most prominent representatives were Robert E. Park, Albion W. Small, Ernest W. Burgess and Roderick D. Mackenzie).

The sociology of the media has studied different historical developments, especially those in the United States and Europe. Firstly, scholars have focused their researches on public opinion and media effects. The media effects study has been a very important topic in all fields of media studies and, in particular, in US communication research (whose most influential authors are Harold Lasswell, Paul F. Lazarsfeld, Elihu Katz, and Robert K. Merton).

In the European approach, media sociologists have avoided a strong "media-centered" perspective, preferring to study the relationships among media and power, social and political institutions, class, gender, democratic life, etc. The question of "power," in particular, constitutes one of the key aspects in the cultural studies approach to sociology of the media (in particular in studies by the influential Birmingham's Centre for Contemporary Cultural Studies). Denis McQuail, one the most influential scholars in the sociology of the media, identifies two types of media power and six main features. The two types refer to the so-called models of hegemony and that of pluralism, while the six main characteristics through which the media can exercise power are: (1) the ability to attract and to direct public attention; (2) the ability to persuade the public in matters concerning opinions and beliefs; (3) the ability to influence behavior; (4) the ability to structure the mechanisms of reality definition; (5) the ability to confer status and social acceptance; and (6) the ability to provide information quickly and to a large audience.

According to Denis McQuail (2010) it is possible to distinguish five areas of research in the sociology of the media: (1) media content studies, traditionally focused on broadcast media (radio and TV) and recently also on social/digital media; (2) political economy of communication, in particular the questions of media ownership and of the role of the public media service; (3) the social effects of the media; (4) the impact of media on democracy and on social institutions; (5) the capacity of the media to reshape and to transform the public sphere and/or the public spaces (Habermas 2006; Volkmer 2014).

The sociology of the media can also be categorized into two different perspectives: (a) the transmission paradigm, in which all the studies funded on a top-down model of communication can be collected (i.e., the first era of the US communication research and the effects model, which affirmed the existence of a causal relationship between media messages and public behavior, as it happens in the *magic bullet theory*); (b) the dialogic paradigm, in which we can place all the approaches based upon a circular model of communication and the consideration of the existence of active audiences (i.e., British Cultural Studies, Audience Studies, the latest tendencies of the *uses and gratifications* approach, etc.).

In recent years, the sociology of the media has strengthened its epistemological status but, at the same time, it has accentuated the process of hybridization and contamination with other disciplines. From the methodological point of view, the most recent studies have abandoned the theoretical disputes between quantitative and qualitative, adopting the so-called *mixed methods* and making extensive use of triangulation (a technique facilitating the validation of data through cross-verification from different sources, usually two or more).

SEE ALSO: Culture, Sociology of; Democracy; Internet, the; Political Sociology; Social Media and Virtual Communities

References

Habermas, J. 2006. "Political Communication in Media Society: Does Democracy Still Enjoy an Epistemic Dimension? The Impact of Normative Theory on Empirical Research." *Communication Theory* 16 (4): 11–26.

McQuail, D. 2010. *Mass Communication Theory*. London: Sage.

Thompson, J.B. 1995. *Media and Modernity: A Social Theory of the Media*. Cambridge: Polity Press.

Volkmer, I. 2014. *The Global Public Sphere: Public Communication in the Age of Reflective Interdependence*. Cambridge: Polity.

Further Reading

Burton, G. 2005. *Media and Society: Critical Perspectives*. Maidenhead: Open University Press.

Hall, S, ed. 1997. *Representation: Cultural Representation and Signifying Practices*. London: Sage.

Medical Sociology

William C. Cockerham

University of Alabama at Birmingham, USA

Medical sociology, sometimes referred to as health sociology, is the study of the social causes and consequences of health and illness (Cockerham 2017a). Major areas of investigation include the social determinants of health and disease, causes of health disparities between different groups in society, the social behavior of patients and healthcare providers, the social functions of health organizations and institutions, the social patterns of healthcare utilization, the relationship of healthcare delivery systems to other social institutions, and social welfare policies regarding health. What makes medical sociology important is the critical role social factors play in determining or influencing the health of individuals, groups, and the larger society. Social conditions and situations not only promote and, in some cases, cause illness, but also enhance prospects of disease prevention and a healthy life.

The earliest works in medical sociology in the United States were carried out by physicians who recognized the importance of social factors in medical work, not sociologists who tended initially to ignore the field. This changed in the late 1940s when large amounts of federal funding became available to support joint research projects between sociologists and medical doctors in order to improve the quality of care for the post-World War II population. At its inception, work in medical sociology was oriented toward finding outcomes relevant for clinical medicine. A potential problem in the early development of the field was dependence on medicine for direction, research opportunities, and permission to study medical settings. However, this situation never fully materialized, as medical sociologists adopted an objective and independent approach to the study of healthcare, both as a supportive discipline and critic when warranted. The practice of medicine became one of its major subjects of inquiry, including the doctor–patient relationships and the organization of healthcare delivery systems. Medical sociologists, in turn, brought their own topics to the study of health, such as social stress, health lifestyles, and the social determinants of disease. Medical sociology is now one of the largest and most active groups doing sociological work in North America and Europe, and the field has expanded to Africa, Asia, India, and Latin and South America. Almost one of every ten American sociologists is a medical sociologist.

Talcott Parsons

A critical event in the development of medical sociology as an academic field was the appearance of Talcott Parsons' book, *The Social System,* in 1951. This book was written to explain a complex structural-functionalist model of society and introduced his concept of the sick role as a social relationship with its own norms, values, and behaviors embedded in the pattern of interaction that takes place between patients and their physicians. Parsons had become the best-known sociologist in the world and having a theorist of his stature provide the first major theory in medical sociology called attention to the young subdiscipline – particularly among academic sociologists. Anything he published attracted interest. Not only was Parsons' concept of the sick role a distinctly sociological analysis of sickness, but it was widely believed by many sociologists at the time that Parsons was charting a future course for all of sociology through his theoretical approach. This did not occur, however, as Parsons' influence faded over time and structural-functionalism was abandoned as a useful theory in sociology. Nevertheless, Parsons brought medical sociology intellectual recognition that it needed in its early period by endowing it with theory and opening up a robust discussion about his concept of the sick role.

The Post-Sick-Role Era

Following Parsons, the next major area of research was medical and nursing education. Howard Becker and his associates published *Boys in White* (1961), a study of medical school socialization conducted from a symbolic interactionist perspective. This study became a sociological classic and was important for both its theoretical and methodological content. The techniques in participant observation provided a basis for subsequent research on doctor–patient interaction, the organization of work in hospitals, death and dying, and subsequent innovations in both theory and research methods.

    With the introduction of symbolic interaction into a field that had previously been dominated by structural-functionalism, medical sociology became a major arena of debate between two of sociology's major theoretical schools at the time. This debate helped stimulate a virtual flood of publications in medical sociology in the 1960s. The symbolic interactionist perspective temporarily dominated a significant portion of the literature. One feature of this domination was the numerous studies conducted with reference to labeling theory and the mental patient experience. Sociologists expanded their work on mental health to also include studies of stigma, stress, families coping with mental disorder, and other areas of practical and theoretical relevance. For example, Erving Goffman's *Asylums* (1961), a study of life in a mental hospital, presented his concept of "total institutions" that stands as a significant sociological statement about social life in an externally controlled environment. An abundant literature emerged at this time that established the sociology of mental disorder as a major subfield within medical sociology (Cockerham 2017b).

Period of Maturity: 1970–2000

Between 1970 and 2000 medical sociology emerged as a mature sociological subdiscipline. This period was marked by the publication of two especially important books, Eliot Friedson's *Professional Dominance* (1970) and Paul Starr's *The Social*

Transformation of American Medicine (1982). Friedson formulated his influential "professional dominance" theory to account for an unprecedented level of professional control by physicians over healthcare delivery that was true at the time but no longer exists. Starr's book won the Pulitzer Prize and countered Friedson's thesis by examining the decline in status and professional power of the medical profession as large corporate healthcare delivery systems oriented toward profit effectively entered an unregulated medical market. This situation was countered by the growing intervention of the federal government in healthcare delivery that began earlier in the mid-1960s with the passage of Medicare and Medicaid. Thus the medical profession emerged as just one of many important groups in society – federal and state governments, employers, health insurance companies, patients, pharmaceutical and other companies providing medical products – maneuvering to fulfill their interests in healthcare.

Another major work was Bryan Turner's *Body and Society* (1984) which initiated the sociological work on this topic. Theoretical developments concerning the sociological understanding of the control, use, and phenomenological experience of the body, including emotions, followed. Much of this work was been carried out in the United Kingdom and features social constructionism as its theoretical foundation. Social constructionism has its origins in the work of the French social theorist Michel Foucault and takes the view that knowledge about the body, health, and illness reflects subjective, historically specific human concepts and is subject to change and reinterpretation. Other areas in which British medical sociologists have excelled include studies of medical practice, emotions, and the experience of illness.

From the 1970s through the 1990s, medical sociology flourished as it attracted large numbers of practitioners in both academic and applied settings and sponsored an explosion of publications based upon empirical research. Major areas of investigation included stress, the medicalization of deviance, mental health, inequality and class differences in health, healthcare utilization, managed care and other organizational changes, AIDS, and women's health and gender. Several books, edited collections of readings, and textbooks appeared.

However, the success of medical sociology also brought problems in the 1980s. Research funding opportunities lessened and the field faced serious competition for existing resources with health economics, health psychology, medical anthropology, health services research, and public health. These fields not only adopted sociological research methods in the forms of social surveys, participation observation, and focus groups, but some employed medical sociologists in large numbers. While these developments were positive in many ways, the distinctiveness of medical sociology as a unique subdiscipline was nevertheless challenged as other fields moved into similar areas of research. Furthermore, some of the medical sociology programs at leading American universities had declined or disappeared over time as practitioners retired or were hired away. Yet the overall situation for medical sociology was positive as the job market remained good, almost all graduate programs in sociology offered a specialization in medical sociology, and sociologists were on the faculties of most medical schools in the United States, Canada, and Western Europe.

The 1990s saw medical sociology move closer to its parent discipline of sociology. This was seen in a number of areas with medical sociological work appearing more frequently in general sociology journals and the increasing application of sociological theory to the analysis of health problems. An increasingly integrated alignment with general sociology was to be expected because of their commonalities – especially those of theory and methods. Contemporary medical sociology came to have a rich and abundant literature with its own theories specific to the subdiscipline, some of which are based on perspectives shared with sociology at large, and others that are unique to its subject matter. While medical sociology drew closer to sociology, sociology in turn moved closer to medical sociology because of its status as one of the largest and most active sociological specialties.

The Twenty-First Century

In the twenty-first century, medical sociology appears to be in the early stage of a paradigm shift away from a past focus on methodological individualism (in which individuals are the primary unit of analysis) toward studies of social structural influences on health and a growing utilization of theories with a structural orientation (Cockerham 2013). Much of the current research involves investigation of the health disparities that exist between social classes, races, and other disadvantaged people, as well as investigating the social determinants of health and disease in which social factors often have causal roles. The term "social determinants of health" refers to the social practices and conditions (such as lifestyles, living and work situations, neighborhood characteristics, poverty, and environmental pollution), socioeconomic status (income, education, and occupation), stressful circumstances, and discrimination, along with the economic (e.g., unemployment, business recessions), political (e.g., government policies, programs, and benefits), and religious (e.g., piety, proscriptions against smoking and drinking) factors that affect the health of individuals, groups, and communities – either positively or negatively. Social determinants not only can have a causal role in fostering illness and disability, but conversely promote prospects for coping with or preventing disease and maintaining health.

Social determinants research includes studies such as those of "neighborhood disadvantage" that investigate unhealthy urban living conditions, structurally induced lifestyles that affect health, and the adverse health effects of racial discrimination and gender inequality. Another growing area of research are studies linking sociological and genetic variables, especially studies of gene–environment interaction. The rapid progress in genetics following completion of the Human Genome Project in 2003 has attracted considerable attention from medical sociologists because breakthroughs in genetics have significant social consequences. This is seen not only in sociological research showing how social environments affect genes, but also with respect to bioethical issues concerning privacy and gene ownership, prenatal genetic screening, and cloning.

The current era has witnessed a sharp decline in influence of sociology's three formerly dominant theoretical perspectives – structural-functionalism, conflict theory, and symbolic interaction – and their replacement by newer theories in both sociology and medical sociology reflecting more contemporary views and social realities (Cockerham 2013). Currently, there are several middle-range theories active in medical sociology. These include social constructionism, social capital, the stress process, life course theory, fundamental cause theory, health lifestyle theory, intersectionality, medicalization, and others.

Also important is the ready availability of advanced statistical techniques allowing researchers to categorize people on the basis of their health behaviors (latent class analysis) and also to determine the separate effects of successive or multiple levels of social structures on the health of individuals. The latter includes not only hierarchal level modeling and similar techniques, but measures of biomarker data to uncover the effects of social structural variables on physiological outcomes such as allostatic load, inflammation, or glucocorticoid secretion. Regardless of theoretical preference, medical sociology today has the methodologies to more fully account for structural effects on the health of the individual.

Ultimately, what allows medical sociology to retain its unique character is (1) its utilization and mastery of sociological theory in the study of health and (2) the sociological perspective that accounts for collective causes and outcomes of health problems and issues. No other field is able to bring these skills to health-related research and analysis. Today it can said that medical sociology produces literature intended to inform medicine and policy makers, but research in the field is also grounded in examining health-related situations that inform sociology as well. Medical sociology no longer functions as a field whose ties to the mother discipline are tenuous, nor has it evolved as an enterprise subject to medical control. It now works most often with medicine in the form of a partner and, in some cases, an objective critic. However, medical sociology owes more to medicine than sociology for its origin and initial financial support, so the relationship that has evolved is essentially supportive. As medical sociology continues on its present course, it is likely to remain as one of sociology's core specialties as the pursuit of health increasingly becomes important in everyday social life.

SEE ALSO: Aging, Sociology of; Body, the; Demography and Population Studies; Disability, Sociology of; Emotion, Sociology of; Medicalization; Mental Health and Illness; Organizations, Sociology of; Sport, Sociology of; Work, Occupations and Professions, Sociology of

References

Becker, H., B. Greer, E. Hughes, and A. Strauss. 1961. *Boys in White: Student Culture in Medical School*. Chicago: University of Chicago Press.

Cockerham, W. 2013. "Sociological Theory in Medical Sociology in the Early Twenty-First Century." *Health and Social Theory* 11 (3): 241–255.

Cockerham, W. 2017a. *Medical Sociology*, 14th ed. New York: Routledge.

Cockerham, W. 2017b. *Sociology of Mental Disorder*, 10th ed. New York: Routledge.

Friedson, E. 1970. *Professional Dominance*. Chicago: Aldine.

Goffman, E. 1961. *Asylums*. Garden City, NJ: Doubleday Anchor.

Parsons, T. 1951. *The Social System*. Glencoe, IL: Free Press.

Starr, P. 1982. *The Social Transformation of American Medicine*. New York: Basic Books.

Turner, B. 1984. *Body and Society*. Oxford: Blackwell.

Medicalization

Peter Conrad

Brandeis University, USA

In its simplest form medicalization means "to make medical." More broadly, medicalization means how previously nonmedical conditions become defined and treated as a medical problem, usually as a disease or disorder. Sociologists who study medicalization are usually not interested in whether a condition is "really" a medical problem, but rather focus on how a problem becomes defined as medical and with what consequences. Many examples exist including alcoholism, addictions, ADHD, normal sadness, PMS, sleep disorders, childbirth, aging, obesity, infertility, learning disabilities, erectile dysfunction, gender dysphoria, cosmetic surgery, and numerous others. Conceptually, we see medicalization in terms of broader categories such as deviance (e.g., many mental disorders, addictions), normal life events (e.g., menopause, aging), and enhancement (e.g., breast enhancements).

The origins of the issues surrounding medicalization can be found in the works of mid-century sociological giants Talcott Parsons, Erving Goffman, and Michel Foucault. However, with an occasional exception, these writers didn't use the term medicalization, although they analyzed phenomena that would later be termed as medicalization. The first sociological use of the term can be attributed to Jesse Pitts, in his 1968 *International Encyclopedia of the Social Sciences* article on "Social Control: The Concept," where he discussed the medicalization of deviant behavior. The most common sociological origin of a wider spread interest in medicalization was Irving K. Zola's (1972) often cited article "Medicine as an Institution of Social Control." He saw the origins of medicalization in the expansion of the jurisdiction of the medical profession and conceptualized it as medical social control. Conrad's (1976) research on what is now called ADHD was among the first to focus research on the processes of medicalization. In the past 40 years scores of scholars have conducted research on various aspects of medicalization (see Conrad 1992, 2007, 2013).

Along with medicalization, there are examples of demedicalization. The most often mentioned is the demedicalization of homosexuality. From the mid-nineteenth century through the mid-twentieth century, homosexuality was seen as a form of mental illness that required treatment. After several years of protest by gay activists, the American Psychiatric Association voted in 1973 to remove homosexuality as a diagnosis from the official diagnostic compendium, which eventually led to a virtually complete

Core Concepts in Sociology, First Edition. Edited by J. Michael Ryan.
© 2019 John Wiley & Sons Ltd. Published 2019 by John Wiley & Sons Ltd.

demedicalization of homosexuality. There are a few other examples of efforts at demedicalization, such as masturbation, which was considered a disease (as onanism) through the early twentieth century and the recent attempts to reconceptualize some types of autism as "neurodiversity." But there is no question that there is far more medicalization than demedicalization.

One can also point to at least five characteristics of medicalization, which show the range of medicalization (see Conrad 2013 for more detail). (1) The (medical) definitional issue is central; how a problem is defined is key to what is done about it. (2) There are degrees of medicalization. Some conditions are fully medicalized (e.g., schizophrenia, epilepsy) while others are marginally medicalized (e.g., sexual addiction, internet addiction), and still others are in-between (e.g., opioid addiction). Thus the acceptance of medicalization is often someplace on a continuum. (3) Medicalized categories are elastic; they can expand or contract. When ADHD emerged in the 1970s, it was limited to children in primary school age 6–12. But by now it has expanded to adolescent and adult ADHD, with a focus on inattention more than hyperactive behavior. Diagnostic categories like hysteria have sharply narrowed in the past decades and are rarely used. (4) Physician involvement is variable, and sometimes only marginally necessary. Alcoholism, for example, was medicalized largely through the efforts of Alcoholics Anonymous, with little participation of physicians or the medical profession. (5) As noted above, medicalization is bidirectional, but the medicalized direction far outstrips the demedicalized direction.

The underlying drivers of medicalization are varied and changing. In the first place, health and medicine is a large part of the US GNP; in 1950 it was 4 percent, in 2016 it is approaching 18 percent. In the second place, in the United States (and elsewhere) the only way to get reimbursed for human services is through health insurance, and the only way to get insurance reimbursement is to have a medical diagnosis and a related medical treatment. This creates an incentive to provide a medical diagnosis to human problems. Thus, in a general sense, medicine and the benefits from obtaining a diagnosis are important aspects underpinning the increase in medicalization. Until the 1980s, most analysts of medicalization focused on the role of the medical profession as a major factor in expanding medical jurisdiction. But in the past few decades, sociologists have broadened their analysis and pointed to the "shifting engines of medicalization": medical technology (especially the pharmaceutical industry); the rise of consumers and medical markets; and the increased role of managed care and health insurance (Clarke et al. 2006; Conrad 2007).

For sociologists, medicalization is not necessarily a good or bad thing for society. It should be studied like any other social process (e.g., industrialization, secularization). The question to ask is what are the origins and consequences of medicalization for society. One major social concern with medicalization is the pathologization of everything; turning all human difference into some kind of medical pathology. Related is a concern of the rise of medical definitions of "normality"; this is especially evident in the pharmaceutical promotions of drugs for treating various medicalized conditions. This has led to the growth of various types of medical markets, especially pharmaceutical (like anti-depressants) and surgical (such as for obesity and various kinds of cosmetic surgery). There are still concerns, raised first by Zola nearly 50 years ago, that medicalization increases the specter and amount of medical social control.

Medicalization continues to expand and if anything the issues are more widespread today than they were in past years. Sociologists are beginning to study the increasing globalization of medicalization, and examining how diagnoses and treatments migrate from places like the United States to other countries (Conrad and Bergey 2014). It is important to understand the impact of the internet and the multinational pharmaceutical industry in this process, and interesting to see how medicalization is manifested in various cultures.

SEE ALSO: Body, the; Deviance; Medical Sociology; Stigma

References

Clarke, Adele, Laura Mamo, Jennifer Fosket, Jennifer R. Fishman, Janet K. Shim, and Elianne Riska. 2006. *Biomedicalization: Technoscience, Health and Illness in the US.* Durham, NC: Duke University Press.

Conrad, Peter. 1976. *Identifying Hyperactive Children: The Medicalization of Deviant Behavior.* Boston: DC Heath.

Conrad, Peter. 1992. "Medicalization and Social Control." *Annual Review of Sociology* 18: 209–232.

Conrad, Peter. 2007. *The Medicalization of Society: On the Transformation of Human Conditions into Treatable Disorders.* Baltimore: Johns Hopkins University Press.

Conrad, Peter. 2013. "Medicalization: Changing Contours, Characteristics and Contexts." *Health Sociology on the Move: New Directions in Theory,* edited by William Cockerham. Oxford: Blackwell.

Conrad, Peter, and Meredith Bergey. 2014. "The Impending Globalization of ADHD: Notes on the Expansion and Growth of a Medicalized Disorder." *Social Science and Medicine* 122: 31–43.

Zola, Irving K. 1972. "Medicine as an Institution of Social Control." *Sociological Review* 20: 487–504.

Mental Health and Illness

Emily Allen Paine and Tetyana Pudrovska

University of Texas, Austin, USA

Mental health and mental illness are defined and debated across multiple fields of inquiry, including psychiatry, psychology, social work, and sociology. While other fields primarily focus on biological and intrapsychic (internal) processes related to mental wellness and distress, sociological research contributes key insights into the ways in which larger social forces shape mental health.

In this overview, we review some of the most important themes in sociological research on mental health, specifically: the roles played by stress processes, identity, and social networks. Although the number of mental health diagnoses are numerous and ever evolving, in this review we focus on depression, distress, suicidality, and alcoholism. We review differences within and across racial, gender, and sexual identity groups, as well as the sociological theories working to explain disparities in prevalence of symptoms and diagnoses.

Stressors and Support

A large body of sociological research on mental health focuses on the integral role stressors play in creating distress. Stressors primarily include chronic stressors, or ongoing conditions such as exposure to poverty or discrimination over time, as well as acute stressors, or life events and traumas – for example, the loss of a spouse, or assault (see Pearlin et al. 2005). Longitudinal research shows that stressors lead to higher levels of distress – a key measure of mental health. In social research, distress is typically measured using sets of survey questions that work together to determine whether one experiences symptoms of depression or anxiety, as well as the degree to which these symptoms may impact one's day-to-day life.

Stressors are theorized to diminish mental health by disrupting physiological and psychological processes, which in turn may lead to behavioral changes. For example, a job loss may cause immediate distress by triggering diminished feelings of self-esteem and a perceived loss of control over one's life. It may also trigger a prolonged "fight or flight" response, including spikes in adrenal hormones, which may (over time) alter the ability of the autonomic nervous system to regulate important hormones. These changes may in turn lead people to seek relief in behaviors such as increased alcohol consumption, which may ultimately prolong distress. However, distress may also compel individuals toward mental health-promoting behaviors, such as exercise and social connection. Resilience to stressors, or the likelihood that stressors will *not* lead to risky health behaviors and elevated distress levels, is strongly linked to social support. A major contribution of sociological research is the importance of social support in ameliorating the impact of stressors.

Social support includes one's number of social ties (such as spouses, family, friends, and colleagues) as well as the quality of these connections. Social ties work to protect mental health from stressors in multiple ways. In the face of hardship – such as job loss – social connections can provide, for example, both emotional support and instrumental support to help buffer the impact on mental health. A spouse may offer emotional support in the form of care and love – helping diminish the likelihood of low self-esteem or mattering. A colleague may provide instrumental support by helping secure a new job, thus lowering the chances of an acute stressor leading to the chronic stress associated with prolonged unemployment or poverty. In these ways and more, social connections help attenuate the effects of stressors. Likewise, social ties are positively associated with overall health and longevity. Because physical illness itself predicts high levels of stress, social networks work through multiple pathways to reinforce health, including mental wellness.

Considerations Within and Across Groups

Insight into how social forces shape disparities within and across groups comprises another leading contribution of sociological mental health research. Given that thousands of mental health diagnoses exist and are constantly evolving, disparities in global mental health – unlike, for example, disparities in levels of high blood pressure – are more difficult to measure across groups. Nonetheless, existing research shows significant differences by gender, race, and sexual and gender identity.

Gender

Women are more likely to be diagnosed with affective disorders such as depression and anxiety compared to men; however, men are more likely to experience alcoholism and suicide. Multiple theories exist to explain these differences. One primary theory argues that women's higher levels of distress result from their disadvantaged social status in relation to men (see Bird and Rieker 2008). Moreover, the social construction of women as biologically inferior to men, paired with the historical medicalization of women's bodies, is argued to encourage the pathologization of women's emotions. Cultural ideas of masculinity related to risk-taking are theorized to normalize men's engagement in drinking, high-risk behaviors, and underreporting of emotional distress. Women are more likely than men to seek healthcare in general, and men are more likely to be doctors. All together, these trends suggest that rather than a biological root to observed gender disparities in mental health, men may under-report and be under-diagnosed for mood disorders and distress, whereas women may be over-diagnosed.

Others argue, however, that different cultural scripts related to successful masculinity and femininity both sort men and women into unequal positions in society and lead to stressors differentially impacting men and women's mental health (see Bird and Rieker 2008). For example, while increasing levels of responsibility and authority in the workplace is shown to decrease depression for men, a recent study found that women in positions of job authority report *more* depressive symptoms than women and men without authority in the workplace (Pudrovska and Karraker 2014). The authors argue that cultural ideologies of femininity measure women in relation to their nurturance and selflessness such that incongruent responsibilities (like hiring, firing, and determining pay level) create distressing role conflict for women. Women in these positions also report increased levels of discrimination related to role conflict.

Race

Exposure to individual and structural-level racism, or race-based discrimination, is a chronic stressor for racial minorities, and inhibits their access to conditions that promote mental wellbeing (e.g., high paying jobs). For example, blacks in the United States have lower documented rates of mood disorders and distress compared to whites in the United States (Williams et al. 2007). Likewise, in the United States, whites are more likely to experience suicidality compared to blacks. Ongoing exposure to hardship lends blacks in the United States greater resilience in the face of stressors, thus buffering the effect on mental health. However, such a hypothesis is difficult to test, and – given that blacks in the United States also have fewer protective social ties compared to whites – conflicts with social support theory. Moreover, studies using biomarkers to measure physical "age" suggest that exposure to racism results in significant physical health disadvantages for blacks in the United States – as further evidenced by their significantly shorter life expectancy compared to whites (see Geronimus et al. 2006). To complicate things further, one study found that while less prevalent, depression among blacks in the United States was more often severe, disabling, and untreated compared to depression among whites (Williams et al. 2007); this finding suggests that disparities may be the result of under-reporting and under-diagnosis of mental illness among blacks. Furthermore, the reversal of across-race mental health trends within sexual and gender identity populations – wherein black sexual and gender identity minorities are *more* likely to attempt suicide compared to their white counterparts – reminds us of the importance of intersectionality – the holistic consideration of one's multiple social identities, as well as within-group differences – when examining mental health disparities.

Sexual and Gender Identity

Sexual and gender identity minorities (SGMs) are more likely to be diagnosed with depression and anxiety and more likely to report high levels of distress and suicidality, in large part due to acute and chronic exposures to sexual stigma and discrimination. Significant gaps in suicidality between heterosexual and gay men have been found in multiple places; in places where discriminatory laws target sexual minorities, these gaps are larger (Hatzenbuehler et al. 2014). Given the association between structural and individual-level discrimination and poor mental health, we can expect to see mental health disparities between SGMs and heterosexuals and cisgender peoples increase or decrease in response to shifting political and cultural attitudes and positions toward LGBT people.

Life Course Considerations

Finally, mental health diagnoses and reports of distress are more common during some periods of the life course than others, and mental health tends to fluctuate in response to significant life course events and transitions (see Pearlin et al. 2005). For example, becoming a parent, losing a parent, physical illness, divorce, and losing a spouse are all associated with increased levels of distress. The longevity and impact transition related to stress, however, is largely associated with access to social support and the presence or absence of concomitant stressors. Although cross-sectional studies show that older adults tend to report worse mental health compared to younger adults, whether this pattern is driven by age or cohort effects remains unclear (and requires the use of prospective studies).

Future Directions

Current scholars of mental health increasingly promote gender-as-relational, intersectional, and biopsychosocial approaches to the study of mental health. A gender-as-relational approach illuminates the ways in which cultural ideals of gender are enacted and reified through relational contexts. Intersectional approaches, as mentioned, emphasize the importance of attending to multiple social identities and understanding differences not only between but within groups in order to determine the social processes and conditions that shape mental health. Finally, biopsychosocial approaches argue for the combined attention to biomarker measures, psychological processes, and social conditions for identifying and explaining mental (and physical) health disparities. Future research into mental health issues will continue to grapple with how social forces and processes provide the conditions for mental health and illness within and across different social groups.

SEE ALSO: Body, the; Gender; Homophobia and Heterosexism; Identity; Life Course; Race and Ethnicity; Sexualities; Social Psychology; Stigma

References

Bird, C., and P. Rieker. 2008. *Gender and Health: The Effects of Constrained Choices and Social Policies.* New York: Cambridge University Press.

Geronimus, A.T., M. Hicken, D. Keene, and J. Bound. 2006. "'Weathering' and Age Patterns of Allostatic Load Scores Among Blacks and Whites in the United States." *American Journal of Public Health* 96 (5): 826–833.

Hatzenbuehler, M.L., A. Bellatorre, Y. Lee, B. Finch, P. Muennig, and K. Fiscella. 2014. "Structural Stigma and All-Cause Mortality in Sexual Minority Populations." *Social Science & Medicine* 103: 33–41.

Pearlin, L.I., S. Schieman, E.M. Fazio, and S.C. Meersman. 2005. "Stress, Health, and the Life Course: Some Conceptual Perspectives." *Journal of Health Social Behavior* 46 (2): 205–219.

Pudrovska, T., and A. Karraker. 2014. "Gender, Job Authority, and Depression." *Journal of Health and Social Behavior* 55 (4): 424–441.

Williams, D.R., H.M. Gonzalez, H. Neighbors, R. Nesse, J.M. Abelson, J. Sweetman, and J.S. Jackson. 2007. "Prevalence and Distribution of Major Depressive Disorder in African Americans, Caribbean Blacks, and Non-Hispanic Whites: Results from the National Survey of American Life." *Archives of General Psychiatry* 64: 305–315.

Military Sociology

Ryan Kelty[1] and David R. Segal[2]

[1] *U.S. Air Force Academy, USA*
[2] *University of Maryland, USA*

Militaries have been among the most powerful social institutions for millennia. However, this institution has received limited attention from sociologists. Even so, some sociologists from the earliest thinkers have studied the military from a societal perspective. Many of the founding scholars addressed the military – though not as central foci in their theories and/or empirical study. Marx noted the critical function of the military as a capitalist tool that facilitated imperialistic exploitation for economic gain. Durkheim discussed the military as an institution that produced challenges for social solidarity and stability. Perhaps the most well-known focus on the military among early sociologists came from Weber's thinking about bureaucracy, derived from his study of the Prussian military, and his claim that the state held a monopoly on the legitimate use of violence within a society. The next generation of sociologists concerned with the military maintained a focus on macro-level analysis of the military institution and its consequences in society (see Segal and Burk 2012 and Segal and Ender 2008 for overviews of origins of sociology focused on the military).

For much of the first half of the twentieth century the study of military sociology was dormant. In America this reflected the historical practice to not maintain a large standing military outside of wartime (Segal and Burk 2012). World War II would serve as a catalyst for the emergence of modern military sociology, and in doing so shift the subfield from its historical roots in Europe to the United Sates. During the massive mobilization of American society for the war effort, the US military commissioned teams of social scientists to study the military and its members with an eye toward better understanding the strengths and challenges of its operations and in developing a more robust understanding of the effects of military service. One of the outcomes of this research was the multivolume series *The American Soldier* (Stouffer et al. 1949), which shifted the focus of the field from the institution to the soldier and began to explore micro-level aspects of service members' experiences during the war, such as promotion rates, experiences in combat, and living conditions. It also examined attitudes related to wartime service and mental health outcomes. Importantly, the questionnaire-based aspect of much of the American Soldier study was critical in establishing the subfield of survey methodology.

Core Concepts in Sociology, First Edition. Edited by J. Michael Ryan.
© 2019 John Wiley & Sons Ltd. Published 2019 by John Wiley & Sons Ltd.

The initial spark of modern military sociology during and immediately after World War II faltered in the 1960s when America's involvement in the Vietnam War made the military unpopular in general, but more so among those in the more liberal-minded college and university ranks. Despite these challenges, the large standing military after World War II and the Cold War motivated several to maintain a focus on the military. This effort was matched by similar scholars in other Western democratic states. It wasn't until the end of the Vietnam War and the transition from a conscripted military to one based on voluntary participation that military sociology again began to build. In the European context, the fall of the Soviet Union and the transition to all-volunteer militaries catalyzed similar growth.

Primary areas of inquiry in military sociology reflect the range of the discipline. Examples at the macro level include citizenship and military service, civil–military relations, military manpower and recruiting, the military as a profession, use of civilians in military organizations, diversity in the military, and military families. At the micro level military sociology explores topics such as group cohesion, attitudes toward military service, gendered relations (including harassment and assault), attitudes toward the enemy, and effects of different leadership styles. While the subfield in the twentieth century found its home predominantly in the United States, in recent decades the center of gravity appears to be shifting back to the field's historical European roots.

Several major international associations support scholarship in military sociology. The Inter-University on Armed Forces & Society (IUS), established in the 1960s at the University of Michigan, which later moved to the University of Chicago, is an international, interdisciplinary organization of scholars focused on military and security issues that meets biennially, and publishes the journal *Armed Forces & Society*. Recently an offshoot organization, IUS-Canada, emerged and hosts meetings on off-years of the main IUS. Another major association in which military sociology scholars find a home is the Research Committee on Armed Forces and Conflict Resolution (RC01) of the International Sociological Association, founded in 1970. The European Research Group on Military and Society was established in 1986 and is "devoted to collaborative research on military and society." Recently ERGOMAS began a relationship with the peer-reviewed online journal, *Res Militaris*, featuring articles in French and English. Aside from providing outlets for presenting research at conferences and in affiliated journals, these organizations provide opportunities for networking with other scholars and developing strong collaborative research projects that are increasingly multinational in focus. Over the last decade, military sociologists have worked with the Eastern Sociological Society to establish successful mini-conferences in military sociology at their annual meetings, drawing scores of researchers from the United States and abroad. Several other national and regional associations also have specific sections or working groups that support scholars of military sociology.

Research in military sociology allows us to better understand the military institution, and the causes and consequences of military organization and actions in society. Military sociology informs broader issues of sociological significance such as civil–military relations, ethics in cross-cultural research, and theoretical and methodological issues and practices that will help to advance sociological inquiry in general. Given the types and durations of conflicts anticipated in the twenty-first century, most nations' militaries are likely to be quite active. Military sociology is poised to provide much-needed insight and critique to inform the best ways forward for military organizations, their host societies, and for the people who serve in uniform and their families.

SEE ALSO: Organizations, Sociology of; Work, Occupations, and Professions, Sociology of

References

Segal, David R., and James Burk. 2012. "Editors' Introduction." In *Military Sociology*, edited by David R. Segal and James Burk, xxv–xlvii. Thousand Oaks, CA: Sage Publications.

Segal, David R., and Morten G. Ender. 2008. "Sociology in Military Officer Education." *Armed Forces & Society* 35 (1): 3–15.

Stouffer, Samuel A., Edward A. Suchman, Leland C. DeVinney, Shirley A. Star, and Robin M. Williams, Jr. 1949. *Studies in Social Psychology in World War II: The American Soldier*. Princeton, NJ: Princeton University Press.

Modernity

Gerard Delanty[1] and Aurea Mota[2]

[1] University of Sussex, UK
[2] University of Barcelona, Spain

The idea of modernity concerns the interpretation of present time in terms of a reposition-ing of the present in relation to the past and to the future. It refers to major transformations that led to the making of the modern world and the formation of new imaginaries concern-ing the possibility of the autonomy of human beings. The term modernity did not arise until the nineteenth century and was very much reflected in the major historical upheavals of that century, especially in the way these were experienced by people in Europe and the Americas. One of the most famous uses of the term was in 1864 when the French poet Baudelaire (1964: 13) wrote: "By modernity I mean the transitory, the fugitive, the contin-gent." This notion of modernity was an expression of the literary movement of modernism and captured the dynamic movements and fast-moving currents in modern society, in particular those that conveyed the sense of renewal and the cosmopolitanism of modern urban life. It also signaled the spirit of creativity and individualism that was taken up by the avant-garde movement. However, the term has a wider currency beyond its cultural and artistic signification. It captures the revolutionary impetus of modern industrial capitalistic society. Marx and Engels in the *Communist Manifesto* in 1848 invoked the spirit of moder-nity with their account of the rise of capitalism as the condition in which "all that is solid melts into air."

Within classical sociology, Max Weber captured some critical aspects of the modern transformation by the concept of rationalization, which had an enhanced importance in shaping the ways that human beings think and act in modern society. The notion of modernity in classical sociological theory expressed the transformation observed in political institutions as well as in the economic and societal transformation of Western societies. Georg Simmel is generally regarded as the figure who first gave a more rigor-ous sociological description of modernity in his account of everyday social life in the modern metropolis. For Simmel, as for Walter Benjamin, modernity is expressed in diverse "momentary images" or "snapshots." Modernity is the condition of the frag-mentation of modern society, on the one side, and, on the other, one of new possibili-ties and forms for culture, made possible, for example, by the camera and the cinema. These technologies led to such momentary images and the related sense that nothing is durable and solid but that everything is fleeting. Thus there is nothing like a modern condition that is able to crystallize itself in a specific spatial context. It is a condition

Core Concepts in Sociology, First Edition. Edited by J. Michael Ryan.
© 2019 John Wiley & Sons Ltd. Published 2019 by John Wiley & Sons Ltd.

that is open to new forms. This is a critical aspect that was asserted by late twentieth-century critiques including postmodern theories.

Modernity can be defined as a condition of awareness that nothing is settled for once and for all and that therefore the future is not predetermined. It expresses the idea that the present is not determined by the past, especially by the recent past. Most conceptions of modernity have announced a rupture of present time from the past, generally the recent past. The modern is the present time; it is the "now" and "the new." The consciousness of the new is common to most cultural, philosophical, and political expressions of modernity from the eighteenth century onwards. The modernist movement in literature, the arts, and architecture strongly emphasized a spirit of newness, purity, and the break from tradition. The social and political ideas of what Reinhart Koselleck (2004) referred to as the *Sattelzeit,* the period from 1750 to 1850, provide the main reference points for modernity, the *Neuzeit.* This period, which saw the formation of key conceptual and structural changes, made possible the emergence of modern society as a new kind of society that sought to reach beyond itself, beyond what had previously been contained within the "space of experience." In the terms of Koselleck, the "horizon of expectation" was considerably expanded beyond the "space of experience," which was also broadened. The discovery of the notion of "progress" in this period, which he attributes to Kant, marks the point at which new expectations become possible and not limited by previous experience. For Koselleck, experience and expectation are key registers of a shift in historical consciousness. Koselleck's theory of the emergence of modernity in terms of a particular kind of time consciousness has been very influential. It suggests a notion of modernity that is defined in categorical terms rather than reducing it to a particular period or epoch. The *Sattelzeit* can be seen as the period when modernity took shape in Europe but is not confined to this period. However, Koselleck's account conflated modernity with its European expression. Despite their co-emergence and entanglement, they need to be conceptually separated. One aspect of the notion of modernity that is striking is that it reflects a strong faith in the capacity of human agency to shape society in light of guiding ideas and in knowledge.

It is also important to highlight the connection between technological advancement and the "civilizational mission" of Western countries during the colonial period in the second half of the nineteenth century. The emergence of discourses and institutional practices in relation the affirmation of human beings in European contexts took place at the same time when colonial domination extended over much of Africa and Asia. Thus it came about that modernity was a leading idea in the struggle for emancipation and for the affirmation of more inclusive states in the European context, but it was also used as the reason for the affirmation of domination and exploitation of other supposed backward areas of the world. The postcolonial critique that emerged by the 1950s emphasized this connection in calls for new genealogies of the modern age.

The idea of modernity also signals an epistemological condition that announces the loss of certainty and the realization that certainty can never be established for once and for all. It is a term that can also be taken to refer to reflection on the age, rather than being coeval with a specific era. For Habermas, modernity is related to the capacity of modern society to contest power through communicative means. Developments in postmodern thought suggest a view of the modern as a reflective moment within the modern, rather than a new era, a particular kind of consciousness rather than a societal condition as such. Modernity is thus a condition that is essentially open as opposed to being closed or a specific societal formation. For this reason, the concept of modernity should be seen as an alternative to the notion of modernization insofar as it draws attention to a diversity of forms and the capacity for self-transformation.

While much of the literature on modernity outside of sociological theory has tended to emphasize the cultural dimensions of modernity, it should be noted that it is also a social and political condition that goes beyond the European assumptions that have tended to accompany the debates. In recent years there has been a huge literature on modernity as a global and a plural phenomenon. Much of this derives from the work of S.N. Eisenstadt (2003), who developed the notion of "multiple modernities" whereby modernity is based on different civilizational trajectories. The older assumptions of modernity as essentially a product of European or Western civilization have been much criticized in wider-ranging scholarship that has emerged from, for instance, comparative historical sociology, transnational and global history, postcolonial theory, and cosmopolitanism. While Eisenstadt gave the notion of modernity a wider and more global relevance, the tendency in recent years has been less centered on its civilizational characteristics insofar as these relate to the emergence of the major Eurasian civilizations of the Axial Age. Eisenstadt's own work also gave the European variant of modernity undue significance in shaping other varieties of modernity. The civilizational dimension cannot be entirely neglected in any kind of global comparison, as Johann Arnason (2003) has shown. The multiple forms that modernity takes can be related to civilizational trajectories, but there are also endogenous logics of development and the entanglement of these with exogenous ones. In place of the notion of multiple modernities has now come a new emphasis on varieties of modernity and on entangled modernities, since the divergent forms of modernity do not develop without interaction with other forms.

SEE ALSO: Colonialism and Postcolonialism; Globalization; Marxism; Postmodernism and Poststructuralism

References

Arnason, P. Johann. 2003. *Civilizations in Dispute: Historical Questions and Theoretical Traditions*. Leiden: Brill.

Baudelaire, Charles. 1964. "The Painter of Modern Life." In *The Painter of Modern Life and Other Essays*. London: Phaidon Press.

Eisenstadt, S.N. 2003. *Comparative Civilizations and Multiple Modernities: A Collection of Essays by S.N. Eisenstadt,* Vols. 1 and 2. Leiden: Brill.

Koselleck, Reinhart. 2004. *Futures Past: On the Semantics of Historical Time*. New York: Columbia University Press.

Further Reading

Gaonkar, D.P., ed. 2001. *Alternative Modernities*. Durham, NC: Duke University Press.

Wager, Peter. 2012. *Modernity*. Cambridge: Polity Press.

Nationalism

Helen Rizzo

The American University in Cairo, Egypt

The importance of understanding nationalism becomes apparent when it is at its worst, such as in times of crises or ethnic conflict which can result in racism, xenophobia, ethnic cleansing, civil war, or genocide. However, it is also ordinary, part of our everyday lives, and deeply rooted in our consciousness. Michael Billig coined the term "banal nationalism" to describe how nationalism is reproduced daily, for example, through the mundane use of symbols such as flags, national anthems, and currency. Because nationalism is a complex set of beliefs and practices that are neither inherently good nor bad, finding one accepted definition in the social sciences is extremely challengingly.

However scholars tend to agree that the concept of nationalism is a modern one, emerging in the eighteenth and nineteenth centuries. Craig Calhoun (1993: 216) argues that nationalism is also part of an international discourse. "Claims to nationhood are not just internal claims to social solidarity, common descent, or any other basis for constituting a political community. They are also claims to distinctiveness vis-à-vis other nations, claims to at least some level of autonomy and self-sufficiency, and claims to certain rights within a world-system of states ... In other words, however varied the internal nature of nationalisms ... they share a common external frame of reference." One that is a product of modernity.

While academic treatments of nationalism, mostly by historians and philosophers, began in the early twentieth century (1918–1945), sociologists and political scientists did not join the debate until after World War II, particularly in the 1960s. The period between 1945 through the late 1980s was a period when the debates surrounding nationalism diversified due to the rise of several schools of thought that attempted to explain the emergence of nations and nationalism including primordialism, perennialism, instrumentalism, modernism, and ethno-symbolism. Since the 1980s, new interdisciplinary approaches, such as postcolonialism and feminism, have tried to transcend the classical debates by arguing for the necessity of incorporating the colonial experience, race, gender, and sexuality into the discussions.

One of the earliest approaches, primordialism, sees the nation and nationalism as natural, not social, phenomena. Smith (1995: 31) summarized the argument: "... one is born into a nation the same way s/he is born into a family." In contrast, perennialists argue that nationalism as a political movement and ideology is modern; the roots of

Core Concepts in Sociology, First Edition. Edited by J. Michael Ryan.
© 2019 John Wiley & Sons Ltd. Published 2019 by John Wiley & Sons Ltd.

nations are not "natural." However, they still look for ethnic roots in an earlier historical, premodern period similar to primordialists. At the other end of the spectrum, instrumentalists see the nation and nationalism "… as a form of power rather than a powerful entity …" (Puri 2004: 44). Inspired by Marxist thought, they argue that nationalist identities are the result of human manipulation and social engineering. They contend that nations are created by political and intellectual elites to advance their own interests.

In the 1960s, modernist approaches emerged in response to the primordial, perennial, and instrumentalist paradigms. What modernists have in common is that they argue that nationalism and nations developed out of recent historical processes rather than being natural or products of early history. Thus the conditions that produced modernity also gave rise to nationalism and nations. These conditions were a result of the social, economic, and political changes that emerged in the eighteenth and nineteenth centuries including capitalism, industrialism, imperialism, the American and French revolutions, development of the bureaucratic state, urbanization, and secularism. Modernists believe that the nation and nationalism emerged as a new kind of community to address the disruptions in social life brought on by modernity. However modernists were not a monolithic group. Debates intensified from the 1960s through the 1980s over which factors were the most important in explaining nationalism. There were those who argued for economic transformations (neo-Marxists Tom Nairn and Michael Hechnter), for the state and political transformations (John Breuilly, Anthony Giddens, Eric Hobsbawm, Michael Mann, and Charles Tilly), for cultural responses to modernity (Anthony D. Smith and Ernest Gellner), and for nationalism as invented practices (Eric Hobsbawn and Benedict Anderson).

Criticisms of the modernist paradigm came from two camps: ethno-symbolism and culturalist approaches. Ethno-symbolism, the earlier approach, emerged in the 1980s as a compromise between primordialism/perennialism and modernism. Based on the works of John Armstrong, Anthony D. Smith, and John Hutchinson, ethno-symbolism takes the past seriously when discussing the formation of nations, particularly their ethnic roots. While recognizing that premodern ethnic groupings are socially and historically constructed, they argue that ethnic identities change more slowly than modernists assume. Once created, these identities can persist over generations, influencing how modern nations are formed at the same time as ethnic identities are being transformed by modernity.

While ethno-symbolists are a relatively homogenous group, critiques of modernist approaches in the culturalist paradigm are more diverse. With its roots in cultural studies established in the late 1950s, 1960s, and 1970s, culturalists have taken a critical stance toward nationalism since the late 1980s. Building on Hobsbawn's and Anderson's insights on nationalism as invented practices, their contributions to nationalism studies fall under four broad areas: nationalism as decentralized power (Michael Billig and Homi Bhabha), nationalism as anti-colonial resistance (Partha Chatterjee and Frantz Fanon), nationalism as racial resistance (black nationalism in South Africa and the United States), and nationalism as gendered (Nira Yuval-Davis, Floya Anthias, Kumari Jayawardena, Deniz Kandiyoti, Cynthia Enloe, Anne McClintock, Valentine Moghadam, Suad Joseph, and Sylvia Walby) and sexualized (Jyoti Puri).

In addition to sexualities, future directions in nationalism studies include its intersections with other interdisciplinary fields such as citizenship studies, diaspora studies, migration and refugee studies, and globalization studies.

SEE ALSO: Citizenship; Colonialism and Postcolonialism; Identity; Immigration, Migration, and Refugees; Modernity

References

Calhoun, Craig. 1993. "Nationalism and Ethnicity." *Annual Review of Sociology* 19: 211–239. DOI:10.1146/annurev.so.19.080193.001235.
Puri, Jyoti. 2004. *Encountering Nationalism*. Malden, MA: Blackwell Publishing.
Smith, Anthony D. 1995. *Nations and Nationalism in a Global Era*. Cambridge: Polity Press.

Further Reading

Özkirimli, Umut. 2000. *Theories of Nationalism: A Critical Introduction*. London: MacMillan Press.
Yuval-Davis, Nira. 1997. *Gender and Nation*. London: Sage.

Organizations, Sociology of

Stewart Clegg

University of Technology Sydney, Australia

The "golden days" of the sociology of organizations occurred in the 1950s, when scholars such as Selznick, Crozier, Gouldner, Etzioni, Blau and Scott, and Goffman were contributing classic case studies. If the 1950s were the era of great sociological case studies, the 1960s became the era in which the dominance of structural contingency theory occurred, with the work of the Aston School in the United Kingdom and Blau and Schonherr in the United States. The 1970s were a time of bifurcation in the English language scene: in North America approaches such as population ecology, which was quantitative and population-level based, dominated, while institutional theory was just emerging to flower fully from the 1980s onwards.

Against other disciplines, such as economics, with its stress on efficiency as the main variable explaining organizations, or contingency approaches, which regarded effectiveness as the key variable explaining why a given contingent structure would be adopted, institutional theorists argued for the importance of cultural factors that signal the legitimacy of an organization as the major determinants of strategic choice in determining structural design. Meyer and Rowan argue that legitimacy often comes wrapped up in "institutional myths" that help organizations gain or maintain legitimacy. Organizations adopt institutionally acceptable forms and practices to ensure organizational survival based on legitimacy. Formal structures of legitimacy may reduce efficiency so organizations often decouple their technical core from legitimizing structures.

DiMaggio and Powell saw institutional pressures as increasing the homogeneity of organizational structures. Firms will adopt similar structures as a result of three types of pressures. Coercive pressures come from legal mandates from the state or organizations whose resources they are dependent on. Mimetic pressures to copy successful forms arise because of perceived social capital attaching to the mimicked form. Normative pressures arising from professionalization see similar practices become widely standard across organizations that employ professionals. These three pressures give rise to institutional isomorphism. The institutional perspective rapidly became the dominant approach in North American and then the wider sociology of organizations from the 1980s onwards. Key texts emerging from institutional theory, such as Scott's *Institutions and Organizations,* achieved paradigmatic textbook status.

Core Concepts in Sociology, First Edition. Edited by J. Michael Ryan.
© 2019 John Wiley & Sons Ltd. Published 2019 by John Wiley & Sons Ltd.

The appearance in 1996 of the first edition of the *Handbook of Organization Studies* (Clegg, Hardy, and Nord 1996) saw a stocktaking of the current state of the field which was updated in 2006, with some additions and deletions. Perhaps the most notable deletion was the absence of contingency theory, which was fading in relevance. Subsequently, the appearance of more specialist volumes within the newly institutionalizing field of organization studies signaled the increasing professionalization of the new field in volumes such as the *Handbook of Organizational Institutionalism* (Greenwood et al. 2008) and the nomenclature of organization studies became widely generalized to cover much work that was often implicitly, if not explicitly, sociological.

One part of the emphasis in sociologically inspired teaching and research in the business schools has been translating mainstream sociology theory ideas studies to the more pragmatic orientations of the field of the sociology of organizations. Key figures for the process of translation have been Giddens's *The Constitution of Society: Outline of the Theory of Structuration* and Bourdieu's *Outline of a Theory of Practice*, which helped germinate many empirical studies of practices and their structuration.

Research Committee 17, The Sociology of Organizations, of the *International Sociological Association* is the main "official" sociological home for researchers. Annual volumes culled from contributions to other conferences are of considerable interest for the sociology of organizations (see, for example, Hernes and Maitlis 2010; Carlile et al. 2013). In addition to journals such as *Administrative Science Quarterly*, *Organization Studies*, *Organization*, and *Organization Science*, which are major outlets for sociology of organizations research, there are many journals that combine specialist interests in organizations with other substantive areas such as *Culture and Organizations*, *Gender, Work and Organizations*, and *Organizations and the Environment*.

Publications and theoretical developments suggest an underlying healthiness: the series in *Research in the Sociology of Organizations*, now published by Emerald, is prestigious; the major theoretical currents in organization studies are clearly sociologically embedded, such as institutional theory, even if increasingly their main proponents are not; major works such as the edited volume on *The Oxford Handbook of Sociology and Organization Studies: Classical Foundations* (Adler 1999), continue to be published, as do evident teaching anthologies.

Sociological approaches to organizations often are aligned with critical post-Marxist perspectives emerging from fields such as Labour Process theory in the encounter of some of its leading figures, such as Hugh Willmott and Mats Alvesson, with the many kinds of nonhistorical subject that were not defined solely by the identity of being "working class." These subjectivities and identities were theoretically illuminated, especially, by work in the tradition of Foucault and Giddens. Various strands of feminist, postcolonial, and Foucauldian-inspired scholarship dominate critical perspectives. These more radical approaches to the dominant functionalism emerged in the 1970s and spilt out into both a more differentiated politics than that solely of class and a more diverse set of theories than those only of the Marxist-related literature. One effect of the emergence of these counter-currents was that older approaches that dominated the field 30 or so years ago, such as structural contingency theory, seem increasingly to be regarded as irrelevant by contemporary scholars. Today, although sociologically influenced approaches have developed in the Business School environment that increasingly employs sociologists of organizations, it is rare that the discipline of sociology per se is being presented in the classroom. The trick is to show the relevance of sociology through the questions it can ask and answer, something in which institutional theory has been very successful. The dominance of new institutional theory and its key concepts such as institutional work, logics, and entrepreneurship can be expected to maintain their centrality; increasingly, institutional theory, in its various complexities, is the normal science paradigm for the field.

In the last decade there has been a return to more classical approaches to the sociology of organizations with a renewed interest in inequality, indicated by the *Administrative Science Quarterly's* (*ASQ*) Virtual Feature issue (see http://asq.sagepub.com/site/misc/VirtIss/ASQVSI2.xhtml). A good guide to other topical areas is provided by the *ASQ's* Editors Choice pages (see http://asq.sagepub.com/cgi/collection), which spotlights work on topics such as affect and emotion, strategy and corporate governance, and social movements, amongst several others. The renaissance of historical approaches, represented in collections by Buchelli and Wadhwani (2014) and Maclaren, Mills, and Weatherbee (2015), suggests that the future of the sociology of organizations will increasingly form around matters of process and historical comparison. Dominant approaches to methods are likely to continue to be hybrid, with a qualitative bias. In conclusion, we can expect that work that situates itself in relation to various currents of sociology, very broadly conceived, will continue to be produced, with institutionally embedded, historically oriented, and critical perspectives continuing to flourish.

SEE ALSO: Class; Culture, Sociology of; Economic Sociology; Gender; Modernity; Rationalization, Bureaucratization, and McDonaldization; Work, Occupations, and Professions, Sociology of

References

Adler, Paul, ed. 1999. *The Oxford Handbook of Sociology and Organization Studies: Classical Foundations.* Oxford: Oxford University Press. DOI:10.1177/0170840610380526.

Buchelli, Marcelo, and Daniel Wadhwani, eds. 2015. *Organizations in Time: History, Theory, Methods.* Oxford: Oxford University Press. DOI:10.1093/acprof:oso/9780199646890.001.0001.

Carlile, Paul R., Davide Nicolinin, Ann Langley and Haridimos Tsoukas, eds. 2013. *How Matter Matters: Objects, Artifacts, and Materiality in Organization Studies,* Vol. 3. Oxford: Oxford University Press. DOI:10.1093/acprof:oso/9780199671533.001.0001.

Clegg, Stewart R., Cynthia Hardy, and Walter Nord, eds. 1996. *The Sage Handbook of Organization Studies.* London: Sage Publishing. DOI:http://dx.doi.org/10.4135/9781848608030.

Greenwood, Royston, Christine Oliver, Roy Suddaby, and Kerstin Sahlin-Andersson, eds. 2008. *The Sage Handbook of Organizational Institutionalism.* London: Sage Publishing. DOI:http://dx.doi.org/10.4135/9781849200387.

Hernes, Tor, and Sally Maitlis, eds. 2010. *Process, Sensemaking, and Organizing,* Vol. 1. Oxford: Oxford University Press. DOI:10.1093/acprof:oso/9780199594566.001.0001.

Maclaren, Patricia, Albert Mills, and Terrance Weatherbee, eds. 2016. *The Routledge Companion to Management and Organizational History.* New York: Routledge. DOI:10.4324/9780203550274.

Patriarchy

Bronwyn Winter

University of Sydney, Australia

The term patriarchy, which is of Greek origin, literally means "rule of the father." Historically, the patriarch was the male head of the extended household, which he ruled autocratically, and by extension, of the village, tribe, or church. Radical feminists of the so-called second wave in the 1960s and 1970s used the term to describe the ideologies and structures of our modern societies (regardless of their political or economic system, regardless also of culture, ethnicity, class, or religion), which have the male domination of women at their core. It is this recasting of the term that is at the origin of its modern sociological meaning: the male domination of women, a unique political relationship that has its origins in the family and constitutes men and women as distinct social groups.

The term was first used in this way by Kate Millett, one of the founding figures of radical feminism, in her then revolutionary book *Sexual Politics* (1970). She chose the term advisedly, to foreground the ways in which the patriarchal system operates. Unlike other social relations, with the possible exception of slavery, the political relationship that is patriarchy is built first within the private sphere, namely, the family, and all public-sphere oppressions of women derive from that original oppression. In this, patriarchy is akin to a feudal system, as Millet noted – a characterization which echoes that of Simone de Beauvoir, whose seminal work *The Second Sex* ([1949] 2010) was hugely influential in the development of second-wave feminism. Beauvoir likened male domination of women to slavery and identified women as a group as a form of *caste*. Unlike the slave, however, and unlike other racialized populations, Beauvoir noted that women have no "homeland," no "elsewhere" outside the society in which they live to which they can turn their minds as a promised place of liberation. There is no other country for women; hence Beauvoir's choice of the term *caste* as the most appropriate in her opinion. Millett and other early radical feminists preferred the term *class*, recalling Marx's framing of the antagonism between the capitalist class and the proletariat. Some years subsequently, in 1978, French radical lesbian sociologist Colette Guillaumin (1995) described the subordination of women as *sexage*, a term reminiscent of the French term for slavery, *esclavage*.

This second-wave feminist deployment of the concept of patriarchy revolutionized thinking about the social relations between men and women. In particular, it laid open the public/private distinction that serves patriarchal social relations by protecting the primary seat of patriarchal control – the family – from scrutiny or critique. Such a system could only function through maintenance of that distinction and through a worldview in which only men count as fully human, such that male appropriations of women's bodies, time, and labor, enforced not only through laws and cultural norms but also through sexual and reproductive impositions and physical, psychological, and economic violence, did not appear clearly as such. Patriarchy, so described, is structural, systemic, ideological, and indeed global: it permeates all levels of society and all aspects of relations between men and women, and indeed between men and men and between women and women.

Although widely adopted subsequently by other strands of feminism and within social and political sciences more generally, the term has not escaped criticism. The most substantial historical disagreement – and the one that has drawn a line between radical and socialist feminists – is over whether capitalism or patriarchy is the root of all other oppressions, with some socialist feminists arguing a "dual-systems" theory (Eisenstein 1978), or more recently, whether several different intersecting forms of domination or discrimination (gender, class, race, and so on) form part of one system of oppression.

A further dissent comes from political theorist Carole Pateman, who in *The Sexual Contract* (1988) suggested that the French Revolution transformed the patriarchal regimes of pre-contemporary societies into the fraternal (or fratriarchal) regimes of today: the rule of the father has given way to the rule of the brothers. The distinction, however, is in some respects moot: the core relationship of male domination of women remains, and the term *patriarchy* remains the most commonly used and most recognizable term for summing up that relationship.

SEE ALSO: Family and Kinship, Sociology of; Gender; Inequality, Gender; Intersectionality; Masculinities

References

Beauvoir, Simone de. [1949] 2010. *The* Second *Sex*, translated by Constance Borde and Sheila Malovany-Chevallier. New York: Knopf.

Eisenstein, Zillah, ed. 1978. *Capitalist Patriarchy and the Case for Socialist Feminism.* New York: Monthly Review Press.

Guillaumin, Colette. 1995. "The Practice of Power and Belief in Nature, Part I: The Appropriation of Women." In *Racism, Sexism, Power and Ideology*, 176–207.

Millett, Kate. 1970. *Sexual Politics.* New York: Doubleday.

Pateman, Carole. 1988. *The Sexual Contract.* Stanford, CA: Stanford University Press.

Political Sociology

Alan Scott

University of New England, Australia

The current division of labor within the social sciences is not set in stone. It is the historical outcome of institutional and intellectual developments that also display national variation. In Britain the social sciences emerged out of political history and philosophy, and social research, often driven by philanthropy. In Continental Europe, where social and political science is closely associated with the training of national administrative elites, it emerged largely out of law. In the United States, where there is a strong tradition of political liberalism (egalitarianism plus small government), social research modeled itself early on the natural sciences (see Anderson 2003). In each case, the social sciences are closely associated with processes of nation-state formation and with the state's need to make society "legible" – and thus governable – by standardizing and collecting data (see Scott 1998).

One key intellectual development that had impact well beyond national borders was the so-called "methods dispute" (*Methodenstreit*) among economists in Germany and Austria around the turn of the twentieth century. On the one side stood those economists who saw their discipline as a historical science concerned with the development of national economies; on the other those representatives of what became the Austrian School, who argued for economics as a positive science concerned with the discovery of universal laws and the building of abstract models. The latter's victory had implications for the social sciences as a whole. It "left politics as a residue [...] and created a domain for a separate science of politics" (Anderson 2003: 17). The same can be said of "the social" and sociology. As is commonly the case with academic disciplines, the strategy was then to identify an object around which the discipline could form and over which a monopoly claim could be asserted. Thus political science emerged as the study of governments, parties, and political systems, while sociology sought to establish "society" as an independent object of academic research. Any system of categorization creates "matter out of place"; matter that falls across or between the categorical schema and with which the schema cannot adequately deal. So too it is with disciplines. If political and social systems are separate and autonomous fields of knowledge, what happens to the connections between those systems? How are we to understand the relationship between "the political" and "the social"; between state and civil society?

Core Concepts in Sociology, First Edition. Edited by J. Michael Ryan.
© 2019 John Wiley & Sons Ltd. Published 2019 by John Wiley & Sons Ltd.

Within this disciplinary order, political sociology, like political economy, is concerned with those areas of investigation that are not well integrated within the historically transmitted division of disciplinary labor because they lie between and/or across disciplinary boundaries and, for precisely this reason, are marginal. Glancing through the contents list of major handbooks of political sociology (e.g., Janoski et al. 2005; Amenta, Nash, and Scott 2012) confirms this impression. These volumes typically include both topics that would not look out of place in similar works in political science (e.g., democracy and democratization) and those that are marginal to both relevant disciplines (e.g., the relationship of gender, ethnicity, or religion to politics and to the state). But this perhaps gives the impression that political sociology is a mere potpourri of themes that are, or were at some point, neglected. This impression is reinforced when we remember that political sociology is not characterized by a common theoretical approach or methodology. The variety of approaches that are to be found within contemporary social science generally – e.g., Marxism, rational choice theory, constructionism, neo-institutionalism – are mirrored in political sociology.

To counter this impression, a first approximation to understanding political sociology might be to view it as a distinctive approach primarily concerned with (i) the social basis of politics (e.g., the class and other cleavages that underlie voting patterns) and (ii) the ways in which the state and politics shape and impact upon social relations (e.g., the way citizenship rights shape social identities). Rather than assert the kind of monopolistic claims over a distinct object of analysis that characterizes the dominant logic of disciplinarity, trans- or cross-disciplinary fields seek to identify the connections between areas of investigation that can be easily lost in the process of discipline formation. This is evident in two themes that have been central concerns within political sociology: social movements and processes of state formation. It is worth considering each briefly.

Social movements represent precisely the kind of object that lies neatly within neither the sphere of the political nor the social. Unlike political parties – which have been a staple of political science since its inception – social movements are not highly integrated into politics or institutionalized within the political system. But nor are they apolitical social phenomena outside the sphere of politics. They are manifestations of "organized civil society," or what Durkheim called "political society"; a sphere intermediate between individuals and informal groups on the one hand, and the more formal institutions of the state on the other. It is thus neither a surprise nor a coincidence that the systematic study of social movements should have found its natural home within political sociology. The kinds of analysis that have developed to account for social movements similarly illustrate the concern with the intersection of politics and society. Thus one strand of social movement analysis emphasizes the social and cultural aspects of social movements by focusing on the role of cultural identity and/or emotions in shaping collective action, while another – coming from the opposite direction – shows how formal political institutions create (nationally) distinct "political opportunity structures" that influence the strategies – and thus the organizational form – adopted by social movements in pursuing their political objectives. While the former emphasizes the affective and non-instrumental aspects of the formation of collective identity and action, the latter emphasizes the elements of instrumental and strategic rationality that effective political action demands. But even this distinction between the affective and the instrumental is not so clear-cut. Protest, for example, is not merely a manifestation of a political demand; it also builds a sense of community and identity. Finally, social movements illustrate one further feature of the relationship between politics and society: the fluidity of its boarders. By politicizing themes – from the employer–employee relationship (once considered a contractual matter) to LGBT rights – that were previously thought of as lying within the private (contractual or personal) sphere, social movements constantly challenge our understanding of what the social or the political really are, and where the boundaries between them lie.

State formation illustrates political sociology's concern with topics neglected by political science and/or sociology in a somewhat different way. As political science sought post-World War II to establish itself – particularly in the United States – as a modern science grounded in methodologically sound social research, the notion of "the state" came to be viewed as a relic of an earlier disciplinary stage; as a mystification immune to serious empirical research. Its place was to be taken by such notions as the "political system," thought to be more amenable to empirical enquiry. It was left to historical and political sociologists such as Barrington Moore Jr., Theda Skocpol, and Charles Tilly to reintroduced the state as a legitimate theme in social analysis, the publication of Evans and colleagues' *Bringing the State Back In* in 1985 being the pivotal moment. In doing so, these sociologists incidentally built a bridge between contemporary debate and classical social theory in its pre-disciplinary form by reviving a concern with the definition of the state and the role of the monopoly of violence, pacification, and warfare in state making. These questions had been of central concern in late nineteenth- and early twentieth-century social theory; notably, of course, in the work of Max Weber and contemporaries such as the historian Otto Hintze. Thus, political sociology is not merely *cross-* or *trans*-disciplinary; it is in some respects *pre*-disciplinary, or at least harks back to a time before social-scientific disciplines had staked their monopolistic claims.

But the element of continuity between political sociology and strands of thought influential long before the emergence of modern social sciences can be traced back even further with perhaps still more radical implications. As some influential postwar political scientists recognized, political sociology is more than the "sociology of politics" in that it introduces normative questions of the kind that have traditionally occupied political theory into the more empirically minded social sciences. Thus far, it has been suggested that political sociology is concerned with the *connections* between the social and the political, but if we trace its origins back far enough into political theory we soon find ourselves at a point in which there was no meaningful distinction between "the political" and "the social." Correspondingly, we find a line of argument in political sociology which, as Sartori suspected and feared, takes an altogether dissenting view on the division of labor between the social sciences. This is a position that we might instantly associate with poststructuralist thought and/or with Foucault, but in fact, there is a long tradition of such radical disciplinary doubt within political sociology. For example, in the 1960s the then highly influential, and now no-less deeply unfashionable, French political sociologist Raymond Aron admonished sociology for its neglect of technical instruments of state (laws, constitutions, etc.) and for "failing to take into account the partial autonomy of the political order" (Aron [1961] 2004: 218) while simultaneously doubting the feasibility of a political science that conceived of its object as disembedded from social relations and social forces.

Finally, political sociology is an area in which the limits to the capacity of academic disciplines to set their own agenda are particularly apparent. For example, social movements do not simply represent an *object* of political–sociological analysis, but also a key *stimulus* that co-shapes the field. Of course, this is true, to varying degrees, of the social sciences generally – think for example of the influence of feminism or communitarianism in political and social theory, and in sociology. But political sociology is an area of investigation in which, in an immediately evident fashion, not merely the boundaries between disciplines are questioned, but the boundary between academic and scientific research and social and political action is itself challenged. Dilemmas of degrees of engagement and detachment are thus particularly evident.

Political sociology is thus more than a collection of themes, or simply an approach or perspective. It is one of those fields of social scientific investigation that – like political economy – does not sit comfortably within the, itself unstable, disciplinary division of labor; which displays a high degree of continuity with classical social and political theory; and in which the mutual influence of political practice and academic debate are particularly transparent.

SEE ALSO: Citizenship; Democracy; Economic Sociology; Marxism; Military Sociology; Modernity; Nationalism; Power and Authority; Social Movements and Social Change

References

Amenta, E., K. Nash, and A. Scott, eds. 2012. *The Wiley Blackwell Companion to Political Sociology*. Oxford: Wiley Blackwell.

Aron, R. [1961] 2004. "The Dawn of Universal History." In *Politics and History*, edited by Miriam Bernheim Constant. New Brunswick, NJ: Transaction Publishers.

Anderson, L. 2003. *Pursuing Truth, Exercising Power: Social Science and Public Policy in the 21st Century*. New York: Columbia University Press.

Evans, P.B., D. Rueschemeyer, and T. Skocpol, eds. 1985. *Bringing the State Back In*. Cambridge: Cambridge University Press.

Janoski, T., R. Alford, A. Hicks, and M.A. Schwartz, eds. 2005. *The Handbook of Political Sociology: States, Civil Societies and Globalization*. Cambridge: Cambridge University Press.

Scott, J.C. 1998. *Seeing Like a State: How Certain Schemes to Improve the Human Condition Have Failed*. New Haven, CT: Yale University Press.

Popular Culture

Beryl Langer

La Trobe University, Australia

Popular culture, ostensibly defined by its appeal to large numbers of people, eludes clear definition outside the context in which it is used. The complexity of the word "culture" (Williams 1983: 87) is compounded by its combination with "popular." It is not a neutral term, but one framed by aesthetic and political judgment as either "mindless entertainment for the masses" or "meaningful amusement for 'the people.'" In that "culture" refers to both texts and objects made by cultural producers and the shared meanings and practices of social actors, the range of what is included in the field of "popular culture" is vast – everything from television, film, music and computer games to shopping, gardening, online gambling, sport, and social media. Popular culture is thus an object of study in a number of subfields within sociology as well as in neighboring disciplines (anthropology, history) and interdisciplinary fields like cultural studies, gender studies, and media studies.

Sociology's approach to popular culture was initially framed in terms of the opposition between "community" and "society" through which the transition to modernity was conceptualized by the discipline's founders. Whereas ethnic and rural folk cultures were seen as reinforcing "community," the commercial entertainment available to urban workers was deemed a social and moral threat. While anxiety about popular pleasures did not begin with industrialization, sociological anxiety was inflected through disciplinary concern with questions of *social order* posed by the transition to industrial modernity, of which both sociology and popular culture in its mass-produced form were a part. In the writings of early Chicago School sociologists, for example, popular culture (radio, movies) was associated with commercial exploitation of needs once met communally – its texts seen as offering cheap thrills and passive escapism (Wirth 1938: 22), its practices (e.g., the Taxi Dance Hall) seen as fraught with moral danger (Cressey [1932] 1968).

Mid-twentieth-century sociological discussion of popular culture was shaped by the "high culture–mass culture" debate. Conservative arguments about cultural decline intersected with the "culture industry" thesis of Frankfurt School Marxism in defining the music, movies, and (later) television enjoyed by mass audiences as inferior to either the folk cultures of pre-industrial society or the art, literature, and music that constituted "high culture." While conservative critics attributed cultural decline to the taste-leveling

Core Concepts in Sociology, First Edition. Edited by J. Michael Ryan.
© 2019 John Wiley & Sons Ltd. Published 2019 by John Wiley & Sons Ltd.

impact of democracy, critical theorists of the Frankfurt School attributed it to capitalism. According to the "culture industry" thesis, Hollywood and Tin Pan Alley produced escapist trash which affirmed capitalist values, subjecting workers to exploitation and domination outside the factory as well as within. Entertainment was simply the "prolongation of work" (Horkheimer and Adorno [1947] 2002: 109), offering no escape from the alienated logic of capitalist production.

A less anxious and less pejorative approach emerged in the course of the 1960s, as researchers engaged with popular culture from the inside rather than from a position of cultural superiority. Popular culture was normalized as part of everyday life rather than pathologized as a social problem, and focus shifted to the connection between cultural taste and social class. Herbert Gans (1974: vii), for example, defended popular culture against the charge that it was not really "culture" at all, arguing that popular culture "reflects and expresses the aesthetic and other wants of many people" and was therefore a "culture," not a "commercial menace." He identified five different "taste cultures," each with its own aesthetic standards and each associated with particular class and educational backgrounds, and argued for a cultural democracy in which "all taste cultures are of equal worth" (Gans 1974: xi). According to French sociologist Pierre Bourdieu (1984), however, the hierarchies of class and culture were mutually reinforcing, and designation of popular culture and those who consumed it as "vulgar" was central to the legitimation of class distinction. Class and its connection to popular culture was also central to research carried out at the Birmingham Centre for Contemporary Cultural Studies, but the focus there was on the appropriation and use of popular culture as a form of *resistance* to the dominant order rather than its legitimation. That the class–culture relation might be even more complex was suggested by Peterson's "cultural omnivore" thesis, which located "cultural distinction" in consumption of both high and popular culture rather than high culture alone.

In the past three decades the revolution in digital technology has produced a cultural field which can no longer be understood in terms of a distinction between two kinds of culture, one "popular," the other "elite." The internet offers instant access across all genres to anyone with a computer (and the technical, cultural, and linguistic capabilities needed to access digital content) and facilitates circulation of content to niche markets across the globe. The fact that "ordinary people" can post material – whether on social media like Facebook or in blogs and YouTube uploads – makes popular culture participatory in ways that could not have been predicted by mid-twentieth-century commentators. Future directions in the sociology of popular culture will be determined by the theoretical and methodological negotiation of this technological transformation.

SEE ALSO: Capital: Cultural, Social, and Economic; Consumption; Culture, Sociology of; Everyday Life; Internet, the; Media, Sociology of the; Social Media and Virtual Communities

References

Bourdieu, Pierre. 1984. *Distinction: A Social Critique of the Judgement of Taste.* London: Routledge & Kegan Paul.

Cressey, Paul. [1932] 1968. *The Taxi-Dance Hall: A Sociological Study in Commercialized Recreation and City Life.* New York: Greenwood Press.

Gans, Herbert. 1974. *Popular Culture and High Culture: An Analysis and Evaluation of Taste*. New York: Basic Books.

Horkheimer, Max, and Theodor Adorno. [1947] 2002. *The Dialectic of Enlightenment*. Stanford, CA: Stanford University Press.

Williams, Raymond. 1983. *Keywords*. New York: Oxford University Press.

Wirth, Louis. 1938. "Urbanism as a Way of Life." *American Journal of Sociology* 44 (1): 1–24.

Postmodernism and Poststructuralism

Julie M. Albright

University of California, USA

Postmodernism and poststructuralism exist at once as philosophies and as critiques, encompassing many disparate ideas and practices. Postmodernism is characterized by a shift in sensibilities in the arts, music, architecture, and other social fields and includes a move from form to artifice, structure to surface, purity to pastiche, and substance to image or simulation. It is both a historic epoch and a style. Poststructuralism is less about shifting aesthetic sensibilities and more about a rethinking of *structuralism*, a set of theories emanating out of linguistics which aims to understand human culture and behavior as reflective of a scaffolding of language which exists *sui generis*; structuralism was later critiqued by the poststructuralists for its rigidity and ahistoricism.

Many argue that Western history has been divided into three major epochs: the premodern, the modern, and the postmodern. The premodern era occurred during the Dark Ages, when the Catholic Church controlled knowledge and "Truth," as ordained by God. Later, emerging scientific discoveries like the compass began to break down that singular worldview, as travel and exploration revealed other ways of knowing. Catholic cleric Nicolaus Copernicus later developed heliocentric theories of celestial mechanics, challenging the church's contention that the sun revolves around the Earth. The church rejected these theories, causing him to set them aside. Some 50 years later, Galileo Galilei built a telescope to demonstrate that the Copernican heliocentric theories were indeed correct; he was later tried for heresy during the Inquisition, and ordered to refrain from holding, teaching, or defending these ideas. The printing press spread many of these scientific discoveries. Francis Bacon developed a "scientific method" which relied upon observation, experimentation, and analysis rather than religious dogma. René Descartes' (1596–1650) philosophy focused on rational thought and the senses ("Cogito, ergo sum" – "I think, therefore I am") which became known as *Cartesian Dualism*. Science became the cornerstone of modernism, which eventually grew into the dominant worldview, secularizing Western societies in its wake.

Modernism continued to evolve through the twentieth century, bringing with it advances in psychoanalysis, medicine, and physics, and ushering sweeping social

Core Concepts in Sociology, First Edition. Edited by J. Michael Ryan.

change, including urbanization and the rise of the modern capitalist industrial state. Its momentum was fueled by the promise of "progress" built upon science and reason. Modernism reached an apex in the atomic era of World War II, with the dropping of two nuclear bombs on Hiroshima and Nagasaki, leaving hundreds of thousands dead, and cities devastated and radioactive. In Europe in 1945, the Allied powers liberated the German concentration camps and discovered six extermination camps in Poland resembling high-tech industrial factories, their sole purpose the systematic extermination of millions of Jews. In light of the devastation brought about by the nuclear bombing of Japan, the destruction of Europe, and the atrocities committed by Hitler and the Third Reich, both religion and modernity seemed to have failed. The spread of television placed a new emphasis on image and consumerism. Modernist architecture, art, and design associated with the Third Reich began to wane. The Dean of the Berlin Bauhaus, modernist architect Mies Van der Rohe, described the modernist sensibility as "Less is More": It encompassed form following function, simplification, and a lack of ornamentation. A newly emerging postmodern sensibility, summed up by architect Robert Venturi, was, "Less is a bore": It was playful, its adherents reveling in irony, ornamentation, and a pastiche of styles.

For postmodernists and poststructuralists, especially those in post-World War II France, deconstructing the linkages between power and knowledge became a critical project. Many also addressed the rapid change in social structures, impacted by rapid urbanization, television, and emerging digital technologies. Earlier attempts at understanding society included structuralism: founded by linguist Ferdinand de Saussure in the early twentieth century, de Sassure ([1916] 1960) theorized that human culture could be understood by examining the underlying structure of language. Saussure termed his studies *semiology*. His book on the subject, called *Course in General Linguistics,* was published by his students posthumously in 1916. His work influenced French anthropologist Claude Levi-Strauss, whose 1949 book *The Elementary Structures of Kinship* ushered in structural anthropology and inspired intellectuals in a variety of fields. Sociologist Roland Barthes began to transition away from structuralism in the 1960s, undertaking a deconstruction of everyday, mundane phenomenon, ranging from striptease to the latest Citroen.

Jean Baudrillard was a lightning rod in the postmodern movement: His work was playful, ironic, and fanciful. He became fascinated by American culture, particularly consumer culture and the media, opinion polling, and environmental design, epitomized by the artifice of Las Vegas and Disneyland. Baudrillard was interested in simulation and simulacra; he coined the term "hyperreality," describing it as "more real than real," for which there is no natural referent: It is, as he put it "always already reproduced." Examples include videotaped workout routines and suburban tract housing; in each case there exists no original, only endless reproduction.

Gilles Deleuze and Felix Guattari were influential in both poststructural and postmodern circles. They interrogated medical discourses as a system of domination and social control and conducted an analysis of desire in society. Their book *Anti Oedipus* (1972) was a poststructural critique of Marxism and Lacanian psychoanalysis. Their proposed "schizo analysis" – as an alternative to psychoanalysis – centered on an emphasis on multiplicity, plurality, and decenteredness. They view desire as revolutionary and productive and hence the centerpiece of control in modern societies. The process of repressing desire they term *territorialization,* while freeing desire from these repressive social forces is *deterritorialization* or *decoding.*

Michel Foucault was another influential poststructuralist. In *An Archeology of Knowledge* (1969) and *Discipline and Punish: The Birth of the Prison* (1975), he undertakes an "archeology of knowledge," interrogating notions of sane and insane, normal and abnormal, while tracing their origins and evolution over time. In *Discipline and Punish* (1995), Foucault examines the relationship between discourse and power, which he termed *power/knowledge,* and how technologies of surveillance are used to discipline identity, desire, and the body. Later, in *The History of Sexuality* (1976), he explored how discourses are used to produce normal versus abnormal sexualities. Foucault implicated the fields of psychiatry, sociology, criminology, and architecture (utilizing Betham's Panopticon) in the proliferation of new techniques of power.

Fredrick Jameson (1930–) is one of the few notable theorists from the United States working in the postmodern tradition. Trained in Marxism, he later developed his own neo-Marxist analysis of the postmodern era. Like other postmodernists, Jameson was influenced by the anti-war and New Left political movements. In his key text *Postmodernism, or the Cultural Logic of Late Capitalism* (1999), Jameson outlines the historical development of postmodernism, describing it as the spatialization of culture under the pressure of organized capitalism.

Like Jameson, François Lyotard's theoretical roots were in Marxism, but he later strayed away from that approach; unlike other social theorists, Lyotard clearly connected himself to postmodernism. In his book *The Postmodern Condition: A Report on Knowledge* (1993), Lyotard examines the connections between knowledge, technology, and science in societies. He postulated that the postmodern condition is characterized by an incredulity toward legitimating metanarratives. Lyotard posits that we need knowledge, or what he calls *petit récit* – small, local, and specific. He theorized the postmodern era as a time in which what counts as knowledge will be that which could be translated into binary code and stored in computerized databases, presaging knowledge production today in the digital era.

Postmodernism and poststructuralism seem to have fallen out of favor and some theorists posit we have entered a "post-postmodern" era (see Nealon 2012). Others say we are "hypermodern" (see Lipovetsky 2005), characterized by hyper-consumption and the hypermodern individual, who is typified by movement, pleasure, and hedonism, yet who is filled with anxiety as belief systems that previously brought comfort erode away. Others have proclaimed postmodernism dead because it embodied a "victim" mentality due to its connection to social movements like feminism, or through its questioning of dominant social narratives, disintegrating into nothingness via relativism. Still others have criticized it for a lack of rigor, stating that it envelops so many different concepts and meanings that it is rendered meaningless. Although several attempts have been made to theorize a post-postmodern era, none of the new labels have entered the mainstream lexicon. Postmodernism has now largely fallen out of favor within academia, supplanted by its progeny: queer theory, feminism, new historicism, and diaspora studies among others.

SEE ALSO: Body, the; Colonialism and Postcolonialism; Modernity; Sociological Theory; Space and Place

References

de Saussure, Ferdinand. [1916] 1960. *Course in General Linguistics*. London: Peter Owen.
Foucault, M. 1995. *Discipline and Punish: The Birth of the Prison*. New York: Vintage.
Lipovetsky, G. 2005. *Hypermodern Times*. Cambridge: Polity Press.
Nealon, J.T. 2012. *Post-Postmodernism, or, The Cultural Logic of Just-in-Time Capitalism*. Stanford, CA: Stanford University Press.

Further Reading

Baudrillard, J. 1983. *Simulations*. New York: Semiotext(e).
Kellner, D. 1988. "Postmodernism as Social Theory: Some Challenges and Problems." In *Theory, Culture and Society*, Vol. 5, 239–269. London: Sage.
Poster, M. 1998. *Jean Baudrillard: Selected Writings*. Stanford, CA: Stanford University Press.

Poverty

Tracy Shildrick

University of Leeds, UK

Poverty has been a persistent feature in economically advanced societies, despite much policy intervention to try to alleviate it in many countries around the world. Within sociology interest in poverty and inequality goes back to the foundations of the discipline and in recent decades the realization that overall increases in wealth have done little to alleviate poverty have also kept the subject alive. Despite this longstanding interest, poverty as a specific term tends to ebb and flow in terms of its popularity within the discipline. A quick trawl of the key UK sociology journal *Sociology* at the time of writing revealed 441 articles with the word *poverty* in the full text (July 2016). This compares with 1559 with the words *social class* and 828 citing *inequality* in the full text. In the United States, the term poverty has tended to remain relatively more consistently popular and the relative prevalence and popularity of the term poverty is probably, at least in part, related to the shifting social and political context. In the United Kingdom, the term has become increasingly marginalized and stigmatized and has been largely deleted from political discussions, apart from occasional references to child poverty. In the United States there has been a longstanding acceptance that poverty exists, whereas in the United Kingdom there has been a much greater tendency to simply deny the existence of poverty. It is also the case that much sociological thinking on poverty resides within broader discussions, for example, social class, or is sometimes hidden behind different concepts and terminology, for example, social exclusion or economic marginalization.

At the heart of much sociological research is the relationship between structure and agency and how the two operate to influence life chances. It is this division that lies at the heart of work that seeks to explain the causes of poverty. There has been a strong emphasis in some of this work around individual pathology as a key cause of poverty. Early variants tend to point toward the so-called "residuum" identified by Booth in 1889 which constituted those apparently feckless and criminal people who were poor and who were argued to be distinct from the supposedly more respectable working classes. Ideas about poverty that stress individual behavioral explanations for the condition have endured, albeit in slightly different guises, for a very long time and show no sign of diminishing. In the 1960s, poverty remained despite increasing general prosperity.

Core Concepts in Sociology, First Edition. Edited by J. Michael Ryan.
© 2019 John Wiley & Sons Ltd. Published 2019 by John Wiley & Sons Ltd.

Hence, it was the "rediscovery of poverty" in the United Kingdom and the "war on poverty" declared by President Johnson in the same period in the United States that led to renewed attempts to try and understand its endurance. Lewis's studies of Puerto Rican families and their experiences of poverty focused on the "cultures" adopted by those experiencing poverty. Lewis argued that it was the cultures of the poor that were responsible for keeping them in poverty and worked against people adopting other patterns of behavior that might allow them to move away from poverty. The "culture of poverty" thesis was influential and in the United States in particular it took on a racial or racist dimension. In the United Kingdom similar ideas took hold in this period with Conservative member of parliament Keith Joseph putting forward the notion of a "cycle of deprivation." At the time there was criticism and skepticism (Rutter and Madge 1976), but these ideas continue to appeal to both political figures and large swathes of the general public. In the 1980s the pathological and behavioral approach resurfaced under the guise of the new terminology of the "underclass." Again in the United States the arguments about a supposed underclass had a particular racial aspect to them. In the United Kingdom, it was the US social commentator Charles Murray who brought this idea to the fore (Murray 1992). Whilst most sociological work has generally been very critical of these sorts of ideas, they remain popular and have been influential with governments in many countries in giving weight to particularly punitive policy responses to those experiencing poverty and in promoting stigma toward those experiencing the condition.

Critiques of these individualist and moral approaches to understanding poverty have tended to focus on the structural context in which poverty occurs. In the United States, since the emergence of the Chicago School of sociological (and later criminological) research in the 1920s, there has been an emphasis in sociology on the lives and experiences of the urban poor. With the Chicago School it was the importance of particular places and the ways in which social and economic changes meant some locales experienced more concentrated poverty than others that was a key focus. The availability of jobs and the quality of employment has also been a key focus of work on poverty. In both the United States and the United Kingdom, although not a new phenomenon, in-work poverty (often referred to popularly as the "working poor") has become an important area of research as more and more people find themselves working but unable to move away from poverty (Shildrick et al. 2012). In seeking to illuminate both the structural causes and effects of poverty, research has highlighted the operation of not just labor markets and the opportunities they may offer to escape or experience poverty, but also the operation of the education system and the nature of welfare provision. The decline of welfare provision, coupled with austerity cuts in countries like the United States and the United Kingdom, have meant that the effects of poverty are being felt ever more widely. In the United Kingdom a recent report highlighted the increase in cases of destitution (Fitzpatrick et al. 2016) whereby individuals are deemed to be unable to "afford to buy the essentials to eat, stay warm and dry and keep clean" (ibid.). Where sociological thinking has been especially useful is in showing how different elements of living in poverty, not just the lack of economic resources, but also the associated limited housing choice, poorer health, and access to services for example, can all work together to limit opportunities and make the prospect of escape from poverty less likely (Townsend 1976). Hence, in contrast to the individual approaches, these sorts of explanations tend to argue that the persistence of poverty through the generations is a problem, but it is one caused by structural and environmental factors rather than individual behaviors. It has been through close-up ethnographic research that sociologists have best been able to demonstrate this.

In one such example from the United States, Sanchez-Jankowski illustrated the ways in which predominantly poor communities exhibit much stability and continuity, with residents showing much care and resilience, albeit in harsh and difficult circumstances (2008). The United Kingdom has a similar history of rich ethnographies that illuminate the complexities of living with poverty. From the classic earlier studies to a number of contemporary ethnographies, accounts frequently show in detail the resilience and tenacity of the lived realities of poverty as well as the sheer hard work required to simply get by.

Poverty features strongly in sociology and is a key aspect of much sociological research and thinking. Whilst poverty as a term has tended to be less popular with sociologists there is an overriding interest in how we can explain and understand the lives of those who experience poverty. The fact that poverty itself endures, and indeed seems to be increasing in recent times, is perhaps enough to ensure that the topic will retain its place in sociological thinking for the foreseeable future.

SEE ALSO: Capital: Cultural, Social, and Economic; Capitalism; Class; Class, Capitalist; Development, Sociology of; Economic Sociology; Homelessness; Inequality, Global; Marxism; Social Justice; Stratification and Inequality

References

Fitzpatrick, S., G. Bramely, F. Sosenko, J. Blenkinsopp, S. Johnsen, M. Littlewood, G. Netto, and B. Watts. 2016. *Destitution in the UK*. York: JRF.

Murray, C. 1992. *The Emerging British Underclass*. London: IEA.

Rutter, M., and N. Madge. 1976. *Cycles of Disadvantage*. London: Heinemann.

Sanchez-Janowski, M. 2008. *Cracks in the Pavement: Social Change and Resilience in Poor Neighbourhoods*. Berkeley: University of California Press.

Shildrick, T., R. MacDonald, C. Webster, and K. Garthwaite. 2012. *Poverty and Insecurity: Life in Low Pay, No Pay Britain*. Bristol: Policy Press.

Townsend, P. 1979. *Poverty in the United Kingdom*. London: Allen Lane and Penguin Books.

Power and Authority

Ashley Harrell and Shane Thye

University of South Carolina, USA

Power and authority are distinct but related ideas in sociology. One can have power without authority (e.g., a rogue-nation dictator) or authority without power (e.g., a lame-duck president). The two concepts are independent, yet they often go together. We first address the concept of power before turning to a discussion of authority. Then, we consider classic research connecting the two.

Power has been conceived in various ways, but all emphasize the relations between individuals (see Thye and Kalkhoff 2014 for an extensive overview of theories of power). Historically, power has been defined in terms of *control* or *benefit* (Willer 1999). Sociological definitions of power typically begin with Max Weber, who defines power in terms of *control*. For Weber, power is "the probability that one actor within a social relationship will be in a position to carry out his own will despite resistance" ([1918] 1968: 53). Social theorists who view power as the capacity to punish (or reward) others – see for example, Molm's (1988) punishment power – also fall within this domain. Other social theorists link power more directly to *benefit*. For instance, in contemporary social-exchange theory, power is (i) a structural capacity linked to exclusion or dependence, or (ii) a concrete event in which one individual benefits at the expense of another. The former is referred to as structural power or power potential, and the latter as power use or power exercise.

Power dependence theory (Emerson 1972) links power to the notion of dependence. Formally, the power of A over B (P_{AB}) is equivalent to the dependence of B on A (D_{BA}), such that $P_{AB} = D_{BA}$. Dependence, in turn, is linked to the availability of exchange partners and the extent to which individuals value goods in those relations. For example, drug dealers are powerful to the extent that they are the exclusive supplier of drugs and that addicts place a high value on those narcotics. Both factors make drug users more dependent on dealers than the converse. A similar idea is found in Willer's (1999) elementary theory, which links power to the capacity to exclude others from valued resources. Thus, in a classic auction where A is selling something to two bidders (B), A has power because one of those bidders will ultimately be excluded from the exchange.

Authority, like power, is a function of one's social position. *Authority* is generally defined as the legitimate or socially approved right to exercise power – including making decisions, giving orders or commands, or enforcing obedience given one's social position. Though authority and power are often used interchangeably, power can be used with or without authority. For instance, a vigilante group may have the power or ability to punish a criminal – but only the judicial system has the authority to do so. While power can be exerted via force or coercion, authority depends on subordinate groups agreeing to the use of power by the powerful.

Weber ([1918] 1968) conceptualized three different forms of authority, and saw each form of authority as a different *strategy* to legitimize rulers' use of power in a political system. *Charismatic authority* is based on the special skills or unusual characteristics of powerful individuals. These person-specific qualities inspire loyal and obedient behavior in followers. For example, a cult leader who claims to make prophecies or possess exclusive knowledge relies on charismatic authority. *Traditional authority* rests on established customs or traditions, such as the inheritance of power from one generation to the next. It is accepted because it is part of history or tradition; a monarchy where kings' authority is given by birth is one example. Finally, *rational–legal authority* is power use legitimized through formal, established rules and regulations. Nations with constitutions give authority to specific positions in a system, and the people who hold those positions, via written rules and laws. Weber predicted that rational–legal authority would ultimately become the dominant form of authority, as societies became more rationalized and bureaucratic.

Perhaps the most iconic demonstration of the confluence of power and authority are the Milgram studies of the 1960s (see Milgram 1974). The studies were inspired by Nazi war crimes, in particular Adolf Eichmann's claim during the Nuremburg trials that he was "just following orders" when executing and torturing thousands of POWs. Milgram wondered if everyday citizens would be willing to inflict severe pain via electric shock (a form of punishment power) on an unsuspecting "learner" in a memory experiment if asked to do so by a legitimate authority. Prior to the experiment, healthcare professionals estimated that fewer than 1 in 1000 people would deliver the highest possible shock of 450 volts to the learner. Remarkably, the results demonstrate that up to 65 percent of subjects delivered the maximum possible shock when urged to do so by an authority figure. The results of the now-infamous Milgram experiments illustrate that obedience to a legitimate authority is an extraordinarily powerful form of social control. More importantly, the study casts explanatory light on how ordinary people can exercise power at the hands of malevolent authorities in situations of dire consequences.

SEE ALSO: Political Sociology; Social Psychology; Sociological Theory; Structure and Agency

References

Emerson, Richard. 1972. "Exchange Theory, Part II: Exchange Relations and Networks." In *Sociological Theories in Progress*, edited by Joseph Berger, Morris Zelditch, and Bo Anderson, Vol. 2: 58–87. Boston: Houghton-Mifflin.

Milgram, Stanley. 1974. *Obedience to Authority: An Experimental View*. New York: Harper & Row.

Molm, Linda D. 1988. "The Structure and Use of Power: A Comparison of Reward and Punishment Power." *Social Psychology Quarterly* 51: 108–122.

Thye, Shane, and Will Kalkhoff. 2014. "Theoretical Perspectives on Power and Resource Inequality." In *Handbook of the Social Psychology of Inequality*, edited by Jane McLeod, Ed Lawler, and Michael Schwalbe, 27–48. New York: Kluwer-Plenum.

Weber, Max. [1918] 1968. *Economy and Society*. Berkeley: University of California Press.

Willer, David. 1999. *Network Exchange Theory*. Westport, CT: Praeger.

Public Sociology

Esther Oliver

University of Barcelona, Spain

Public sociology means opening dialogues with broader audiences with the purpose of going beyond the academy and deepening the way both sociologists and publics understand public issues and social sciences. According to Michael Burawoy, "Public Sociology brings sociology into a conversation with publics, understood as people who are themselves involved in conversations" (Burawoy 2005: 7).

Public sociology is one part of the sociological division of labor proposed by Burawoy. According to Burawoy, the division is composed of policy sociology, professional sociology, public sociology, and critical sociology. The differences among these sociologies are better understood if we answer two questions:

Question 1: *Sociology for whom?* This question leads sociologists to think about the type of audiences with whom to talk. Open dialogues with wider, extra-academic audiences take place in policy and public sociologies. Dialogues only with academic audiences take place in professional and critical sociologies.

Question 2: *Sociology for what?* This question leads sociologists to reflect on the type of knowledge to be achieved from sociology. Instrumental knowledge (from professional and policy sociologies) is traditionally linked to serving the interests of power or addressing a goal or purpose. Reflexive knowledge (from critical and public sociologies) addresses mainly the value premises of society and of the sociological profession.

Each type of sociology contains its own complexities. There are differences and tensions but also many connections and complementarities among the four types. Sociologists can develop more than one of these types simultaneously during their lives. According to Burawoy, "my normative vision of the discipline of sociology is of reciprocal interdependence among these four types (an organic solidarity in which each type of sociology derives energy, meaning, and imagination from its connection to the others)" (Burawoy 2005: 15).

Policy sociology is in the service of a goal defined by a client. Policy sociologists' main role is to find solutions to problems that concern their clients or to scientifically legitimate solutions that have been already reached. By contrast, in public sociology, the research agenda is the result of dialogue between the sociologist and the public. Policy sociology and public sociology are often complementary.

Core Concepts in Sociology, First Edition. Edited by J. Michael Ryan.
© 2019 John Wiley & Sons Ltd. Published 2019 by John Wiley & Sons Ltd.

Professional sociology provides methods, techniques, scientific knowledge, and theoretical frameworks; therefore, it provides legitimacy and expertise for public and policy sociology. Finally, critical sociology examines the implicit and explicit foundations of the research programs of professional sociology to make the field aware of its own gaps or biases and to promote new research agendas.

Understanding the concept of public sociology also requires deepening the distinction between traditional and organic public sociology.

In traditional public sociology, sociologists write for wider audiences about matters of public importance, but the publics are invisible and passive: there is no interaction between the scholars and the audiences. Since the beginning of the discipline, many sociologists have written scientific work that has been read beyond academia. These works have become vehicles for public discussion.

In organic public sociology, sociologists interact with visible and active publics, such as social movements, trade unions, or human rights groups. Organic connections are defined as part of the sociological life, making visible the invisible, and establishing dialogues with old and new publics, which are in a constant process of creation and transformation.

Traditional and organic public sociologies are complementary and inform each other. Main debates in society, for example, are influenced by the work of sociologists with their audiences, while activism or social movements influence the way sociologists collaborate with social agents and create knowledge. These different public sociologies reflect not only different publics but also diverse commitments from sociologists to society.

Michael Burawoy is the key author for understanding what public sociology is. His presidency of the American Sociological Association in 2004 marked a turning point in the way sociology is framed, first in the United States, and later globally. His presidential addresses to the ASA in 2004, published in the *American Sociological Review* (Burawoy 2005), defined the main characteristics of public sociology through eleven theses. However, public sociology had been practiced long before the term became popular in the discipline. C. Wright Mills, Alvin Gouldner, W.E.B. DuBois, and David Riesman, for example, were already considered public sociologists.

Burawoy made public sociology visible. Public sociology existed from the origins of the discipline, but the canons of specialization required by the academy had marginalized the field. Burawoy's concept of public sociology calls for a return to the original sociological spirit, taking knowledge back to those from whom it came (Burawoy 2005: 5), without denying the relevance of professional sociology. He appeals for understanding of the complementarities of public and professional sociology, highlighting the scientific basis of public sociology but also its moral and political engagement with society.

Burawoy's profound analysis connected for the first time the very different scholars doing public sociology today and constituted a new global framework for sociology worldwide. This endeavor was strengthened during his presidency of the International Sociological Association (2010–2014). Since then, public sociology has expanded around the world. All continents have scholars undertaking public sociology in very diverse contexts, major journals in the field, such as *Social Problems, Social Forces, Critical Sociology, The British Journal of Sociology, American Sociologist,* and *Current Sociology,* have published special issues on public sociology, and main international conferences in sociology have special sessions on public sociology.

Consequently, public sociology creates many intellectual debates within the discipline today about the audiences, the goals, the methods, and the benefits or drawbacks of each type of sociology. At the same time, however, the project of public sociology has called forth various criticisms from scholars concerned, for example, about the risk that public sociology will politicize sociology or about the impossibility of building synergies or complementarities between professional and public sociology, among others. Scholars also argue that public sociology is based on a false premise of uniformity of the moral and political agenda of sociologists or question that public sociology has an idealistic perception of the audiences and the public.

Indeed, public sociologists face many obstacles. The reality of public sociology worldwide is diverse and variable, depending on the political and social context each country is living at every moment. Each public sociologist has complicated dilemmas when he or she decides to be committed to the public in the development of his or her scientific work: to practice different sociologies simultaneously and to answer to different audiences through sociological work; to cope with emotional engagement or to develop research in a politicized environment; to guarantee the complementarity between objectivity and social engagement or to deal with the implications at the personal level to develop public sociology about controversial issues; the difficulties linked to the development of public sociology within the university context in specific countries; the challenge of dealing with potential reprisals when power structures are challenged; the development of public sociology in contexts with political violence; the reinforcement of a local public sociology from a global context; the engagement of diverse publics with the different types of sociologies; the methodological challenges to guarantee an ongoing dialogue between scholars and all types of audiences, even the traditionally silenced or the subaltern communities.

In facing these dilemmas, globally and locally, public sociology is giving "a sense of purpose" to the sociological work that many junior and also senior scholars are doing. The connections among scholars of public sociology united by Burawoy's contributions have given a breath of fresh air to the discipline. Indeed, many scholars who had been relegated for years to the margins of the academy because of their personal commitment to society through their work have found a way to be socially and politically committed to their professional and scientific goals, while receiving the international and academic recognition they deserve for their rigorous work as public sociologists.

When the world is facing devastating problems that undermine the most basic principles of humanity, public sociology acquires new strengths to contribute from science and, through open dialogue with diverse social agents, to provide answers to alleviate these tensions worldwide. The exercise of public sociology is defending civil society against the collusive relation of the state and the market, "just as sociology arose with civil society in the 19th century to oppose market anarchy and political tyranny" (Burawoy 2014: 153). Sociology is, indeed, "becoming active in the public sphere and becoming a social movement itself, while simultaneously holding on to its scientific basis" (Burawoy 2014: 153).

SEE ALSO: Knowledge, Sociology of; Social Justice; Social Movements and Social Change; Sociological Imagination; Sociology

References

Burawoy, Michael. 2005. "For Public Sociology." *American Sociological Review* 70 (1): 4–28. DOI:10.1177/000312240507000102.

Burawoy, Michael (Guest Editor). 2014. Special Issue: "Precarious Engagements: Combat in the Realm of Public Sociology." *Current Sociology* 62 (2). Monograph 1, March.

Further Reading

Clawson, Dan, Robert Zussman, Joya Misra, Naomi Gerstel, Randall Stokes, Douglas L. Anderton, and Michael Burawoy, eds. 2007. *Public Sociology: Fifteen Eminent Sociologists Debate Politics & the Profession in the Twenty-First Century*. Berkeley and Los Angeles: University of California Press.

Qualitative Methods

Amir Marvasti

Penn State Altoona, USA

What is broadly recognized as qualitative methods is an exciting and generally accessible approach to investigating social life. From the onset, it is important to note that qualitative research is represented by a wide range of practices. Its meaning and implementation vary considerably, both in terms of procedural guidelines and theoretical conceptualization. For many, qualitative methods are an attractive choice because they allow for the representation of research findings in a a an accessible way, they can be carried out using a small sample and typically a small budget, and can produce profoundly insightful and "deep" understanding of issues from the perspective of the "people on the ground." Another related advantage is its potential for allowing researchers to get closer to the topic of investigation and enter a more meaningful encounter with the research participants.

The most elementary forms of qualitative research were most likely practiced by early novice Western, particularly British, anthropologists in the form of travel logs that described various encounters with what they viewed as exotic cultures. These travel logs gradually form the basis of "ethnographic" and/or "observational research" (discussed below). Subsequently, in the United States, qualitative research became associated with the Chicago School of Sociology, particularly with early ethnographic research conducted by W.I. Thomas, Park, and others. Over the next few decades, qualitative research grew in popularity and became a mainstay of many disciplines ranging from education to nursing and management (for a detailed history of research interviews, in particular, see Platt 2012).

Theory

It is important to think of qualitative methods as an extension, or the flip side, of a theoretical enterprise, as opposed to a distinct body of research practices. More specifically, how qualitative research is conducted explicitly or implicitly reflects assumptions about the nature of reality and the possibilities for representing that reality. One way to

Core Concepts in Sociology, First Edition. Edited by J. Michael Ryan.
© 2019 John Wiley & Sons Ltd. Published 2019 by John Wiley & Sons Ltd.

think of the theoretical foundations of qualitative research is in terms of a continuum with constructionism on the one end and positivism on the other. With the latter, the underlying assumption is that social reality can be captured in concrete factual terms and represented to others more or less as it happened. So a face-to-face interview, for example, can be designed to collect a respondent's true feelings. According to this approach, the interview could then be transcribed and analyzed in the form of variables to test cause and effect relationships, such as how attitude X is related to behavior. On the other end of the theoretical continuum, constructionists would see the interview itself as part of an interaction through which meanings and realities are constructed and negotiated. The interview, in this context, is not a method of data collection as much as it is an occasion for meaning making. Note that the positivism–constructionism dichotomy is useful for instructional purposes. In practice, few studies adhere to a rigorous theoretical regime. Instead, they fall somewhere in the middle of the continuum where both positivistic and constructionist concerns enter the equation – whether explicitly or implicitly.

Methods

As noted earlier, qualitative methods constitute a diverse universe. However, for the most part, certain themes tend to dominate the research and in some ways other practices are variations on the same theme. A central focus of qualitative methods is discerning the quality of experience and representing its complexity and variation. To do so, preference is given to direct and open-ended responses from research participants, ideally in "natural" settings or contexts.

Interviews

The interview is perhaps the most common type of qualitative data collection. At its most basic level, an interview is a type of social exchange in which one person, the interviewer, is largely charged with asking questions, and the other person, the interviewee or the respondent, is expected to provide answers (Gubrium and Holstein 2002). That said, interviews vary considerably in terms of their format and length. Some qualitative interviews might be based on very concrete, or closed-ended questions where the interviewer follows the same format with little variability. Other interviews might be based on more open-ended questions that allow the respondents to elaborate on their responses, making the interview more "in depth." A similar dimension of the interview is the degree of flexibility in role taking in the context of the interview. For example, some researchers might allow for the respondents to ask them questions about their own personal backgrounds whereas others would follow a script to the letter. How an interview is conducted is a reflection of the theoretical assumptions that inform the research design. Structured interviews grow out of a positivist view where variations or rewording of interview questions are seen as a source of bias that distorts the truth of the interview. Open-ended and in-depth interviews go along with the constructionist view of the world where variations and improvisations enhance and clarify the meaning-making process.

Ethnographic Research

Ethnography is a very popular and quintessentially qualitative research method. The most basic component of ethnographic research is the gathering of data in a place, research site, called the field. While the field can be a very specific place in some cases, a homeless shelter, for example, the actual boundaries of the field can contract or expand over the course of a research project. In the case of the homeless shelter, the field could expand into surrounding streets and city parks. Another component of field work is deciding one's "membership role" (Adler and Adler 1987) in the field. Here the choices range from being a "complete observer" (detached observer) to a "complete participant" (full immersion in the goings-on in the field). Another consideration in fieldwork is establishing rapport with the research participants. This is important for two reasons. First, rapport translates into access or entry into the various dimensions of the field. Second, rapport qualitatively alters that nature of data collection, with greater rapport producing more in-depth, better, data.

Beyond observations, ethnographic research could also include data collection through interviews, or ethnographic interviews. While the actual conduct of the ethnographic interviews may be very similar to research interviews in general, they do offer the added advantage of being sited, providing context and cues for soliciting and interpreting the interview. For example, interviewing the homeless outside an emergency shelter allows the respondents to literally point to their surroundings and include reference to objects and physical space in their responses. In this context, an interviewee might say, "I was sleeping on that bench over there when I was robbed."

Lastly, auto-ethnographies are a form of ethnography that highlights the researcher's own voice and experiential encounters with the topic under analysis (Ellis and Bochner 2000). In essence, an auto-ethnography is field research where the distance between researcher and the people under observation is bridged so that they become one and the same. However, there is much variation in the way this type of research is conceptualized and practiced (see Anderson 2006).

Content Analysis

Qualitative methods can also be used to gather and analyze data from textual and visual sources, such as official documents, books, magazine, and movies. For the purpose of content analysis, observations are sampled from a larger pool of material. Typically, the observations are then coded into categories or themes. The final step is to list the themes and the frequency of their occurrence. In some cases, content analysis can be combined with descriptive and inferential statistics (quantitative data analysis) to test cause-and-effect hypotheses. For example, using content analysis one can test the hypothesis that local news coverage of crime is more likely to include an offender's picture if she is a woman. This would involve gathering a sample of news stories about crime, coding the offenders' gender in each story and whether or not his or her image appeared in the story, and finally comparing the male and female stories to see which was more likely to include an offender's image. In this example of content analysis, the initial data is qualitative but it is quantified for the purpose comparisons and hypothesis testing. In other types of content analysis, textual data is grouped and thematized without being reduced to numerical categories. For example, the same crime stories can be analyzed in terms of their discursive content or constructions of gender as a central feature of the news story.

Sampling

The careful selection of research participants is an important consideration for qualitative researchers. However, they are less likely to utilize random sampling techniques for this purpose. This is in part because qualitative research is usually not intended to produce findings that are generalizable to a larger population. Instead, qualitative research typically generates in-depth knowledge about a handful of cases. To this end, qualitative sampling techniques rely on respondents who have special knowledge and interest in the topic under analysis. For example, ethnographers rely on informants to help them become acclimated to the nuances of the field. Similarly, in cases where the study population is small or highly secretive, researchers may use convenience and snowball sampling to recruit participants.

Analysis

Once qualitative data is collected, the next challenge is making sense of it all. The work of analyzing qualitative data relates to the theoretical discussions presented earlier. If the goal is to establish cause-and-effect relationships, it is possible to code and quantify qualitative data into measurements and variables, which can then be analyzed using statistical techniques. However, given that most qualitative studies rely on small samples, as a general rule, they are not suited for generalizations about a larger population. The more common approach to qualitative data analysis is to use "thick descriptions" (Geertz 1988). Qualitative descriptions tend to be detailed, contextualized, and theoretically informed accounts of the research observations. A more systematic form of qualitative data analysis is "grounded theory" (Charmaz 2008). In its most basic form grounded theory analysis involves reducing large amounts of descriptive data into themes and theories. Other forms of qualitative analysis include narrative analysis (discerning the story content and structure) and conversation analysis (meticulous examination of verbal exchanges and their relationship to the social construction of reality under consideration). Regardless of the particular form of analysis being employed, making sense of qualitative data tends to be a reflexive or circular process where the research findings gradually and continuously emerge from the empirical observations and in turn inform the researcher's subsequent observations and focus.

Validity

Qualitative researchers share a common concern with their quantitative counterparts about the accuracy or validity of their findings. For example, through a process called "respondent validation," researchers return to their research participants and ask them to comment on the findings. This is to ensure the respondents' accounts are accurately captured and reflected in the final analysis. Another validity check for the purpose of qualitative analysis is "triangulation" (Denzin 1970), which involves examining the same issue from multiple perspectives. For example, life at a homeless shelter can be viewed from the perspective of the clients, the staff, and the volunteers. This creates both a richer, deeper understanding of the topic and counters any potential bias caused by relying too much on any one perspective or voice. Finally, inter-coder reliability allows for multiple analysts to compare and challenge each other's interpretations and coding of the same data. Through this process any wildly disparate interpretations of the same data would have to be discarded, reframed, or at least reconciled.

Writing

Most qualitative researchers give special attention to how their observations are ultimately shared with a larger audience in writing or other formats. Whereas quantitative research is typically represented through a very formulaic approach, qualitative researchers are afforded a wider range of possibilities. For example, in addition to the traditional format (introduction, methods, results, and conclusion), qualitative researchers can represent their work as story or a narrative, or they can publish it as a multimedia content on the web (Vannini 2012). Like data analysis, writing in qualitative research also has a theoretical and reflexive dimension. Rather than being viewed as a simple process of recording and reporting facts as they happened, in the context of qualitative research writing itself can be viewed as an extension of the analysis where the author has to carefully reflect on the choices made about conveying and framing his or her observations, with each choice having its own consequences and reflecting a different dimension of the kaleidoscope of social reality under consideration.

Technology and Qualitative Research

Technological innovations will likely alter the practice of qualitative research in three important ways. First, recording devices have become exceedingly more affordable and reliable (Lee 2004). Whereas the traditional ethnographer may have been equipped with pencil and pad (and perhaps a bulky film camera) in the field, new researchers essentially have unlimited recording capacity with their smartphones. This in turn means a significantly larger portion of the goings-on in the field (or the research interview) may be recorded and brought back for the purpose of analysis and representation. Second, online spaces (social media, chat rooms, blogs, etc.) provide fertile sites for collecting data and making contact with virtual communities around the world. These venues can also serve as outlets for sharing research findings (possibly in multimedia format) with a worldwide audience at little or no cost. Additionally, the open format of online spaces allows for real-time feedback from research participants and other interested parties. Third, the digital format of the data itself (whether text or visual) lends itself to more systematic and rapid analysis using various types of computer software (e.g., NVivo).

SEE ALSO: Constructionism vs. Essentialism; Epistemology; Ethnography; Ethnomethodology; Everyday Life; Quantitative Methods; Social Media and Virtual Communities; Social Network Analysis; Sociological Theory; Sociology

References

Adler, Patricia, and Peter Adler. 1987. *Membership Roles in Field Research*. Newbury Park, CA: Sage.

Anderson, Leon. 2006. "Analytic Autoethnography." *Journal of Contemporary Ethnography* 35 (4): 373–395.

Charmaz, Kathy. 2008. "Constructionism and the Grounded Theory Method." In *Handbook of Constructionist Research,* edited by Jay Gubrium and James Holstein, 397–412. New York: Guilford Press.

Denzin, Norm. 1970. *The Research Act in Sociology*. London: Butterworth.

Ellis, Carolyn, and Arthur P. Bochner 2000. "Autoethnography, Personal Narrative, Reflexivity: Researcher as Subject." In *Handbook of Qualitative Research*, 2nd ed., edited by Norman K. Denzin and Yvonna S. Lincoln, 733–768. Thousand Oaks, CA: Sage.

Gubrium Jay, and James Holstein. 2002. "From the Individual Interview to Interview Society." In *Handbook of Interview Research: Context and Method*, edited by Jay Gubrium and James Holstein, 3–32. Thousand Oaks, CA: Sage.

Lee, Raymond. 2004. "Recording Technologies and the Interview in Sociology, 1920–2000." *Sociology* 38: 869–889.

Platt, Jennifer. 2012. "The History of the Interview." In *The Sage Handbook of Interview Research: The Complexity of the Craft*, edited by Jay Gubrium, James Holstein, Amir Marvasti, and Karyn McKinney, 9–26. Los Angeles: Sage.

Vannini, Phillip, ed. 2012. *Popularizing Research: Engaging New Media, Genre, and Audiences*. New York: Peter Lang Publishing.

Quantitative Methods

Guillermina Jasso

New York University, USA

As a scientific discipline develops, it achieves increasing exactness, accuracy, and parsimony. Ideas about the subject matter of the discipline become clearer; the essential operations and relations come more sharply into focus, and the epicycles fall away. This increasing clarity both arises from and spurs quantitative expression.

Of course, disciplines develop at different rates. Some phenomena resist scientific description. And, within discipline, theory and empirics, though deeply intertwined, also develop at different rates. Fortunately, the methods of both theoretical analysis and empirical analysis rest on a common foundation of logic, mathematics, and statistics. And thus "quantitative methods" – like "qualitative methods" – are methods for both theory and empirics, and methodological advances in one are advances for both.

This entry first considers briefly theory and empirics, then moves to three major elements in models of sociological phenomena – variables, functions, distributions.

Sociological Theory

Of the many types of theory, three are especially useful in a scientific discipline, and they are intimately linked to empirics. Two of these are deductive, the third nondeductive. The two deductive forms have similar structure. They each begin with a small set of premises which yield a number of deduced consequences. In the first deductive form – the gold-standard hypothetico-deductive form invented by Newton – the premises (often called postulates) are Popperian "guesses about the structure of the world," and the deduced consequences (often called predictions) range to farflung domains; tests of the predictions reveal the postulates' fidelity to the real world. In the second deductive form, the premises are true or subject to human/social control, and the deduced consequences follow necessarily whenever the premises hold; the empirical task is to discern the conditions under which the premises hold. In the nondeductive form, propositions are constructed by linking terms in a theory and observable outcomes; the empirical task is to test the propositions.

All three theory forms embed variables and relations between variables. Of course, the two deductive forms are somewhat more elaborate, for both the premises and the deduced consequences are often themselves relations between variables, so that there are three kinds of relations overall – $X \rightarrow Y$ relations in the premises, $X \rightarrow Y$ relations in the deduced consequences, and a set of superordinate relations between the $X \rightarrow Y$ relations in the premises and the $X \rightarrow Y$ relations in the deduced consequences.

Moreover, because there are variables, there are also distributions of these variables, together with all the parameters of interest, such as mean, median, and inequality. Further, in many applications, matrices also arise naturally – e.g., when a set of observers each assigns a just wage to a set of workers.

Sociological Empirics

The three theory forms summarized above lead naturally to empirical work. But they are not the only engine or pathway to empirical work. Despite the predilection for "theory-informed" empirical work, there is an important place for extra-theoretical empirics. Sometimes the simple act of "playing" with variables, combining and re-combining them in alternate ways, can produce new empirical knowledge. Indeed, sometimes this new empirical knowledge becomes the premise for a new theory.

Besides testing propositions and exploring additional relations between variables, empirical work spans further activities, including measurement, as well as estimation of frequency distributions and matrices.

Variables

Variables are the building blocks of sociology. They may describe quantitative or qualitative characteristics of persons or social entities. For simplicity, consider characteristics of persons. There are two kinds of personal characteristics, quantitative characteristics – of which there can be more and less, or higher and lower – and qualitative characteristics – for which there is no inherent ordering. Both play important parts in sociology, an idea pioneered by Blau.

Quantitative characteristics can be further distinguished along two dimensions. First, they can be cardinal (like income) or ordinal (like athletic skill). Second, they can be continuous (like land) or discrete (like number of children).

Other sociologically relevant dimensions of variables include additivity, transferability, and goodness/badness. For example, material possessions are additive and transferable; beauty and intelligence are nonadditive and nontransferable; number of children is transferable in the variable "number of children in a household" but not in "number of children born to a particular couple."

Quantitative characteristics of which more is preferred to less are called goods, and quantitative characteristics of which less is preferred to more are called bads. For most people, income is a good and time in prison is a bad. However, there are "contrarians" who differ from their fellows, and they may be in good company; for example, two formidable saints, St. Teresa of Avila and St. Francis of Assisi, both regarded money as a bad.

Variables – Theoretical Measurement

Theoretical measurement involves choosing the set of numbers to represent a quantitative variable. For example, happiness may be represented by the set of positive numbers – happiness growing from negligible to large amounts – or it may be represented by the full real-number line – happiness extending from extremes of unhappiness through a zero point to extremes of happiness. In justice research, the justice evaluation is represented by the real numbers, with zero representing the point of perfect justice, negative numbers representing degrees of unjust under-reward, and positive numbers representing degrees of unjust over-reward; the larger the absolute value of the number, the greater the injustice. Ordinal characteristics, like beauty or athletic skill, are represented by relative ranks within a group or population. Of course, choosing the set of numbers to represent a quantitative variable is self-evident for some variables – like number of children – and almost as easy for money variables, where the only decisions to be made involve currency (say, dollars or yen) and denomination (say, hundreds, thousands, or millions).

Variables – Empirical Measurement

Empirical measurement involves a procedure for approximating magnitudes of quantitative variables and for affixing numbers to categories of qualitative variables. For example, magnitude estimation techniques used in factorial surveys ask respondents to choose the number corresponding to the magnitude of the respondent's assessment of a particular situation, such as the respondent's justice evaluation about a particular combination of reward and rewardee. Relative ranks are straightforward to measure; simply arrange the persons in a group or population in ascending order on an ordinal variable, then divide the absolute rank by the quantity $(N+1)$, where N denotes the size of the group or population. It is worth noting that cardinal variables have many useful properties in empirical research, and thus it is important to resist the temptation to collapse them into categories.

Relations Between Variables – Functions

The heart of an idea about how the social world works is usually a proposition linking two or more variables. Such propositions connect an outcome – or dependent variable – to the input(s) which generate(s) it – the independent variable(s).

Functions – Theoretical Specification

In theoretical work the chief task is to specify the function with as much fidelity to a priori reasonings as possible. This entails careful thought about the presumed effect of each input on the outcome. Is the X–Y relation increasing or decreasing? Is the X–Y relation linear or nonlinear? If nonlinear, is it changing at an increasing or decreasing rate? Carefully working through these questions will enable the theorist to specify the form of the function. Sometimes prior reasoning leads quickly to a particular form; other times further reasoning and/or mathematical work is needed. For example, reasonings from classical writers suggest that the justice evaluation J increases as the actual reward A increases and decreases as the just reward C increases; this is a general form compatible with several specific forms. Reasoning further about properties that the justice evaluation function should satisfy leads to a specific functional form which uniquely satisfies two important properties – scale invariance (by which the justice evaluation remains unchanged whether the actual reward and the just reward are multiplied by a constant, as when expressed in one or another currency or denomination) and additivity (by which the effect of the actual reward on the justice evaluation is independent of the just reward, and the effect of the just reward on the justice evaluation is independent of the actual reward): $J = \ln(A/C)$. This log-ratio form turns out to have many other useful properties, including loss aversion, the property that deficiency is felt more keenly than comparable excess. Further work leads to a new expression including a kind of scaling constant called the signature constant and denoted θ, whose sign indicates whether the observer frames the reward as a good (+1) or a bad (-1) and whose absolute value represents the observer's expressiveness: $J = \theta \ln(A/C)$.

Of course, some processes cannot be adequately described by a single function but instead require a multi-equation model. The full justice model, for example, incorporates not only the justice evaluation function but also the actual reward function, just reward function, and justice consequences function. For example, a simple two-equation justice model used in empirical research includes not only the justice evaluation function shown above but also a just reward function in which the outcome is the just reward (C in the justice evaluation function) and the inputs are the determinants of the just reward (such as schooling, experience, etc.).

Functions – Empirical Specification

The empirical specification adds an error term to the theoretical specification, for example: $J = \theta \ln(A/C) + e$. The empirical specification is now ready for use in a variety of empirical analyses. For example, if the data include observations on J, A, and C for a number of rewardees, the empirical specification above can be linearized to the form $J = \theta \ln(A) - \theta \ln(C) + e$, with the restriction that the two coefficients must be equal, so that regression of J on $\ln(A)$ and $\ln(C)$ yields estimates of θ, thus providing information on whether the respondent frames the reward as a good or a bad as well as the respondent's expressiveness. Interestingly, if the data include only observations on J and A, regression of J on $\ln(A)$ not only yields estimates of θ but also makes it possible to estimate the just reward the respondent implicitly assigns to each rewardee. Further, the two-equation model sketched above leads to an equation in which J is regressed on both $\ln(A)$ and the determinants of C, yielding estimates of θ and, after some algebraic manipulation, of the effects of the determinants of C.

Functions – Empirical Estimation

The goal is to obtain estimates with the best possible properties. To that end, the researcher considers alternative estimators, such as ordinary least squares, generalized least squares, weighted least squares, fixed effects, random effects, etc., reasoning carefully about their properties in the particular estimation context.

The Magical Second Derivative

The second derivative, which describes the rate of change (whether constant or increasing or decreasing) of the effect of an input on an outcome, unlocks many secrets – that wages increase at an increasing rate with investments, that status increases at an increasing rate with status characteristics like income or beauty, that the justice evaluation function produces loss aversion, that sociobehavioral outcomes generated by the same input fall into three sets distinguished by the second derivative.

Of course, not all sociological relations are monotonic. For example, two nonmonotonic forms of immigrant selection are the U-shaped pattern, indicating that the probability of migrating is highest at the lower and upper extremes of the distribution of schooling or income, and an inverse U-shaped pattern, indicating that the probability of migrating is highest at an intermediate level of schooling or income.

Variable's Array – Distributions

Some variables are so important that their distribution – all by itself, without any link to another variable – provides a picture of society. The quintessential case is income. The income distribution reveals the minimum and maximum incomes; the mean, median, and mode(s); the proportion below the mean; and, importantly, the inequality. Also deeply suggestive is the distribution of justice evaluations, revealing the extremes of unjust under-reward and unjust over-reward; the proportions under-rewarded, fairly rewarded, and over-rewarded; and the overall shape of the distribution. For sociology, with its emphasis on inequality and stratification, it is important to study carefully the frequency distributions and inequality measures of the main variables of interest.

Theory and Distributions

Much can be done a priori. As discussed above, in the section on variables, the initial theoretical work includes discerning whether the variable is cardinal or ordinal, continuous or discrete, and choosing the set of numbers to represent it. These features constrain the distributional families that can be used as modeling distributions in theoretical work. For example, income distributions are usually modeled by positive variates, such as the lognormal and the Pareto, and not by variates that sit on the whole real-number line, such as the normal or the logistic. In contrast, distributions of ordinal variables are modeled by the rectangular distribution.

Of course, input–outcome relations start with the distribution of the input and then, using the function that connects input and outcome, obtain the distribution of the outcome. For example, when status S (which, like the sense of justice, is intimately tied to identity and the self) is modeled as the Goode-Sørensen function of relative rank r – viz., $S = \ln(1/(1-r))$ – and thus the input is modeled by the rectangular, the status distribution is a negative exponential. Justice evaluation distributions assume a larger variety of shapes because the justice evaluation depends on two inputs rather than one and the two inputs can be cardinal as well as ordinal. A simple beginning with four actual reward distributions – lognormal, Pareto, and power-function for cardinal rewards and the rectangular for ordinal rewards – quickly yields several families of justice evaluation distributions – the normal and positive/negative exponentials in the case where the just reward is a constant (such as equality), and, in the case where the actual and just rewards are both drawn from the same initial variates, more normals plus the (asymmetrical) Laplace and (quasi)logistic.

The three major associated functions of a probability distribution – cumulative distribution function, probability density function, quantile function – provide alternate ways of visualizing the distribution and working with it. The quantile function is especially useful in sociology, as it presents the value of a variable as a function of its relative rank, for example, the income amount as a function of the income relative rank.

In some substantive contexts, it is useful to link quantitative and qualitative variables. For example, linking income and nativity (where one is born) makes it possible to explore the subdistributions of income within native and foreign-born subsets and to link measures of overall income inequality with measures of cross-group income disparity. To illustrate, it has been shown that in a specified class of distributions, overall inequality and cross-group gaps go hand in hand; as inequality increases in one, it increases in the other.

Empirics and Distributions

Much can be learned by careful inspection of the distribution of each variable in an empirical analysis. In particular, it is useful to calculate inequality measures in cardinal variables and to graph distributions. For graphing, the quantile function (QF) is especially useful, as its graph is informative even with small-sized data sets. Moreover, its graph reveals important properties. For example, the flatter the graph of the quantile function, the lower the inequality; and peaks in the probability density function appear as points of inflection in the QF graph.

Some Desiderata

As sociology grows, it becomes important to learn more about bads. The level of knowledge about goods is large and growing; for example, frequency distributions and inequality measures for goods are ubiquitous. Less is known, however, about the frequency distributions and inequality of variables many observers regard as bads, such as risks of disease, risks of unemployment or atypical employment, and debt and other liabilities.

Looking Ahead

Quantitative methods can be the sociologist's best friend. They can provide laserlike accuracy and high levels of parsimony. They cross analytic levels, from the most micro of micro levels – like the constituent elements of thoughts, judgments, and sentiments – to the most macro of macro levels – like planets in speculative contrasts of future human populations. They can aid greatly to build theories and spin out their often long deductive chains. They can make possible the unification of theories, showing the essential unity of seemingly disparate processes and effects. They can provide ever-increasing clarity to the accumulating knowledge about human behavioral and social phenomena.

SEE ALSO: Epistemology; Identity; Qualitative Methods; Social Justice; Social Psychology; Sociological Theory; Stratification and Inequality

Further Reading

Jasso, G. 2006. "Factorial Survey Methods for Studying Beliefs and Judgments." *Sociological Methods and Research* 34: 334–423.

Jasso, G., and S. Kotz. 2008. "Probability Distributions." In William A. Darity Jr. (ed.), *International Encyclopedia of the Social Sciences*, 2nd ed., Vol. 6, 491–498. Detroit: Macmillan Reference USA.

Johnson, Norman L., Samuel Kotz, and N. Balakrishnan. 1994–1995. *Continuous Univariate Distributions*. New York: Wiley. Second edition of two volumes in original compendium of 1969–1972.

Kennedy, Peter. 2008. *A Guide to Econometrics*, 6th ed. Malden, MA: Blackwell.

Stuart, Alan, and J. Keith Ord. 2010. *Kendall's Advanced Theory of Statistics*, Vol. 1, *Distribution Theory*, 6th ed. Originally by Sir Maurice Kendall. New York: Oxford University Press.

Race and Ethnicity

John Stone

Boston University, USA

Questions of race and ethnicity have intrigued humanity for centuries, but were often under-represented or largely ignored during the formative years of modern sociology. Economic and political revolutions absorbed the attention of many of the pioneers of the discipline so that the central importance of racial and ethnic stratification in almost all societies around the world was rarely given the attention that it deserved. A few exceptions stand out with the writings of Ibn Khaldun, Montesquieu, Alexis de Tocqueville, Harriet Martineau and, later, W.E.B. DuBois shifting focus onto these vital issues. In the United States, pioneering sociologists were often associated with rationalizing the slave system – it is interesting to note that among the first books to name the discipline in their titles were George Fitzhugh's *The Sociology of the South* (1854) and Henry Hughes's *Treatise on Sociology* (1854), both paternalistic rationalizations for maintaining the institution rather than analyzing its true nature and consequences. On the other hand, Alexis de Tocqueville in *Democracy in America* (1835, 1840) and Harriet Martineau in *Society in America* (1837), classic texts on American society, did focus considerable attention on the central role of slavery in the 1830s and in the suffering of Native Americans as they were continuously dispossessed of the lands in the westward expansion of the new nation.

It was not until the earlier decades of the twentieth century that sociologists started to fully integrate racial and ethnic factors into the mainstream of their discussions of social interaction and social change, but it was still seen as a residual category to such fundamental divisions as class, status, and power. The rise of the Chicago School, including the studies of urban living in a milieu that combined extensive migration from diverse European societies combined with the exodus of millions of African-Americans from the segregated Jim Crow states of the South, provided a laboratory for the analysis of patterns of ethnic and racial conflict and competition. Robert Ezra Park, W.I. Thomas and Florian Znaniecki, Charles Johnson, Louis Wirth, and Everett Stonequist, all followed in the tradition started by DuBois in Philadelphia just before the turn of the century, in developing theories, models, and empirical data to understand the changing nature of race and ethnic relations in the twentieth century. These included attempts to arrive at a systematic approach to assimilation among white immigrant groups in Park's

Core Concepts in Sociology, First Edition. Edited by J. Michael Ryan.
© 2019 John Wiley & Sons Ltd. Published 2019 by John Wiley & Sons Ltd.

poorly named "race relations cycle"; a classic study of Polish migration on both sides of the Atlantic; pioneering research on life in the black community and the 1919 race riots in Chicago; and classic works exploring the experience of minorities, anti-Semitism, and marginality as central features of American and other societies.

The European pioneers of sociology had an even more marginal concern with the subject despite the central issue of imperialism and the colonial expansion of European powers across the globe throughout the nineteenth century and early decades of the twentieth century. For Marx, the obsession with class relationships and his overly deterministic model of historical change left little room for understanding the true importance of race, ethnicity, and nationalism, that was to intersect with the communist revolutions in the century after his death. If religion was the "opium of the masses," then racism and nationalism were their heroin and cocaine. Max Weber, on the other hand, did provide some valuable insights into the complexity of race and ethnicity, and a basic theory that applied the process of monopolization, an idea borrowed from his economic studies, to the random meetings of peoples with different levels of power throughout history. This combination of forces helped to explain the variations in boundaries and boundary markers found among different racial and ethnic groups around the world. Durkheim's work had rather less concern with the key problems and concepts relevant to this area, despite some interesting ideas linking behavioral patterns to social change and social integration. His insights have proven most interesting to racial, ethnic, and national interactions at the small group (meso) and personal (micro) levels.

Sociological studies in the later decades of the twentieth century have developed a broader range of perspectives, though many of them are still rooted in the basic formulations of the earlier period. Out of the Marxist-materialist approach, more flexible models have been proposed to counteract the obvious deficiencies of theories that ignore or downplay the reality of racial, ethnic, and national attachments. These are the direct descendants of the debates about the "national question" after the Bolshevik Revolution and the struggles against imperialism in much of Africa, Asia, and Latin America. Wallerstein's World System theory is an outgrowth of Lenin's idea of "imperialism: the highest stage of capitalism," transposing the class struggle in one society onto a global scene. Thus the proletariat consists largely of Third-World workers, while the divisions in Marx's simple bifurcation is complicated to include a range of petite bourgeois and semi-peripheral groups and societies, thus making the overall model more plausible. More traditional approaches can be found in writers like Miles and Phizacklea (1984) who essentially subscribe to a reductionist form of analysis, linking "race" relations to international migration and the operation of global employment practices. Other variants give greater accord to the independent role of racial affiliations, either as a rallying cry of oppressed peoples often linked to the history of slavery and colonialism, or to variants of nationalism associated with African, Asian, or Latin American liberation and ethno-nationalist movements. All sorts of combinations can in practice be found, as perhaps best seen in the pioneering writings of W.E.B. DuBois. In his approach, DuBois moved from the bold assertion that the "problem of the twentieth century would be the problem of the color line" (1903) to a variety of strategies incorporating Pan Africanist and socialist ideas as he grew older and became increasingly skeptical of America's capacity to change during the first six decades of the twentieth century.

The two world wars of the twentieth century and the impact that these major conflicts had in precipitating global changes in the world power structure generated interest in a variety of fields that demanded sociological attention. Genocide and genocidal massacres ceased to be seen as temporary deviations from the "civilization process," the surprising resurrection of nineteenth-century "progress theory" that flies in the face of so much evidence, from the massacres in King Leopold's Congo at the turn of the century – graphically chronicled by Park in his first career as a journalist – to the Armenians after the collapse of the Ottoman Empire in 1917, the Nazi Holocaust in the 1940s, millions dying in the break-up of India later in the decade, and slaughters in Biafra, Cambodia, and Rwanda, just to mention a few of the most horrific cases. The recurrent nature of such massacres, and their appearance in so many different places and under such diverse circumstances, require explanations that transcended specific cases. Ideas like the "banality of evil" and "obedience to authority" combined with more macro-level disturbances to normal social, economic, and political life, seemed to be present in many of the outbreaks of such violence. Leo Kuper's *Genocide: Its Political Use in the Twentieth Century* (1983) and Michael Mann's *The Dark Side of Democracy* (2005) are two of the more comprehensive attempts to compare and contrast major genocides of the twentieth century.

While a significant part of the mainstream analysis of race and ethnicity explored the specific institutions and movements associated with such divisions in societies around the world, attempts were made to synthesize the outcome of much of this research in a number of diverse directions. Scholars like Michael Banton (1982) and Michael Hechter (1987) tried to merge extensive research in Europe and Africa under the framework of rational choice theory. Taking a somewhat different strand of economic theory from that chosen by most Weberians, this approach stressed an individualistic calculus in a field that is often seen as heavily collectivist in nature. By stressing the role of ethnic and racial competition and the manner in which the competition takes place, either on an individual basis or at the group level, this analysis suggests that the former tends to erode group boundaries while the latter enhances them. Thus by taking a different analogy from economic theory, stressing competition rather than monopolization, market forces are viewed as the solvent of group conflict rather than its instigator. Another form of competition has also been developed but this time linked to sociobiological theories. Pierre van den Berghe, building on the influential writings of E.O. Wilson and others, has sought to apply theories developed to explain much of the behavioral patterns of social insects like ants and bees, to account for the strength of group ties and racial and ethnic conflicts. Because of the history of racial theorizing, most sociologists have looked on such theories with a great degree of skepticism and feel that trying to "reduce" such conflicts to genetic "selfishness" raises more questions than it answers. We can anticipate similar problems with the popular field of neuroscience should similar reductionist arguments attempt to link racial and ethnic violence to specific activities of the brain.

Far removed from these perspectives are those that claim to provide insight into race and ethnic dynamics through a variety of other lenses. Critical race theory, intersectionality, systemic racism theory, racial formation theory, along with many variants of these ideas, all claim to capture fundamentally different elements of racial and ethnic relationships. For example, intersectionality, associated with many feminist writers like Kimberlé Crenshaw and Patricia Hill Collins, is an attempt to give greater prominence to gender and other divisions and the complex cross-pressures and unique locations of inequality resulting from multiple identities.

Another interesting development focuses attention on the demographic changes both within societies and between them. Richard Alba's argument in *Blurring the Color Line* (2009) suggests that population changes among American ethnic communities provide one possible mechanism that may fundamentally shift the power relations between the current white majority and the ever-expanding communities of color. While some might object to this image of "blurring the color line" as an "assimilationist" future for America's increasingly diverse society, it can equally be seen as an important variable in the power struggle to fulfill the true message of the "American Creed." While few would argue that population size per se is a sufficient condition for greater racial equality, it may well be a necessary component for moving beyond the racist past of American society. On a global scale, similar shifts in both population dynamics and economic development, as the world moves toward a multipolar political and economic structure, may also change the balance of power among societies comprising very different racial and ethnic populations. The rise of China, India, Brazil, Indonesia, and Nigeria being some of the most prominent examples of societies behind the "new world disorder."

While changes of this kind can be the subject of variable interpretations, some theorists have chosen to stress other issues when seeking to understand the full range of racial, ethnic, and social changes. In the United States, and particularly in the wake of the Obama presidency, debates about the true significance of this undoubtedly important symbolic event have resulted in very different conclusions. The appeal of ideas about "post-racialism," particularly to many who had spent decades opposing policies and movements toward greater racial justice and inclusion, could be seen as an ironic twist of fate, thus leading conservative politicians and Supreme Court justices to object to what they termed "reversed racism" to undermine the continuation of affirmative action policies or the maintenance of laws designed to ensure equal voting rights. As Bonilla-Silva (2006) demonstrated, the superficial paradox of "racism without racists" had become the new norm for those opposed to measures designed to reduce racial divisions. At a more subtle level, questions were also being raised about the salience of group affiliations and the need to avoid overemphasizing collective identities. Thus "ethnicity without groups" and the earlier notions of "symbolic ethnicity" provided an interesting corrective to those insisting on seeing the world perpetually divided into hostile collective categories. Nevertheless, the continuing significance of race in so many societies and the levels of nationalist and interstate conflicts, resulting in genocides and other mass slaughters, provide evidence of the salience of race, ethnicity, and nationalism in the twenty-first century.

SEE ALSO: Citizenship; Colonialism and Postcolonialism; Culture, Sociology of; Demography and Population Studies; Globalization; Identity; Immigration, Migration, and Refugees; Inequality, Racial and Ethnic; Social Movements and Social Change; Stratification and Inequality

References

Banton, Michael. 1982. "The Two Ethnicities 1." *Journal of Intercultural Studies* 3 (2): 25–35.
Bonilla-Silva, Eduardo. 2006. *Racism Without Racists: Color-Blind Racism and the Persistence of Racial Inequality in the United States*. Lanham, MD: Rowman and Littlefield.
Dubois, W.E.B. 1903. *The Souls of Black Folk*. Chicago: A.C. McClurg & Co.
Hechter, Michael. 1987. "Nationalism as Group Solidarity." *Ethnic and Racial Studies* 10 (4): 415–426.
Miles, Robert, and Annie Phizacklea. 1984. *White Man's Country: Racism in British Politics*. Longwood Press Ltd.

Further Reading

Collins, Patricia Hill, and Sirma Bilge. 2016. *Intersectionality*. Cambridge: Polity Press.
Elias, Sean, and Joe Feagin. 2016. *Racial Theories in Social Science: A Systemic Racism Critique*. New York: Routledge.
Stone, John, and Polly Rizova. 2014. *Racial Conflict in Global Society*. Cambridge: Polity Press.
Stone, John, Rutledge Dennis, Polly Rizova, Anthony Smith, and Xiaoshuo Hou. 2016. *The Encyclopedia of Race, Ethnicity and Nationalism*. 5 vols. Oxford: Wiley Blackwell.

Rationalization, Bureaucratization, and McDonaldization

George Ritzer

University of Maryland, USA

Weber's broadest concern was his overarching theory of rationalization. His paradigm case for that process was the bureaucracy and the process of increasing bureaucratization in which it was embedded. The issues of bureaucracy and bureaucratization per se grew less important over time, in part because the bureaucracy itself was growing less important, especially in comparison to Weber's early twentieth-century Germany.

Weber's belief, circa the turn of the twentieth century, was that the bureaucracy was *the* paradigm of the rationalization process. However, while that might have been true at the time, in the late twentieth century it was becoming clear that there were other, maybe even far better, paradigms of that process, especially the fast food restaurant.

While Weber had a great deal to say about rationalization, he offered no clear definition of it and tended to shy away from defining it in general terms. Rather, he focused on types of rational action and types of rationality – practical, theoretical, substantive and, most importantly, formal rationality. The latter was most important to Weber because it embeds rationality in larger structures like the bureaucracy. It is this type of rationality that arose only in the West and tended to make it such a distinctive civilization. While Weber generally discusses specific types of rationality, there are places where his overarching theory is clear: "(In) the whole process of rationalization ... especially in the bureaucratic state machine ... discipline inexorably takes over ever larger areas as the satisfaction of political and economic needs is increasingly rationalized" (Weber [1921] 1978: 1156).

A review of Weber's work on (formal) rationalization led Ritzer (1983) to the conclusion that formal rationality had five basic characteristics: *calculability* (a focus on that which can be counted or quantified), *efficiency* (finding the best means to whatever end is sought), predictability (having systems operate in the same way from one time or place to another), replacement of human with non-human technologies (e.g., automated technologies, robots), and control over uncertainties (especially those related to humans as primarily customers or workers). In addition, there is a sixth, derivative, trait – the irrational consequences of rational actions, or the "irrationality of rationality."

Core Concepts in Sociology, First Edition. Edited by J. Michael Ryan.

In Ritzer's (2015) work on the *McDonaldization of Society*, he argues that the fast food restaurant, especially McDonald's, had replaced the bureaucracy as the paradigm of the rationalization process and that its fundamental principles were, in fact, the five characteristics of rationalization identified by Weber. McDonaldization *is* the rationalization process in a more contemporary form. Thus, *McDonaldization* is defined as the "process by which the principles of the fast food restaurant are coming to dominate more and more sectors of American society as well as of the rest of the world" (ibid: 1).

In its basic form, McDonaldization is a descriptive theory of the principles of rationalization, as well as their proliferation globally. In the latter form it is also a theory of globalization. For example, O'Byrne and Hensby (2011) see McDonaldization as one of eight major theories of globalization.

However, McDonaldization is more than a descriptive theory and like Weber's theory of rationalization has a critical component. Weber was well-attuned to the irrationalities of rationality, most notably the "iron cage" that the rationalization process was in the process of creating and from which there was less and less chance of escape. Ritzer deals with that idea under the heading of the irrationality of rationality, but also with a number of other irrationalities that are explicit and implicit in Weber's bureaucratized society as well as in the McDonaldized society. They include, most generally, incalculability, inefficiency, unpredictability, loss of control over technology (and being controlled by it), and increasing uncertainty. Beyond that a number of other, more specific, irrationalities are dealt with including disenchantment, homogenization, and dehumanization.

Overall, Weber's theory of rationalization remains highly relevant, even though it needs to be adapted – as do all theories – to contemporary realities and changes. While less important today, the bureaucracy remains an example of the rationalization process and of its importance in the contemporary world. The approximately 36,000 fast food restaurants in the McDonald's system, to say nothing of the many more that are part of other fast food chains such as Kentucky Fried Chicken and Burger King, are themselves part of larger bureaucratic organizations. However, the bureaucracy as a structural form is past its prime, while the fast food restaurant model continues to be ascendant. That model, too, will age, decline, and perhaps even die. Fast food restaurants, like bureaucracies, are bricks-and-mortar structures, but the future belongs to those that are largely, if not wholly, digital in nature.

While it involves material delivery and has even recently experimented with bricks-and-mortar structures, Amazon.com is largely a digital organization that is growing increasingly ubiquitous. While it may be different from bureaucracies and fast food restaurants, it is definitely part of the larger process of rationalization. Indeed it is far more rational than its predecessors and raises rationalization to a whole new level. For example, while the fast food restaurant pioneered "putting the customer to work" (Ritzer 2015: 70–73), or turning consumers into prosumers, this has been brought to a whole new level on digital sites where prosumers do virtually all of the work. In this sense, and many others, the process of rationalization is not only alive and well, but growing in force and influence.

SEE ALSO: Capitalism; Consumption; Economic Sociology; Globalization; Internet, the; Organizations, Sociology of; Work, Occupations, and Professions, Sociology of

References

O'Byrne, Darren, and Alexander Hensby. 2011. *Theorizing Global Studies.* New York: Palgrave.

Ritzer, George. 1983. "The McDonaldization of Society." *Journal of American Culture* Spring: 100–107.

Ritzer, George. 2015. *The McDonaldization of Society,* 8th ed. Thousand Oaks, CA: Pine Forge Press.

Weber, Max. [1921] 1978. *Economy and Society.* 2 vols. Berkeley: University of California Press.

Religion, Sociology of

Ryan T. Cragun

University of Tampa, USA

The sociology of religion has been a core subdiscipline of sociology since the discipline's beginning. Early approaches to studying religion varied substantially. Some early scholars emphasized problematic elements of religion, considering religion to be inferior to other epistemologies (Comte) or as an impediment to economic progress by impeding the development of class consciousness (Marx). Other scholars saw religion as the sacralization of societal values (Durkheim) or as an important contributor to societal development and the rise of new economic systems (Weber). Just as sociology has shifted its focus over time from comparing and contrasting more developed societies with less developed societies, the sociology of religion has increasingly grown to focus on the experience of religion itself or the relationship between religion and other aspects of modern society, like gender, sexuality, and health.

As with many topics in sociology, religion can be somewhat challenging to define. Durkheim proposed an overly broad definition of religion by suggesting that religion is that which is sacred in society. Many sacred phenomena (e.g., scriptures, altars, mosques) are, of course, associated with religion, but many things people consider to be sacred (e.g., flags, sports teams, and art collections) are not part of what most people would consider to be religion. Weber offered a less broad definition that, while still problematic in some regards, is more in line with what most scholars would consider to be religion: collective beliefs related to the supernatural. The two components to this definition, "collective" and "supernatural," are key to understanding the phenomenon of religion. Supernatural refers to that which is above or beyond nature. If nature is that which can be sensed, detected, or measured, then the supernatural is that which cannot be sensed, detected, or measured. The supernatural would include gods, demons, angels, spirits, ghosts, leprechauns, unicorns, gnomes, and so on. Religion is collective in the sense that it refers to shared beliefs. If a single person believes they are a god and no one else does, that person is typically considered to have a mental health issue. If, however, an individual claims they can communicate with a god and has followers who also believe that person is in communication with a supernatural entity, that shared belief system is considered a religion. In short, religion has to be shared beliefs that are in some way related to the supernatural. This understanding of religion is broad enough to include most traditional religions (e.g., Buddhism and Islam) but not so broad as to include other ideologies, like nationalism or fascism, which lack a supernatural element.

Sociologists who study religion are interested in many dimensions of the phenomenon. At a very basic level, sociologists are interested in the experience of being religious and what it means to people to be religious. A common sociological term to describe experiences with religion is "religiosity," which broadly encompasses the many ways that religion is manifest in peoples' lives. Sociologists of religion now understand that religiosity is complex and multidimensional. For instance, identifying as part of a religion, like Catholicism, can be central to someone's identity, but that individual may never attend Catholic religious services. Someone could not believe in a god or higher power (i.e., atheism) or believe that it is impossible to know whether a god or higher power exists (i.e., agnosticism), yet feel a close connection with, occasionally attend, and be a member of, for instance, a Jewish synagogue. Some individuals affiliate with religions and attend religious services where their sexual or gender identity is considered sinful and deviant, yet they still find value in the experience of religion (Sumerau, Cragun, and Mathers 2016). The lived experience of religion is complex, and often reflects the incongruent nature of human beings.

Another aspect of religion that has interested sociologists is how religion evolves. As noted above, Durkheim observed that religions often reflect the structure and values of society. In tribal societies with more egalitarian power structures, religions were often polytheistic, with many gods that were also egalitarian (Durkheim 1995). As societies grew more complex and hierarchical, so, too, did religions, with chief gods (e.g., Zeus) or even a single god (i.e., monotheism) who held significant power. In some societies, religion is an integral part of culture and difficult to disentangle from both the social structure (e.g., the Hindu caste system) and from societal values and daily life (e.g., Shinto in Japan). In other societies, religion is just one aspect of culture and is increasingly not obligatory (e.g., Christianity in much of Europe).

Religions can also evolve relative to their relationship to the government and their perceived legitimacy. Religions that are closely allied with the government and often have obligatory membership in that society are referred to as state churches. Religions that are more distanced from governments and are voluntary are typically referred to as denominations. New religions that split from existing religions – typically with the aim of returning to what is perceived to be an earlier and less corrupt form of the parent religion – are referred to as sects or sectarian movements. New religions that spring up more spontaneously without a clear parent religion and with a charismatic leader are referred to as new religious movements. Each of these ideal types of religions varies in terms of its perceived legitimacy and its relationship to the government. Religions can evolve from one type (e.g., a new religious movement like early Christianity) into another (e.g., the Catholic Church).

Another way to classify religions is to think about them along a liberal/conservative continuum. Liberal religions have accepted that modern technology and science present challenges to their beliefs and values and, as a result, they have adjusted those beliefs and values. For instance, most members of the Church of Sweden and the United Methodists accept evolution and therefore view the Bible as an inspired book that often draws upon metaphors rather than seeing it as a literal history. On the conservative end are religions that are more resistant to modern ideas, like Pentecostalism and Mormonism.

These religions tend to be more patriarchal in their polity and more literalist in their understanding of scripture. Religions that hold literalistic understandings of scripture, claim they have exclusive access to truth, and encourage black and white or right and wrong thinking are often called "fundamentalist" religions. Religious fundamentalists are typically those who are responsible for religion-inspired violence and terrorism (Juergensmeyer 2003).

While there have always been individuals in societies who question the religious order and religious beliefs, it has become much more common and acceptable for individuals to switch religions or leave religion altogether since religion ceased to be obligatory and became voluntary. This is a relatively recent development in Western societies (though was arguably possible before the widespread adoption of Christianity; Whitmarsh 2016). As a voluntary institution in some societies (but not in others, like many predominantly Muslim countries today), sociologists have explored the factors that contribute to religious growth and decline. One of the most prominent theories that explains religious growth and decline is secularization. Secularization theory suggests that modernization (i.e., advances in technology, human rights, philosophy, democracy, equality, and science) causes problems for religious belief systems. Modern modes of thinking can run counter to religious beliefs, rituals, and power structures, undermining religiosity and leading to secular states, institutions, and people. Secularization theory helps explain declining levels of religiosity in many Western countries since the nineteenth century.

As religiosity has declined, the focus of sociologists of religion has turned to that which is not religion but related to, which is referred to as nonreligion. Individuals who in surveys about religious affiliation report that they have no religious affiliation are typically categorized as "nonreligious" or as religious "nones." The rise of the nonreligious has been quite dramatic in most Western countries over the last century or so. In the United States, this rise has been quite recent. In 1990 in the United States, 7 percent of adult Americans reported no religious affiliation. As of 2014, 23 percent of adult Americans reported no religious affiliation. The nonreligious are the fastest growing "religious" group in most highly developed Western countries around the world due to people disaffiliating from religion at high rates. However, relatively low birth rates among the nonreligious suggest that other religious groups, like Islam and Hinduism, will continue to grow at a faster rate than will nonreligion for the foreseeable future (Hackett et al. 2015).

Related to the growth of nonreligion is the growing prevalence of spirituality. Spirituality has been notoriously difficult to conceptualize, as people – including researchers – have very different conceptions of what it means. Some scholars have argued that spirituality is broad enough to include a sense of meaning, regardless of whether that meaning is devoid of any religious or supernatural beliefs. When conceptualized that broadly, spirituality, not surprisingly, appears to be important for things like physical and mental health. However, when spirituality is limited in its scope to supernatural beliefs and behaviors outside of the context of organized religion (e.g., holding a belief in reincarnation or believing all humanity is spiritually linked), spirituality appears to have a limited relationship with other phenomena (Cragun et al. 2016). The debates between scholars as to how to define spirituality aside, a growing number of people are choosing to identify as "spiritual but not religious." It is not entirely clear what is driving the moderate increase in this identification. Obviously one contributing factor is the growing number of people who do not affiliate with religious organizations. But whether people are identifying as spiritual because they hold supernatural beliefs or because they want to avoid the discrimination that often faces nonreligious individuals in societies that continue to value religion is uncertain.

Much of the research in the sociology of religion has both a Western and Christian focus. Future research on religion needs to move beyond highly developed, Western, and currently or formerly Christian countries. In some non-Western countries, conducting such research is challenging due to governmental restrictions on religion. Given the growing awareness and acceptance of LGBTQ+ individuals, more research is needed to understand how these individuals think about, participate in, avoid, and are accepted by religions. Another important line of research will be to better understand the growth of nonreligion and how such individuals think about existential issues. The relationship between religion, terrorism, and politics also warrants continued research. Given the rapid changes taking place in religion around the world, there will be a continued need for the sociology of religion.

SEE ALSO: Epistemology; Modernity; Science and Technology, Sociology of

References

Cragun, Deborah, Ryan T. Cragun, Brian Nathan, J.E. Sumerau, and Alexandra C.H. Nowakowski. 2016. "Do Religiosity and Spirituality Really Matter for Social, Mental, and Physical Health? A Tale of Two Samples." *Sociological Spectrum* 36 (6): 359–377.

Durkheim, Emile. 1995. *The Elementary Forms of Religious Life.* New York: Free Press.

Hackett, Conrad, Marcin Stonawski, Michaela Potančoková, Brian J. Grim, and Vegard Skirbekk. 2015. "The Future Size of Religiously Affiliated and Unaffiliated Populations." *Demographic Research* 32 (27): 829–842. DOI:10.4054/DemRes.2015.32.27.

Juergensmeyer, Mark. 2003. *Terror in the Mind of God: The Global Rise of Religious Violence,* 3rd ed. Comparative Studies in Religion and Society. Berkeley: University of California Press.

Sumerau, J. Edward, Ryan T. Cragun, and Lain A.B. Mathers. 2016. "Contemporary Religion and the Cisgendering of Reality." *Social Currents* 3 (3): 293–311. DOI:10.1177/2329496515604644.

Whitmarsh, Tim. 2016. *Battling the Gods: Atheism in the Ancient World.* Reprint edition. London: Vintage.

Risk

Rolf Lidskog

Örebro University, Sweden

Risk is a relatively new concept for sociology, but its importance and use has been rapidly growing. Sociology stresses that risk is always socially embedded; it is always situated in a social context and necessarily connected to actors' activities. However, in much thinking about and handling of risks they are often treated as separated from society in the sense that they are lifted out of their social context and are dealt with as something uninfluenced by activities, technologies, and instruments that serve to map them.

The concept of risk developed originally within a technical framework where risk is understood as the product of the probability and consequences of an adverse event. It is here measured and calculated through various scientific instruments, and predictive models are elaborated in order to take action to minimize risks (either reduce their likelihood or mitigate their consequences). Due to the difference between experts' evaluation of risks and public's perception of risk, behavioral and social scientists started to explain how different groups and individuals perceived risks, stressing the role contextual factors play for laypersons' risk perception.

Many sociologists seek a more sophisticated way to understand the clash between experts' and the public's understanding of risk than drawing a sharp line between risk as defined and assessed by experts and as understood by the public. The *social amplification of risk* model is an example of this. This model understands risk as a signal (an event or phenomena) that passes different social stations that amplify or attenuate this signal. Risk analysis can explain the original signal, but it is social sciences that have to investigate the processes of amplification which in turn result in different consequences. The approach explains why certain hazards and events that experts assess as low risk may receive public attention, whereas other hazards that experts consider more severe receive less attention. Examples of the former are the many "food scares," which are willingly reported by media because they can be framed as potentially urgent and dramatic dangers to human health. Other health risks, such as that posed by domestic radon (exposure at home and work resulting in increased risk of lung cancer), have not given rise to much public and political concern. Another example is toxicologists' warnings about cocktail effects of chemicals (long-term effects of low-dose exposure to

Core Concepts in Sociology, First Edition. Edited by J. Michael Ryan.
© 2019 John Wiley & Sons Ltd. Published 2019 by John Wiley & Sons Ltd.

a combination of chemicals), which hitherto have not resulted in any greater societal response. By encompassing different factors on different levels, the social amplification of risk model presents a dynamic and multilayered view on how risk awareness develops.

Another sociological understanding stresses *the social construction of risks*; that risks always exist in and are shaped by their contexts. The implication is that technical risk analysis and experts' assessments of risks are only one of many possible ways to define and evaluate risks. This means that neither experts' nor the public's forms of risk awareness are wrong, only that they are related to their specific contexts. Thus, risks are here seen as social phenomena in their own right, constructed by institutions and organizations in order to understand the world and make it manageable. Instead, risks should be seen as social phenomena in their own right, constructed by institutions and organizations to understand the world and make it manageable. Thus, sociology has an important contribution to make, not only to make people's risk evaluation understandable or to explain why certain risks have received such attention, but also to reveal how experts' risk assessments are dependent on their contexts. This is important because risk is a way to order reality and make it calculable, thereby creating a space for action and decision-making.

Yet another distinct sociological understanding of risk stresses that we are approaching a *risk society*. Most appositely articulated by the German sociologist Ulrich Beck, macro-structural factors are fundamentally transforming our current society. This new and coming risk society differs clearly from the industrial society in that it focuses on the environmental question and the distribution of risks instead of the social question and the distribution of wealth. Hitherto risks had been possible to perceive as adverse but manageable side effects of the production of wealth. But now risks have become more widespread and serious than ever before; for the first time in history, society involves the potential for human-made global catastrophes. Even if this theory has been vividly discussed, many sociologists share the standpoint that risks have become an organizing principle for society. To reflect on future consequences of human action is nothing new in history, but it is a new phenomena that almost all aspects of social life have been pervaded by thinking and organizing in terms of risk.

To conclude, a sociological understanding of risk means to place it in its social context. There are no risks "out there" in the sense of being independent of the society in which they emerge, are measured, and monitored. To develop sociological knowledge on risks implies instead to contextualize risks; to associate them with specific actors, institutions, and settings. The sociology of risk should therefore not be restricted to the investigation of risk perceptions, but should also study definitions and usage of risks, including how these are framed and regulated.

SEE ALSO: Environment, Sociology of the; Epistemology; Frames, Narratives, and Ideology; Science and Technology, Sociology of

Further Reading

Beck, Ulrich. 1992. *Risk Society: Towards a New Modernity*. London: Sage.
Bernstein, Peter. 1996. *Against the God: The Remarkable Story of Risk*. New York: John Wiley and Sons.
Giddens, Anthony. 1990. *The Consequences of Modernity*. Cambridge: Polity Press.

Lidskog, Rolf, and Göran Sundqvist. 2013. "The Sociology of Risk." In *Essentials of Risk Theory*, edited by Sabine Roeser, Rafaela Hillerbrand, Per Sandin, and Martin Peterson, 75–105. New York: Springer.

Lupton, Deborah. 2013. *Risk*, 2nd ed. London: Routledge.

Pidgeon, Nick, Roger E. Kasperson, and Paul Slovic, eds. 2003. *Social Amplification of Risk*. Cambridge: Cambridge University Press.

Science and Technology, Sociology of

Gary Bowden

University of New Brunswick, Canada

The sociology of science and technology is a subdisciplinary specialization focused on the cultures, networks, and social structures characteristic of scientific and engineering activity and the social and cultural consequences of those activities. Although interest in technology can be found in the writings of Marx and other early social theorists, it was Robert Merton's mid-twentieth-century research on science which defined the area as a coherent subdiscipline. Merton's functionalist description of science as a social institution harmonized with the justifications provided by logical positivist historians and philosophers of science for the truth of scientific theories and observations. When historian Thomas Kuhn fundamentally undermined this view by showing how changes in scientific knowledge were, in part, a product of social processes, sociologists shifted their gaze from the institution of science to the content of the knowledge produced by that institution, leading to a new sub-specialization – the sociology of scientific knowledge. Theoretical insights about the production of scientific knowledge were extended to technology, resulting in the body of knowledge known by the current label – the sociology of science and technology. This line of research, which raised fundamental questions about the epistemology and ontology of scientific knowledge, became the conceptual core of many interdisciplinary science and technology studies programs and culminated in the 1990s debates known as the "science wars." As the theoretical debate between objectivism and constructivism subsided, the field became more eclectic. Recent areas of research focus include race and gender, authority and expertise, democracy and participation, health and pathology, risk and uncertainty, globalization, and environmental protection.

Merton, Logical Positivism, and Science as an Institutional System

The history and philosophy of science existed as established areas of scholarly activity long before the sociology of science. Focused on the distinctive nature of scientific knowledge, positivist philosophers argued that the scientific method, involving the

Core Concepts in Sociology, First Edition. Edited by J. Michael Ryan.
© 2019 John Wiley & Sons Ltd. Published 2019 by John Wiley & Sons Ltd.

systematic collection of information derived from sensory experience and interpreted through reason and logic, was the only source of truth. Robert Merton gave a sociological twist to the historical question of why the scientific revolution occurred in Europe rather than other times or places. In an argument similar to Weber's analysis of the link between the Protestant Ethic and the rise of capitalism, Merton showed that seventeenth-century English scientists were predominantly Protestant and argued that Protestant values provided a religious justification for their scientific activities.

Merton's later work focused on the operation of science as a social institution by describing both its normative structure and its distinctive reward system. The "ethos of modern science" consisted of four institutional norms: universalism (the institution of science should provide equality of opportunity for all scientists because the validity of scientific knowledge is independent of the personal attributes the scientists), communalism (scientific knowledge should be shared rather than kept private in order to promote collective collaboration), disinterestedness (scientists should act for the benefit of the collective enterprise rather than for their own personal gain), and organized skepticism (scientific claims should be critically scrutinized by the scientific community before being accepted as valid).

Scientists adhere to the norms of communalism and disinterestedness because of the reward system of science. By sharing their findings they gain recognition and prestige within the field. The idea that professional status rather than financial reward was the factor driving scientists led Merton's students to study the citations in scientific articles in order to develop quantitative measures of recognition. The large databases of scientific articles used for their bibliometric analysis of citation patterns were the precursors of the electronic databases of journal articles now used in libraries throughout the world.

A central feature of the Mertonian paradigm was the way it complemented logical positivism and, hence, circumscribed the features of scientific activity subject to sociological scrutiny. Adherence to the collective norms of the scientific institution led scientists to follow the procedures of the scientific method and get results that were true. Thus, sociology had nothing to say about the production of valid scientific knowledge. It was only when social pressures led scientists to deviate from the norms of science, as in the case of Lysenkoism, that sociological factors became relevant.

Rapid developments in science and technology, in part the result of the shift from "little science" to "big science" described by Derek de Solla Price, fueled the economy following World War II. Where early science was practiced on a small scale by individual scientists, big science refers to large-scale projects, such as the Manhattan Project to develop the atomic bomb, typically funded by governments and involving a large number of scientists working in big laboratories with big budgets and large expensive pieces of equipment. In order to understand this transition and provide recommendations to governments on how to effectively fund scientific and technological research that would contribute to social and economic development, sociologists began to study science and technology policy.

Kuhn, the Sociology of Scientific Knowledge (SSK), and the Science Wars

In the 1960s philosophers and historians challenged the logical positivist understanding of scientific change. Kuhn, through close examination of the Copernican Revolution and other major shifts in scientific understanding, documented the role of sociological factors in scientific development. This insight opened the production of scientific knowledge to sociological scrutiny and led to the symmetry thesis argument – social factors were relevant for understanding the production of both valid and erroneous knowledge.

Over the next several decades sociologists engaged in an intense theoretical debate about how to make sense of this situation. If scientific knowledge is contingent and has interpretive flexibility, in other words is not determined entirely by empirical observation interpreted through reason and logic, then there must be a social process that accounts for the treatment of some knowledge claims as valid and others as invalid. Notable approaches and their major proponents included the Strong Programme (Barry Barnes, David Bloor, Steven Shapin), the Empirical Programme of Relativism (Harry Collins, Trevor Pinch), new literary forms (Michael Mulkay, Steven Woolgar), and actor–network theory (Bruno Latour, Michel Callon). Laboratory studies, the practice of studying scientists at the lab-bench, became an important methodological strategy. It allowed sociologists to directly observe the actions of the scientists and engineers rather than rely on their written or verbal accounts of those actions. Another major development was the technological turn. Ideas developed for understanding the production of scientific knowledge were extended to include the development of technological artifacts. Examples include the social construction of technology (Wiebe Bijker, Trevor Pinch) and the emphasis on technoscience among actor–network theorists. These approaches questioned technological determinism, the notion that technology is an autonomous force affecting social development.

Over time SSK theories became more and more epistemologically radical. Competing theory groups argued acrimoniously and the claim that scientific knowledge was just another social construction was attacked by scientific realists in a series of debates known as the science wars. These debates, coupled with the recognition that their constructionist arguments were providing intellectual cover to climate-change deniers and other reactionary interests, led Latour and others to re-evaluate their epistemological stance and admit a role for nature in the production of scientific knowledge.

The Era of Empirical and Topical Diversification

Following the science wars, the field entered a period of eclecticism and continuing diversification which has continued to this date. Research in SSK disproportionately emphasized physics and related sciences because they were seen as the hardest area in which to establish the claim that scientific knowledge was socially constructed. Current research in SS&T covers a much broader swath of scientific and technological activity, with notable emphasis on environmental science, medical science, genomics, and emerging technologies such as social media, medical technologies, biotechnology, and nanotechnology. Another major theme is the way in which boundaries are drawn and the purposes served by the resulting distinctions. Among the boundaries examined are those between science and nonscience, experts and laypersons, science and politics, science and the law, and the social and natural. Feminist and postcolonial critiques of science and technology, perspectives which emerged among scholarly communities focused on the experiences of particular marginalized groups, have become major strands of research in contemporary SS&T. In a similar way, links with other sociological subdisciplines, such as social movements, international development, political sociology, medical sociology, economic sociology, and the sociology of law, have emerged.

SEE ALSO: Development, Sociology of; Economic Sociology; Environment, Sociology of the; Knowledge, Sociology of; Medical Sociology; Political Sociology; Power and Authority; Social Movements and Social Change; Sociological Theory

Further Reading

Hackett, Edward, Olga Amsterdamska, Michael Lynch, and Judy Wajcman, eds. 2007. *The Handbook of Science and Technology Studies*, 3rd ed. Cambridge, MA: The MIT Press.
Latour, Bruno. 1987. *Science in Action: How to Follow Scientists and Engineers Through Society*. Cambridge, MA: Harvard University Press.
Merton, Robert K. 1973. *The Sociology of Science*. Chicago: University of Chicago Press.

Self, the

Peter L. Callero

Western Oregon University, USA

The concept of *self* is widely employed by sociologists to represent (a) the way in which individual persons come to understand who they are in relation to others, and (b) the way in which individual actions are motivated, planned, and adjusted within a social setting. In this sense, the self is simultaneously both an object and a subject.

As an object, the self represents the totality of a person's thoughts and feelings about their experience in the world. It answers a fundamental question required of all social encounters: Who am I in relation to other?

As a subject, the self is an agent, actively engaged in the processing of social information, interpreting the reactions of others, responding to the demands of interaction, while at the same time working diligently to construct and maintain the self as object.

George Herbert Mead (1934) is largely credited with developing this particular understanding of the self. Mead referred to the self as object as the *Me*, and the self as subject as the *I*, and he stressed the necessary codependence of these two complementary dimensions. In the same way that a coin must always have two sides, there is no Me without an I, and no I without a Me. To know who we are as a social object, we need to be actively engaged as a knowing subject. But because one cannot be subject and object at exactly the same moment, we are constantly switching back and forth between acting as a subject and assessing who we are as an object.

This reflexivity can be understood as an internal conversation between the I and the Me. It is a dialogue in which the active and spontaneous I, always speaking in the present, becomes the socially recognizable Me of our always developing past. In this way, our sense of self influences our behavior, and our behavior in turn influences our sense of self. Sometimes the influence is immediate, as when we make behavioral adjustments on the fly, altering our words, gestures, and actions while engaged in a conversation, or attempting to solve a problem. Other times we might have some distance from our past actions, as when we think more generally about who we are, what we have done, and who we would like to be in the future. In both instances, our understanding of self remains more or less a reflection of our social experience.

This is the so-called *looking-glass self* where others' reactions to our behavior serve as the mirror that we use to see our own reflection. In other words, we are able to assess

Core Concepts in Sociology, First Edition. Edited by J. Michael Ryan.
© 2019 John Wiley & Sons Ltd. Published 2019 by John Wiley & Sons Ltd.

our self as an object in society indirectly by interpreting the meaning of others' response to our behavior. We are in essence asking ourselves: How do I appear to be from someone else's point of view? Here it is important to note that the *others* that we use as the mirror come in many different shapes and sizes. At times it will be a very specific other, such as a friend, a relative, a teacher, or boss, while at other times it will be a more *generalized other* such as one's family, church, or society, where similar points of view come together as an organized whole.

All healthy human persons are born with the capacity for selfhood but, from a sociological perspective, no one is born with a self. The self forms gradually and in conjunction with the mastery of symbolic communication. In the same way that individual language development presupposes a community of language users, the self emerges from the actions and interactions of persons with already established selves. Explaining how this developmental process transpires has been one area of focus in research on the self. In this line of investigation, considerable attention is devoted to *role-taking* as a central mechanism in the production of selves.

Role-taking occurs when an individual imaginatively takes the position or perspective of another person, group, or culture. It begins when the infant learns to imitate or mimic the gestures and vocalizations of a caregiver. As proficiency with symbols grows, the child gradually learns to visualize life as another person, creates make-believe friends, and acts out characters with costumes, toys, and dolls. Over time, the overt role-playing of childhood play becomes more skillful, complex, and hidden from view. When fully formed and mature, the role-taking process is a common and mostly automatic cognitive process that enables cooperation through the merging of perspectives and the development of shared meaning. But this does not mean that all persons employ role-taking with the same degree of proficiency. A number of studies have shown, in fact, that role-taking accuracy is associated with social status, and individuals who hold low status positions tend to be more accurate role-takers.

One major focus of research and debate on the self concerns the content or elements used in the construction of the self as object. Questions include: How do social forces influence the selection and interpretation of the content of the self? What are the social and psychological consequences of positive and negative evaluations of the content? And how is social inequality implicated in the construction of the self? Most research in this area of study concerns the way in which identity categories structure the self. For sociologists, the identities of most interest are those that define social positions and group affiliations (e.g., race, ethnicity, gender, social class, sexuality, the nation-state), as well as *collective identities* that represent affiliation with activist movements organizing for political and cultural change. But in modern society, where the reins of tradition have been loosened, the resources for self-construction are multiple and diverse and might also involve material objects (clothing, automobiles, houses), alterations of the body (piercings, tattoos, plastic surgery), or computer technology (Facebook, avatars). Understanding how these diverse resources intercept, overlay, and are prioritized for individual persons is another key research question. Here there is some evidence to suggest that storytelling and the use of cultural narratives is critical to the maintenance of a coherent sense of self in modern society.

Another major area of research investigates the self as a mechanism or process through which behavior is controlled and motivated. How are self-views negotiated in particular situations? How do we manage to maintain a consistent view of self when social situations shift and change around us? How do we use social settings and social relationships to craft preferred interpretations of the self? One prominent program of research in this area has found evidence that the self operates as a type of control system, where internalized self-meanings (identity standards) function much like a thermostat. If a particular situation feels uncomfortable, inauthentic, or inconsistent with one's preferred identity meaning, the self will be motivated to alter the situation, or modify behavior in attempt to receive positive verification of established identity meanings. But if social forces consistently work against identity verification, the self will be motivated to change and may eventually accept a new identity standard that is more consistent with the social environment.

For nearly a century, sociologists influenced by symbolic interactionist theory have employed the concept of self as a critical conceptual bridge connecting individuals and society. In this tradition (the tenants of which have been described above), the self is understood to be an emergent product of social relations and a key mechanism in the organization of social life. While this view of the self is dominant, it is not the only socio-logical interpretation. Another prominent approach emerged in the 1970s in opposition to traditional scholarship on the self. The *postmodern perspective*, as it has been called, rejects the assumption that individuals are in possession of a true, unified self, and challenges the idea that persons are rational actors with independent consciousness.

The postmodern argument begins by emphasizing the fact that conceptions of self vary dramatically across history and among cultures. Given this variability in understanding of selfhood, how can we assume that any single explanation is accurate? Might the social sci-entific approach to the self be reflecting the bias and dominance of Western civilization? In light of these concerns, postmodern analyses prefer to "deconstruct the self" and show how all explanations of the subject, even scientific ones, favor interpretations embedded in the discourse of powerful institutions. Rather than looking for common features of a universal self, it is argued that sociologists should instead describe how actors produce meaning in local settings in ways that give rise to particular understandings of subjectivity.

It is worth noting, however, that when the postmodern critique of the self was initially developed it made little reference to the work of George Herbert Mead and most post-modernists did not directly engage symbolic interactionist theory. Today, there is a greater appreciation of the overlap between the two theoretical perspectives. While it is true that cultural interpretations of the self vary dramatically, this debate often confuses the social construction of identity categories (content of the self) with the universal process of self-objectification and recognition. While identities may come and go, human persons remain both subject and object in all societies.

SEE ALSO: Emotion, Sociology of; Identity; Knowledge, Sociology of; Postmodernism and Poststructuralism; Social Psychology; Socialization; Symbolic Interactionism

Reference

Mead, George Herbert. 1934. *Mind, Self, and Society*. Chicago: University of Chicago Press.

Further Reading

Burke, Peter J., and Jan E. Stets. 2009. *Identity Theory*. New York: Oxford University Press.
Callero, Peter L. 2003. "The Sociology of the Self." *Annual Review of Sociology* 29: 115–133.
    DOI:10.1146/annurev.soc.29.010202.100057.
Elliot, Anthony. 2014. *Concepts of the Self*. Cambridge: Polity Press.

Sexualities

Barry D. Adam

University of Windsor, Canada

Origins of the Study of Sexualities

The study of sexualities is a relatively recent, but now flourishing, area in sociology. Though sexuality studies can be traced as far back as the late nineteenth century in the Western academy, it was long considered a topic for biological and medical investigation or was subsumed under the mantle of family, marriage, and morality. While these paradigms remain strong even today, the recognition of sexualities as sociocultural practices emerged over time. While still firmly grounded in biological and naturalistic presumptions, German scholars in the early twentieth century began to document considerable variation in human desires, interactions, and practices both in Europe and around the world. The Institute for Sex Research (*Sexualwissenschaft*) under the direction of Magnus Hirschfeld in Berlin cumulated much documentation about human sexuality during its 14 years of existence, but the institute and much of its legacy was destroyed by the Nazis in 1933. In the same period, Sigmund Freud and subsequent schools of psychotherapy opened new avenues for thinking about sexual development and variation beyond the strictly biological.

In the postwar period, work in anthropology and history cast more light on the wide variability of cultural forms in family, kinship, and sexuality calling into question traditional notions of sexuality as determined simply by instinct, biology, or "nature." With the advent of the feminist and gay and lesbian movements of the 1960s and 1970s, taken-for-granted arrangements of heterosexual courtship, family dynamics, and gender propriety came under critical scrutiny, leading to the formation of more properly sociological questions. Feminist critiques took on the gendered politics of nuclear families. Gay and lesbian critiques rejected the categorization of same-sex desire and relationships as sin or sickness. The underlying sociological questions became: How do social arrangements shape desire? How do states, economies, and social institutions regulate and privilege certain forms of family and sexuality? What are the viable options people are discovering for living their intimate and erotic relations? With these, the Freudian presumption that sexual instinct was the prime cause underlying psychology and society was overturned by the question of how culture, society, and history infuse the formation and expression of desire.

Core Concepts in Sociology, First Edition. Edited by J. Michael Ryan.
© 2019 John Wiley & Sons Ltd. Published 2019 by John Wiley & Sons Ltd.

A new generation began to explore these kinds of sociological questions, often starting with symbolic interactionist frameworks and moving over time into social constructionist and Foucauldian approaches. Notable pioneering work that took sexual variation, and homosexuality in particular, out of the sociology of deviance and into interactionist analysis were Mary McIntosh's article, "The Homosexual Role," in *Social Problems* (1968), John Gagnon and William Simon's book, *Sexual Conduct* (1973), and Kenneth Plummer's *Sexual Stigma* (1975). Plummer went on to become the founding editor of the influential journal, *Sexualities*. Jeffrey Weeks's magisterial trilogy, *Coming Out* (1977), *Sex, Politics, and* Society (1981), and *Sexuality and Its Discontents* (1985) offered a theoretically sophisticated history of gay and lesbian Britain, becoming influenced by Michel Foucault's *The History of Sexuality*, the first volume of which was published in English in 1978. The sociology of sexualities remained deeply engaged in the intellectual currents of the day in gender, family, and gay and lesbian studies, as well as with sexuality studies in related disciplines like anthropology and history. In 1983, Philip Blumstein and Pepper Schwartz published *American Couples*, the first study of its kind to contrast the internal dynamics of heterosexual and same-sex couples and, in 1984, Carol Vance's volume, *Pleasure and Danger*, laid out a wealth of feminist reflections on sexualities.

Broad-based survey research also began to take up sexuality questions. The first major survey since the Kinsey report, initiated by Edward Laumann, John Gagnon, Robert Michael, and Stuart Michaels, endured attacks by the Christian right and defunding by US senators, but finally appeared as *The Social Organization of Sexuality* in 1994. The survey has since become a staple in public opinion polling regarding, for example, homophobic attitudes or attitudes to same-sex marriage. Sexuality questions have more recently been added into national health surveys, often with the assistance of funding for HIV research, generating a new range of data.

On these foundations, the sociology of sexualities has grown from peripheral status to one of the growth areas in the field and became the conference theme for the American Sociological Association for the first time in 2015.

Sexualities and Social Theory

Today sexuality studies reflect some of the major themes in social theory of our era. Works by major sociological theorists like Anthony Giddens in *The Transformation of Intimacy* (1992), Ulrich Beck and Elisabeth Beck Gernsheim in *The Normal Chaos of Love* (1995), and Zygmunt Bauman in *Liquid Love* (2003) tend to place sexuality under the post-Durkheimian sign of increasing disorder, disembeddedness, and uncertainty. "Where people gradually cast off the commitments, dictates, and taboos of premodern society they began to put new hopes in love, but equally found themselves in new predicaments," argue Beck and Beck Gernsheim (1995: 45). These theorists observe trends in Western societies toward de-traditionalization, the loss of familiar signposts for relationship formation, new freedoms and equality in relationship expectations, and individual control over one's own body and sexuality. The result, Giddens contends, is the rise of the "pure relationship" that is voluntary, consensual, mutually beneficial, and egalitarian but also judged by the standard of individual utility and shorn of familial and institutional supports (or pressures) that once held relationships together for the long term. Sexuality becomes yet another element disembedded from family, elevated as an individual pleasure, and freighted with heightened expectations for personal fulfilment.

By contrast is the work of Judith Stacey in *Brave New Families* (1990) or Jeffrey Weeks in *The World We Have Won* (2007). They view these trends through a more celebratory lens as a proliferation of options, the flourishing of diversification, and the piecing together of gender, desire, and relationship in a range of new configurations. These trends herald the overcoming of patriarchy and heteronormativity, counteract the disciplinary forces of state and religion, and empower people to express the forms of sexuality and intimacy that best fit their needs. For Weeks (2007), "Increasingly the contemporary world is a world we are making for ourselves, part of the long process of the democratization of everyday life ... The sexual and intimate revolutions of our time are largely the result of ... grass-roots transformations."

Macro-Sociology of Sexualities

In the 2000s, sexuality studies have moved from being viewed as a somewhat suspect prurient interest marginal to the sociological core to being regarded as a fundamental dimension for understanding social interactions, structure, and inequalities. A major area of inquiry has been the intersection of sexualities and the state. Public debates about sexual violence against women have prompted research on the ways that judicial systems construct consent, implicitly excuse or naturalize male aggression, and actively reproduce an inequitable sexual order. Public debates over the equality claims of lesbian, gay, bisexual, and transgender people, particularly same-sex marriage, have highlighted the role of the state in institutionalizing heteronormative sexual arrangements and in disciplining citizens who choose other options. Gayle Rubin's classic 1984 article, "Thinking Sex," pointed out the moral and political hierarchies that continue to privilege some sexualities as "natural" and subject others to stigma, regulation, and punishment. A good deal of work has since been done exploring how states regulate sexualities through immigration, the military, the criminal justice system, and welfare policy, thereby constructing privileged forms of citizenship defined by sexuality as well as by race, gender, and social class. Gary Kinsman's *The Regulation of Desire* (1987, 1996) and Margot Canaday's *The Straight State* (2009) are notable works in this area. Roger Lancaster's landmark book, *Sex Panic and the Punitive State* (2011: 14) examines the depth and extensiveness of state regulation of sexualities as "the menace posed by the inscrutable evil of the (implicitly black) rapist, the (implicitly homosexual) paedophile, or the (supposedly irremediable) child abuser prods ever more extreme ... increasingly irrational security measures." Ranging over the satanic abuse and day-care panics of the 1980s in the United States, child abuse scandals afflicting the Roman Catholic Church around the world, and rise of sex offender registries, Lancaster documents the pervasiveness of the carceral state, thereby challenging sociohistorical visions of sexuality as a story of liberal progress toward greater freedom and enlightenment.

At the same time, analysis of the underlying social forces that lead to repression or emancipation is a central concern of sociology and sociological tools have much to offer in making sense of struggles over sexuality. Social movement analysis has long sought to explain the social origins of discontent, key elements of social mobilization, and the larger array of social forces that determine the success or failure of aggrieved populations in pressing their demands. Same-sex marriage has posed intriguing questions on how best to sort through the complex social, political, and cultural ingredients that have gone into the long struggle of LGBT movements (e.g., Verta Taylor and Mary Bernstein, *The Marrying Kind?*, 2013). Work on LGBT movements themselves (e.g., Barry D. Adam, *The Rise of a Gay and Lesbian Movement*, 1987, 1995), on public conflicts over sex education in schools (Janice Irvine, *Talk About Sex*, 2002), and conservative movements that have fought hard to retain traditional sexual hierarchies (Arlene Stein, *The Stranger Next Door*, 2001) have all sought to identify the underlying forces that fuel these conflicts.

In the 2000s, many of these conflicts have moved onto the global stage. The global impact of neoliberal economic policies, the rise of the internet and instantaneous global communication, increased air travel, and transnational migration have all had their effects on sexualities as well. Current scholarship has been investigating how these forces have been influencing the proliferation of LGBT identities around the world (Dennis Altman, *Global Sex*, 2000) and changing how people understand their sexualities and identities (Peter Drucker, *Warped*, 2016). It has also been looking into how sexuality plays a role as a motivator in migration and tourism (Lionel Cantu, *The Sexuality of Migration*, 2002). But perhaps most striking has been the emergence of a global divide, often played out in policy debates at the United Nations, between Europe, North and South America, and Australia, who envision themselves as modern and progressive, versus much of Africa, the Caribbean, Russia, and the Middle East, who envision themselves as the guardians of morality, tradition, and indigenous culture. In the former, women's and LGBT equality rights have come quite recently to be constructed as signs of enlightenment and democracy; in the latter, as evidence of social chaos and loss of rightful patriarchal and religious authority. This development is ripe for sociological inquiry. The exceptions and ambivalent cases to this overall trend may prove to be particularly illuminating. South Africa and postcolonial French and Portuguese states in Africa have been liberalizing while former British colonies have mounted new waves of persecution. Catholic Ireland has adopted same-sex marriage by referendum; Catholic Poland reaffirms traditionalism. The United States itself is an ambivalent case as "religious freedom" laws work through state legislatures to re-authorize discrimination against LGBT people in the wake of Supreme Court approval of same-sex marriage. Caught in this global politic are sexual minorities attempting to navigate conflicts over the meaning of Muslim sexual identities in both Muslim-majority nations and in diaspora (Jasbir Puar, *Terrorist Assemblages*, 2007; Momin Rahman, *Homosexualities, Muslim Cultures and Modernity*, 2014). Increasing attention is as well being turned to the ways in which sexualities enter into constructions of race and racism in Asian and African populations in the United States (Joane Nagel, *Race, Ethnicity and* Sexuality, 2003; Patricia Hill Collins, *Black Sexual Politics*, 2005).

Ethnographies of Sexualities

Edward Laumann et al. (1994) postulated that there are five different regional sexual cultures in the United States based on national data collected on attitudes to a number of sexual issues. In a later study based in Chicago, Laumann and other colleagues (*The Sexual Organization of the City*, 2004) refined that analysis further to show how sexual markets and cultures varied by neighborhood, particularly where African-American, Latino, or

LGBT people predominated. Ethnographic studies raise questions about how sexual subjectivities are generated and transformed over time and place. In an era of smartphones, webcams, and dating apps that have made a wide range of sexual imagery instantly accessible even (or especially) to youth and has allowed the formation of networks and virtual communities among an expanding number of once-isolated people, there is a new sense of possibility and access to sexual discourse and connection than ever before. Perhaps paradoxically the internet era has helped some people identify themselves as "asexual" in a world where sexual imagery and possibility can be experienced as pressure or obligation. Sociology is only beginning to document the effects of these changes on emergent sexual subjectivities.

Adam Green's (2014) Bourdieu-inspired analysis of "sexual fields" points to the ways that the spaces of sexual sociality generate hierarchies of desirability that in turn influence notions of attractiveness and erotic capital. A good deal of ethnographic work has appeared in recent years exploring sexual communities and the intersections of sexualities with social institutions. These include studies that: take non-monogamy out of the category of "cheating" into the realm of sexual and relationship innovation (Meg Barker and Darren Langdridge, *Understanding Non-Monogamies*, 2010), look at schools cultures as generators of sexual values (C.J. Pascoe, *Dude, You're a Fag*, 2007), and examine religion and workplace as sites of struggle over sexuality (David Rayside and Clyde Wilcox, *Faith, Politics, and Sexual Diversity in Canada and the United States*, 2011; David Rayside and Gerald Hunt, *Equity, Diversity, and Canadian Labour*, 2008). Or they study the cultures of sex work (Wendy Chapkis, *Live Sex Acts*, 1997; Elizabeth Bernstein, *Temporarily Yours*, 2007), drag (Leila Rupp and Verta Taylor, *Drag Queens at the 801 Cabaret*, 2003), or BDSM (Margot Weiss, *Techniques of Pleasure*, 2011). A quickly growing recent area of work concerns the sexualities of transgender people.

Sociological study of sexualities also intersects with other large bodies of research, most notably in criminology, health, and cultural studies. A very sizeable research tradition inquires into sexual violence, hate crimes, and more recently the criminalization of HIV. Though HIV studies tend to be vast area of publication with only limited overlap with sexuality studies per se, it generates an immense amount of data relevant to sociology about sexual practices, sexually transmitted infections, changing sexual mores around safer sex, and sexual interaction and cultures of HIV-positive people.

SEE ALSO: Body, the; Constructionism vs. Essentialism; Deviance; Family and Kinship, Sociology of; Feminist Theory; Gender; Homophobia and Heterosexism; Identities; Masculinities; Social Movements and Social Change; Stereotypes, Prejudice, and Discrimination; Stigma

References

Beck, Ulrich, and Elisabeth Beck-Gernsheim. 1995. *The Normal Chaos of Love*. Cambridge: Polity.
Green, Adam, ed. 2014. *Sexual Fields*. Chicago: University of Chicago Press.
Lancaster, Roger. 2011. *Sex Panic and the Punitive State*. Berkeley: University of California Press.
Laumann, Edward, John Gagnon, Robert Michael, and Stuart Michaels. 1994. *The Social Organization of Sexuality*. Chicago: University of Chicago Press.
Weeks, Jeffrey. 2007. *The World We Have Won*. London: Routledge.

Further Reading

Aggleton, Peter, and Richard Parker. 2010. *Handbook of Sexuality, Health and Rights.* New York: Routledge.

DeLamater, John, and Rebecca Plante. 2015. *Handbook of the Sociology of Sexualities.* New York: Springer.

Seidman, Steven, Nancy Fischer, and Chet Meeks. 2007. *Handbook of the New Sexuality Studies.* New York: Routledge.

Social Justice

Valerie Chepp

Hamline University, USA

Social justice refers to efforts aimed at promoting a fair society that challenges inequality and oppression, and values diversity. Specific social justice concerns – such as racial, economic, gender, and environmental justice – fall within this definition.

Social justice has been central to sociology since the discipline's inception. For over a century, questions about what constitutes a fair society, how social inequality is reproduced and challenged, and how institutions and interactions structure groups' experiences with oppression and self-determination have shaped the field. A passion for social justice has motivated many to pursue a career in sociology.

In the early twenty-first century, the term "social justice" has gained significant visibility in the sociological lexicon. Journal articles, journals, special issues, anthologies, book chapters, and entire monographs are devoted to social justice research, theory, and praxis. Social justice subjects are integral to sociological curriculums and course topics. A commitment to social justice is reflected in the discipline's professional structure: several American Sociological Association sections are dedicated to promoting social justice, and entire organizations and conferences are coordinated around social justice (e.g., Society for the Study of Social Problems and Association for Humanist Sociology). It is not unusual to see sociology job descriptions explicitly seek a specialization in social justice, and academic programs and centers focused on social justice are becoming more commonplace on college campuses, many of which find homes or affinities within sociology departments.

While the *purview* of social justice has been ever-present, a clear definition of and unique sociological contribution to the concept has yet to be fully articulated. Other intellectual traditions, such as philosophy, religion, and legal scholarship, have deep roots in justice studies. For centuries, scholars and practitioners in these fields have debated, delineated, and described the meaning of justice from their disciplinary vantage points. Having emerged more recently, sociology has a shorter disciplinary history and truncated track record of self-reflection.

A survey of some of the major disciplinary dimensions shaped by social justice ideas – inside and outside the academy – can help further define this essential sociological concept. Within academic sociology, the discipline's contribution to social theory, and

Core Concepts in Sociology, First Edition. Edited by J. Michael Ryan.
© 2019 John Wiley & Sons Ltd. Published 2019 by John Wiley & Sons Ltd.

specifically critical and conflict theories, reflect a strong commitment to social justice. Marxist theory and, later, the Frankfurt School, are prominent examples. Within these schools of thought, the critique of power and resource imbalances among different social groups, along with an analysis of social change, points to an unspoken working definition of social justice. Sociology's influence on other (inter)disciplines has given rise to more recent theoretical traditions with a social justice bent, including critical race, LatCrit, feminist, and queer theories.

A commitment to social justice also informs research methods commonly used in academic sociology, such as feminist methodologies and participant action research. These methods seek a more egalitarian approach to the traditional researcher–subject power relationship, and aspire to produce knowledge that will benefit research participants, as well as contribute to disciplinary knowledge and professional credentials.

Social justice topics are frequently at the center of academic teaching and scholarship in sociology. These topics are far too extensive to exhaustively name, but include the rich tradition of sociological studies of social inequality and the myriad ways inequality is reproduced and challenged through social interactions and institutional arrangements. The rise of intersectional scholarship – another intellectual innovation nurtured by sociological insight and a social justice agenda – has pushed the discipline's approach to teaching and researching inequality in more nuanced and productive directions. Teaching and research about social movements and change is another reflection of the discipline's interest in and commitment to better understanding actions that result in a more socially just society.

Social justice ideas have also informed sociology's strong presence and long tradition outside of the academy. Burawoy (2005) shows how social justice goals influence the public and policy dimensions of sociology. People working in these sectors – such as advocacy groups, lawmakers, professional academics, and public intellectuals – draw upon sociological knowledge to shape policy outcomes, inform public debates, and speak to a wide audience through popular media outlets. Beyond policy and public spheres, social justice objectives factor prominently into applied and vocational aspects of sociology, which include the fields of social work, activism, community organizing, direct service provision, relief and humanitarian aid work, civic engagement, and volunteerism. Throughout this work, sociological insight is deployed to achieve more equitable and humane social outcomes, often giving special attention to the socially marginalized.

Taken together, these social justice dimensions of sociology highlight core features that distinguish social justice as an essential sociological concept. Social justice is *action-oriented*, aimed at social change that results in a fairer, more tolerant, and equitable society in which all social groups are equipped with resources and capacities for self-determination and freedom from oppression. Diverse group representation in institutional decision-making processes is a key component of this social justice equation (Young 1990). The wellbeing of those at the bottom of the social hierarchy is of great concern, as are the unfair privileges, power, and resources concentrated at the top. Embedded in these actions for change is the sociological recognition that individuals and groups are members of a larger social union; different sociological perspectives reflect this core insight. For instance, in social functionalist terms, the good living of everybody results in a more balanced and successful society; thus, social injustice is dysfunctional (McGowan 1940). In intersectional terms, fighting one form of oppression necessitates the dismantling of other forms to ensure the individual and collective wellbeing of all people (Combahee River Collective [1977] 1995). A social constructivist perspective illustrates how different groups come to define justice and injustice, and how these ideas get structured into social institutions and interactions, thereby enabling or constraining various forms of collective action organized around social justice and wellbeing (Parker 2014).

These sociological perspectives are distinct from philosophy's interest in, for example, identifying guiding principles of justice, religion's interest in making a moral case around justice, or legal scholars' interest in determining appropriate punishment for injustice. Whether working inside or outside the academy, the sociologist's extensive knowledge of the social laws governing human interactions and institutional structures position the discipline well for making a unique contribution to social justice. Sociology reveals the various and complicated ways that the individual's welfare fits into the general welfare of society, and how one's own self-interests and wellbeing are linked to that of the larger social unit. This knowledge can foster a society in which institutions are more diverse and equitably structured, and the freedom, dignity, and wellbeing of all people is ensured.

SEE ALSO: Intersectionality; Public Sociology; Risk; Social Movements and Social Change; Stratification and Inequality

References

Burawoy, Michael. 2005. "For Public Sociology." *American Sociological Review* 70 (1): 4–28. DOI:10.1177/000312240507000102.

Combahee River Collective. [1977] 1995. "A Black Feminist Statement." In *Words of Fire: An Anthology of African-American Feminist Thought*, edited by Beverly Guy-Sheftall, 232–240. New York: New Press.

McGowan, Raymond A. 1940. "Social Justice and Sociology." *The American Catholic Sociological Review* 1 (2): 68–73.

Parker, Stuart. 2014. "'This Isn't Right!': A Sociological Approach to Social Justice." *Journal of Social Justice* 4. Online at: http://transformativestudies.org/wp-content/uploads/This-isnt-right.pdf.

Young, Iris Marion. 1990. *Justice and the Politics of Difference*. Princeton, NJ: Princeton University Press.

Social Media and Virtual Communities

Gaspar Brändle

Universidad de Murcia, Spain

The number of people who have access to the internet (which as of 2016 exceeds three billion globally) and are active social media users (which as of 2016 exceeds two billion globally) is rapidly growing around the world. More than just occasional users, many individuals have integrated these practices into their daily routines, making a study of such practices of growing interest. While there are still significant gaps in terms of access and use, there has undoubtedly been a substantial change in the way many of us communicate and interact, multiplying the possibilities of increasing social capital by establishing links with other people without the necessity of kinship bonds or geographical proximity.

Social media are a group of mobile and web applications that allow contact between people via the mediation of technology and enable the creation and exchange of user-generated content. Kaplan and Haenlein (2010) establish six groups of social media: collaborative projects (e.g., Wikipedia), blogs and micro-blogging (e.g., Twitter), content communities (e.g., YouTube), social networking sites (e.g., Facebook), virtual game words (e.g., World of Warcraft), and virtual social worlds (e.g., Second Life).

There are hundreds of social media which allow a wide range of practices such as the dissemination of information, peer communication, networking, friendship and support, providing a sense of belonging, etc. They serve to help the pursuit of individual and group goals, and their recent success is based on their capacity to allow people to organize and mobilize themselves. While there are multiple social benefits derived from the use of social media, there are also new problems associated with such usage. For example, many people are subject to an absolute dependence derived from the need to always be online, or what is commonly known as FOBO syndrome (fear of being offline). There has also been a dramatic shift in individuals' sense of privacy, which has introduced new potential threats to personal security and privacy.

One of the outcomes of contact between individuals through social media involves the creation of virtual communities. To Rheingold (1993), virtual communities are groups of people with shared interests who interact online with technology mediation. Within this general description we may also include a wide variety of communities that differ significantly in their structure and function. For example, although at least some of the interaction must be generated online, in several of these communities some of the interaction takes place offline as well, thereby creating combined communities. Such communities may have a more formal and institutionalized nature or they may be created spontaneously; it may be that the interests and goals shared by members are manifest or they may be more blurred; there can be huge numbers and global dimensions or there can be a relatively small number of members at a local level; bonds between members may be weak and merely instrumental or stronger and intense due to emotional components, etc. We are, therefore, faced with very different virtual communities with specific rules and dynamics but which, in general, come to enable new and greater opportunities for social interaction.

One positive aspect of these types of communities is that they can accommodate many more active members than face-to-face communities since participation is not restricted to delimited geographical and temporal boundaries, thereby generating a near limitless number of communities where people can enjoy and develop new spaces for virtual sociability.

In virtual communities the referents of belonging are arguably becoming more flexible, allowing increasing variations regarding group loyalty and membership. Thus, membership in a given community can be shared and practiced simultaneously with membership in other communities in a myriad of combinations. In this context, relationships have the potential to lose much of their former face-to-face intensity and often also allow more lax criteria for group inclusion and exclusion. But even when membership could be ephemeral and the possibility of members meeting face-to-face is slim, there is an increasing ability to belong to virtual communities with others who share a common interest or commitment.

This new way of relating and being grouped together, even with strangers, is also characterized by the establishment of certain affective bonds; the spread of feelings of commitment and solidarity; the collaborative production of common resources that are shared via open access in the digital environment; the emergence of values such as trust and altruism; decentralization and horizontality of relationships, etc. The internet thus becomes a privileged space for personal involvement from which it is possible to build relationships and a sense of community.

SEE ALSO: Capital: Cultural, Social, and Economic; Community; Internet, the; Media, Sociology of the; Science and Technology, Sociology of

References

Kaplan, Andreas M., and Michael Haenlein. 2010. "Users of the World, Unite! The Challenges and Opportunities of Social Media." *Business Horizons* 53 (1): 59–68.
Rheingold, Howard. 1993. *The Virtual Community: Homesteading on the Electronic Frontier*. New York: HarperPerennial.

Further Reading

Etzioni, Amitai, and Oren Etzioni. 1997. "Communities: Virtual vs. Real." *Science* 277 (5324): 295. DOI:10.1126/science.277.5324.295.
Social Media + Society. SAGE Journals. Online at: http://sms.sagepub.com.
Wellman, Barry, Anabel Quan Haase, James Witte, and Keith Hampton. 2001. "Does the Internet Increase, Decrease, or Supplement Social Capital? Social Networks, Participation, and Community Commitment." *American Behavioral Scientist* 45 (3): 436–455.

Social Movements and Social Change

Colin Bernatzky and David A. Snow

University of California, Irvine, USA

From petitions to protests, from celebratory marches to targeted acts of political violence, the presence of social movements in daily life is palpably apparent to even the uninitiated observer. Despite being readily identifiable, however, social movements can at times feel rather difficult to define, given their immense depth and breadth of causes, targets, and tactics. Broadly understood, social movements are the embodiment of collective grievances through which individuals stake claims of advocacy or resistance toward relevant authorities for the purpose of producing desired shifts along social, political, or cultural fault lines. Predating even the Greco-Roman era, social movements have served as a driving force in the engine of history and continue to function as critical carriers of social change. Here, we will lay out the different theoretical lenses through which scholars have conceptualized social movements and their attendant phenomena; tease out the shared characteristics of social movements as well as their distinguishing features of differentiation; and highlight the focal themes and questions that guide the study of social movements.

As with many other sociological concepts, there is little consensus about how to most adequately and accurately define social movements. Some scholars understand social movements in terms of their organized, strategic, or rational character, while others opt to examine the ideological components of movements or the coalitional or networked properties of movements. In a more recent turn, scholars have analyzed movements in terms of their politicized characteristics and their contentious relationship to political regimes and/or the state as movement targets. Others, meanwhile, have sought to expand the definitional boundaries of social movements so as to include collectivities that exert challenges to institutional, organizational, and cultural domains that are not strictly political or otherwise directed at state apparatuses. Fortunately, this lack of universality does not require scholars to prioritize one definition above all others, as each conceptualization provides a distinct framework to understand social movement phenomena; what is more important is to remain cognizant of how one's selected definition emphasizes and accents certain characteristics over others. Regardless of which conceptual tools are used, there are several key characteristics that are likely to be present across all social movements. First, whether they are seeking or opposing change, social movements are fundamentally *change-oriented*, although this orientation can vary greatly in terms of the direction, magnitude, and level of change. Second, it follows that movements thus act as a *challenge to or defense of existing institutional and/or cultural structures*. Third, in defending or challenging such structures, movements typically exert pressure from *outside the confines of institutional channels*, even though they may also simultaneously work within these channels. Fourth, while social movements often have marked effects on individual attitudes and behavior, movements are *collective, not individual*. Fifth, as collective enterprises, movements entail *some degree of organization*, which can range from a loose coalitional network to a more concretized social movement organization (SMO). Sixth, and finally, social movements are not randomly occurring phenomena but are *temporally and spatially bound*.

Unsurprisingly, the considerable variation that is possible along each of these six shared axes accordingly results in a wide range of movements that differ from each other in important ways. Perhaps the most obvious point of differentiation is the degree of change sought – that is, whether movements strive to preserve, reform, or revolutionize the status quo. This distinction has been noted by several scholars, including Smelser's (1962) characterization of movements as either *norm-oriented* (e.g., seeking specific system changes, such as marijuana legalization or stricter gun control laws) or *value-oriented* (e.g., seeking deeper cultural or structural change that fundamentally shifts conceptualizations of power, personhood, or sovereignty, such as the Civil Rights Movement or the American Revolution). Similarly, Wallis (1984) offers a comparable classification of movements as being either *world-affirming* or *world-rejecting*. This dichotomy is perhaps most evident when considering religious movements, but can be extended to other contexts as well. Jim Jones' Peoples Temple, best known for its associated mass suicide in its compound in Guyana, typifies a world-rejecting movement, as does the orientation of anarcho-primitivists, survivalists, or the Situationist International.

Of course, movement-driven change occurs not just in terms of direction or magnitude, but also with respect to the different levels of society through which change takes place. Aberle (1966) derived a four-cell typology to capture this variation, characterizing movements as either *alternative, redemptive, reformative,* or *transformative*. Alternative and redemptive movements aim to produce change on an individual level either in part or in full, respectively. We might think of self-help movements such as Landmark as representative of the former, whereas Hare Krishnas or those abiding by straight-edge lifestyle practices are indicative of the latter. In this typology, reformative movements are in line with the norm-oriented movements described above, while transformative movements are analogous to value-oriented or world-affirming movements.

Scholars have also differentiated movements along historical lines, examining how movements might be clustered based on their place in the arc of history and change-oriented goals and tactics. In an early conception of this approach, Mannheim (1946) drew distinctions between four movements in the modern historical epoch: *chiliastic movements*, typified by peasant uprisings and religious movements; *liberal humanitarian movements*, encapsulated by the French and American revolutions; *conservative movements*, associated with the rise of fascism and Nazism; and *socialist movements*, which are expressed by international communism and labor movements. Drawing on this historical analytical lens, Turner (1969) noted how each of the four movement types differed in their sense of injustice, arguing that the liberal humanitarian and socialist movement perspectives had lost their galvanizing potential, and that a new movement type – characterized by dignity, identity, and self-worth – was emerging in their place. This analysis foreshadowed the advent of theorizing about what are now known as *new social movements*. In contrast to those movements focused on material and economic gains, such as labor movements, new social movements are characterized by their concern with rights, access and/or lifestyle issues. These movements – which include environmental concerns, animal rights, feminism, men's rights activists, and LGBT movements – are perhaps among the most prominent to us in the contemporary Western world.

Building on the examination between social movements and historical change, Tilly (2006) argued that movements must be understood not only in terms of the period in which they exist, but by their *repertoires of contention*, or the strategies and tools they use to advance their claims. Repertoires of contention vary across historical and political context; with the dawn of the internet and virtual modes of communication, we are arguably witnessing the emergence of a new "digital" repertoire of contention.

Not only do repertoires of contention differ across context, but they differ in content – that is, strategies and tactics – as well. Perhaps the most noticeable distinction in this regard is between violent and nonviolent movements, although the definitional boundaries of this binary are frequently contested by and within movements themselves: factions within the animal liberation movement or black bloc anarchism, for example, typically frame their destruction of property as nonviolent in that it does not target human life. This social acceptability of a movement's tactics is illustrated by McAdam, Tarrow, and Tilly's (2001) distinction between *constrained contention* and *transgressive contention*, with the former approach working within institutional channels and the latter deploying tactics that are "either unprecedented or forbidden within the regime in question" (8).

At present, the central orienting questions pertaining to the study of social movements have been guided by four key points of inquiry, the first of which considers the *emergence* of movements. Given that movements are not random but rooted in time and space, what are the conditions that enable or constrain both the articulation of grievances and the subsequent emergence of movements? Much attention has been paid recently to theories of political opportunity structures, which examine how political contextual factors support the emergence of movements; at the same time, it remains equally important to understand not only the context but the conditions which are generative of the initial grievances themselves.

The second focal point of inquiry concerns processes of *recruitment and participation*. Who joins a particular movement, and why? In what ways do they participate? Why do some individuals dive headlong into a movement while others in similar circumstances remain distant or tempered in their enthusiasm? Scholars have made a variety of contributions in this arena, examining factors such as the efficacy of emotion and affective relationships as potent methods of recruitment or the role of framing strategies that target specific constituents.

The third guiding question relates to the ongoing *dynamics* of social movements. Once movements have emerged and mobilized participants, what is the character of their daily on-the-ground experience? How are movements organized? How do they make decisions and negotiate conflicts? Such broad questions have generated a plethora of research, such as analysis of internal group dynamics and the question of leadership, how social movement organizations (SMOs) are structured, movement participation and endurance, and how movements engage in resource mobilization to achieve their ends.

The fourth and final motivating question is perhaps of greatest importance to scholars and activists alike: what are the *outcomes, effects, and consequences* of movements? In short, what do movements accomplish, in what ways, to what effect, and for which constituencies? While some consider movement effects to be largely epiphenomenal – that is, a byproduct of broader social forces which were already and independently underway – by many accounts movements do indeed play an important role in shaping and directing the arc of social, cultural, and political change. Moreover, the success of a movement has more recently been theorized not merely in terms of its externalized effects (e.g., achieving the desired outcome), but in its consequences on shaping policy processes or altering participants' personal biographies.

Of course, the story of social movement research does not end with this overview, as new warrants and theoretical frameworks continue to generate novel contributions and directions that complement, challenge, and extend the existing body of literature. We wish to draw particular attention to just a few of the promising developments in this regard. First, there is an increasing focus being paid to settings that exist beyond the domain of left and progressive movements found in Western democratic contexts, which have traditionally been the focal point for social movement scholarship. Thus, we are encouraged by research that expands the scope of study to include new cultural and geographical contexts as well as political orientations, particularly in light of phenomena such as the Arab Spring or the rise of movement activity among the far right and so-called "alt-right." Relatedly, it may also be fruitful to direct deeper attention to the relationship between culture, movements, and social change, particularly with respect to the ways in which movements are embedded within and exert influence upon cultural fields. That is to say, movements often revitalize or assemble cultural elements (be they cultural products, practices, or values) as a means of embracing, modifying, or rejecting particular aspects of culture.

Finally, the relationship between social movements and social change is too often reduced to the realm of conventional politics, neglecting to account for the immense influence of nonpolitical movements as well as their effects on nonpolitical contexts. For example, the first nationwide social movement in the United States arose not in response to political institutions but from religious forces that emphasized an explicitly moral dimension, calling upon citizens to bear witness to the sins of slavery and intemperance. Throughout history individuals have collectively engaged in activities and outcomes that are not principally concerned with state apparatuses, ranging from feminist protest within the military and Catholic Church to ungoverned agrarian communities in Southeast Asia.

Or, in response to years of advocacy from Mothers against Drunk Driving, the Harvard Alcohol Project created a designated driver campaign which integrated messaging directly into TV scripts, a strategy that ultimately led to reduced fatalities as well as the proliferation of designated driving as a commonly accepted concept. Thus, social movements launch history into trajectories of change that are often unknowable and unanticipated, or can only be understood by scholars in time.

SEE ALSO: Citizenship; Frames, Narratives, and Ideology; Identity; Nationalism; Political Sociology; Social Network Analysis

References

Aberle, D. 1966. *The Peyote Religion Among the Navaho*. Chicago: Aldine.

Mannheim, K. 1946. *Ideology and Utopia*, translated by L. Wirth and E. Shils. New York: Harcourt, Brace and Co.

McAdam, D., S. Tarrow, and C. Tilly. 2001. *Dynamics of Contention*. Cambridge: Cambridge University Press.

Smelser, N. 1962. *Theory of Collective Behavior*. New York: The Free Press.

Tilly, C. 2006. *Regimes and Repertoires*. Chicago: University of Chicago Press.

Turner, R.H. 1969. "The Theme of Contemporary Social Movements." *British Journal of Sociology* 20: 390–405.

Wallis, Roy. 1984. *The Elementary Forms of the New Religious Life*. London and Boston: Routledge.

Further Reading

Snow, D.A., and S.A. Soule. 2010. *A Primer on Social Movements*. New York: W.W. Norton & Company.

Social Network Analysis

Christina Prell

University of Maryland, USA

The twenty-first century is characterized by a variety of social relations that shrink the world, make it smaller, and help bring geographically distant individuals into close contact with one another. Studying social networks helps make sense of this complexity. Social network analysis (SNA) is a methodological approach, complete with analytical concepts and a range of formal math and statistical models, for studying the structural features and patterns of networks. Combined with data on actors' attributes, sociologists have used SNA to reveal a number of interesting patterns that link features of social networks to actors' outcomes. Why do some managers get higher salaries than others? Why are some students more likely to complete high school? And why are some individuals more likely to become smokers than others? Sociologists have explored these questions (and a range of others) through social network analysis.

SNA emerged from multiple interactions within and across disciplines. Historical accounts tend to agree that the field was more or less started through the efforts of Jacob Moreno, a student of psychiatry from Vienna. However, sociologists have been instrumental in shaping the discipline from its earliest days. For example, Ferdinand Tönnies (1855–1936) and Émile Durkheim (1858–1917) who both discussed social relations, and Georg Simmel (1858–1918), a German sociologist who argued that macro-level structures, such as institutions, and social phenomena, such as international war, could all be understood by focusing one's attention on the micro configurations like triads and dyads.

Sociologist George Homans wrote a classic work entitled *The Human Group* (Homans 1950), which explained how tied partners engage in a variety of exchange relations. His book laid the groundwork for the sociological theory known today as social exchange (or network exchange). Another prominent sociologist was James Coleman, whose treatise, *Foundations of Social Theory* (Coleman 1990), outlined an expansive theory of social action, where social networks and the structuring of those networks play a prominent role. Peter Blau, a contemporary of Coleman, developed an important core concept within the field, that of *homophily*, a concept pertaining to the idea that similar people are attracted to one another, and is illustrated by the phrase, "birds of a feather flock together." James Davis wrote a number of pieces in the 1960s and 1970s exploring clustering in empirical networks, and, with the help of Leinhardt and Holland, he

Core Concepts in Sociology, First Edition. Edited by J. Michael Ryan.
© 2019 John Wiley & Sons Ltd. Published 2019 by John Wiley & Sons Ltd.

developed the sociological concept of *transitivity*, which refers to the idea that "a friend of my friend is also my friend."

Harrison White pushed SNA forward via his advances in *roles and positions* analysis. With his colleague Francois Lorrain (Lorraine and White 1971), he published a seminal piece, entitled "Structural Equivalence of Individuals in Networks," which introduced the notion of *structural equivalence*, i.e., the idea that two actors are the same (equivalent) to the extent that they share the same relations to the same others. In this article, Lorrain and White discuss the importance of analyzing *complete* networks, i.e., networks consisting of a bounded set of actors and all relations between them. Through analyzing such complete networks, Lorrain and White were better able to identify structural *positions* within networks, i.e., which actors clustered together (shared a position) because of the similarity of their ties to others.

Many of White's PhD sociology students are notable sociologists within the SNA field. Mark Granovetter has written one of the most cited articles within and outside sociology, i.e., the famous "The Strength of Weak Ties" article (Granovetter 1973). Philip Bonacich's development of two centrality measures – *eigenvector* centrality and *power* centrality – are well known and used across disciplines. Finally, Barry Wellman, whose empirical research on community studies, social support, and the internet have been widely cited and have contributed to popularizing social network analysis across a range of disciplines.

Modern Developments in Social Networks

The 1980s and 1990s saw an increasing interest in developing statistical network models. The most famous of these are the family of models referred to as exponential random graph models (ERGMs). With ERGMs, the social network is treated as the dependent variable, and the analyst is looking to explain the network structure via both endogenous and exogenous network effects. A similar set of models developed for longitudinal network data has been created by Tom Snijders. These models are referred to as stochastic actor-oriented models (or SAOMs). Here, changes in network structure are analyzed over time alongside changes in actors' behaviors. Actors in the observed network are assumed to be evaluating his/her positions and striving to find the best, i.e., optimum, configuration of relations. This evaluation process on the part of the actor happens via an exponential function of the actor's position, in a very similar way as the p* model. There are a number of benefits to using these statistical models for network data, among these being the study of micro–macro linkages, and hypothesis testing.

SEE ALSO: Economic Sociology; Quantitative Methods; Social Psychology; Stratification and Inequality

References

Coleman, J.S. 1990. *Foundations of Social Theory*. Cambridge, MA: Belknap Press of Harvard University of Press.

Granovetter, M. 1973. "The Strength of Weak Ties." *American Journal of Sociology* 78: 1360–1380.

Homans, George Caspar. 1950. *The Human Group*. London: Routledge and Kegan Paul.
Lorraine, F., and H.C. White. 1971. "Structural Equivalence of Individuals in Social
  Networks." *Journal of Mathematical Sociology* 1: 49–80.

Further Reading

Kadushin, Charles. 2012. *Understanding Social Networks: Theories, Concepts, and Findings*.
  New York: Oxford University Press.
Prell, Christina. 2012. *Social Network Analysis: History, Theory, and Methodology*.
  London: SAGE.
Simmel, Georg. 1907. *Philosophie des Geldes*. 2. verm. Aufl. ed. Leipzig: Duncker & Humbolt.

Social Psychology

Maria C. Ramos and Lynn Smith-Lovin

Duke University, USA

Social psychology is the study of individuals, their interactions, and their relational contexts. It draws on a broad set of theoretical perspectives and addresses a variety of substantive topics. Most contributions to social psychological scholarship come from sociology and psychology. This has led to considerable debate on the relationship between psychological and sociological social psychology. In general, psychologists tend to focus on intra-individual processes (e.g., cognition, perception, and decision making) in relationship to social interactions. By contrast, sociologists often emphasize processes that connect the individual with larger groups and social institutions (e.g., families, the government, religion) and structures that connect individuals to one another. Since the same phenomena are often studied through the lenses of different social psychological approaches, the field might be best understood by examining its major theoretical frameworks.

Theoretical Frameworks

Social psychology spans a wide range of theoretical approaches from diverse intellectual origins. They differ in their assumptions about the nature of individuals. The major frameworks have led to a number of coherent theoretical research programs. The evolution of most theories in social psychology can be traced to the following major theoretical paradigms: cognitive and biological social psychology, symbolic interactionism, social exchange, and justice frameworks.

Cognitive and Biological Social Psychology

Cognitive and biological social psychology includes two broad explanatory accounts of social experience: explanations based on biological foundations and explanations based on mental states. Explanations based on biological factors focus on the neural and genetic underpinnings of social and affective processes. Social neuroscience and genetics are examples of perspectives within this category. Evolutionary theory (including both evolutionary psychology and sociobiology) applies the principles of adaptation and natural selection from evolutionary biology to understand social phenomena. For example, some work on this vein has explored the role of nepotism as a mechanism for natural selection. This approach contrasts with other perspectives that see nepotism as resulting from culture-specific beliefs.

Explanations based on mental states include the social–cognitive, personality, and dual-process approaches. The social–cognitive approach emphasizes how people store, process, and use information about other people and social situations. Research illustrating this perspective includes studies of the cognitive processes behind racial stereotyping. Personality scholars hold that differences in relatively stable cognitive and affective characteristics underlie behavior. Examples of research using this approach include studies of the different strategies that introverts versus extroverts use for obtaining social support. Another cognitive approach, the dual-process perspective, posits that some social phenomena involve the operation of two distinct mental processes: one of them being highly automatic, intuitive, affective, and fast, and the other being more deliberative, analytical, and slow. Thus, people's responses to situations will vary according to the type of mental process activated (automatic versus deliberative). For instance, some studies examine the persuasive effect of messages linked to whether the message engages automatic versus deliberative cognitive processes.

Social identity theory is a theory of group processes that incorporates cognitive principles of categorization. Its origins lie in the work of Henry Tajfel and his associates, who showed that categorization into groups is a sufficient condition for acquiring a social identity as a member of a group. For Tajfel, social identity based on group membership is a source of intergroup conflict. Indeed, one of the main empirical findings of the theory suggests that commitment to a group is linked to in-group favoritism (also known as in-group bias).

Symbolic Interactionism

Symbolic interactionism holds that social institutions are created and sustained through repeated, meaningful interactions. Meaningful interactions are understood as experiences individuals interpret through language and other symbols. Symbolic interactionism emerged as a reaction to perspectives that approached the individual–society relationship in a "top-down" fashion, focusing on the impact that macro-level forces have on the individual. By contrast, symbolic interactionism proposed a "bottom-up" approach, with emphasis on how people make sense of their world and how face-to-face interactions create and sustain social patterns, organizations, and institutions. For example, symbolic interactionism might approach the macro-level phenomenon of gender discrimination in the workplace by examining the experiences and face-to-face interactions that perpetuate the pattern.

Symbolic interactionism originated from a variety of influences, including the work of the Scottish moral philosophers and Adam Smith. However, George Herbert Mead is often referred as the most central figure in advancing this perspective. Mead's fundamental contribution was his account of the self as emerging from symbolic interaction. Later, Charles Horton Cooley studied the process by which the self recognizes itself as an object through his notion of *the looking glass self.* According to this notion, our self-perception is based on how we think others perceive us.

Ethnomethodology, another development within symbolic interactionism, focuses on the taken-for-granted, routine aspects of social life that create order in society. According to this view, members of society accomplish order by engaging in coordinated, concerted, and procedural behaviors. Examples of these everyday behaviors that create order are standing in line for a service or driving on a freeway. Harold Garfinkel conducted breaching experiments that aimed to disrupt an everyday social norm in order to unveil people's reactions to those violations. For instance, in a famous breaching experiment, the experimenter plays a game of tic-tac-toe with a participant. The participant makes the first move. Then, the experimenter erases the participant's mark, moves it to another cell, and makes his own mark. Finally, the experimenter observes people's reactions to the disruption with the intent of revealing existing social norms.

Erving Goffman's seminal works on dramaturgy and the presentation of self became a cornerstone of symbolic interactionism. His work expanded the prevailing emphasis of symbolic interactionism at the time from a focus on how others perceive actors in a situation to considering the actors' influence on how others perceive them. The notion of a proactive individual capable of managing impressions led to further ideas about the negotiated nature of roles. This also meant that situations were continually redefined as interactions unfold. Howard Becker moved these ideas on the definition of situations further through the development of labeling theory. This theory holds that the labels or terms used to describe individuals have a profound impact on their behavior.

During its evolution, symbolic interactionism took three main trajectories based on the works of Herbert Blumer, Manford Kuhn, and Sheldon Stryker. Herbert Blumer coined the term "symbolic interactionism." For Blumer, society is unstructured and in constant flux. He saw every interaction as agentic and unpredictable. For this reason, Blumer regarded qualitative methods as the only suitable tool for examining social life. By contrast, Manford Kuhn and Sheldon Stryker saw society as patterned and relatively stable, and used quantitative methods to understand the relationship between individuals and society. Kuhn and his colleagues attempted to measure perceptions of the self through surveys. Sheldon Stryker's structural symbolic interactionism proposed that different positions within the social structure led to distinct expectations of behavior (through internalized role-identities). Identity theory was later expanded to include identities from roles, group memberships, and personal self-conceptions.

The most notable contemporary developments of symbolic interactionism are an internal branch of identity theory and affect control theory. Identity control theory grew directly from the structural symbolic interactionism tradition. The theory deals with how multiple identities operate in situations. Affect control theory is a formal, mathematical theory of interaction. It posits that the labels people use to define a social situation evoke affective meanings. According to the theory, individuals tend to interact in order to maintain their original definition of the situation and the affective sentiments associated with it.

The expectation-states tradition constitutes another contemporary set of theories that bridge symbolic interactionist ideas and the social exchange tradition (see below). Even though this tradition developed out of the exchange tradition (with group members exchanging deference for higher performance inputs) rather than from symbolic interactionism, many parallels exist with interactionist thought. The basic tenet of the expectation-states tradition is that people take cues from others that allow them to form expectations of "who" those people are and interact accordingly. Some subtheories in this tradition include status characteristics theory and status construction theory. Status characteristics theory deals with the formation of expectations based on socially evaluated categories of people (e.g., occupation, race, or gender). Instead, status construction theory explains how status beliefs emerge from interactions in which there is an association between a non-valued characteristic and resources that aide performance.

Social Exchange

The social exchange framework was influenced by utilitarian economics, anthropology, and psychology. As a result, some theories within this framework use a rational choice approach model (actors are consciously oriented toward maximizing outcomes), while others are inclined toward a learning model (actors respond to consequences of past actions). Social exchange was established as a distinct perspective within social psychology in the late 1950s with the work of George Homans, Peter Blau, John Thibaut, and Harold Kelley. Common to all these authors was a view of interactions and social behavior as exchanges, and an interest in the forms of association that result from these exchanges. Based on the insights of these authors, Richard Emerson published his power-dependence theory in 1972.

Rather than developing a broad theory of social behavior, Emerson elaborated a relatively small set of specific propositions. This made the empirical test of the theory a more tractable task. Power-dependence theory became a fruitful research program still active today. The theory focused on the relationship between power and social structure. Two distinguishing features of the theory were particularly influential for subsequent developments. First, power was viewed not as a property of actors, but as a feature of relations. Second, the concept of power was integrated with notions of social network analysis. Power became understood as a potential dependent on the resources an actor can access through his connections.

The modern social exchange framework sees interactions as exchanges of resources. Its main foci of study include the connections between the exchanging actors, the resources exchanged, the outcomes of the exchange, sometimes the conditions of the exchange and the processes that occur during it (e.g., power dynamics, coalitions). The social exchange framework begins with some fundamental tenets. First, actors can be individuals or organizations – any entity capable of acting as a unit. Second, actors are self-interested and oriented toward obtaining valued resources. Third (and perhaps most importantly), exchange structures are the types of *connections* that actors have. Exchange structures can go beyond dyads to include networks of different sizes and shapes. The process of exchange is the way the interaction unfolds during the exchange. For example, in negotiated transactions actors make decisions together to reach an agreement. By contrast, in reciprocal transactions actors perform behaviors that benefit the other without knowing when or whether the other actor will reciprocate or not. Variation in exchange structures and processes results in differences in access, control, and use of resources. The *social* exchange framework differs from many economic approaches in that it assumes that successive exchanges are interdependent, meaning that the outcomes and processes of previous exchanges influence future ones.

Emerson's power dependence theory gave rise to several research programs that joined exchange theories with empirical tests. Karen Cook, Toshio Yamagishi, and others directly built on Emerson's ideas by investigating the distribution of power in networks based on patterns of exchange relations. These authors also contributed to the study of trust in exchanges. Linda Molm focused on the study of non-negotiated and reciprocal exchanges. In addition, she has investigated fairness, affect, and commitment in exchange networks. The work of Edward Lawler studied conflict resolution in negotiation and bargaining. He has also developed a theory of relational cohesion and a theory of the role that emotions play in exchange called the affect theory of social exchange. David Willer, Barry Markovsky, and their colleagues developed network exchange theory to quantify the power of positions in diverse exchange networks. Shane Thye, Michael Lovaglia, and other scholars have made links between power and status.

Justice Frameworks

Justice frameworks examine people's conceptions of justice, and their perceptions and reactions to injustice. Justice theories deal with distributive, procedural, and interactional justice. Work on distributive justice arose in the 1960s and 1970s, and examined the norms people use to determine what is a fair distribution of resources among individuals in a group, community, or society. Thus, distributive justice focuses on the fairness of the *outcomes* of resource allocation. By contrast, procedural justice is concerned with the fairness of the decision rules employed to allocate resources. Thus, procedural justice focuses on the fairness of the *process* of resource allocation. Interactional justice examines the treatments individuals receive during the decision-making process. Often, interactional justice is understood as an aspect of procedural justice. However, the correct categorization of interactional justice is a subject of considerable debate. The last two decades have witnessed the flourishing of works that intersect the distributive and procedural branches (usually under the umbrella of organizational justice). Even though the questions these approaches deal with are deeply intertwined, a unified theoretical framework is still a work in progress.

The basic justice model underlying both distributive and procedural justice proposes that a combination of individual factors (e.g., beliefs, personal characteristics) and situational variables (e.g., organizational context) influence people's perceptions and reactions to injustice. Most research in the justice literature uses this common framework, focusing on specific aspects of it. For example, some work has explored emotional reactions to perceptions of injustice. Other research has dealt with assessments of injustice in work environments and from the viewpoint of subordinates versus authorities. Over the years, the justice literature has proposed a number of principles that individuals might take into account to assess the fairness of a situation (e.g., equity, equality, and need). Research in this vein has investigated factors that might determine which principle would be preferred.

Guillermina Jasso, a central figure in the justice literature, proposed a theory of distributive justice. This became the first formal model of observers' assessments of justice. The justice evaluation function is the key contribution of Jasso's theory. According to Jasso, observers' perceptions of injustice are a function of comparisons between the just reward and the actual reward obtained by an individual. Current developments of the theory attempt to establish links between justice, status, and power.

Within the procedural justice literature, John Thibaut and Laurens Walker proposed a model under which people prefer fair procedures since they guarantee fair distributions of resources. This model is often referred to as the instrumental model. A decade later, in 1985, Allan Lind and Tom Tyler advanced the relational model of procedural justice. The underlying assumption of this model is that individuals seek to be valued members of their groups and tend to prefer procedures that will also benefit other members. More recently, in 2000, Michael Wenzel suggested a model of procedural justice based on identity processes. In his view, people will perceive and react to injustice to the extent to which they identify themselves as members of the group that received unfair treatment. These ideas are closely related to a branch of the expectation-states theoretical framework, in which an abstract reference standard based on category membership ("people like me") is used to evaluate justice.

Conclusion

Social psychology studies individuals and their interactions to understand a broad range of phenomena, such as the organization of the self, everyday interactions, group processes, and the formation of collective behavior. All of these topics can be addressed through different theoretical frameworks. While the field is noted for its systematic theoretical development, boundaries are not clear-cut and scholars can (and often do) integrate distinct perspectives to study a given phenomenon.

SEE ALSO: Emotion, Sociology of; Self, the; Symbolic Interactionism; Identity; Power and Authority; Sociological Theory

Further Reading

Burke, Peter J., ed. 2006. *Contemporary Social Psychological Theories*. Stanford, CA: Stanford University Press.
DeLamater, John, and Amanda Ward, eds. 2013. *Handbook of Social Psychology*. Dordrecht: Springer.
Gawronski, Bertram, and Galen V. Bodenhausen, eds. 2014. *Theory and Explanation in Social Psychology*. New York: Guilford Publications.

Socialization

Jeremiah C. Morelock and John B. Williamson

Boston College, USA

Socialization

Socialization is a central mechanism throughout social life. It is the process by which individuals learn how to act in accordance with social norms, structures, and institutions (Grusec and Hastings 2015). This learning process happens in many ways and has many sources. Socialization can be direct, through instruction by others, or indirect, through observation and experience. Society is diverse, and people are likewise socialized according to different norms, specific to their social positions and group memberships. People are socialized according to differences in culture, race, class, gender, religion, ethnicity, family role, occupation, and subculture. Socialization also changes for everyone over the life course. Life course theory emphasizes how people are shaped as they age through changing social contexts (Morgan and Kunkel 2016). For example, being a young child in a family carries with it different social expectations than being an adult parent in a family. To grasp how people are socialized, it is very useful to understand how socialization typically changes throughout life.

Over the life course, people enter into new roles in new institutions. Each time they undergo such changes, they face the challenge of adjusting to new social circumstances, which requires conforming to a new set of social expectations. We encounter new agents of socialization, people, and institutions that teach us how to act in society. In early childhood, for example, parents and other immediate family are the primary agents of socialization. Children learn how to speak and act through imitating what they see their parents do, and through what their parents teach. Children are also socialized through media, for example through children's television and music. Media exposure tends to be regulated by parents, so they can filter what influences the child receives. The school is also a major agent of socialization for children. At school children learn how to be a student in a classroom, to sit quietly, follow the teacher's instruction, complete assignments, raise their hands, and get along with peers.

Peers and the media may be present all throughout the life course, yet typically they are most prominent as agents of socialization during adolescence. During this time

Core Concepts in Sociology, First Edition. Edited by J. Michael Ryan.
© 2019 John Wiley & Sons Ltd. Published 2019 by John Wiley & Sons Ltd.

school continues to train children to go on to college or enter the workforce, which in young adulthood present new sets of roles, rules, and social norms. Young adults may enter new family roles and identities as spouses or parents. In mature adulthood, work and family are likely to be the most prominent agents of socialization. Parental roles continuously change as children grow and workers may be promoted to higher positions with more responsibility. It is possible for a sense of stagnation to set in during middle age that leads some to acts of deviance, rebelling against social expectations for middle-aged parents and workers, and indulging in excitements normally associated with younger people. Older adults may take on new family roles as grandparents. Increasingly, older adults will be less capable of taking care of others, and more in need of receiving care from others. Throughout life, socialization is a constantly evolving process and experience.

Talcott Parsons, iconic theorist of structural functionalism, placed socialization in a key position in his social theory. For Parsons, when social institutions are functioning correctly, individuals become properly socialized into the behaviors and values of their social contexts. They internalize social expectations, and act accordingly without having to think much. If socialization is incomplete, deviance may result. Deviance may also result when individuals are successfully socialized into deviant subcultures. Gang-related socialization during youth in poor urban centers has long fostered various forms of adolescent deviance. Not long ago affluent workers in some of the major banks in the United States were socialized by their co-workers to knowingly engage in illegal actions that contributed in a major way to the great recession of 2008. Emile Durkheim theorized that when society changes quickly and people are unable to fulfill roles in society that they expect, anomie results: socialization no longer functions to provide people with coherent norms to follow. Functionalist Robert Merton adapted the theory of anomie specifically to the issue of crime. He proposed criminal behavior results from structural strain, when people are socialized to believe they should be capable of attaining life goals for which the social system does not provide them adequate opportunities (Giddens et al. 2013).

George Herbert Mead, an early theorist who contributed to symbolic interactionism, also placed processes of socialization in a central position of his theory of society. In his social behaviorism, he discussed how identity develops in the context of social relationships. We learn about who we are and what we should do through a constant processing of social signals throughout day-to-day life, interpreting the significant gestures of others around us as they respond to our behaviors. Socialization is also important for conflict theorists. Conflict theorists emphasize how we are socialized into accepting unequal positions in society, and how we are differently socialized according to race, class, gender, and other differences by which we are stratified. Pierre Bourdieu says people learn to adopt the habitus – habits and norms – of the social groups to which they aim to maintain a position (Calhoun et al. 2012). Private tastes are adopted and expressed to symbolize to ourselves and others what groups we belong to within larger structural social hierarchies. In all of these perspectives, socialization is a central component. It is integral to any comprehensive theory of society.

SEE ALSO: Culture, Sociology of; Deviance; Family and Kinship, Sociology of; Life Course

References

Calhoun, Craig, Joseph Gerteis, James Moody, Steven Pfaff, and Virk Indermohan, eds. 2012. *Contemporary Sociological Theory*, 3rd ed. Malden, MA: Wiley.

Giddens, Anthony, Mitchell Duneier, Richard P. Appelbaum, and Deborah Carr. 2013. *Introduction to Sociology*, 9th ed. New York: Norton.

Grusec, Joan E., and Paul D. Hastings, eds. 2015. *Handbook of Socialization: Theory and Research*, 2nd ed. New York: Guilford.

Morgan, Leslie A., and Suzanne R. Kunkel. 2015. *Aging, Society, and the Life Course*, 5th ed. New York: Springer.

Sociological Imagination

Christopher Andrews

Drew University, USA

Coined by C. Wright Mills (1959), the "sociological imagination" describes an imaginative way of thinking about the intersection of biography and history, or an awareness of how individuals' specific circumstances and life experiences are linked to or reflective of larger social and historical forces.

The first lesson of this imagination, Mills argued, is that individuals can only understand their own circumstances and chances in life by also becoming aware of those of others facing similar circumstances at the same time. This means conceptualizing one's own life as ordinary – to see one's intensely private and personal experiences as typical of the era and place one lives. But it also means avoiding the "traps" of narrower explanations of circumstance that fail to account for social and historical forces.

Writing during a period of enormous change in postwar 1950s America, Mills described a sense among people of increasingly feeling "trapped" in their private lives by "seemingly impersonal changes in the very structure" of society, unable to understand or control the larger social and political forces shaping their everyday worlds. What people needed, Mills argued, was the "quality of mind" or capacity to see the "connection between the patterns of their own lives and the course of world history," linking individuals' personal lives to larger social and historical trends. This, Mills argued, would allow people to distinguish between "personal troubles of milieu" and "the public issues of social structure," or individual and social problems.

Unemployment, for example, may be a personal hardship, but when millions of people lose their jobs – as they did during the Great Depression – unemployment becomes a public issue. Likewise, when a society finds that nearly half of marriages end in divorce, it suggests a structural problem rooted in the institution of marriage or related institutions (e.g., work and gender) rather than simply individual difficulties. Accordingly, because every problem people face is not structural or systemic in nature, Mills suggests we use the sociological imagination to distinguish between the troubles of individuals and social problems facing the larger public.

While one can find traces of the sociological imagination in Mills's earlier writings, more recently scholars have used it to examine the shifting social contract between employers and workers (Rubin 2012), the conflation of financial crises with individual

Core Concepts in Sociology, First Edition. Edited by J. Michael Ryan.
© 2019 John Wiley & Sons Ltd. Published 2019 by John Wiley & Sons Ltd.

greed (Hansen and Siamek 2010), and the resistance of institutions to social and demographic changes (Gerson 2009). Widely cited in both introductory textbooks and journal articles, the sociological imagination is likely to continue to have an enduring influence on the discipline of sociology.

SEE ALSO: Everyday Life, Sociology

References

Gerson, Kathleen. 2009. "Changing Lives, Resistant Institutions: A New Generation Negotiates Gender, Work, and Family Change." *Sociological Forum* 24: 735–753. DOI:10.1111/j.1573-7861.2009.01134.x.

Hansen, Laura L., and Movahedi Siamak. 2010. "Wall Street Scandals: The Myth of Individual Greed." *Sociological Forum* 25: 367–374. DOI:10.1111/j.1573-7861.2010.01182.x.

Mills, C. Wright. 1959. *The Sociological Imagination*. New York: Oxford University Press.

Rubin, Beth A. 2012. "Shifting Social Contracts and the Sociological Imagination." *Social Forces* 91: 327–346. DOI:10.1093/sf/sos122.

Sociological Theory

Jeffrey Stepnisky

MacEwan University, Canada

As used in contemporary sociology, the term "theory" has many meanings (Abend 2008). Most often, though, when sociologists use the term they mean the overarching intellectual perspectives that sociologists use to explain, understand and, in some cases, transform the social world. These perspectives include within them claims about society (What is society? What are its most important features?), knowledge (What can be known about society? How can it be known?), and human nature (Is there a human nature? What drives human behavior? What is the relation between human nature and society?).

Types of Sociological Theory

Within this broad definition, sociologists have attempted to classify different types of theories. There have been many such classification schemes (Helmut Wagner (1963) lists at least five). By way of example, this entry addresses only a few.

Writing in the 1970s and 1980s, Ritzer (1975) argued that sociology had three main theoretical paradigms, or types of theory. The *social-fact paradigm* grew out of Emile Durkheim's sociology but also includes perspectives like conflict theory and structural-functionalism. Theories of this kind focus on the analysis of macro-structures and institutions. The *social-definition paradigm* grew out of Max Weber's interpretive sociology, but also includes perspectives like symbolic interactionism and social phenomenology. These theories place the socially meaningful action of the individual at the center of analysis. Finally, the *social-behavior paradigm* grew out of behavioral psychology, but also includes theories like exchange theory. It studies the objective, observable causes (such as rewards and punishments) of patterned behavior. Though this typology no longer captures the full range of sociological theories, it represents a form of "meta-theoretical" analysis that attempts to assess the state of sociology. Indeed, the purpose of classification is to ask questions like: What kinds of theories are available for sociological analysis? Do these theories adequately address all aspects of social life? Does sociology have theoretical blind-spots?

Core Concepts in Sociology, First Edition. Edited by J. Michael Ryan.
© 2019 John Wiley & Sons Ltd. Published 2019 by John Wiley & Sons Ltd.

Another classificatory scheme organizes sociological theories according to the episte-mology (i.e., theory of knowledge) that they assume. For example, Jürgen Habermas (1968/1972) distinguished between three types of knowledge: empirical-analytic, hermeneutic, and emancipatory.

Empirical-analytic knowledge is associated with positivist philosophy and science, and is modeled on the natural sciences (e.g. biology, chemistry, physics). It advocates neutrality (the sociologist's point of view should not be reflected in their theories), tries to develop causal explanations of behavior, and seeks universal, law-like theories that can be used to predict future action. In this view, a strong distinction is drawn between theory and data. Theory mirrors, or at best organizes through interconnected proposi-tions, that which is discovered in the world itself. Though each had a different interpre-tation of positivism, representatives of this kind of sociology typically include Auguste Comte, Herbert Spencer, and Emile Durkheim, as well as proponents of exchange theory and rational choice theory.

The *hermeneutic* theory of knowledge, which usually appears under the more encom-passing term interpretive theory, argues that humans are self-interpreting, culturally constituted beings (Taylor 1985). While positivist approaches embrace the methods and ideals of the natural sciences, interpretive theories reject the methods and ideals of the natural sciences. Interpretive theorists argue that the defining quality of humans is their shared ability to use symbols or, more specifically, language. Where the positivist sees language (and hence theoretical claims) as something that reflects what is in the world, the interpretive theorist sees language as something that gives expression to, and shapes, the world. The task of interpretive sociologists is to show how the meaning systems of different societies, and subgroups within those societies, gives rise to the possibility of particular kinds of action. The hermeneutician tries to imagine the life-world of other people by interpreting the meaning systems in which they live. Examples of this kind of theory include Weberian cultural analysis, symbolic interactionism, and social phenomenology.

Finally, Habermas contrasted emancipatory knowledge, or critical theory, to both positivism and hermeneutics. Critical theories are based in a critique of oppressive social systems. Their goal is to liberate people from oppressive social systems. They are grounded in what neo-Marxist Antonio Gramsci called a philosophy of praxis: theory should enable meaningful social change that addresses the concerns of people's lived realities. Critical theorists expose systems of domination across many social institutions and social forms: economic, gender, sexuality, and ability, to name a few. In contrast to positivism and hermeneutics, critical theories have an explicit political bent to them. Examples of this approach include Marxism, feminist theory, and queer theory.

While classificatory schemes provide conceptual focus, there are also problems with them. For one, no classification scheme can capture the variety of theories on offer at any one time. This became increasingly apparent as the numbers of different theories, representing a wide variety of epistemological positions, proliferated in the latter half of the twentieth century. Moreover, by collecting diverse sets of ideas within broad types, theories are necessarily oversimplified. For example, differences between perspectives are often over-emphasized and similarities overlooked. Also, starting in the 1980s, inspired by postmodern philosophy, sociologists became increasingly skeptical of any attempts to organize or systematize knowledge. Classification schemes frequently leave out, or misrepresent, positions on the periphery, like, at least historically, feminist theory. No doubt, sociologists and social theorists continue to work with some of the categories developed as part of these kinds of analysis. It still makes sense to refer to differences between, for example, positivist theories and emancipatory theories, even if the distinctions are sometimes blurred. However, the *formal* practice of developing of classificatory schemes seems to have peaked in the 1980s.

History of Sociological Theory

Another approach is to treat theory as the study of the history of ideas about society. Rather than viewing theories as classifiable, static perspectives, this view treats theory as a historically grounded, and constantly changing, body of knowledge.

Classical Sociological Theory

People have made observations about what we now think of as sociological phenomenon for thousands of years. In his account of the history of sociology, Alan Sica (2012) described sociological ideas found in the writings of Confucius, Thucydides, Aristotle, Ibn-Khaldun, Niccolò Machiavelli, and Thomas Hobbes, among others. Yet, the field of sociology proper, and consequently sociological theory, did not emerge until the 1800s, following the development of the concept of "society." Charles Taylor (2003: 19) argued that the concept of society first emerged when philosophers Hugo Grotius, John Locke, Adam Smith, and Jean-Jacques Rousseau started to develop the idea that the human world is composed of relations between individuals, or what Taylor calls relations of "mutual benefit." These relations between persons make up what we now call the social sphere. The social sphere or, as Taylor also calls it, the *modern social imaginary*, is composed of four institutions. The *economy*, as described by Adam Smith, is the institution in which people exchange goods and services. The *public sphere* is a "common space in which the members of a society ... meet through a variety of media ... and thus ... form a common mind ..." (Taylor 2003: 70). The institution of the *sovereign people* refers to a self-defining collective, for example, the nation, that exercises political rule over itself. Finally, emphasizing the importance of consumer culture to modern society, Taylor argued that *fashion* is an institution that fosters interpersonal exchange through "mutual display" (565).

Classical sociological theory developed in the wake of this modern social imaginary. It was an attempt to describe this new *social* order, and elaborate the methods by which this order can be studied. French scholar Auguste Comte coined the term sociology in 1839, introduced a positivist philosophy of social analysis, and developed the Law of Three Stages. According to the Law of Three Stages, societies pass through theological and metaphysical stages to arrive at the positivist stage – the endpoint of social development. The Law of Three Stages is exemplary of the kind of grand sociological narratives that were common to classical sociological theories. Society was defined as an entity unto itself and different societies were thought to possess different qualities that change over time. Another grand narrative of social development was offered by Comte's English contemporary, Herbert Spencer. Drawing on evolutionary theory, Spencer provided an organismic theory of society. Society is like a biological organism composed of multiple structures which perform particular functions. Over time, the structures present in a given society change and become better adapted to their environment.

Over the last 50 years, Karl Marx, Emile Durkheim, and Max Weber have emerged as the core of the classical sociological canon. Each of them conceptualized society in unique ways that have shaped how sociologists conceive of and study society. Marx, responding to political economists such as Adam Smith, and drawing on German romantic philosophy (Georg Hegel and Ludwig Feuerbach) developed a *dialectical–materialist* account of social change which placed human labor at the center of analysis. For Marx the history of human society is the history of the changing relationships between the owners of means of production (bourgeoisie) and those who must work for the owners of the means of production (proletariat). This conflict culminates in modern capitalist society, which, in Marx's analysis, under the weight of growing economic inequality, will give way to communism.

Durkheim was a *social realist*, which means he thought of society as a thing-in-itself that is irreducible to other phenomena. In Durkheim's view, Marx and his followers focused too much on economic and political forces, and failed to provide a scientific understanding of properly social phenomena: values, norms, culture, collective consciousness, and the division of labor. Durkheim also fought against scholars who reduced sociology to psychology. For example, Durkheim's nemesis, Gabriel Tarde, argued that sociological phenomena were nothing more than the byproduct of interpersonal imitation. In defiance of this view, Durkheim insisted that the world possessed "social facts" that are distinct from individual behavior, and that these social facts are the proper subject matter of sociology. For example, in *Suicide*, Durkheim showed that suicide rates could be explained by analyzing social phenomena such as economic change (industrialization and the division of labor) and religious belief (Catholicism versus Protestantism).

Weber was a *methodological individualist*, which means that unlike Durkheim he did not think of society as a thing-in-itself. Rather his approach focused on individual action. The task of the sociologist is to understand the meaning systems that guide human action and therefore influence the course of history. For example, in the *Protestant Ethic and the Spirit of Capitalism* Weber argued that the religious doctrine of Protestant Calvinism encouraged disciplined, ascetic behavior which, alongside material factors, were the foundation for the development of capitalist economies. Though Weber did not think that social scientists could discover broad social laws (like those sought by Comte), he nevertheless offered a depiction of human societies drifting, over time, toward increasingly disenchanted, bureaucratically organized forms. In contrast to Marx's hope for an inevitable communist revolution, and Durkheim's faith in the corrective powers of social science, Weber gave us the image of modern society as a suffocating "iron cage."

These three figures aside, there were many other sociologists in the classical period who contributed different visions of society. For example, while Marx, Durkheim, and Weber offered primarily macro-sociological accounts of modern society, Georg Simmel and George Herbert Mead contributed micro-sociological theories of society (though each of them, especially Simmel, also described macro-sociological aspects of society). Simmel focused on interpersonal interactions, and Mead is notable for having placed the self at the center of his analysis. Charlotte Perkins Gilman offered a feminist theory grounded in an evolutionary perspective. She emphasized the sexuo-economic relationship, and argued that gender and sex inequality are not peripheral issues of interest to women alone, but rather shape the entire modern order. To understand gender is to understand modern society. Despite her prominence as a public speaker and author, historically, Gilman (as well as other feminist thinkers) was not included in the sociological canon and only now is being recognized by the sociological mainstream as a theorist of significant accomplishment. So too, African-American sociologist W.E.B. Du Bois, despite having founded, at Atlanta University, one of the earliest sociological laboratories, has been neglected. While Gilman placed gender at the center of her concept of society, Du Bois argued that the "color line" (i.e., race) was the defining feature of modern society, both in America and around the world.

Contemporary Sociological Theory

Though distinctions between classical and contemporary theory vary, classical theory is usually defined as the set of sociological theories that developed between the early 1800s and World War II, and contemporary theory anything after. The case for such a distinction is made in various ways. For one, the devastation caused in Europe by World War II, as well as the migration of many intellectuals (especially Jewish intellectuals) from Europe as a result of the war, caused sociology's center of gravity to shift from Europe to the United States. Though in the latter half of the twentieth century sociological theory shifted back to Europe (with the work of people like Giddens and Bourdieu), through the mid-twentieth century sociological theory had a distinctly American flavor and gave rise to theories such as *structural–functionalism*, *conflict theory*, and *symbolic interactionism*. Theorists associated with these schools included Talcott Parsons, Robert Merton, Ralph Dahrendorf, and Herbert Blumer. Also, the 1950s and 1960s saw the emergence of consumer culture and a range of technologies (e.g., the television, refrigerator, washing machine, and automobile) that transformed the make-up of everyday life.

One of the major developments of the contemporary period was the expansion of micro-sociological perspectives through, among other approaches, symbolic interactionism, exchange theory, and rational choice theory. Particularly notable contributions came from Erving Goffman, who is credited with establishing the foundations for *dramaturgical theory*, when he argued that social life could be likened to a theatrical performance. Harold Garfinkel's *ethnomethodology* covered similar micro-sociological terrain except that he came out of the phenomenological philosophical tradition. He argued that "members" in a particular social order regularly construct, or constitute, the conditions of possibility for their own continued social existence.

The expansion of micro-sociological theories led to the development of another theoretical problem that captured the attention of sociological theorists in the 1970s and 1980s. Historically, sociologists had developed theories that primarily were either macro-sociological or micro-sociological. The question now arose: Is it possible to develop theories that address macro-sociological problems and micro-sociological problems at the same time? Or, as it was framed in Europe, is it possible to develop theories that bridged the structure–agency gap? One example of an effort to solve this problem was Anthony Giddens's *structuration theory*. Giddens argued that human action is both agentic and structured at the same time. Actions are patterned (structured), but these patterns only come into existence through people whose actions reproduce these patterns. The micro–macro or agency–structure divide was also addressed by Pierre Bourdieu with his concepts of *habitus* and *field*, Jeffrey Alexander in his *multi-dimensional* sociology, and Norbert Elias in his *figurational* sociology, among others.

The mid- to late twentieth century also brought new forms of social critique. Neo-Marxist theories, especially those developed by members of the Frankfurt School (many displaced from Germany to America during the war years), and the Birmingham School of cultural studies, offered critiques of mass media and the consumer society. In addition, the 1950s and the 1960s saw the rise of civil rights movements which placed social problems of gender and racial inequality front and center. This too affected the way that sociologists theorized the social world, increasingly turning away from theories developed by "dead white men" to those developed from a diversity of social locations. Though theories of race are gaining, only now, serious attention in mainstream sociological theory, the work of mid-twentieth-century psychiatrist, philosopher, and social theorist Frantz Fanon has done much to establish the basic categories of race analysis, especially the relationship between processes of racialization and colonialism.

Feminist theory also found new impetus with the founding in 1975 of feminist theory journals like *Signs*, and the development of theories focused on the lives and experiences of women and social minorities. Dorothy Smith, for example, developing the idea of *standpoint theory*, argued for an approach based in the lived experiences of women. This not only offered a critique of abstract, "masculine" forms of theory, but drew attention to the importance of embodiment as an analytic category. Also coming from a standpoint perspective, Patricia Hill Collins brought intersectional analysis to sociology. This approach drew attention to the way in which particular experiences, and knowledges, are created by people's positions at the intersection of various social locations (e.g., race, class, gender, ability, sexuality). In recent years, feminist theory has expanded significantly and, under the influence of queer theory, has come to question gender categories themselves. Led by theorists like Judith Butler, queer theorists argue that gender, sexuality, and identity are not natural facts, but social practices structured by dominant power relations.

Any review of the history of sociological theory would be incomplete without mention of the impact of postmodernism. Inspired by the writings of mostly French intellectuals (Jacques Derrida, Gilles Deleuze, Jean-François Lyotard, Jean Baudrillard), postmodern perspectives became influential in the 1980s and 1990s. These argued that developments in mass media and the consumer culture have created social forms, and persons, that can no longer be accounted for through the categories of "modern" sociological theories. Postmodernists argue that concepts like truth, value, selfhood, and even social structure are outdated concepts. Society and self are not stable phenomena that can be captured in theory, but fluid ever-changing entities. Indeed, for postmodernists theory itself is a social process that carries within it ideological presuppositions and power relations. Though few would now call themselves postmodernists, or embrace the nihilism (i.e., there is no truth, and theory is just a language game) associated with the most radical postmodern perspectives, the challenge to sociology is clear: sociologists cannot take the knowledge that they produce for granted, and theories must regularly account for the social processes that give rise to sociological knowledge in the first place.

In the twenty-first century the numbers and kinds of sociological theory have continued to expand. Though the range of approaches is too vast to summarize, there are a number of particularly unique and influential perspectives. Globalization theory has been important to sociology since the 1980s with some theorists, like Ulrich Beck, arguing that the nation-state is no longer the appropriate unit of analysis for sociology. This should be replaced by the study of global flows and cosmopolitan identities. Another influential perspective is the aforementioned queer theory and the related approach of affect theory. These investigate how emotion, desire, and, in particular, sexual desire organize social life. The importance of science and technology to the constitution of modern and postmodern societies has been emphasized by actor–network theory which, among other points, argues that modern societies are not exclusively human creations, but are made up through configurations of human and nonhuman actors, such as technology (e.g., the automobile, the computer) and animals. This perspective dovetails with posthumanist perspectives which also deconstruct the human-centeredness of previous approaches.

While many of these new theories draw upon ideas developed over the last two hundred years, they clearly respond to problems unique to the twenty-first century, thus underlining the dynamism and continuing relevance of sociological thought.

SEE ALSO: Ethnomethodology, Feminist Theory, Marxism, Modernity, Structure and Agency, Symbolic Interactionism

References

Abend, Gabriel. 2008. "The Meaning of 'Theory.'" *Sociological Theory* 26 (2): 173–199.
Habermas, Jürgen. 1968/1972. *Knowledge and Human Interests*, translated by J. Shapiro. Boston: Beacon Press.
Ritzer, George. 1975. "Sociology: A Multiple Paradigm Science." *The American Sociologist* 10 (3): 156–167.
Sica, Alan. 2012. "A Selective History of Sociology." In *The Wiley-Blackwell Companion to Sociology*, edited by George Ritzer, 25–54. Hoboken, NJ: Wiley Blackwell.
Taylor, Charles, 1985. "Self-Interpreting Animals." In *Human Agency and Language: Philosophical Papers 1*, 15–44. New York: Cambridge University Press.
Taylor, Charles. 2003. *Modern Social Imaginaries*. Durham, NC: Duke University Press.
Wagner, Helmut. 1963. "Types of Sociological Theory: Toward a System of Classification." *American Sociological Review* 28 (5): 735–742.

Sociology

Elizabeth Hartung[1] and Peter Kivisto[2]

[1] *California State University Channel Islands, UK*
[2] *Augustana College, USA*

Sociology can be defined as the scientific study of human interaction, groups, social institutions, cultural factors, and forces causing order and change in society. This definition is both broad and general, and it reflects the fact that very little if anything in the human world does not fall under its domain. As sociologist Neil Smelser (1994: 8) characterized this, it means that sociology's "scope is enormous; in principle, there is a sociology of virtually everything under the sun." Sociology, however, is only one of several social sciences, and thus needs to be seen in terms of other disciplines concerned with the social world: psychology, economics, political science, geography, history, and anthropology among others.

What distinguishes sociology from psychology, economics, political science, geography, and history is that it is more expansive than they are. In the case of psychology, the primary focus is on the individual personality; psychologists seek to understand mental states and processes. While some psychologists look at interaction in small groups, the discipline arguably does not attempt to address matters related to institutions, and social forces or, in short, those things that operate at the macro level. Nevertheless, the insights of psychology inform sociology, as for example in efforts to rethink the idea of the authoritarian personality in light of the rise of right-wing populism in the United States and Western Europe in the second decade of the twenty-first century.

Economists and political scientists define their respective object domains in terms of the economic and political institutional spheres respectively, and thus do not look at society as a whole the way the discipline of sociology as a whole does. Economists and political scientists are specialists with a highly concentrated subject matter, while sociologists can in contrast be seen as defining their subject matter in broader terms. That said, there is considerable overlap between sociology and these two social sciences. This can be seen by the fact that two important areas of specialization in sociology are political sociology and economic sociology.

Geographers emphasize a spatial approach to social interaction, looking at such matters as land resource use, settlement patterns, and population distribution. The concentration on space is a limiting factor in determining what does and what does

Core Concepts in Sociology, First Edition. Edited by J. Michael Ryan.
© 2019 John Wiley & Sons Ltd. Published 2019 by John Wiley & Sons Ltd.

not fall under the purview of geography. Again, sociology has a more expansive vision of its proper subject matter. However, as recent scholarship on transnationalism makes clear, sociologists share geography's interest in place, space, and borders (Waldinger 2015).

History, by definition, is primarily interested in the past, rather than the present, which is not to say that historians do not study the past in order to inform us about how the present came into being and how the past continues to be implicated in the present. Some practitioners of traditional historiography do not make use of a social scientific approach to its subject matter, but instead as in historical biographies or histories of specific events such as the Civil War construct narrative accounts that are primarily concerned with the particularities of the person or event under investigation. Such historians are not particularly interested in attempting to draw generalizations from the specific case. Other historians, however, operate very much like social scientists, and indeed they make extensive use of concepts, theories, and methods derived from the social sciences, especially sociology. These particular practitioners of the discipline of history are proponents of social history, which has great affinity with historical sociology.

As will become clear below, the founding figures of sociology were deeply immersed in historical inquiry, as they attempted to understand how modern societies had emerged out of their premodern pasts. However, for many contemporary sociologists, granting greater emphasis on the sheer complexity of the present has meant that they have devoted somewhat less attention to the past compared to their predecessors. However, there are many sociologists intent on further developing a historically grounded sociology. One of the recent giants in this effort was the late Charles Tilly (1981), his work straddling the two disciplines so seamlessly that he was often seen as simultaneously a historian and a sociologist.

Anthropology and sociology have a somewhat unique relationship because they share an interest in the expansive vision of the social whole, combined with a desire to understand particular parts of any society in relationship to other parts and to the whole society. Even when not making explicit connections between the specific arena of social life being studied and the larger societal context, the assumption is that the former should be seen as situated in the latter. In addition, there is considerable overlap between the two in terms of the theories and methodologies they employ. This is not to say that they are merely interchangeable. In fact, it is not simply that sociologists are more inclined to rely on quantitative date while anthropologists prefer qualitative study. Rather, even in engaging in ethnographic work, one can detect at least subtle differences in approach.

The major difference between the two disciplines is a reflection of their different histories. Sociology arose in the nineteenth century most directly in response to the impact of the emergence of modern industrial societies. Anthropology took off around the same time, but in response to the impact of the European colonization of vast parts of the globe. Going out to the colonies, anthropologists took as their subject matter traditional, preindustrial societies. Sociologists ended up often treating nation-states as societies while anthropologists confined their understanding of society to smaller entities, often tribes.

Since many of the societies once studied by anthropologists have undergone far-reaching changes and have become part of the industrializing modern world, many anthropologists have turned their attention to modern urban and industrial societies. As a result, there is considerable overlap between sociology and anthropology at the present time, with the likelihood that the old boundaries distinguishing the two social sciences will be renegotiated in the future.

Sociology and the other social sciences differ from the natural sciences, chemistry, physics, biology, and geology because of the crucial differentiating feature of their subject matter. Human beings are "meaning-creating creatures," involved in creating and interpreting the world around them. From the perspective of sociologists who stress the significance of human agency *as well as* the constraining and enabling features of social structures, the task of sociology is to learn how this is accomplished and this means that sociologists are called upon to interpret the ways people interpret their social situations. For those sociologists focusing on social structures, it is not interpretation per se that they seek to explore, but rather the larger causal forces at play in making possible distinctive webs of meaning in particular times and places.

Given the distinctive subject matter of sociology, it is a fair question to ask whether or not sociology is necessary, and if so, why? What makes it unique? What can it tell us about its particular subject matter and how can we benefit from its insights? Sociologist C. Wright Mills answered these questions over a half-century ago in his well-known book, the *Sociological Imagination* (1959). According to Mills, the "sociological imagination" allows us to understand how personal troubles are connected to, and indeed are the consequence of, larger social and historical issues. In Mills (1959: 6) own words, "The sociological imagination enables us to grasp history and biography and the relations between the two within society." Mills clearly thought that sociological knowledge was a valuable tool in addressing social problems by adding scientific insights into their causes and potential solutions. This idea of sociology reflects a view that it is a moral science, and thus a view that sociologists are guardians of the common good. Such an understanding has in recent years informed ongoing discussions about what has been termed "public sociology" (Jeffries 2009).

Sociologists do not work in a vacuum. They are part of a community of researchers that is devoted to the task of advancing our understanding of various aspects of society. This community includes contemporaries and sociologists from the past. Thus, in addressing any sociological topic, sociologists inevitably turn to the work of others, reacting to and building upon a historical tradition with deep historic roots, but which most commentators agree took off in the nineteenth century.

The French social thinker Auguste Comte is often described as the founder of sociology, in part because he coined the term "sociology." Along with him, many other individuals contributed to the emergence of modern sociology, a short list of which would include Herbert Spencer, Harriet Martineau, Albion Small, William Graham Sumner, Gabriel Tarde, Ferdinand Tönnies, William Graham Summer, and Lester Ward. However, of all the figures in the early history of sociology, three stand out as the most important, having achieved canonical status: Karl Marx (1818–1883), Max Weber (1864–1920), and Emile Durkheim (1858–1917). In different ways, this trio has shaped and continues to shape the way sociologists view the social world.

Marx never claimed to be a sociologist, never held a university appointment, was hated by many because of his radical political and economic views, and frequently was unable to find publishers interested in publishing his writings. Despite all of this, his legacy has richly informed sociology as well as a number of other disciplines. Marx lived during what historians have called the "age of revolution." He witnessed a dramatic transformation of European social, economic, and political life, and sought to understand it. Much of his life was spent in exile, first in France and then in England, with a brief stay in Belgium sandwiched between the two. His ideas reflect a distinctive synthesis of key intellectual developments occurring in three of the countries where he at various times resided: philosophy from Germany, the socialist ideas of French social thinkers, and British economic thought. Out of this unique blend emerged an astute analysis of the dynamics of capitalist industrial society.

In his view, capitalism is predicated on an economic system that produced the oppression of the working class by the capitalist system (and not just directly by the owners of industrial enterprises). Marx contended that the exchange of labor for wages was an unequal one in which the capitalist got more in the bargain. Capitalist success necessitated the economic exploitation of workers. At the same time, Marx thought that capitalism was a progressive force and the capitalist class was, in its own way, revolutionary. This class had vastly improved communication and transportation systems. It had stimulated scientific and technological developments, with the result being that in its relatively brief history, its achievements far surpassed those of all previous historical periods (Marx and Engels in Tucker 1972: 337–338).

The main problem with capitalism was that not everyone would be a beneficiary of these developments. A society in which everyone would benefit would have to be a classless society, and this type of society, which he called either socialist or communist, could only come about as a result of the revolutionary activities of the most oppressed class in capitalism: the working class. Marx was optimistic about the prospects of a transition from capitalism to socialism.

In many ways he proved to be a critical and insightful analyst of developments in Western Europe during his lifetime, but some of his predictions about long-term trends proved to be inaccurate. Most significantly, revolution did not take place where it was expected, and the class structure of industrial societies changed in many ways he had not anticipated – in particular the rise of the professional middle class. Despite these shortcomings, Marx remains valuable to us insofar as capitalism continues to produce both winners and losers. His insight into the dark side of capitalism still informs sociological analysis, as recent concerns about growing inequality attest (Jones 2016).

Max Weber was a major figure involved in the development of sociology in Germany. If Marx was optimistic about the future, Max Weber's assessment of modern industrial civilization was deeply pessimistic. Weber did not share Marx's economic arguments or his view about the revolutionary potential of the working class. He thought Marx overemphasized economic factors at the expense of cultural and political ones. In short, Weber was definitely not a Marxist. Nevertheless, Weber agreed with many of Marx's criticisms of capitalism, but he did not think that socialism would be a viable solution. The reason was that, in both systems, technology was harnessed to machine production in the interest of increasing productive capacity. More significantly, organizations would be transformed in both systems into a new form of administration, which Weber referred to as a bureaucracy. In his view, the modern age is the age of bureaucracy.

Bureaucratic organizations were necessary in industrial societies, because such societies require efficiency, calculability, predictability, and control, or in short, a process he termed rationalization. Contrary to the belief that bureaucracies are inefficient, the notion of "red tape," Weber saw them as the most efficient form of organization possible in industrial society. But bureaucracies stifle individual initiative and creativity. Weber considered such organizations to be a threat to freedom. Moreover, they are based on a hierarchical chain of command, and are therefore not democratic. Bureaucratization encourages a dehumanized attitude that seeks to reduce emotions and irrationality from decision making. In such a world, one of the consequences is secularization, which means that religion loses some of its power and influence. Some people in such societies can come to believe that they are threatened by the prospect of a world that is ultimately meaningless, while others find the prospect of being free from religion a liberating idea. The members of modern societies are divided not only about the implications of secularization, but about whether it is an inevitable consequence of modernity.

Weber saw little chance of exiting or fundamentally changing this bureaucratic world. Thus, near the end of *The Protestant Ethic and the Spirit of Capitalism* ([1904–5] 1958: 181), he depicted the modern bureaucratic world as an "iron cage." This metaphor reflected his deep concern that the modern industrial world poses a serious threat to individuality and freedom. While most contemporary sociologists who see themselves as in some sense heirs of Weber do not share his deep pessimism, many have concluded that he, in fact, correctly identified the main trends of modern history. Thus, as we seek to understand the world we live in – a world profoundly changed by technological innovations that impact the class structure – his ideas about industrial society, though derived from an earlier stage of development, continue to have relevance.

Emile Durkheim was a pivotal figure in the establishment of sociology in France, and his ideas were to play an important role in the way sociology developed internationally. His analysis of industrial society was quite different from that of Marx. In *The Division of Labor in Society* ([1893] 1964), the divisions referred to are not Marx's social classes, but instead the divisions into various professional specializations that were becoming characteristic of contemporary society. It was this division, he argued, that marked the movement from preindustrial society to industrial society.

Durkheim posed the difference between preindustrial and industrial societies in terms of two opposing kinds of social solidarity: "mechanical" and "organic." He described preindustrial societies as mechanical and industrial societies as organic. Preindustrial societies have simple social structures with very little division of labor. Individuals and families had to perform a wide variety of tasks necessary to sustain their lives, including obtaining the food, clothing, and shelter they needed to survive. In this situation, the solidarity binding people together was based on a set of shared values, rather than being based on interdependency. By contrast, modern societies have complex social structures and a very highly developed division of labor. The specialization of work, and with it the expansion of the professions, is needed because people are not capable of grasping all of the knowledge required to sustain their lives. The result is that we rely more and more on others. For example, the automobile is a vital mode of transportation for most people, and yet most of us cannot repair our cars when something goes wrong. Due to the interdependence of people in modern societies, Durkheim thought that they are appropriately seen as organic.

Durkheim was concerned about various social problems that arose in modern societies. He was especially concerned about a condition he termed "anomie" which meant a condition characterized by a lack of widely accepted norms that could be used to guide individual behavior. In a famous early empirical study of suicide, Durkheim identified anomic suicide as one of the most common types of suicide in modern society. Anomie was depicted as akin to a disease, but Durkheim, as a "physician to modern society," felt that it was possible to find a cure for this illness and to find solutions to other contemporary social problems.

American sociology also emerged during the late nineteenth and early twentieth centuries. One of the characteristic features of many early American sociologists was their interest in social reform. Like Durkheim, they thought that sociology could play a significant role in alleviating the social problems of the day. Sociological studies of these problems could provide vital information needed in the formulation policies designed to improve conditions.

Early sociologists addressed a wide range of social issues. For example, Edward Alsworth Ross, at the University of Wisconsin, was concerned with the undue concentration of wealth in giant corporations, and he endorsed the progressives and populists of the era who urged breaking up the giant trusts and expanding the government's role in regulating business. At Brown University, Frank Lester Ward promoted an applied sociology that was intended to help reduce conflicts among various social classes. Concerned that modern industrial society undermined the bases of community, he considered one of the important tasks of sociology as that of helping to find ways to revive a vibrant community life.

The rapid industrialization of the United States during the early part of the twentieth century brought with it the large-scale migration of peoples from around the world and brought African-Americans out of the rural South and into the urban North. Not surprisingly, early sociologists and social reformers paid particular attention to matters related to the consequences of economic change, urbanization, and race and ethnicity. One of the most influential sociologists to pursue such a line of inquiry was Robert E. Park, who became the head of the sociology department at the University of Chicago and from that position exerted considerable influence on American sociology between World War I and World War II. Park's career as a muckraking journalist, a member of an anti-colonial reform association, and as the personal secretary of Booker T. Washington, the founder of Tuskegee Institute, provided him with rich life experience that informed his views of what sociology should be about. He was a pioneer in the sociology of cities and racial and ethnic relations. Moreover, he was instrumental in promoting participant observation or ethnography as a research methodology, encouraging his students to provide richly descriptive accounts of various slices of the metropolis. Influenced by this approach, students at Chicago wrote about a wide variety of topics including urban race relations, ghetto life, gangs, prostitution, and mental illness.

There has been a belated appreciation of the contributions of another individual during this era: W.E.B. DuBois. During his long life, DuBois played a key role in black protest against racial oppression. He was, for example, the longtime editor of the NAACP's magazine, *The Crisis*. While hailed as an important black intellectual and leader, his contribution to sociology is less well known. He was however, the first African-American to receive a PhD from Harvard University and the first black sociologist. DuBois began his career attempting to employ sociological training in studying the African-American community. His study of the African-American community in Philadelphia combined survey research and descriptions of slum life to examine such issues as family structure, housing, education, income, and occupations. While today this work is seen as a landmark in the early history of empirical research, it was unfortunately largely ignored when it first appeared (Morris 2015).

Contemporary sociology has built on a tradition, one that involves those scholars widely embraced as canonical early on as well as those that it took much longer to include in the canon due to marginalization along racial and gender lines. These foundations have served as the basis for the development of the discipline, which today is a "big tent" containing numerous theoretical approaches and differing research methodologies. The differences on both theoretical and methodological fronts involve various choices and preferences of sociologists. Whereas some focus on agency – people actively constructing their social reality – others stress the significance of social structures in both constraining and enabling various outcomes. Whereas some think sociology should pattern itself on the natural sciences, others think it should be closer to history, with its awareness of the uniqueness of events in specific times and places. Some want to get at the macro-level picture, while others stress the importance of the micro level, and still others operate in between at the mezzo level. The result theoretically is that numerous approaches are employed, including: conflict, critical, ethnomethodology, exchange, feminism, functionalism, neo-Marxism, phenomenology, postmodernism, rational choice, structuration, symbolic interactionism, and systems theory. Likewise, methodological approaches vary, including survey research, ethnography, archival work, and content analysis.

Regardless of approach, equipped with the sociological imagination that links scientific inquiry to humanistic concerns, sociologists inquire into countless aspects of the social world. Their collective concerns range from the local to the global, including both the familiar and the unfamiliar. Sociologists help to appreciate both the impact of society on each of us, and the ways we – individually and collectively – create, sustain, and change our social surroundings. By gaining a better understanding of how society both constrains and limits us, while also enabling us to do things we could not do if we lived like Robinson Crusoe outside of society, we come to better realize the value of society and our obligation to insure its wellbeing.

References

Durkheim, Emile. [1893] 1964. *The Division of Labor in Society*. New York: The Free Press.
Jeffries, Vincent, ed. 2009. *Handbook of Public Sociology*. Lanham, MD: Rowman & Littlefield.
Jones, Gareth Stedman. 2016. *Karl Marx: Greatness and Illusion*. Cambridge, MA: The Belknap Press of Harvard University Press.
Mills, C. Wright. 1959. *The Sociological Imagination*. New York: Oxford University Press.
Morris, Aldon. 2015. *The Scholar Denied: W.E.B. DuBois and the Birth of Modern Sociology*. Oakland: University of California Press.
Smelser, Neil. 1994. *Sociology*. Cambridge, MA: Blackwell Publishers.
Tilly, Charles. 1981. *As Sociology Meets History*. New York: Academic Press.
Tucker, Robert. 1972. *The Marx–Engels Reader*. New York: W.W. Norton.
Waldinger, Roger. 2015. *The Cross-Border Connection: Immigrants, Emigrants, and Their Homelands*. Cambridge, MA: Harvard University Press.
Weber, Max. [1904–5] 1958. *The Protestant Ethic and the Spirit of Capitalism*. New York: Charles Scribner's Sons.

Space and Place

John R. Logan

Brown University, USA

Space and place are both very concrete and very abstract notions. They are concrete in the following way. Space is often thought of in terms of physical space. The widespread use of satellite-based geographic positioning systems (GPS) has made us very aware of location as a set of geographic coordinates. Indeed coordinate systems have always been crucial to systematic mapping. GIS maps that make it possible to visualize spatial patterns and to make the measurements required for spatial analysis absolutely rely on measuring longitude and latitude on the surface of the earth. Places, in turn, are usually studied as elements of a built environment, although the term can also apply to natural environments. In many studies a place is defined by its composition (e.g., its density, home values, ethnic makeup) and treated as a unit of analysis without attention to meanings or symbols or consequences of that composition. Both terms can refer to quite tangible components of the physical context in which people live and interact.

Both terms also are abstractions from these physical realities, and this is how they become more informative for social science. Place is relevant to social life because everything happens somewhere, all action is embedded in place and may be affected by its placement. Abbott (1997: 1152) links this insight to the classical Chicago School, stating "that one cannot understand social life without understanding the arrangements of particular social actors in particular social times and places ... Social facts are *located*." In the urban political economy tradition every place is socially constructed with a history and a future; where people are placed affects their fortunes and adds structure to their lives; place-based interests are at the heart of much collective and political action (Logan and Molotch 1987). In either theoretical perspective a place is not fully constituted by what one can see in a given locale, the buildings and streets and people. What is essential about a place is that it has meaning. The idea that places have social and symbolic meaning has found its way into many areas of scholarship, from urban sociology to what is now termed "geo-humanities."

The wide application of this notion of place has potential to minimize the relevance of space. For example Gieryn (2000: 465) dismissed space as "what place becomes when the unique gathering of things, meanings and values are sucked out." Another approach is to identify spatial characteristics with attributes of larger areal units. From this

Core Concepts in Sociology, First Edition. Edited by J. Michael Ryan.
© 2019 John Wiley & Sons Ltd. Published 2019 by John Wiley & Sons Ltd.

perspective Voss (2007) argues that traditional demography through the mid-twentieth century was "spatial" in the sense that it was the study of ecological units like cities and counties. A shift of focus to individuals and individual-level processes (associated with increased availability of data at this level) pulled demography away from its spatial origins until the advent of multilevel modeling gave us methods to distinguish between processes at the individual and aggregate levels. This use of a spatial vocabulary seems to suggest that counties are spatial but people are not. In a more careful formulation Entwisle (2007) treats people as spatial in the sense that they make choices about where to live, that they move and that their movements can collectively result in changes in place characteristics and restructure their social networks. Yet she also has in mind the literature on place effects, and she uses the term "spatial" mainly to refer to places as local "social and spatial" contexts.

It is more useful to conceive of the spatiality of places in terms of relationships between places (Logan 2012). Space refers not only to specific physical locations (place coordinates on a grid system) but also to *where things are or where they happen in relation to others*. There is an implicit spatial reference in almost all studies of places. If a place is a certain residential district, its spatial element is its location in relation to other places: is it near the center city or out in the suburbs, is it close to a transit line, how long does it take to get to the daycare center, what else is in the vicinity? Concepts that are critical to spatial thinking – distance, exposure and access, scale, and boundaries – are all rooted in relative locations.

- Distance is the core concept in many sorts of spatial research, so central that it is incorporated in the First Law of Geography, which holds that "everything is related, but near things are more related than distant things" (Tobler 1970: 236). Consequently when place attributes like racial composition or organizational density are mapped, the map demonstrates that there is a spatial pattern, often a clustering of similar areas.
- "Proximity to" or "distance from" is often understood in terms of inequalities in exposure or access. Some places are more exposed to hurricanes because of their proximity to the coast or to air pollution because of their proximity to congested roads. Some places have better access to jobs or to prenatal clinics or to mass transportation. These attributes can be thought of as characteristics of the place itself, but they are inherently spatial.
- Spatial scale refers to the geographic scope of the place or phenomenon that is being studied. We use terms like neighborhood or zone to identify a territory that is not a single point or address on a map. Such terms seem natural, but they introduce a spatial question: what is the geographic scale of the territory? Political studies often deal with world regions or nation-states. River basins and valleys define territories for environmental research. Metropolitan labor markets, cities, and more local areas within cities are important to urban analysis.
- The boundary is a more complex spatial concept. Despite the proximity between two adjacent places, easily measured by distance, these places can be sharply separated by a boundary. The boundary could be related to the natural environment like a river, or the built environment like a six-lane highway, or a political construct like the city line. Many boundaries are socially constructed, so it is useful for social scientists to think of processes of boundary formation or bridging.

• Another commonly discussed spatial process is diffusion. If a disease spreads from neighborhood to neighborhood, or country to country, that represents a dynamic process in which spatial boundaries are being crossed. If an innovation like a musical style or a method of birth control spreads from one part of the country to other parts, we may expect it to follow a distinctive spatial path rather than appearing randomly in different locales. Some mechanisms of communication or influence seem more likely to affect nearby places, and diffusion is a term that encompasses such a process.

It is difficult to think about spatial patterns or processes without reference to places. Spatial social science is about relations between places, however these are defined. The distinctive element in what may be called the "spatial turn" in social science is that increasingly scholars are also attuned to the spatiality of places.

SEE ALSO: City, the; Demography and Population Studies; Everyday Life; Globalization; Urban Sociology

References

Abbott, A. 1997. "Of Time and Space: The Contemporary Relevance of the Chicago School." *Social Forces* 75: 1149–1182.

Entwisle, B. 2007. "Putting People into Place." *Demography* 44: 687–703.

Gieryn, T. 2000. "A Space for Place in Sociology." *Annual Review of Sociology* 26: 463–496.

Logan, J.R., and H.L. Molotch. 1987. *Urban Fortunes: The Political Economy of Place.* Berkeley: University of California Press.

Logan, J.R. 2012. "Making a Place for Space: Spatial Thinking in Social Science." *Annual Reviews of Sociology* 38: 507–524.

Tobler, W.R. 1970. "A Computer Movie Simulating Urban Growth in the Detroit Region." *Economic Geography* 46: 234–240.

Voss, Paul R. 2007. "Demography as a Spatial Social Science." *Population Research and Policy Review* 26 (5–6): 457–476.

Sport, Sociology of

Jay Coakley

University of Colorado, Colorado Springs, USA

The sociology of sport is a young, global, organizationally autonomous (sub)discipline in which research and theory focus on sports as social phenomena and on the relationships between sports and the social and cultural contexts in which they are created, sustained, and changed by individuals and groups. Although it is grounded primarily in the theory and methods of sociology, the field has been constituted by scholars trained and housed in a variety of disciplinary contexts, including sociology, physical education, kinesiology, media and communications, health sciences, and sport management, as well as women's, ethnic, physical cultural, leisure, policy, and disability studies.

Despite the emerging visibility, popularity, and social and cultural importance of sports and related physical activities, the sociology of sport has not been strongly embraced by the major professional associations of sociology, physical education, or other well-established disciplines. This is not surprising given that sports are explicitly embodied activities, and university-based knowledge domains are grounded in historical and cultural traditions that assume mind–body distinctions.

The implicit and enduring acceptance of Cartesian mind–body dualism has sustained a university-based intellectual culture that has ignored bodies or relegated them to the "repair shops" located in university medical schools or departments concerned with anatomy and body mechanics. Unlike scholars in Asian cultures, where widely used ontological approaches assume mind–body integration as the foundation for being human, scholars in Europe, North America, and most English-speaking regions of the world have been slow to study the actions and relationships of human beings as embodied, and slow to take seriously embodied activities, such as physical play and games and their institutionalized expressions in sports. For example, the Higher Education Funding Council for England recommended in 2009 that funding should not go to research on sports and other trivial topics having no real-world relevance.

This intellectual climate has made sports and other forms of physical culture risky topics for research and teaching among scholars concerned with professional recognition, status, and security in much of higher education. Additionally, there has been relatively little institutional support and funding for sociologists and physical educators who study sports as social phenomena. An exception to this has occurred in some nation-states where there is a cabinet-level ministry of sport concerned with policies and practices involving the physical activity and wellbeing of citizens and the systematic development of national athletes and teams in international competitions. When there is an emphasis on the former, those who study physical activities and sports as social phenomena receive support, if not funding for research having policy implications.

Origins of Sociology of Sport

Only institutionalized over the past half-century through the formation of professional associations worldwide, the substantive intellectual roots of the sociology of sport are scant and shallow. Play and games were mentioned by a few European and North American social scientists between 1880 and the 1950s, but sports received scarce attention during those years. In a notable exception, Thorstein Veblen discussed emerging Ivy League college sports in *Theory of the Leisure Class* published in 1899. Max Weber mentioned English Puritan opposition to sports in his 1904 and 1905 volumes of *The Protestant Ethic and the Spirit of Capitalism*, and William Graham Sumner discussed "popular sports" in *Folkways*, published in 1906. Willard Waller devoted attention to the "integrative functions" of sports in US high schools in *The Sociology of Teaching* in 1932. But even these scholars mentioned sports only in passing, and they failed to inspire others to view sports as legitimate topics of study (Page 1973).

Theodor Adorno's student Heinz Risse was the first notable scholar to refer to a "sociology of sport" when he published *Sociologie des Sports* in 1921. But another 40 years passed before a few scholars in Europe and North America rediscovered sports as social phenomena. This occurred in connection with the gradual rationalization of sports during the twentieth century and was partially fueled by recognition among some scholars that social issues raised by the Cold War, along with the civil rights, women's, and student movements during the 1960s and 1970s were especially obvious in sports (Edwards 1969; Stone 1972; Coakley 1987). The formal birth of the field occurred in 1965 when a group of scholars from diverse disciplinary and national backgrounds formed the International Committee for Sport Sociology (ICSS) Warsaw, Poland, and sponsored publication of the *International Review for Sport Sociology* (*IRSS*) and the first international conference in Cologne in 1966.

Growth and Current Status

The sociology of sport grew steadily into the twenty-first century as professional associations were formed in North America, East Asian countries, including Korea, Japan, Taiwan, and China, and most recently, in South America. This, combined with the diversity of research in the field, has attracted scholars with research interests that may not be supported the traditional disciplines of sociology and physical education.

As the field has grown so too have the definitions of sports used by researchers. Initially, sport was defined as "an embodied, structured, goal-oriented, competitive, contest-based, ludic, physical activity" (Loy and Coakley 2015). But many in the field felt that this definition ignored the fact that sports are social constructed, contested, and dynamic physical activities that people create, sustain, and regularly include in their collective lives. Therefore, they may include tai chi practiced in a Beijing park, capoeira practiced in a plaza in Rio de Janeiro, parkour practiced in a Paris neighborhood, windsurfing on the water of Australia's Gold Coast, or skateboarding on the concrete surfaces of an inner city.

Although the sociology of sport has embraced research on informally organized alternative, recreational, and lifestyle sports, research tends to focus primarily on the institutionalized, competitive, rule-governed physical activities that have become highly visible components of contemporary cultures.

Theory and Research

Conceptions of sport vary widely across cultures. Therefore, the historical and conceptual links between sports and related phenomena are diverse. As such, sports have been studied in connection with play, leisure, games, recreation, outdoor activities, folk festivals, tourism, physical education, and physical culture in general. Substantive topics have included relationships between sports and gender, race and ethnicity, social class, (dis)ability, socialization process, youth development, education, deviance and violence, the economy, politics and policy, media and communications, and world religions.

A recent study of nearly two thousand articles published between 1977 and 2011 in the three major English-language journals in the field provides a description and analysis of content themes along with the theories, theorists, and research methods used or discussed in the articles (Dart 2014). The most common among the 133 content themes identified were politics/economics, psychology, sex/sexuality, race/ethnicity, media, education, feminism, organization/governing bodies, culture, theory, and body/health. If the gender-related themes were grouped together, gender emerges as the most common theme or topic studied or discussed in the sociology of sport.

The most used and discussed theories and theorists in the articles were feminist theory, Foucault, Bourdieu, Marx, Elias/figurational theory, postmodern theory, symbolic interactionism, poststructural theory, Goffman, and phenomenology. Structural-functionalism was widely used during the 1960s and 1970s, but various forms of critical theory are used most often today. Unsurprisingly, cultural studies, especially the version practiced at the Centre for Contemporary Cultural Studies at the University of Birmingham, has strongly influenced the choices of theories and theorists used in sociology of sport research.

The most used and discussed research methods were content analysis, statistical/quantitative, interviews and focus groups, surveys, ethnographic, questionnaires, auto/biographic, comparative, longitudinal, and mixed method. Quantitative research was more often used during the 1960s through most of the 1980s, but various forms of qualitative research have been favored since the 1990s. This shift is due to restricted access to large samples of respondents, lack of funding to support such access, and media reports that present quantitative data. Today, most quantitative research by scholars in the sociology of sport is done in countries where sport ministries provide access and support, and comparative quantitative studies have become more common in Europe under the sponsorship of the European Union.

Future Directions

Like other social sciences, the sociology of sport is struggling to retain its place in higher education and in knowledge production. Some scholars in the field have suggested that sociology of sport research become so diverse that the field should formally embrace its multidisciplinary character and its broad theoretical foundations and represent itself as "physical culture studies" (Silk and Andrews 2011).

At present, sociology of sport courses at the undergraduate and graduate levels are increasingly offered in sport management programs where they occasionally emphasize applied knowledge presented with an implicit structural functionalist orientation. If this continues, the extent to which critical research and theory currently dominates the field will recede as will a focus on non-commercial, community-based, alternative, and informal sport forms.

SEE ALSO: Body, the; Culture, Sociology of; Everyday Life

References

Coakley, Jay. 1987. "Sociology of Sport in the United States." *International Review for the Sociology of Sport* 22 (1): 63–79.

Dart, Jon. 2014. "Sports Review: A Content Analysis of the *International Review for the Sociology of Sport*, the *Journal of Sport and Social Issues* and the *Sociology of Sport Journal* Across 25 Years." *International Review for the Sociology of Sport* 49 (6): 645–668.

Edwards, Harry. 1969. *The Revolt of the Black Athlete*. New York: The Free Press.

Loy, John, and Jay Coakley. 2015. "Sport." In George Ritzer and J. Michael Ryan (eds.), *Blackwell Encyclopedia of Sociology Online*. London: Wiley.

Page, Charles H. 1973. "Review of *Sport: Readings from a Sociological Perspective*, edited by Eric Dunning (Toronto: University of Toronto Press, 1972)." *American Journal of Sociology* 79 (2): 474–476.

Silk, Michael L., and David L. Andrews. 2011. "Toward a Physical Cultural Studies." *Sociology of Sport Journal* 28 (1): 4–35.

Stone, Gregory. 1972. *Games, Sport, and Power*. New York: Dutton.

Stereotypes, Prejudice, and Discrimination

Michael Pickering

Loughborough University, UK

Stereotypes are evaluative forms of representation which endorse existing patterns of social discrimination. They isolate an alleged characteristic of a social group, class, or category, such as laziness, duplicity, greed, or licentiousness, and insist upon enframing all members of the group or category in terms of this characteristic. The consequence is discriminatory in refusing any other form of description and assessment, and in rendering those stereotyped as inferior in some way or another, especially when compared, either implicitly or explicitly, to those who perpetuate any specific stereotype. Stereotyping always involves this two-way, yet one-sided relationship.

Stereotyping also acts to reinforce prejudice in the negative meaning of this term as seeing or judging others in unfavorable or hostile ways, as for example is the case with racism, ageism, and sexism, though prejudice in itself is neither a necessary precondition nor a necessary result of stereotyping precisely because one can be prejudiced against racism, ageism, or sexism, and wish to see stereotypes associated with them challenged and excluded from future social interaction. Prejudices themselves may need to be critically questioned, qualified, or rejected in the light of experience, but they should not be simply run in with forms of discrimination. Racial prejudice, say, may go hand-in-hand with racial discrimination, but racial prejudice should be challenged because it is racist, not because it is prejudiced. It should be challenged on this basis for at least two reasons: firstly, critique cannot be established solely by showing the existence of prejudice, and secondly, especially when it reinforces discrimination, racism is not merely a problem of cognition, hasty judgment, or lack of evidence. It is far more a problem of the value system which racist stereotyping supports.

The definitional power of stereotypes lies in the essentialist manner of their representation. They allow no alternative, and are absolute in their depiction or placement of others. Their attribution of homogeneity to certain social groups or classes then seems incontestable because it is immutable. In this way they serve to validate an existing social order or cultural hierarchy, as, for example, in the way the "chav" stereotype demonizes certain white working-class people whose poverty is attributed to their own fecklessness, irresponsibility, and lack of ambition or determination, rather than to the social and economic inequalities that divide British society. The stereotype reinforces the symbolic boundaries between social classes through its associations with uncouth behavior, sexual promiscuity, wayward parenting, and tasteless vulgarity in dress and hair style. The "chav" stereotype is simply the latest in a long line of representations whose purpose is to "blame the poor" for their own poverty and make cuts to welfare seem thereby legitimate and justified. At the same time, it illustrates how stereotypes are socially inimical because they affirm and perpetuate structural divisions while circumscribing the identity of those targeted by them.

Stereotypes operate with rigid "us"/"them" distinctions and their ideological force lies in the extent to which they are accepted as natural and inevitable. It is in this way that they reinforce relations of power and inequality. To take another example, in the United States a long-established news practice of exaggerating black crime and ignoring or playing down white crime has served to confirm the stereotype of an innate black male proclivity to criminality, so regularizing discrimination against black men and occluding their social and economic disadvantages in the post-slavery period all the way along to the Civil Rights Movement and beyond. Over the same period, black women have been either pathologically "othered" as the antithesis of white womanhood, or rendered safe and reassuring to white society in the form of the Aunt Jemima stereotype, full of good humor and an obsequious servility. In both film and television, black women were usually cast in the role of a cook or housemaid. The script name varied, but the stereotype was the same, and its legacy has been long.

Despite their potency and entrenchment in social discourse, stereotypes can be critically challenged, and this may eventually lead to their dissolution. In doing so, the monolithic attributes or traits to which whole social categories are reduced should be situated within the structures of power and privilege which they actively uphold. Stereotyping is not just a problem of perception or cognition. It is more importantly a sociological problem, and the point of contesting it is to foster greater scope for both self-determination and social inclusiveness.

SEE ALSO: Homophobia and Heterosexism; Inequality, Gender; Inequality, Racial and Ethnic; Social Psychology; Stigma

Further Reading

Pickering, Michael. 2001. *Stereotyping: The Politics of Representation*. Basingstoke and New York: Palgrave Macmillan.

Jones, Owen. 2012. *Chavs: The Demonization of the Working Class*. London: Verso.

Roberts, Diane. 1994. *The Myth of Aunt Jemima*. London: Routledge.

Stabile, Carol. 2006. *White Victims, Black Villains: Gender, Race, and Crime News in US Culture*. London: Routledge.

Stigma

Matthew Clair

Harvard University, USA

Stigma is an attribute that conveys devalued stereotypes. Erving Goffman (1963: 3) classically defined stigma as an "attribute that is deeply discrediting." A discredited attribute could be readily discernable, such as one's skin color or body size, or could be hidden but nonetheless discreditable if revealed, such as one's criminal record or struggles with mental illness. For Goffman, stigma is a general aspect of social life that complicates everyday micro-level interactions – the stigmatized may be wary of engaging with those who do not share their stigma, and those without a certain stigma may disparage, overcompensate for, or attempt to ignore stigmatized individuals. Most people, Goffman (1963: 138) argued, experience the role of being stigmatized "at least in some connections and in some phases of life." Indeed, Goffman's broad definition of stigma incorporates many contemporary discredited attributes, including what he defined as "tribal stigmas" (e.g., race, ethnicity, and religion), "physical deformities" (e.g., deafness, blindness, and leprosy), and "blemishes of character" (e.g., homosexuality, addiction, and mental illness).

In the decades following Goffman's articulation of stigma, psychologists elaborated stigma's cognitive dimensions and the processes through which it shapes micro-level social interaction. Much of this research has focused on stigmas understood to be related to character, such as mental illness or addiction, or stigmas stereotyped as deviant, such as homosexuality. Psychologists have explored the evolutionary causes of stigma, with some suggesting that stigma serves sociobiological functions by categorizing and excluding individuals who may threaten a community through the spread of disease or perceived social disorder. In addition, social psychologists have focused on the individual-level consequences and coping responses of those who face stigma in daily interactions. This research has documented stigmatization's negative implications for self-esteem, academic achievement, mental health, and physical wellbeing. Research on coping has documented how stigmatized individuals manage their stigmatized identities and cope with specific instances of discrimination that they attribute to their stigma. This research literature is a subset of a larger psychological literature concerned with individual coping responses to stress more broadly. Researchers have enumerated numerous coping responses – such as avoidance, suppression, and identity development – and have identified these responses' inconsistent moderating effects on stress.

Until the turn of the twenty-first century, research on stigma in sociology had been less coherent than its counterpart in psychology. Sociologists relied on the concept when it helped to illuminate a social phenomenon, but rarely did researchers strive to accumulate theoretical knowledge around stigma as a fundamental social process. Link and Phelan's (2001) review of stigma in the *Annual Review of Sociology* initiated a distinctively sociological approach to the study of stigma that since has been refined and elaborated. Drawing on Goffman but incorporating a broader concern for the operation of power in society, Link and Phelan define stigma as the co-occurrence of four processes: 1) labeling human differences; 2) stereotyping such differences; 3) separating those labeled from "us"; and 4) status loss and discrimination against those labeled. By incorporating the role of power and discrimination in their definition of stigma, Link and Phelan articulated an approach to stigma that would enable sociologists to consider how stigma related to fundamental sociological questions, namely those relating to the social creation, reproduction, and consequences of social inequalities.

Sociological approaches to stigma in the ensuing 15 years have considered the different types of, as well as the meso- and macro-level causes and consequences of, and responses to, stigma (see Table 1). With respect to type of stigma, sociologists have focused not only on stigmas related to character, but also – and with greater emphasis than psychologists – on stigmas related to heritable, bounded social categories such as race and ethnicity ("tribal stigmas"). These stigmas are related less to deviance and the violation of social norms and more so to processes of exploitation and domination (Phelan, Link, and Dovidio 2008). Sociological research on the causes of stigma has considered the role of

Table 1 Psychological and sociological approaches to stigma along four categories.

	Micro-level (psychology)	Meso-level (Social psychology and cultural sociology)	Macro-level (sociology)
Causes	Physical and mental disorders, sociobiological and instrumental motivations	Intersubjective and symbolic motivations, cultural motivations, stereotypes	Social closure, power, institutional practices, neighborhood and social segregation, discriminatory laws
Contexts	Body, mind, cognitive schema	Individual perceptions and attitudes, interpersonal relationships	Policies/laws, neighborhoods, workplaces, nation-states, built and natural environments
Consequences	Mental illness, stress, physical illness	Self-esteem, identity, symbolic worth, interpersonal (mis) recognition	Group disparities in mental and physical health, in/out-group membership, economic and social inequality
Responses	Grit, physiological coping, individual management	Interpersonal withdrawal, psycho-social resources, cultural reframing	Social movements, institutional/ organizational change, policy and legal change

the law and institutional practices in the maintenance of stigmatization. Such practices enable stigmatized individuals' exclusion from social networks, neighborhoods, labor markets, the law, and politics. Here, stigma has been understood as both cause and effect: it justifies exclusion of devalued others and, through such exclusion, reifies devalued stereotypes. With respect to stigma's consequences, research in public health has considered the role of stigma as a fundamental driver of population-level health disparities through various mechanisms; for sociologists, one main mechanism is the unequal distribution of material resources given discrimination against stigmatized groups. Sociologists studying responses to stigma have considered collective responses, such as social movements and legal change, as well as what could explain variations in responses across stigmatized groups, interactional contexts, and societies (Lamont et al. 2016).

Contemporary sociological research on stigma continues to draw inspiration from Goffman's core insights on the phenomenon, developing measures to understand how different dimensions of stigma – such as courtesy stigma, structural stigma, or internalized stigma – shape inequalities faced by different groups and their social relations. Future research on stigma could benefit from greater comparison across stigmatized groups. Goffman articulated stigma as a general social process, focusing on how stigmatized individuals often face similar constraints in the management of social interactions, regardless of the particular type of stigma they face. Research comparing the experiences, causes, and consequences of stigma across types would enable a better understanding of the causal role of stigma in the reproduction of social inequality. Future research could also benefit from greater exchange between psychology and sociology, especially with respect to detailing the unique contributions of psychological mechanisms (e.g., stress) as compared to sociological mechanisms (e.g., unequal resources) in the production of health disparities. Finally, sociologists should develop new approaches to studying destigmatization, or the process by which stigmatized groups become less devalued in society. Whereas psychologists have documented the effects of stigma reduction interventions in experimental settings, sociologists largely have been remiss to examine the external validity of such interventions or the sociohistorical transformation of devalued attributes.

SEE ALSO: Identity; Race and Ethnicity; Social Psychology; Stereotypes, Prejudice, and Discrimination; Stratification and Inequality

References

Goffman, Erving. 1963. *Stigma: Notes on the Management of Spoiled Identity*. New York: Simon & Schuster.

Lamont, Michèle, Graziella Moraes Silva, Jessica S. Welburn, Joshua Guetzkow, Nissim Mizrachi, Hanna Herzog, and Elisa Reis. 2016. *Getting Respect: Responding to Stigma and Discrimination in the United States, Brazil, and Israel*. Princeton, NJ: Princeton University Press.

Link, Bruce G., and Jo C. Phelan. 2001. "Conceptualizing Stigma." *Annual Review of Sociology* 27: 363–385. DOI:10.1146/annurev.soc.27.1.363.

Phelan, Jo C., Bruce G. Link, and John F. Dovidio. 2008. "Stigma and Prejudice: One Animal or Two?" *Social Science & Medicine* 67: 358–67. DOI:10.1016/j.socscimed.2008.03.022.

Further Reading

Clair, Matthew, Caitlin Daniel, and Michèle Lamont. 2016. "Destigmatization and Health: Cultural Constructions and the Long-Term Reduction of Stigma." *Social Science & Medicine*. DOI:10.1016/j.socscimed.2016.03.021.

Pescosolido, Bernice A., and Jack K. Martin. 2015. "The Stigma Complex." *Annual Review of Sociology* 41: 87–116. DOI:10.1146/annurev-soc-071312-145702.

Stratification and Inequality

Nico Wilterdink

University of Amsterdam, The Netherlands

Stratification and inequality are central topics of sociological theory and research, and focal issues in politics and public debates. Since the beginnings of the discipline in the nineteenth century, sociologists have dealt intensively with questions concerning the nature, the dynamics, the causes, and consequences of stratification and inequality in different societies and historical periods.

Definitions

While social inequality in the broadest sense comprises all kinds of social differences, it is common in sociology, as in colloquial language, to give the term a more specific meaning: social inequality refers to hierarchical, "vertical" differences, for which the metaphor of high and low (or top and bottom, upper and lower, etc.) is used. People in "higher" positions have more power, prestige and privileges than people in "lower" positions. *Social inequality* can be defined as differences in power, prestige (status) and privileges (rewards, gratifications) between the members of a group, society, or social network.

Social inequality is by definition relational; it is not simply the reflection of given individual differences, a supposed "natural inequality". While personal attributes such as age, sex, height, physical strength or skin color may play a more or less important role in generating, maintaining, and perceiving social inequality, it depends on the nature of social relations – the power relations among groups and individuals, and the social definitions and classifications connected with these relations – whether, to what extent, and how such attributes are elements in inequality structures.

In the concept of *social stratification*, the high–low metaphor is used to refer to the division of a society into different layers or strata. Usually, families or households rather than individuals are taken as the basic units of stratification; members of these units share privileges (which does not preclude substantial inequalities between them), and through kinship relations inequalities are continued over generations. Social stratification may be defined then as social inequality between groupings of families or households through which privileges are passed on from one to the next generation. A society is more stratified the larger the differences in power, prestige, and privileges are, the sharper the boundaries between the strata distinguished, and the smaller the mobility between them.

Variations and Developments in Stratification

While all human societies are characterized by some degree of social inequality, not all are stratified in this sense. Bands of hunters and gatherers were too small and too homogeneous for stratification to evolve. This changed after the introduction of sedentary agriculture, when societies became larger and more differentiated, and ruling groups of priests and warriors began to distinguish themselves from the rest of the population. In agrarian societies, huge inequalities with sharp demarcations between different strata came into being, such as between slaves and slave owners, castes, or estates. *Castes* are groups with a definite status whose membership is determined by birth. A prime example is the intricate caste system that developed in India, legitimated by religious beliefs and rituals. *Estates* are strata that are distinguished by different political and social rights, such as between the clergy, the nobility, and the "third estate" in the European Middle Ages. The dominant stratum in this system was the land-owning nobility, whose membership was hereditary but allowed for some limited entry of new members from other ranks.

In relation to modernization processes since the eighteenth century – political reforms in the direction of equality of legal rights, and industrialization processes that transformed economic relationships – stratification in Western societies changed toward what came to be known as a system of *classes*. Contrary to castes or estates, classes do not have formal boundaries, recognized in law, custom, or religion, nor is their membership officially determined by birth. Class divisions rest primarily on differences in economic position and economic interests, such as between capital owners and industrial workers. Yet in spite of the openness of classes and the absence of well-defined boundaries between them, the chance to attain a certain class position remains quite strongly dependent on the class position of one's family of origin, as sociological research on social mobility has made abundantly clear. In modern societies too, the degree of intergenerational mobility is much smaller than could be expected on the basis of the meritocratic idea of equality of chances.

Dimensions of Stratification and Inequality

While societies differ in the nature and degree of stratification, within each society different principles of stratification and inequality are working at the same time. Social inequality is multidimensional: positions can be ranked according to different dimensions or criteria, and the resulting hierarchies usually do not exactly coincide. The German sociologist Max Weber (1864–1920) made this explicit by distinguishing three forms of stratification, which he termed "classes," "status groups," and "parties." *Classes* in his typology are groupings of people with similar economic market positions, indicated by property, occupation, and income. *Status groups* (*Stände* in German, which can also be translated as "estates") are characterized by successful claims to honor (prestige, status), connected with a distinct lifestyle and a tendency toward social closure, the confinement of informal social intercourse to those who are regarded as social equals. *"Parties"* are associations oriented to the acquisition of power.

Weber's typology has been reformulated in the threefold distinction of class, status, and power as the main dimensions of social inequality. This distinction evokes several questions, however; in particular, how "power" should be conceptualized in relation to the other dimensions. Sociological research usually focuses on the other two dimensions: class position (indicated by occupation, income, and wealth) and social status (as measured by occupational prestige, or based on research on patterns of social interaction and social judgments). These dimensions are often taken together, for example in the index of socioeconomic status (SES), which combines occupation, income, and education. As formal education is an important determinant of occupation and income chances and social status in modern societies, it is taken as an indicator of both the class and the status dimension.

Another way of distinguishing dimensions of stratification and inequality is by reference to different forms of *capital*, conceived as sources of power and privileges. French sociologist Pierre Bourdieu distinguished three main forms: economic, cultural, and social capital, to which he added a fourth one – symbolic capital – referring to signs and symbols of social prestige. Later scholars have suggested a variety of other types, which usually overlap with these four, such as moral capital and political capital. All are pursued both as ends in themselves and as means to accumulate more capital of the same or other types.

The conceptual distinctions by Weber, Bourdieu, and other sociologists reflect the common notion that social inequality is multifaceted, with dimensions and subdimensions that are causally interconnected but cannot be reduced to one another. Discrepancies in rank according to different (sub)dimensions often occur. These *status inconsistencies* may lead to tensions and subsequent efforts to reduce them, particularly when they conflict with normative expectations.

Theoretical Interpretations and Explanations

Various general explanations and theoretical interpretations of stratification and inequality have been advanced. They include (1) *integrationist and functionalist* theories, which regard inequality as functional for society since it serves as a device to ensure conformity to social norms and a stimulus to the fulfillment of functionally important roles; (2) *power-and-conflict* theories, which see the usurpation of power sources by one group at the cost of other groups as the basis of stratification (Marxian class theory being one version); (3) *rational action and exchange* theories, according to which social inequality results from the competitive actions of individuals who pursue their own interests; (4) *interactionist and constructionist* views, which regard social definitions, classifications, and perceptions of inequality as basic to inequality itself; and (5) a *biosocial* approach, which hypothesizes universal patterns of dominance and submission characteristic of the human species, from which variations and changes in social inequality emerge.

These theoretical interpretations do not necessarily exclude one another in all respects, as they focus on different aspects of stratification and inequality. Elements of different perspectives can be and have been combined in more synthetic views (see, e.g., the works listed below under Further Reading).

Current Issues

A central question in sociological debates is how and why stratification and inequality change over time; more specifically, whether there is a dominant tendency of increasing or decreasing inequality, and how to explain this. In the nineteenth century, contrasting views were represented by, on the one hand, Karl Marx, who observed growing class inequalities in capitalist societies, and, on the other hand, the French social and political thinker Alexis de Tocqueville, who argued that Europe would follow the United States in a process of democratization, diminishing inequality, blurring status and class distinctions, and increasing social mobility. Developments in the twentieth century seemed to confirm Tocqueville's predictions for some time, but since about 1980 a tendency of growing inequality, at least in the economic sphere (indicated by estimates of income and wealth inequality), has been observed for most Western societies. At the same time, Western political and economic dominance on the global level has decreased. Both trends have been explained by relating them to processes of globalization, which have favored owners and managers of large companies in comparison to the majority of workers.

It is open to debate what the tendency of growing economic inequality within Western (as well as many non-Western) nation-states means for class relations and status distinctions. In any case, this trend has stimulated renewed interest, among social scientists and the public at large, in social inequality and its causes and consequences. Examples of research into social and psychological consequences of inequality are the much-discussed comparative work by British social epidemiologists Richard Wilkinson and Kate Pickett (2010), and Robert Putnam's widely read study of decreasing social cohesion and growing disparities of life chances in an American community (2015).

SEE ALSO: Capital: Cultural, Social and Economic; Capitalism; Class; Class, Capitalist; Development, Dociology of; Inequality, Gender; Inequality, Global; Inequality, Racial and Ethnic; Marxism; Poverty; Social Justice

References

Putnam, Robert D. 2015. *Our Kids: The American Dream in Crisis*. New York: Simon & Schuster.
Wilkinson, Richard, and Kate Pickett. 2010. *The Spirit Level: Why Equality Is Better for Everyone*, 2nd ed. London: Penguin Books.

Further Reading

Bourdieu, Pierre. 1984. *Distinction: A Social Critique of the Judgement of Taste*. London: Routlede & Kegan Paul (original French edition 1979).
Collins, Randall. 2004. *Interaction Ritual Chains*. Princeton, NJ, and Oxford: Princeton University Press, esp. Chapter 7.
Elias, Norbert, and John L. Scotson. 1994. *The Established and the Outsiders*, 2nd ed. London: Sage.
Lenski, Gerhard. 1966. *Power and Privilege: A Theory of Social Stratification*. New York: McGraw-Hill.

Structure and Agency

Piotr Sztompka

Jagiellonian University, Poland

The question decisive for the identity of sociology as a separate discipline is: what is society? Or in other words, what is its specific subject matter? In a general sense society is a concept applicable to all levels of complexity, or "size" of social objects: families, communities, groups, associations, organizations, nation-states, and even global society. They are arguably all made of the same social fabric, namely human actions and interhuman relations.

But what is the nature of society? For a long time sociologists were trapped between two alternatives: either society is a specific "system," or organism of the supra-individual sort, or it is merely the sum total of multiple individuals. These alternatives were the reflection of a broader set of two illusions: the illusion of reification (society is seemingly some solid entity over and above the heads of individuals and outside of their control), and the illusion of egocentrism (each individual is a seemingly free, autonomous, and separate being). The current view in sociology overcomes this opposition with the help of two combined notions – structure and action – and it emphasizes the dynamic, processual nature of society through the notion of agency.

If we look closely at any society we can see acting individuals and the results or products – whether intended or unintended – of their actions. But individuals are never acting in a vacuum; rather they act in relation to other people and to social products. Individuals are embedded in a network of relations with others and hence any action is influenced by other people – whether individuals are aware of it or not. And, at the same time, individuals also exert influence on those who are linked with them by social relations. From birth to death individuals live with others, side by side with others, together with others; in cooperation and competition, love and hatred, friendship and conflict, peace and struggle. Individuals are always surrounded by "significant others" who influence them and whom they reciprocally influence. This fundamental existential fact is grasped by the concept of structure. In a most general sense structure refers to this network of relations between or among individuals. Society, then, is what happens between or among individuals, the flow of actions along structured space.

Structures can eventually acquire a more lasting and solid quality beyond concrete episodes of human activity, and due to that are able to constrain or facilitate the wider category of actions of large masses of people. There are five types of structures which

Core Concepts in Sociology, First Edition. Edited by J. Michael Ryan.

provide the context for actions. First is the interactional structure consisting of concrete encounters among and between individuals, which can become to some extent solidified by the patterns of interactions, or communications which people tend to follow for some time (e.g., friendship, cooperation, competition, etc.). This type of structure is found in families, organizations, associations, teams, local communities. Second is the axio-normative structure, the system of values and rules which generalize typical relations and endow them with the sanctions as good and proper (e.g., customs, moral precepts, laws), defining what people should, and should not, do toward others and what they can expect from others in return. This type of structure is embodied in institutions (e.g., marriage, employment, trade, government). Third is the ideal structure which consists of shared beliefs and ideas (e.g., political commitments, myths, knowledge about nature and society, ideas about identity as members of wider communities, ethnic groups, or nation-states). Fourth is the opportunity structure, which defines the statuses and roles that people take in society and the relations among them (e.g., occupations and professions, hierarchies of inequality and power). Fifth, there is the material infrastructure, "the containers of social relations" which provide channels into which encounters and interactions are squeezed (e.g., the layout of streets in the city, architecture of buildings, design of offices, arrangement of tables in the restaurant, technical means of communication, or telecommunication).

Any action, i.e., meaningful behavior, occurs in the context of such multiple structures. Arguably, however, action is only either negatively constrained or positively facilitated by such structures; never fully determined by them. Individuals retain a considerable scope of freedom because the causal impact of structures is mediated by human subjectivity; the mechanisms of internalization and interpretation. People act on their personal understanding of relations with others, binding rules, shared beliefs, established statuses and roles, ecology of material space within which they move. Structures limit the chances for some actions and provide opportunities for other actions. How people obey or resist constraints, and take or reject opportunities is arguably subject to their choices, sometimes deliberate and rational, sometimes impulsive and irrational.

Structures do not come from nowhere but instead are a human product, created by actions, and thus can be seen as more solid, lasting sediments of typically or commonly repeatedly taken actions. Here the notion of agency becomes important, defined as the potentiality for producing or modifying structures, sometimes referred to as "morphogenesis" (Archer 2000). On a small scale we exercise agency when we establish acquaintances or friendships in our private interhuman space. On a major scale of public structures, the potential for change belongs to common people who, following some pattern of action in masses and for some time, turn it into a typical custom. The collective actions taken by social movements may revolutionize morality or law. Often the creation of structures is due to particular individuals seen as being endowed with moral, intellectual, aesthetic, or coercive powers: e.g., religious prophets and charismatic leaders, reformers, revolutionaries and legislators, scholars and artists, innovators and trend setters.

Individuals live within the structured interhuman space which had been created for them by their predecessors. They recognize structures, take them into account, internalize them, interpret them, and can abide by or oppose them. At the same time structures can provide resources and opportunities which individuals may use in their actions. By acting within structural constraints individuals reproduce structures. But at least some individuals, at least some of the time, are able through their actions to exercise agency, i.e., to modify or create structures for their own future or for the next generations. This incessant process of producing and reproducing the structured social world has sometimes been referred to as "structuration" (Giddens 1984), or "social becoming" (Sztompka 1991).

SEE ALSO: Epistemology; Everyday Life; Sociology; Sociological Theory; Symbolic Interactionism

References

Archer, Margaret. 2000. *Being Human: The Problem of Agency*. Cambridge: Cambridge University Press.

Giddens, Anthony. 1984. *The Constitution of Society*. Cambridge: Polity Press.

Sztompka, Piotr. 1991. *Society in Action: The Theory of Social Becoming*. Cambridge: Polity Press.

Symbolic Interactionism

Robert Dingwall

Dingwall Enterprises Ltd., UK

The term "symbolic interaction" was first used by the American sociologist, Herbert Blumer (1900–1987), in a chapter on social psychology written for a 1937 undergraduate textbook. During the 1960s, it was adopted as a banner under which various US sociologists distinguished themselves from both structural–functionalism and Marxism. As such, it has often been described as a sect, when it really just continues mainstream thinking in US sociology before World War II. In the United Kingdom, it was imported during the late 1960s and initially associated with radical political movements within the sociology of deviance. More recently, European scholars have become interested in the approach as a way to fill the intellectual vacuum left by the collapse of the Marxist agenda for sociology after the events of 1968.

Symbolic Interaction

Blumer based symbolic interactionism on the philosophical work of G.H. Mead (1863–1931), whose lectures he attended while a graduate student at the University of Chicago. Mead himself described his approach as "social behaviorism" in contrast to the radical behaviorism of the psychologist J.B. Watson (1878–1958). Watson thought that it was unnecessary to have a concept of "mind." Behavior was simply a set of responses to incoming stimuli which did not need to be explained by some intervening process. Mead, however, argued that there was an important difference between the way humans dealt with stimuli compared with the rats, dogs, or pigeons studied by behaviorist psychologists. Animals treated incoming stimuli as signs, direct information about the world that triggered automatic or conditioned responses. Humans normally responded to stimuli as symbols, signals that required cognitive transformation before they could result in actions. Mead stressed the extent to which the meaning of acts was not derived from the actor's intentions. An actor would design an act while imagining the likely response of its expected recipient or audience. However, the meaning of that act would only emerge from the actual response of its recipient or audience – and might be subject to further revision from the producer's subsequent self-correction. Speech, for example,

Core Concepts in Sociology, First Edition. Edited by J. Michael Ryan.

involves organizing the range of sounds producible by the human body into blocks that stand for, or symbolize, the speaker's anticipation of the hearer's response. If these blocks of sound were to work as a means of communication, they must form part of a system shared by both the speaker and the hearer.

In the course of action, then, I say something that I expect you to respond to in a particular way, based on my knowledge of the language that I think we share and my understanding of where you are coming from. In the same way, you respond to what I have said based on your knowledge of the language and your understanding of what you think I might be trying to say. Whatever I might have intended, I find out what I meant from your response. This creates the "looking-glass self": who we are is how other people see us, not how we choose to be seen. In interaction, we are also constrained by our understanding of what an average citizen, the "generalized other," would be likely to be taken to mean if they said the same thing using the same language. Language is the most important component of a social system of symbols, and the means of using them, that we learn in the course of socialization. Mead has an extensive discussion of children's games, for example, and the way they develop a sense of self and mind through social interaction. His core thesis has been summarized as a chain from society or social interaction to the construction of an idea of the self to the construction of mind.

Blumer developed this thinking into a wider critique of 1950s US sociology. He opposed the emphasis of the sociology of the day on social structures at the expense of action, and on survey methods that naively assumed questions would mean exactly the same thing to every respondent. He argued instead that a sociology that was concerned for action and meaning should rely primarily on qualitative methods. This thinking was reflected in the department that he developed at Berkeley from 1952 until his retirement in 1967, and with which he continued to be associated until his death.

Chicago Sociology

In his focus on the legacy of G.H. Mead, however, Blumer established a rather misleading creation myth for symbolic interactionism. Mead's work was a particular version of Pragmatism, which is a distinctively American style of philosophy associated with William James, C.S. Peirce, C.H. Cooley, and Josiah Royce, among others. Many of these scholars studied in Germany where they were influenced by the work of Kant and were familiar with older traditions, particularly the Scottish Enlightenment writings of Francis Hutcheson, David Hume, and Adam Smith. While pragmatism influenced other Chicago sociologists, they also drew heavily on ecological and evolutionary thinking derived from Adam Smith, Charles Darwin, and Herbert Spencer. They read the work of Weber, Simmel, and Durkheim and there was a fluid boundary with anthropology. British social anthropologists like Bronislaw Malinowski and A.R. Radcliffe-Brown were visitors and Lloyd Warner and Robert Redfield were both influential mentors to sociology PhD students.

If we look at the sociologists who trained at Chicago from the 1930s until the early 1950s – and are often labeled as symbolic interactionists – they are actually a rather diverse group. Scholars like Anselm Strauss, Howard Becker, Eliot Freidson, and Erving Goffman drew much less on Mead's thinking than Blumer's narrative implies. Everett Hughes's ecological perspective on work, occupations, and organizations is a marked influence on the first three, while Goffman owes more to Warner, and ultimately Durkheim, than to pragmatism.

There is a shared belief in the importance of qualitative methods, particularly participant observation, which goes back to the foundation of the Chicago department. Everyday life can only be understood by sharing the experience of those producing it. Social systems are the outcomes of social interaction, although they may be experienced as prior, given constraints. The meaning of actions is fluid and indeterminate, constructed in the moment, although also available for reconstruction and renegotiation. Actions take place within institutional contexts that they simultaneously shape, and are shaped by. Where Blumer's formulation focuses on a sociological social psychology, the wider practice of symbolic interactionism is more organizational. Its emphasis on discovery has been particularly attractive in Europe, where both Marxist orthodoxies and the recent German fashion for systems theories have tended to assume answers before conducting research.

Contemporary Symbolic Interactionism

Symbolic Interactionism today forms part of a family of theoretical approaches that draw on the same philosophical roots but have taken different journeys to the present. Four are particularly significant:

Radical Constructionism This is associated particularly with the circle around Norman Denzin and with auto-ethnographers like Carolyn Ellis or Laurel Richardson. These writers mix pragmatism with postmodernism and phenomenology to produce a more introspective approach to the investigation of the self and its engagements with the world through interaction.

Ethnomethodology This is the heir to a parallel philosophical tradition that emerged from the German-speaking world during the 1930s, particularly in the social phenomenology of Alfred Schutz and Aron Gurwitsch and the linguistic philosophy of Ludwig Wittgenstein. There are fundamental differences in the understanding of meaning. Ethnomethodologists are much more skeptical about the possibility of imaginatively understanding action and the processes of interpretation through observation. They argue that sociologists and participants in action can only work with the practices that they see and hear rather than assuming some kind of empathy or *verstehen*. Nevertheless, there are convergences, exemplified in the writings of Robert Emerson and some of the work in science and technology studies.

Organizational Ethnography Relatively little work is now being done on organizations under the brand of symbolic interactionism, although David Maines, Peter M. Hall, and Timothy Hallett have tried to keep this alive. Some of the original contributions to the New Institutionalism program in organization studies drew on the work of Strauss and Goffman but their visibility has declined as organization studies have become more integrated with the business school environment.

Identity Work This is probably the largest body of scholars who would clearly identify themselves as symbolic interactionists. The focus here is on the way that identities are ascribed or accomplished through interaction, particularly in the context of race, gender, and sexual orientation. It is more closely anchored in the Blumerian program which, to some extent, accounts for the view of symbolic interaction as a niche approach.

SEE ALSO: Deviance; Ethnography; Ethnomethodology; Identity; Marxism; Organizations, Sociology of; Postmodernism and Poststructuralism; Qualitative Methods; Social Psychology; Socialization; Structure and Agency

Further Reading

Blumer, Herbert. 1969. *Symbolic Interactionism: Perspective and Method*. Berkeley: University of California Press.

Dingwall, Robert. 2001. "Notes Towards an Intellectual History of Symbolic Interactionism." *Symbolic Interaction* 24: 237–242.

Fine, Gary Alan. 1995. *A Second Chicago School? The Development of a Postwar American Sociology*. Chicago: University of Chicago Press.

Rock, Paul. 1979. *The Making of Symbolic Interactionism*. London: Macmillan.

Urban Sociology

Cate Irvin and Kevin Fox Gotham

Tulane University, USA

Urban sociology is a study of social lives in urban settings and investigates the processes and patterns of urban growth and change, as well as how these processes shape our daily lives. Urbanization transpires when populations shift from rural to urban areas, which has rapidly occurred since industrialization in the 1800s. Today, urban sociologists examine how cities develop, how they are organized, how they change, how they affect people, and what they might look like in the future. Urban sociologists investigate the effects of industrialization, suburbanization, immigration, racial population migration, globalization, federal programs and revitalization drives, and the impacts of large-scale factors on urban development. Urban sociology is not about the central city alone, but embraces a diversity of theories, methods, and scales of analysis to understand neighborhoods and communities, metropolitan regions, and both city and suburban life.

Major Urban Development Patterns

While different countries and regions have undergone distinctive processes of urbanization, we classify modern cities into three major development patterns: commercial cities, industrial cities, and corporate cities. Commercial cities, existing until approximately the 1850s, were small port cities, based on a rural agricultural economy. A small, heterogeneous population of primarily merchants and their service providers lived in urban center. These cities were dense, with a compact layout, since walking was the primary mode of transportation. Additionally, due to their size, there was rarely a separation of work and home, or a separation between the different social classes.

In the 1860s, manufacturing emerged as the primary economic system, and industrial cities dominated the urban environment. During this time, cities began to move inland, which provided more space for factories (e.g., Chicago, Detroit), though many commercial cities also transitioned to an industrial economy. Industrial cities resulted in rapid growth, as populations of workers left the agricultural sector and moved to the city. During these developments, large class and social distinctions emerged, with workers living in residential areas closer to the factories, and the wealthier moving to the outer neighborhoods.

Core Concepts in Sociology, First Edition. Edited by J. Michael Ryan.
© 2019 John Wiley & Sons Ltd. Published 2019 by John Wiley & Sons Ltd.

In the 1920s, the economy began to shift from industrial to service based, creating corporate cities. In corporate cities the manufacturing plants, office spaces, and retail establishments moved from the center to the outer edges of the cities. This resulted in a decentralization of the cities and a growth in the peripheral urban areas and suburban areas. Now, the downtown is no longer the only location of business activities; commutes are no longer only into city cores, requiring new forms of transportation, and during this time the automobile began to develop as a main component of transportation for commuters. During this era, residential segregation continued to increase as the poor urban minorities become concentrated in the inner city, while the middle and working class, along with the wealthy, relocated to the outer areas and suburbs of the city.

At the beginning of the twentieth century, scholars associated with the University of Chicago began developing theories of urban growth and change as a response to industrialization in the United States. Led by researchers including Robert Park, Ernest Burgess, and Robert McKenzie, the Chicago School produced a prodigious number of works; their main emphasis was on community-based studies, primarily examining poor and ethnic minorities, focusing on the study of everyday city life and the cultures of the city.

The Chicago School developed the classical urbanization model, urban ecology, out of the concern with the form and development of the modern American city. This model approached the study of urban life through an analogy with the evolution of plants and organisms to the physical environment. Utilizing two ecological principles (dominance and succession), which operate to establish order and balance in nature, urban ecology explores the relationship between the spatial patterns of the urban form and the social patterns of morality and norms. It argues that social norms are rooted in the relationship between a population and the territory in which they live. Cities become ordered into "natural areas" through processes of competition, invasion, and succession, thus different neighborhoods develop through the adjustments made by inhabitants as they struggle for resources.

Urban ecologists were interested in studies of human behaviors as well as the studies of changing land-use patterns. In 1925, Ernest W. Burgess described the land-use structure of Chicago in terms of *concentric circles*. The business district lies in the center of the city where most of the tertiary employment is located. A ring of factories where many of the industrial activities are located borders this zone. This is then bordered by multiple residential rings, which become more expensive the farther they are from the noise and pollution of the city center.

These theories provided a good model of American urban growth up until the 1960s, and the observed patterns still influence how many cities look today, but the theories encountered a number of critiques as new urban patterns emerged. One major critique is that these studies place too much emphasis on *where* different activities take place, rather than *why or how*. Additionally, this model does not address that competition for space is multidimensional nor does it distinguish among different ways that people show attachment to place (Firey 1947). It is also unclear how "natural groups" acquire and exercise power or even what types of "resources" groups fight over. Furthermore, the Los Angeles School, emerging in the 1980s, claimed that Los Angeles is the paradigmatic American metropolis of the twentieth and twenty-first centuries and did away with the concept of a city being focused on a single "urban core," instead looking at cities as multi-nuclei.

Political Economy of Place

The urban riots of the 1960s further demonstrated issues with the urban ecological model and, as a result, urban sociological analysis shifted away from the ecological approach and toward the urban political economy model. This model, drawing from Karl Marx's analysis of class conflict, rejects the ecological view of the city, instead claiming that city life is controlled by larger institution structures, which cause spatial and class conflicts. Capitalism transforms the city into real estate that is traded for profit, concentrating wealth and power in the hands of a small group of elites. This model views places as commodities, with both use and exchange values. Moreover, place is linked to many other commodities, such as services and goods, that could significantly change one's life chances. In this way, political economists argue that *how* space is used as a commodity creates inequalities of power. This process of urban growth is dependent on the interests of those who want to benefit from increased exchange- and use-values. These growth coalitions (Molotch 1976; Logan and Molotch 1987) include politicians, the metropolitan newspapers, utility companies, transportation officials, institutions, labor unions, retailers, and corporate capitalists, who lobby, manipulate, and pressure the government to help them control and alter the way the city grows.

The Role of Theory in Urban Sociology

Several meanings and definitions of urban theory dominate contemporary urban sociological research on cities and metropolitan life. One definition is broad and views urban theory as a heuristic or sensitizing device to help urban sociologists understand the nature of urban order, change, and stability. In this meaning, urban theories are interpretive tools that address questions such as what is "urban" about urban life, how are cities organized, and how do they change over time? Another more analytical approach defines urban theory as a set of interrelated propositions that allow for the systematization of knowledge, explanation, and prediction of urban reality. In this definition, urban theories specify both causal relations between variables (including models that indicate how causal factors are interrelated) and causal mechanisms responsible for producing these relations. A third meaning of urban theory starts from a critical–normative foundation and views theory as a set of concepts and explanatory tools to examine the operation of urban power structures, identify the causes and consequences of urban inequalities, and clarify the bases of social conflict and struggle in cities. This critical urban theory is problem-centered, embraces a strong social justice and equity component, and aims for urban *praxis* - a fusion of urban knowledge and practice. In this later meaning, urban theorizing is undergirded by a utopian impulse that attempts to illuminate the mechanisms of domination and subordination in cities, and provide a prescription for ameliorative social action and revolutionary change.

There are no timeless, static, or immutable urban theories. Just as urban theories are products of particular times and historical conditions, urban theories change as social movements, social processes, and individuals transform cities and metropolitan areas. Today, urban sociology has theories of urban space, gentrification, residential segregation, ethnic neighborhoods, place attachment, socio-spatial urban restructuring, and so on. Urban sociologists tend to focus on applying, testing, and/or developing theories of cities, space, place, and the urban. Sometimes theorizing means the work urban sociologists do to abstract or generalize empirical findings, or to set them in context. Moreover, there is a widespread belief that empirical work in urban sociology should be driven or informed by theory. Thus, urban journals tend to reject "atheoretical" and "undertheorized" papers, as well as papers that fail to make a theoretical contribution to the literature on cities and urban life. An important intellectual activity for urban sociologists is to "theorize" about urban things like cities, places, communities, and spaces. Indeed, that urban sociology offers "theories" about cities and urban life is arguably what makes it count as a social science and differentiates it from journalistic exposés of cities and accounts that laypersons and poets offer.

Urban Sociology in the Twenty-First Century

As a vibrant and growing subdiscipline with interdisciplinary connections, urban sociology will continue to animate urban studies, drive new research agendas, and influence debates on extra-local processes and change in cities. The future of urban sociology is bright, due to the continued importance of globalization processes, race and class inequalities, and critical theorizing on cities. At the same time, we are entering a post-disciplinary era where distinctions between sociological, geographical, anthropological, and political interpretations and debates have less relevance to understanding urban phenomena (Gotham 2001). There are clearly a variety of interesting futures for urban sociology because of the subdiscipline's multidimensionality, theoretical and analytical diversity, and conceptual richness. Based on past trends and proven strengths, the utility of urban sociology as a field of study lies in reclaiming and refreshing conventional approaches that are sensitive to urban inequality and that recognize the importance of nuanced and sophisticated empirical research. Urban sociologists can respond to the challenge of interdisciplinarity and fragmentation in sociology and related fields of urban studies and urban planning by focusing on perennial issues and topics including sociospatial divisions, poverty and segregation, the interplay of the global and the local in the development of cities, and the nexus of capitalist development and urbanization.

SEE ALSO: City, the; Community; Everyday Life; Space and Place

References

Firey, Walter I. 1947. *Land Use in Central Boston*. Cambridge, MA: Harvard University Press.

Gotham, Kevin Fox, ed. 2001. *Critical Perspectives on Urban Redevelopment*. Volume Six of *Research in Urban Sociology*. New York: Emerald Press.

Logan, John, and Harvey Molotch. 1987. *Urban Fortunes: The Political Economy of Place.* Berkeley: University of California Press.

Molotch, Harvey. 1976. "The City as a Growth Machine: Toward a Political Economy of Place." *American Journal of Sociology* 82 (2): 309–332.

Further Reading

Park, Robert E., Ernest W. Burgess, and Roderick D. McKenzie. 1984. *The City*. Chicago: University of Chicago Press.

Work, Occupations, and Professions, Sociology of

Rudi Volti

Pitzer College, USA

Work is a fundamental human activity. More than simply a means of earning a living, the work that we do plays a large role in how we see ourselves and are seen by others. It is a key determinant of our income, wealth, and social status. It is also a source of many of our friendships. Many aspects of sociological inquiry such as social class, race and ethnicity, gender, and economic relationships are closely tied to the study of work and occupations.

Milestones in the Sociological Study of Work

One of the oldest comments on work appears in the Old Testament. In *Genesis* 3:19 we learn that Adam and Eve's disobedience condemned them to a life where "In the sweat of thy face thou shall eat bread …" A more analytical approach to work appeared in the writings of nineteenth-century sociologists, which often reflected the fundamental changes affecting work and society as result of industrialization. Karl Marx (1818–1883) stressed how the division between the owners of the means of production (capitalists) and those who had only their labor to offer (proletarians) was generating class conflict that inevitably would lead to revolutionary transformation. In his early writings Marx also focused on worker alienation, an issue which continues to be a source of concern today. Emile Durkheim (1857–1917) elaborated on the division of labor, which continues to be a key concept for understanding modern society. Max Weber (1864–1920) also incorporated this concept in his discussion of the key elements of bureaucratic organization, a theoretical approach which continues to be influential today.

During the twentieth century the study of work and occupations grew in empirical and theoretical sophistication. Pioneers of what came to be known as industrial sociology such as Elton Mayo (1880–1949) studied work in natural settings, noting the importance of informal social arrangements in shaping the way work was actually done. Prior to what became known as the human relations movement it was simply assumed that the only source of worker motivation and behavior was the opportunity to make more money.

During the second half of the twentieth century and beyond, our understanding of the nature of work was broadened through cross-cultural research into work and occupations. Of particular interest were anthropological studies of the world's few remaining hunting-and-gathering societies. These studies effectively challenged the assumption that "primitive" people had to endure lives of unremitting toil simply to survive. In fact, inhabitants of these societies devoted relatively few hours each week to gaining their livelihood. This was possible because the ratio of land to people was large, and there was sufficient plant- and animal-based food to support their small numbers. God's harsh injunction to Adam and Eve became a reality only after the invention of sedentary agriculture, which supported far more people per area of land, but at the cost of many more working hours.

Major Themes in the Sociology of Work and Occupations

The sociological study of work and occupations has always reflected the major social, economic, and cultural forces affecting society. One of the most important of these has been the movement of large numbers of women into the ranks of paid employees. In 1940 only 24.3 percent of American women over the age of 16 worked outside the home; in 2014, 57 percent of women were members of the labor force. Although substantial gains have been made, women continue to earn less on average than men. There are a number of reasons for this disparity. Occupational and pay discrimination is surely one of them, but other factors are also important. One of the most significant of these is the interruption of careers caused by the demands of pregnancy and motherhood. Sociologists, economists, and historians have also documented that women, even when employed full time, spend more hours on housework and child care than their male spouses, although there is recent research suggesting that the gap is closing. Yet for all these hindrances, women workers have collectively narrowed the gender-based income gap. In 1979 women workers in the United States averaged 62 cents for every dollar earned by a male worker. By the middle of the second decade of the twenty-first century the female-to-male ratio was 82 cents to the dollar.

The era in which women took up paid labor in large numbers also was characterized by significant gains in civil rights for racial and ethnic minorities. These gains, however, have not been matched by equivalent advances in the distribution of occupations. Although there are many exceptions, African-Americans and Latinos are over-represented in low-income, low-skilled jobs. As with women workers, discrimination is one source of these disparities but not the only one. The lower median educational levels of African-Americans and Latinos, powerfully influenced by present and past discrimination, also affect the distribution of occupations as well as income.

Educational attainments have always been an important source of occupational attainment, never more so than today. But why have formal educational attainments, college degrees in particular, been of such paramount importance in recent years for job placement and subsequent earning power? Economic and technological changes have required a more skilled workforce, but critics also have noted that educational attainments are also used as means of "signaling" the presumed worthiness of a job applicant, irrespective of what he or she has actually learned.

Education, whatever its significance, is an important component of professionalization. The study of professions, beginning with medicine and law but now encompassing many other kinds of work, has been a major concern of the sociology of work and occupations for many years. In the immediate post-World War II era the study of professions centered on the traits that presumably set professions apart from other occupations. These included the nature of the knowledge required, the extent of specialized training, and the internalization of ethical beliefs and their application. In more recent years, sociologists have been less concerned with particular traits and have been more attuned to efforts on the part of professionals and would-be professionals to insulate themselves from competitive, market-based relationships.

Another key issue animating the sociology of work and occupations is immigration, both legal and illegal. Immigration has had both positive and negative consequences. Many immigrants do work that native-born workers are reluctant to do for the wages offered by employers. On the other hand, the competition of immigrants for jobs may depress the wages of unskilled workers, although economists have not reached a consensus on this issue. On a positive note, immigrants have made important contributions to the advancement of a variety of industries and enterprises, resulting in the creation of many new jobs.

Current and Future Influences on Work and Occupations

The forces shaping the future of work and occupations can be discerned to a certain extent, although many surprising future developments are likely. One of the most reliable ways of forecasting the future comes from the study of demographic trends. The populations of all advanced industrial nations are getting older on average, and while the cohort of younger workers is becoming more racially and ethnically diverse. These two trends will be the source of advantages as well as challenges for employers and society as a whole.

A second powerful force is technology, broadly defined as the tools, techniques, and materials through which work is done. At the micro level, organizational and industrial sociologists have conducted many studies on the effects of specific technologies on organizational structures and procedures. At the macro level, technological change is constantly reshaping work and working environments. Although statements about our living amidst "an unprecedented rate of technological change" are overblown, it is indisputable that advances in communications, robotics, and information processing will continue to affect the way that work is done, while at the same time creating new occupations and eliminating some older ones. Fears of widespread unemployment due to technological advance were not realized in the past, nor are they likely to be in the future. Even so, technological change has decimated some industries and geographical regions, while the loss of obsolete jobs and the rise of new ones have contributed to the rising degree of economic inequality that has been evident in recent decades. Technological change has also been changing the distribution of needed workforce skills. An important task for sociologists will be to delineate how the mix of skills is being altered, and to provide insights into how our educational systems need to be adjusted in light of these changes.

Economic globalization often has consequences similar to those caused by technological change. Although a solid argument can be made for the benefits of globalization and foreign trade for the economy as a whole, the same cannot be said about their impact on individual workers and the rise and fall of particular skills. In both cases, many workers who have been displaced need retraining if they are to remain effective members of the workforce. Particularly problematic is the situation of unemployed older workers; too many employers cling to the myth that older workers are not suitable for job training. In general, sociologists can combine with psychologists and economists to delineate the best means of mitigating the negative consequences of globalization and other sources of disruption for work and workers.

Work is a practical activity, but it also encompasses many non-utilitarian aspects of life. In their own work, sociologists should strive to blend both of these aspects of work through the development of new theoretical and methodological approaches, while always being attuned to the problems and needs of the men and women whose everyday labors keep the world running.

SEE ALSO: Capitalism; Class; Class, Capitalist; Education, Sociology of; Organizations, Sociology of

Further Reading

Levy, Frank, and Richard J. Murnane. 2004. *The New Division of Labor: How Computers Are Creating the Next Job Market*. Princeton, NJ: Princeton University Press.

Mishel, Lawrence, Josh Bivens, Elise Gould, and Heidi Shierholz. 2012. *The State of Working America*, 12th ed. Ithaca, NY: Cornell University Press.

US Bureau of Labor Statistics. n.d. "Weekly Update." Online at: www.bls.gov/opub/update.htm.

Volti, Rudi. 2012. *An Introduction to the Sociology of Work and Occupations*. Thousand Oaks, CA: Sage.

Index

Core Concepts in Sociology, First Edition. Edited by J. Michael Ryan.
© 2019 John Wiley & Sons Ltd. Published 2019 by John Wiley & Sons Ltd.